PRAISE FOR

The
BURGER COURT
and the
Rise of the
JUDICIAL RIGHT

"As this important book makes clear, courts, given time, can accomplish—or demolish—a great deal by degrees, leaving their successors to finish the job."

—Jeff Shesol, *The New York Times Book Review*

"Ambitious and engaging. . . . Readers interested in the Supreme Court's role in American society during the second half of the twentieth century will gather significant insight from this book's elegant, illuminating arguments."

—Justin Driver, *The Washington Post*

"When the Supreme Court unanimously ruled against President Nixon in the famous 1974 Watergate tapes case that doomed his presidency, Nixon cursed the justices he had appointed. The myth grew that Nixon had failed to significantly move the Court to right. In their compelling, elegantly written analysis, two brilliant legal scholars (and clear-eyed explainers) convincingly demolish that myth."

—Evan Thomas, author of *Being Nixon*

"[A] landmark new book. . . . Thrillingly intelligent analysis of the ways the Burger Court handled the massive legacy it was handed by the Warren Court. . . . Graetz and Greenhouse are tough but even-handed, dealing equally in personalities and precedents and creating some energetic reading along the way."

—Steve Donoghue, Christian Science Monitor.com

"In this fresh and often surprising return to the Burger Court years, Graetz and Greenhouse show how that court, generally dismissed for failing to reverse the liberal arc of the Warren Court era, embedded significant conservative markers in areas of the law critical to consumers, women, prisoners, business, voters and others. . . . This illuminating trip through history is well worth taking."

—Marcia Coyle, Chief Washington Correspondent,
The National Law Journal, and author of *The Roberts Court: The Struggle for the Constitution*

"This revelatory book resets how we think about the Constitution and the Supreme Court that interprets it. The Court led by Chief Justice Warren Burger is often seen as an afterthought, wedged between the Warren Court and the hard right justices today. . . . With clarity and insight, Michael Graetz and Linda Greenhouse show how the often jumbled doctrines of that time helped produce the America of today."

—Michael Waldman, President, Brennan Center for Justice at NYU School of Law, and author of *The Fight to Vote*

"Although the Burger Court is often viewed as a backwater in Supreme Court history, the authors argue that the court Warren Burger led from 1969–86 was more than a transitional moment between the aggressively liberal Warren Court and the aggressively conservative Rehnquist and Roberts eras. . . . Engaging and authoritative."

—*Los Angeles Times*

"Timely and engaging, Graetz and Greenhouse's study provides a richly detailed look at the high court's jurisprudence on the most heated issues of the past half-century. Even readers who follow the court's work closely will find revelatory reporting."

—Jay Strafford, *Richmond Times-Dispatch*

"Two powerhouse law historians/journalists deliver a major contribution to the history of the Supreme Court."

—*Kirkus Reviews* (starred review)

"Graetz and Greenhouse offer an insightful and intimate view of life and law behind the scenes in the Burger Court. By exploring the debates among the justices on such fundamental issues as women's rights,

abortion, the death penalty, religion, and racial equal[...] [...]
ing new perspectives on the interactions of the justices [...]
of the law in the Court that was created by Richard Nixo[...]

—Geoffrey Stone, Edward H. Levi[...]
Service Professor at the Universit[y...]
and chief editor the Inalienable R[...]

"An insightful and well-researched examination of the Burger Co[...]

—*Library Journal* (starred r[...]

"With crisp intelligence and notable fairness, *The Burger Court and [...]
Rise of the Judicial Right* shows how quickly and profoundly politics ca[...]
reshape the law of the land. The appointment of four conservative justices
in the Nixon years led the Court to gut landmark rulings, empowering
the judicial right in ways that still reign. Michael Graetz and Linda Greenhouse have written an engrossing and excellent book that will lead court
watchers to think in importantly different terms about the Burger Court."

—Lincoln Caplan, Senior Research Scholar,
Yale Law School, and author of *The Tenth Justice:
The Solicitor General and the Rule of Law*

"With remarkable skill, Michael Graetz and Linda Greenhouse show how
the Burger Court eroded the equality that underlay almost all the work of
the Warren Court. . . . This extraordinary book will engage everyone who
cares about the contemporary Supreme Court and its history."

—Laura Kalman, Professor of History,
University of California, Santa Barbara

"Michael Graetz and Linda Greenhouse's wonderful book on the Burger
Court is the best survey and analysis that I have seen of the actions and
implications of the decisions of that Court. It will be indispensable for
scholars as well as ordinary citizens interested in the political and constitutional history of that fraught period of time."

—John Ferejohn, Samuel Tilden Professor of Law,
NYU Law School

"Informative, accessible, and meticulously detailed."

—Glenn C. Altschuler, *The Huffington Post*

The
BURGER COURT
and the
Rise of the
JUDICIAL RIGHT

Michael J. Graetz
and
Linda Greenhouse

Simon & Schuster Paperbacks

New York   London   Toronto   Sydney   New Delhi

Simon & Schuster Paperbacks
An Imprint of Simon & Schuster, Inc.
1230 Avenue of the Americas
New York, NY 10020

First Simon & Schuster trade paperback edition June 2017

SIMON & SCHUSTER PAPERBACKS and colophon are registered trademarks of Simon & Schuster, Inc.

For information about special discounts for bulk purchases, please contact Simon & Schuster Special Sales at 1-866-506-1949 or business@simonand schuster.com.

The Simon & Schuster Speakers Bureau can bring authors to your live event. For more information or to book an event, contact the Simon & Schuster Speakers Bureau at 1-866-248-3049 or visit our website at www.simon speakers.com.

Interior design by Joy O'Meara

Manufactured in the United States of America

10 9 8 7 6 5 4 3 2

The Library of Congress has cataloged the hardcover edition as follows:

Graetz, Michael J., author.
    The Burger court and the rise of the judicial right / Michael J. Graetz and Linda Greenhouse.
        pages cm
    Includes bibliographical references and index.
    1. Political questions and judicial power—History—20th century.
2. United States. Supreme Court—History—20th century. 3. Burger, Warren E., 1907–1995. I. Greenhouse, Linda, author. II. Title.
    KF8748.G69 2016
    347.73'262—dc23   2015031713

ISBN 978-1-4767-3250-3
ISBN 978-1-4767-3251-0 (pbk)
ISBN 978-1-4767-3252-7 (ebook)

For Charles Whitebread and Anthony Lewis
In Memory

Contents

Contents

The
BURGER COURT
and the
Rise of the
JUDICIAL RIGHT

President Nixon is flanked by the departing chief justice, Earl Warren (left) and the new chief justice, Warren E. Burger, on the steps of the Supreme Court after Burger took the oath of office on June 23, 1969.

Introduction

A Counterrevolution Reclaimed

On September 17, 1987, an extravagant celebration took place in Philadelphia to mark the bicentennial of the United States Constitution. A quarter of a million people lined the route for a parade that included a forty-foot replica of a parchment scroll: the Constitution deified. At 4:00 p.m., the hour at which the delegates to the Constitutional Convention had signed the document two hundred years earlier, a man stepped forward to ring a replica of the Liberty Bell. His abundant mane of white hair made him instantly recognizable. It was Warren E. Burger, the retired chief justice of the United States, who had ended his seventeen-year tenure a year earlier for the purpose of presiding over this very observance—which, as it happened, fell on his eightieth birthday.

Burger addressed the crowd: "If we remain on course, keeping faith with the vision of the Founders, with freedom under ordered liberty, we will have done our part to see that the great new idea of government by consent—by We the People—remains in place."[1]

Burger's call to keep faith with the Founders reflected one vision of the project they had launched with their "great new idea." But it was not the only vision. Four months earlier, Justice Thurgood Marshall, who still sat on the Supreme Court, had offered a far more sober take on the meaning of the bicentennial in a speech to a bar group meeting on the Hawaiian island of Maui.

Marshall, the aging hero of the legal campaign to end racial segregation, and the first African American to sit on the Supreme Court, advised his audience to be wary of the "flagwaving fervor" surrounding the bicentennial. "The focus of this celebration invites a complacent belief that the vision of those who debated and compromised in Philadelphia yielded the 'more perfect Union' it is said we now enjoy," Marshall said, adding: "I cannot accept this invitation." The government the Framers devised, he explained, "was defective from the start, requiring several amendments, a civil war, and momentous social transformation" to better realize the promise of a more just society. Credit for the Constitution in its present meaning belonged not to the Framers, Marshall concluded, but "to those who refused to acquiesce in outdated notions of 'liberty,' 'justice,' and 'equality' and who strived to better them."[2]

The competition between these two narratives is in many ways the subject of this book.

———

From his appointment by President Dwight D. Eisenhower in 1953 until his retirement in the opening months of the Nixon administration in 1969, Chief Justice Earl Warren presided over a revolution in constitutional meaning. Official segregation by race came to an end. Criminal defendants acquired enforceable rights against compelled self-incrimination and illegally seized evidence. The political dominance that rural America held over the nation's legislatures was ended by the new jurisprudence of one person, one vote. Organized prayer was ejected from public school classrooms.

The Warren Court's overarching theme was equality. Reviewing his tenure, the chief justice told reporters that his Court's three most important decisions were the reapportionment ruling (*Baker v. Carr*), the desegregation decision (*Brown v. Board of Education*), and the decision requiring that a lawyer be provided to any defendant facing a serious criminal charge who could not afford to hire one (*Gideon v. Wainwright*).[3] All three were in the service of greater equality.

The Court's activism produced public backlash. "Impeach Earl Warren" signs dotted lawns across the South—and elsewhere—for years before the Chief Justice retired in 1969. A sizable portion of the public attributed rising crime rates to judicial leniency. At the start of the 1968 election year, 63 percent told the Gallup Poll that courts were too soft on criminals, up from 48 percent three years earlier.[4] A few months later, the Louis Harris poll reported that 81 percent of voters agreed with the statement that "law and order has broken down in this country." Only

14 percent disagreed.[5] Certainly, not all these uneasy voters saw the Supreme Court as the primary source of crime in the streets—there were, after all, riots in cities across the country—but the poll reflected a widespread sense of vulnerability among the law-abiding public.

Competing signs along a California highway, one calling for the impeachment of Chief Justice Earl Warren in order to "save our republic," and the other, from a local bar association, supporting the chief justice in the name of the rule of law.

These developments made Warren himself, and the Court he led, inviting targets, creating a situation ripe for exploitation by ambitious politicians, Richard Nixon prominently among them. Nixon ran for president in 1968 on an explicitly law-and-order platform; indeed, the Republican Party's official platform prominently declared that "lawlessness is crumbling the foundations of American society."[6] Nixon's target was the Supreme Court—the Supreme Court's record on the rights of criminal defendants and, more submerged but distinctly visible to his intended audience, the Supreme Court on race. During the campaign, Nixon pledged to appoint "strict constructionists" to the bench, telling one Southern audience: "I think some of our judges have gone too far in assuming unto themselves a mandate which is not there, and that is, to put their social and economic ideas into their decisions."[7]

Warren Burger was an ambitious politician in his own way, although he never sought elective office. At the 1952 Republican National Convention, he had been instrumental in delivering Minnesota's delegation to Eisenhower, who rewarded him by bringing him to Washington and naming him assistant attorney general in charge of the Justice Department's Civil Division. In 1956, the president named him to the United States Court of Appeals for the District of Columbia Circuit. On that court, often considered second only to the Supreme Court in its important role in the judicial system, Burger clashed repeatedly with his more liberal colleagues.

He also began giving speeches and writing articles critical of the Supreme Court's criminal law decisions. Although these were fairly scholarly in tone,[8] his private correspondence offers a different picture. On Labor Day 1967, he wrote to his boyhood friend Harry Blackmun that "if I were to stand still for some of the idiocy that is put forth as legal and constitutional profundity I would, I am sure, want to shoot myself in later years." That letter continued: "These guys just *can't* be right. So there is nothing to do but resist."[9] In another letter to Blackmun in March 1969, Burger was sharply critical of the Supreme Court and, referring to President Nixon by his initials, observed: "RN can only straighten that place out if he gets four appointments."[10]

––––––

In short order, Nixon got his four Supreme Court appointments. Warren Burger was the first. Presenting his nominee to a national television audience on the evening of May 21, 1969, the president observed that "I think it could fairly be said that our history tells us that our chief justices had probably had more profound and lasting influence on their times and on the direction of the nation than most presidents have had." [11] Nixon could not have known how prescient that statement would prove to be; it would have hardly seemed possible that just over five years later, Chief Justice Burger's name would be on the unanimous Supreme Court opinion that drove the president from office.

Burger's appointment was followed by those of Harry Blackmun in May 1970 and Lewis F. Powell, Jr., and William H. Rehnquist in December 1971. Blackmun, a judge on a midwestern federal appeals court and friend of Burger's dating back to their shared boyhoods in St. Paul, Minnesota, took the seat that had been vacant since the resignation of Abe Fortas nearly a year earlier. Powell and Rehnquist replaced Hugo L. Black and John Marshall Harlan II respectively; both had abruptly left the Court due to ill health at the beginning of the 1971 term.

Neither Powell nor Rehnquist had ever been a judge. Powell, a partner in a Richmond, Virginia, law firm, had a distinguished legal career, serving as president of the American Bar Association and as head of both the Richmond and the Virginia school boards. Rehnquist, a former Supreme Court law clerk, had been active in Barry Goldwater's presidential campaign in 1964 and left a law practice in Phoenix to join the Nixon administration as assistant attorney general in charge of the Office of Legal Counsel. In that role, he had helped to vet Harry Blackmun as a Supreme Court nominee.

Nixon had no further Supreme Court vacancies to fill, but his influence was now assured with the four appointments that Burger had predicted the president would need. The Burger Court itself was now nearly complete. The only subsequent vacancies during his tenure would be filled by Presidents Gerald Ford, who named John Paul Stevens to succeed William O. Douglas in December 1975, and Ronald Reagan, who in 1981 named Sandra Day O'Connor to replace Potter Stewart, thereby fulfilling a campaign pledge to appoint the first woman to the Court. Stevens was a judge on the federal appeals court in Chicago. O'Connor, who was Rehnquist's law school classmate at Stanford, had held elective office as majority leader of the Arizona State Senate. At the time of her nomination, she was a judge on Arizona's intermediate appeals court. Three justices who were already serving on the Court when Burger arrived—William J. Brennan, Jr., Byron R. White, and Thurgood Marshall—remained after his retirement.

President Nixon and his new chief justice chat in a White House reception room, July 20, 1969. Burger inscribed the photo to Harry Blackmun, then still sitting on a federal appeals court: "For Harry A. Blackmun, incomparable friend of a lifetime with best wishes." In the top left-hand corner, Burger mused: "To be or not to be, that is the question—and now?"

Burger served with twelve colleagues in all. (For brief biographies of the members of the Burger Court and the Court's composition over time, see the Appendix.) For most of his seventeen-year tenure, the Court's dynamic was notably different from what we have become accustomed to today. Instead of two ideologically defined wings with a "swing justice" in the middle whose vote would decide the case, there were two, three, or even four justices who formed the Court's center of gravity and whom lawyers for each side of a case needed to persuade. Membership in this group changed over time as some Burger Court justices changed their ideological stripes. Harry Blackmun, for example, began his tenure as a reliable conservative ally for the chief justice. But he eventually broke with Burger, and when he left the Court in 1994, Blackmun was the most liberal member of the Rehnquist Court. Later, and in less dramatic fashion, Stevens and O'Connor also moved leftward. Burger himself never did, and neither did Rehnquist. They were the two most reliably conservative justices of the Burger Court, just as Brennan and Marshall were the most liberal.

———

When we told friends and colleagues that we were writing a book about the Burger Court, the response was almost universally one of surprise and the question was "Why?" That was understandable. The received learning about the seventeen-year period known as the Burger Court is that it was a chapter of Supreme Court history during which nothing much happened. The title of a collection of essays published in 1983 exemplifies this verdict: *The Burger Court: The Counter-Revolution That Wasn't*.[12] After all, according to this view, the major and most controversial landmark rulings of the Warren Court were still on the books by the time Warren Burger retired. Criminal suspects were still being read their Miranda rights. Organized prayer still couldn't be conducted in public schools.

The Burger Court is often depicted as simply having occupied a transitional role between the aggressively liberal Warren Court and the similarly aggressive conservatism of the Rehnquist Court. It was "primarily a Court of consolidation," according to one well-known Supreme Court scholar, "without an agenda or overriding philosophy."[13]

Our purpose in writing this book is to offer a different view, to reclaim a period of Supreme Court history that has been overlooked and under-studied. As we show in the following chapters, a great deal happened during the Burger Court. How could it have been otherwise? Outside the Supreme Court, the country changed dramatically between Warren Burger's appointment in 1969 and his retirement in 1986. Judges "do not stand aloof and chill on these distant heights," Benjamin N. Cardozo, later a Supreme Court justice, wrote while serving on New York

State's high court. "The great tides and currents which engulf the rest of men do not turn aside in their course and pass the judges by." [14]

Further, the Warren Court had painted in broad strokes: the schools were to be desegregated "with all deliberate speed." It fell to the Burger Court, as it would have fallen to any subsequent Court, to fill in the blanks, to make highly consequential choices that in many ways shaped the society we live in today. To the Burger Court's majority, equality was no longer the pole star, as the chapters that follow demonstrate.

The Court was to spend much energy drawing lines and setting limits. Some of its choices were stark. Yes, busing was a valid tool for integrating the schools, but it and other remedies had to stop at the school district line. The Constitution's guarantee of equal protection couldn't be invoked to attack great disparities in the wealth available to neighboring school districts. The Court interpreted the equal protection guarantee itself as protecting against only deliberate discriminatory action by the government; the need to prove intentional discrimination has cut off constitutional challenges to policies that have obvious, even foreseeably disparate, impacts on racial minorities or women.

The Burger Court faced issues that the Warren Court never had to confront: claims by white workers and white applicants to public universities that they were victims of unlawful or unconstitutional racial discrimination. The Court's responses shaped the debate over "affirmative action" that persists to the present day. The First Amendment right of corporations to spend money in politics comes from a Burger Court precedent on which the Court under Chief Justice John G. Roberts, Jr., majority drew for the 2010 *Citizens United* decision.

True, the Burger Court defied expectations in failing to overturn the Warren Court's leading criminal law precedents. But it left those precedents hollowed out, while also erecting daunting barriers to defendants seeking to vindicate their rights in federal court. The school prayer precedents remain, but Burger Court decisions gave religion and its symbols a more prominent place in the public square.

On the surface, there exists one glaring exception to the Burger Court's conservative profile: women's rights, including the right to abortion. No Warren Court decision suggested that the Constitution's guarantee of equal protection had anything to do with discrimination on account of sex. The Burger Court opened the door to a jurisprudence of sex equality. But the door never opened wide enough to encompass the understanding that discrimination on the basis of pregnancy is a form of sex discrimination—a point that continues to elude the Supreme Court even today. And the right to terminate a pregnancy did not, in the Court's view, include a right to public financial assistance in obtaining an abortion.

The Burger Court decided 2,738 cases with published opinions. In the chapters that follow, we examine only a small proportion of the Court's work—enough, we believe, to prove our premise.

A Note on Supreme Court Procedure

In the pages that follow, we depict the justices at work. For readers unfamiliar with the basics of Supreme Court procedure, we offer this capsule description.

Two basic tasks confront the justices: constructing the docket, and deciding the selected cases. The significance of the first task is often overlooked, but as we shall see, it is itself an important and sometimes intensely contested decision. The Burger Court received about 5,000 new cases each term and chose only about 150 to decide with full argument and signed opinions. (In recent years, the Court has received about 8,000 new cases and has issued only about seventy decisions per term.)

The votes of four justices are required to grant a case, adding it to the docket for argument and decision. Cases not granted are simply listed as "certiorari denied," usually without further explanation. The Court considers the process of selecting cases to be an internal matter and doesn't reveal either the vote or the justices' deliberations on whether to accept a new case. The details we offer about the process that led to the selection of particular cases come from the justices' papers.

During weeks when they are hearing arguments, the justices meet in conference to vote on the disposition of each argued case. (The word "conference" has two meanings at the Supreme Court. The first, more ordinary definition, refers to the private meeting at which the justices discuss and vote on cases; no law clerks or other assistants attend these closed-door sessions. In the other meaning, "conference" refers to the nine justices as a collective, as in "a memo to the Conference.") If the chief justice has voted with the majority, he exercises the prerogative of assigning the majority opinion, either to himself or to another member of the majority. If the chief justice is in dissent, the senior associate justice in the majority gets to make the assignment. During the Burger years, that justice was most often William Brennan.

The decisional process begins, rather than ends, with the majority opinion assignment. The opinion writer needs to retain the agreement of at least four other justices. Discussion of the case at the conference is often quite cursory, and justices whose votes may have reflected general agreement with the outcome may object to how the opinion writer's initial draft proposes to get there. Bargaining often ensues, carried out through multiple opinion drafts. A member of the majority who is left unsatisfied might write a separate opinion, concurring only in the Court's judgment, or might even switch sides, requiring the case to be reassigned to a justice who originally voted in dissent. Occasionally, the Court will issue an unsigned opinion labeled *per curiam*, meaning "by the court." (*Per curiam* need not mean unanimous. *Bush v. Gore*, the 2000 presidential election decision, was issued as a *per curiam* opinion over four dissents.[15])

This process almost never becomes public contemporaneously. We are grateful to those former justices whose collected papers offered us a window into how the Burger Court really worked as it carried out its counterrevolution. (Unlike the president, whose official papers [if not classified] are public documents, Supreme Court justices have complete discretion over where to place their papers, what conditions to set for public access—and even whether to keep their papers at all. The justices' papers we used are cited in the endnotes. Harry Blackmun's papers are at the Manuscript Division of the Library of Congress. Potter Stewart's papers are at Yale University's Sterling Memorial Library. Lewis Powell's papers are at Washington and Lee University; unlike those of the other justices, many of Powell's papers have been digitized and are available on the Washington and Lee library's website. Warren Burger's papers, housed at the College of William and Mary in Williamsburg, Virginia, will remain closed to the public until 2026.)

PART ONE

Crime

In 1970, Lyndon Johnson's attorney general, Ramsey Clark, published a book entitled *Crime in America*, arguing forcefully that the nation's crime problem stemmed from societal conditions, especially inner-city poverty.[1] To address the public's growing concerns about crime, Clark urged the nation to focus on alleviating poverty and rehabilitating wrongdoers. His views reflected much mainstream opinion then but were rapidly becoming archaic. They soon would be emphatically rejected by a fearful public and its representatives. Clark's view of the causes of crime and appropriate policy responses was the last hurrah of a political and legal vision that disappeared with the 1960s.

Crime increased in the 1960s and 1970s, engendering public fear, producing political gains for being tough on crime, and ushering in a dramatic transformation in criminal law and policy. In 1975, James Q. Wilson wrote a bestseller, *Thinking About Crime*, laying crime at the doorstep of "evil" people and insisting that imprisoning more criminals and keeping them in prison longer would produce declining crime rates.[2] Emphasis shifted to incarcerating the guilty. Radical increases in sentences for offenders ensued; sentences in the United States became significantly higher than they had been and much higher than elsewhere.[3] The goal of rehabilitating criminals was abandoned, and retribution came to the forefront of American crime policy. The "War on Drugs" commenced. Victims of crime began to play a central role in the criminal process. Harsher sanctions proliferated. Beginning in 1975, every state enacted mandatory minimum sentences, and many adopted "three-strikes-you-are-out" laws. The federal government, which historically had played a limited role in criminal law, began in the late 1960s expanding the list of federal crimes and, like the states, enacted overlapping and redundant criminal laws and increasingly punitive sentences.

In 1970, less than 0.2 percent of the U.S. population was incarcerated, a number comparable to other developed countries. By 2012 that number had more than tripled to 0.7 percent, and the United States imprisoned a larger share of its population than any other developed country—about five times the average elsewhere. That year more than two million Americans were imprisoned—an increase of more than 700 percent since 1970. In 1970, our nation had two times as many police as prisoners; by 2010 that relationship was the reverse: twice as many prisoners as police.[4] As our criminal law became more punitive, prisons turned into one of the most successful growth industries. The United States has spent $300 billion on new prisons since 1980; we now spend more than $80 billion a year on our jails and prisons.[5] In 2012, we spent an average of more than $31,000 per year for each prison inmate, $50,000 in some states.[6] We became a society wedded to "law and order," incarcerating and executing more of our citizens than any other democratic developed nation. This could not have happened without a seismic political and legal transformation.[7]

How and why did this occur? For starters, the social upheaval and political rebellions of the 1960s led to growing public anxiety that crime and disorder had become common in America. People were on high alert: crime rates were way up. Widely publicized FBI statistics announcing that every year between 1965 and 1969 the crime rate had risen by double digits fed public fears. Civil rights demonstrations, antiwar protests, political assassinations, and urban riots were all linked by the public to the rise in street crime. Many Americans had watched their cities burn in the violent urban riots. In 1965, thirty-four people were killed in the Los Angeles riot; in 1967, forty-three were killed in Detroit, twenty-three in Newark.[8] After Martin Luther King, Jr.'s, assassination in 1968, more than 140 cities went up in flames and were looted. People were afraid to go for a walk after dark. Along with disparate crime rates, this forged a regrettable link between race and crime. African Americans—only 13 percent of the U.S. population—now comprise nearly half of the state and federal prison population. The Department of Justice estimated that a black male born in 2001 had nearly a one in three likelihood of serving prison time.[9]

The turbulent times and pervasive worries about escalating violence inflamed attacks on the Supreme Court's expansion of the constitutional rights of criminal defendants. The Warren Court had affirmed the rights of indigent criminal defendants to counsel, made clear that suspects could maintain their silence and have an attorney present during police questioning, insisted that suspects must be informed of their rights and affirmatively waive them before police interrogation, and excluded from criminal trials evidence that the police had obtained illegally.[10] A large segment of the public had come to blame the Supreme Court for its plight. Politicians of both parties vilified the Supreme Court for being soft on crime and for elevating the rights of criminal defendants over those of the public and the police.[11] In the 1968 campaign for president, George Wallace, the segregationist governor of Alabama, stoked public fears about crime. "Crime has risen in our country at an astronomical rate," he frequently said, "and the court system has ruled that you can hardly convict a criminal. If you are knocked on the head on a street in a city today, the man who knocked you in the head is out of jail before you get to the hospital."[12]

Richard Nixon also exploited the crime issue during his 1968 presidential campaign. Recognizing that crime had become the public's top domestic concern, Nixon frequently stressed his commitment to "law and order." He gave numerous speeches devoted to that subject, married public fears to rising crime statistics, and insisted that freedom from fear was a basic right of every American. Nixon harshly criticized the Warren Court for coddling criminals and hindering law enforcement. He insisted that the time had come "for soft-headed judges and probation officers to show as much concern for the rights of innocent victims of crime as they do for the rights of convicted criminals."[13]

Together, Nixon and Wallace secured 57 percent of the votes that year. Democrats soon refused to concede the law-and-order issue to Republicans: a bidding war began over who could be tougher.

President Nixon promised the public both a different attorney general and a new Supreme Court. He appointed his former law partner and campaign director John Mitchell to replace Ramsey Clark as attorney general. (Ironically, Mitchell would subsequently be convicted of crimes in office.) Then, in 1969, Nixon named Warren Burger to succeed Earl Warren. Burger had come to Nixon's attention through Burger's harsh statements about inordinate protection of criminal defendants and his criticisms of Supreme Court decisions restricting the police and prosecutors. While serving on the federal appellate court in Washington, D.C., Burger in May 1967 delivered the commencement address at Ripon College in Wisconsin. He limited his remarks to "one problem . . . one which, like war, will affect every American and hang over every home and lurk at every dark corner . . . the problem which we might call crime and punishment." Burger then described "society's problem with those who will not obey law," and recited statistics of recent increases in violent crimes: murder, rape, and assault. He complained about how difficult it is "to convict even those who are plainly guilty," and lamented court decisions and legislative enactments "which have enlarged the protections of a person who is accused of crime." His bill of particulars included delayed and lengthy trials, too many appeals and retrials where defendants are "tried and re-tried and re-tried again," and where those convicted are given "almost unlimited procedures to attack [their] conviction or seek reduction of [their] sentence." The "suppression of evidence," he said, unduly discouraged guilty pleas. Notorious Warren Court criminal law cases, he insisted, are "common talk in the best clubs and worst ghettos," and serve to undermine the deterrent effect of criminal law. "Justice," Burger said, "is far too important to be left exclusively to the technicians of the law." [14] Warren Burger's main goal when he took his seat as chief justice of the United States was to roll back rights that Earl Warren's Supreme Court had granted to criminal defendants.

The key question is: how well did Burger succeed? Many previous accounts emphasize that the Burger Court failed to overrule any of the key Warren Court criminal law decisions. When Warren Burger left the Court after seventeen years, the most important and controversial Warren Court criminal law precedents remained standing, despite his efforts to eliminate them. The Burger Court's failure to overrule these decisions has played a central role in shaping the conventional narrative that in the

Burger Court nothing happened. It is the chief reason the Burger Court acquired its reputation as a "counter-revolution that failed." But that is to badly mistake what did happen.

The Burger Court dramatically diminished the scope and impact of the Warren Court precedents: they survived, but only their facade was left standing. Sometimes the Court accomplished this by sharply limiting the effectiveness of the rights granted to criminal defendants. Sometimes the Burger Court simply shut federal courthouses to defendants' claims. These restrictions are the subject of Chapters 2 and 3. But before tackling them, we shall recount the Court's struggles over constitutional challenges to the death penalty. Death penalty cases had reached the Supreme Court before, but the Burger Court was the first to impose serious constitutional scrutiny on capital punishment in America. The role of constitutional constraints on the death penalty became the biggest, most visible, and highly contentious issue of criminal law to reach the Burger Court. That battle reveals much about the Court's—and the nation's— struggle over constitutional criminal law and procedure.

CHAPTER I

The Fall and Rise of the Death Penalty

William Henry Furman was an unlikely fellow to find himself on death row. Early in the morning of August 11, 1967, in Savannah, Georgia, while attempting to burglarize the home of William Micke and his family, Furman shot Micke dead. At his trial, Furman, a black man, claimed his gun accidentally went off when he stumbled while running away. The detective at the scene testified that Furman had said that after Micke had come into the kitchen and tried to grab him, Furman had stopped outside the kitchen door and fired one shot before leaving.[1] The bullet had clearly passed through the kitchen door. It was horrid luck for both men that it killed Micke, a twenty-nine-year-old father of five children. In less than two hours, an all-white jury convicted Furman and sentenced him to death. In Georgia, death sentences were then imposed at the unfettered discretion of a jury sitting in a capital case.

Two other convicts, Lucas Jackson, also from Georgia, and Texas's Elmer Branch, whose death sentences were before the Supreme Court along with Furman's, had been convicted of rape, not murder. The convicts' lawyers all argued that the death penalty was imposed rarely, randomly, and arbitrarily.[2] All three of these cases had one thing in common: each of the men sentenced to death was black, his victim white.

In 1972, the Supreme Court, in *Furman v. Georgia*, halted executions in the United States. The Court concluded that all forty-one states that imposed capital punishment did so in a manner that violated the Constitution's prohibition against "cruel and unusual punishment." The *Furman* decision spared the lives of more than six hundred death row inmates.[3] It

17

was the first occasion in the 185 years since the Constitution was written that the Court had engaged in serious constitutional oversight of capital punishment. In the nearly half century since, *Furman* has been the "lodestar" for Supreme Court death penalty decisions.[4] Some lodestar.

Before *Furman*

The *Furman* litigation was a key piece of a strategy by the NAACP Legal Defense Fund (LDF) and its allies to halt executions throughout the country, a strategy that had enjoyed considerable success. Nineteen sixty-eight was the first year in American history in which no one was executed. When *Furman* reached the Court in 1972, no one had been executed in the United States since June 2, 1967.[5] Even so, death penalty opponents faced long odds against a Supreme Court victory.

In a death penalty case decided just before Earl Warren stepped down in 1969, the Court rejected a claim that Alabama's imposition of a death sentence on an African American for armed robbery was so disproportionate to his crime that it constituted unconstitional cruel and unusual punishment. Ducking that issue, the Court found instead that the defendant's guilty plea had been given involuntarily—a claim he had not even advanced.[6]

The first death penalty challenge in the Burger Court also went nowhere.[7] The following year, the Court took two more cases that raised identical questions: (1) whether a bifurcated trial is required—in which, after a conviction, the jury hears evidence of aggravating and mitigating factors relevant to its decision whether to impose a death sentence—and (2) whether some standards are necessary to limit juries' discretion in imposing death sentences.[8] In both of these cases—one from Ohio, the other from California—the defendant had been convicted of first-degree murder. Both states gave juries absolute discretion whether to impose the death penalty. Ohio determined the defendants' guilt and sentence in a single trial, but California required a separate sentencing procedure following a guilty verdict. Richard Nixon's solicitor general, Erwin Griswold, argued in support of both states. On May 3, 1971, by a 6–3 majority, the Court in *McGautha v. California* decided that states have complete discretion whether to require a bifurcated trial or to impose any limits on jury discretion. Writing for a majority that included Burger, Stewart, White, and Blackmun, Justice Harlan emphasized the difficulties for the Court to set standards limiting jury discretion in capital cases:

> To identify before the fact those characteristics of criminal homicides and their perpetrators which call for the death penalty, and to express those characteristics in language which can be fairly understood and applied by the sentencing authority, appear to be tasks which are *beyond present human ability*. . . . In light of history, experience and the present limitations of human knowledge we find it quite impossible to say that committing to the untrammeled discretion of the jury the power to pronounce life or death in capital cases is offensive to anything in the Constitution.[9]

The *McGautha* decision also concluded that the Constitution did not require that capital trials be bifurcated for separate determinations of guilt and sentence.[10]

Despite the Court's decision, neither of the two convicts was executed. Dennis McGautha, along with more than one hundred death row inmates, was spared when a controversial 1972 decision of the California Supreme Court struck down the death penalty as a violation of that state's constitution.[11] The Ohio convict, James Crampton, was one of the inmates released from death row by the Supreme Court's decision the following year in *Furman*.

On June 28, 1971, less than two months after the *McGautha* decision seemed finally to have resolved capital punishment questions the Court had struggled with for so long, the Court took four more death penalty cases: one from California (which was dismissed after the California Supreme Court struck down that state's death sentence); Elmer Branch's rape case from Texas; and two cases from Georgia, Lucas Jackson's rape case, and William Furman's murder case. Hugo Black, nearing retirement, urged his colleagues to dispose of the "cruel-and-unusual-punishment" issue "once and for all." He must have believed that, with the two Nixon appointees, he finally had a majority to affirm his long-standing position that the Constitution imposes no limits on states' discretion in imposing death sentences.[12] The Court instructed the parties to address only one question: "Does the imposition and carrying out of the death penalty in these cases constitute cruel and unusual punishment in violation of the Eighth and Fourteenth Amendments?" [13]

Furman

Death penalty abolitionists were puzzled about how they might garner the five votes necessary to strike down the states' death penalty statutes. They could count for sure on only three: Douglas, Brennan, and Marshall, the three dissenters in *McGautha* the previous term. Unlike Brennan and Marshall—who concluded that the death penalty was always cruel and unusual punishment and therefore always unconstitutional—Douglas grounded his opposition to the death penalty in its discrimination against minorities. Discrimination, he concluded, made death sentences unconstitutionally "unusual." [14]

Four members of the Court—Stewart, White, Burger, and Blackmun—had been in the six-vote *McGautha* majority that had so recently upheld the California and Ohio death penalty procedures. At the *Furman* conference, Burger and Blackmun again both voted to uphold the death penalty. Blackmun said that if he were a legislator he would vote against the death penalty, and Burger said that, as a legislator, he would vote against imposing death "for some types of crime." Burger added that he would vote against capital punishment for rape. (Burger then elaborated his views in an unfortunate exposition on "mild rape" versus "cruel rape.") Foreshadowing future Court decisions, Blackmun agreed that the death penalty was "harder to uphold" for rape than murder. [15]

The composition of the Court had changed again between *McGautha* and *Furman*. In September 1971, Hugo Black and John Marshall Harlan, in deteriorating health, had resigned, replaced by Lewis Powell and William Rehnquist. But, like their predecessors, neither would vote to strike down the states' death penalty laws. At the *Furman* conference, Rehnquist said that he was not at all "torn by the problem," emphasizing that forty-one states imposed capital punishment. He said that, even as a legislator, he would vote to keep it. [16] Powell agreed with Blackmun that this decision was best left to state legislatures and Congress. So, all four Nixon appointees voted in *Furman* to uphold the death penalty. They insisted—correctly—that the American public had not "repudiated" the death penalty, despite the five-year moratorium on executions.

Nevertheless, in a surprising decision, announced on June 29, 1972, in *Furman v. Georgia*, the Supreme Court struck down the death penalty by a 5–4 vote. In a one-paragraph per curiam opinion, the Court announced that "the imposition and carrying out of the death penalty in these cases constitute cruel and unusual punishment in violation of the Eighth and Fourteenth Amendments." [17] Because the statutes in these cases were similar to those throughout the land, the *Furman* decision halted executions everywhere in the United States. The Court's conclusion was short, but the justices' reasoning was not. Each justice wrote separately, and each member of the majority spoke only for himself. Totaling fifty thousand words spread over 233 pages, *Furman* produced the longest set of opinions in the Court's history.

The surprise was that Stewart and White—who the year before had both voted with the majority to uphold the death penalty statutes in *McGautha*—now decided that the way the death penalty was imposed in the United States was unconstitutional. Stewart and White had very different reasons for striking down capital punishment, but both concluded that its random imposition rendered it unconstitutional. Potter Stewart was especially reluctant to provide the fifth vote to uphold the death penalty and have the blood of more than six hundred death row inmates on his hands. [18]

Stewart's opinion reflected his ambivalence. He emphasized that the Court was not deciding "whether capital punishment is unconstitutional for all crimes and under all circumstances"; he acknowledged the "inconclusive empirical evidence" concerning the effectiveness of the death penalty as a deterrent; and he accepted the penalty's abandonment of rehabilitation of the perpetrator as a goal. [19] Retribution, Stewart said, is constitutionally permissible: the "instinct for retribution is part of the nature of man, and channeling that instinct serves an important purpose in promoting the stability of a society governed by law." [20] But "these death sentences," he concluded in a phrase that soon became famous, "are cruel and unusual in the same way that being struck by lightning is cruel and unusual." [21] The Constitution, he said, "cannot tolerate the infliction of a sentence of death under legal systems that permit this unique penalty to be so wantonly and freakishly imposed." [22]

Justice White took quite a different tack. He intimated that mandatory capital punishment for "more narrowly defined categories of murder, or for rape" might be constitutional. The problem, he said, is that the death penalty was being imposed so rarely that it was not serving as an effective deterrent to crime. "The death penalty," White said, "unless imposed with sufficient frequency, will make little contribution to deterring those crimes for which it may be exacted." [23] To White, more frequent executions were more consonant with the Constitution.

The dissenters were more united in their views. Harry Blackmun wrote a heartfelt opinion to emphasize his personal distaste for capital punishment. "I yield to no one," he said, "in the depth of my distaste, antipathy, and, indeed, abhorrence, for the death penalty." But, like the other Nixon appointees, he regarded the decision whether to impose death sentences as one for legislatures. Blackmun also criticized those in the majority for ignoring the "misery the petitioners' crimes occasioned to the victims, to the families of the victims, and to the communities where the crime took place." [24] Lewis Powell described the majority's decision as having a "shattering" effect "on the root principles of *stare decisis* [respect for precedent], federalism, judicial restraint, and—most importantly—separation of powers." [25] William Rehnquist argued that the majority had strayed far beyond its proper judicial role.

Significantly, Chief Justice Burger, in his dissent, said that the majority's many opinions left "the future of capital punishment in this country . . . in an uncertain limbo." He emphasized that, in addition to the four dissenters in *Furman*, Justices Douglas, Stewart, and White had not firmly closed the door to the death penalty. Only Brennan and Marshall had concluded that the death penalty is always unconstitutional. Burger said, "if state legislatures and the Congress wish to maintain the availability of capital punishment, significant statutory changes will have to be made. . . . Legislative bodies may seek to bring their laws into compliance with the Court's ruling by providing standards for juries and judges to follow . . . or by more narrowly defining crimes for which the penalty is to be imposed." [26]

Much of the nation's press failed to notice this harbinger; many journalists proclaimed the end of the death penalty in America. *The Washington Post* predicted that the death chambers would be dismantled. That prediction could have hardly been more wrong. Privately, Warren Burger and Potter Stewart voiced a similar expectation.

After *Furman*

A fearful nation was paying close attention when the Supreme Court decided the *Furman* case. Politicians throughout the land lambasted the ruling. The day after the Court announced its decision, President Nixon stressed Burger's dissent and insisted that the Court had not ruled out capital punishment.[27] He soon asked Congress to reinstate the federal death penalty for specific crimes, including treason, kidnapping, and hijacking. As Bob Woodward and Scott Armstrong put it in their book, *The Brethren*, Richard Nixon "made the death penalty a foot soldier in his war on crime."[28]

Ronald Reagan, California's governor, had also run for office promising to restore law and order, saying in his first campaign, "our cities are jungle paths after dark." He, too, blasted the Court's ruling and called for reinstatement of the death penalty.[29] Reagan's call was soon heeded by the voters, who by a 2–1 majority amended California's constitution to overrule the State Supreme Court and restore the death penalty. Other governors and state legislators, reflecting the retributive turn in public attitudes, likewise sought political gains by pushing to reinstate the death penalty. Unsurprisingly, many southern politicians regarded *Furman* as a barely disguised Supreme Court attack on racial bigotry in the South and were especially vociferous in attacking the Court. Georgia's racist lieutenant governor Lester Maddox called *Furman* a license for "anarchy, rape and murder."[30] The Georgia legislature voted by an overwhelming margin to bring back the death penalty and, although he questioned its constitutionality, Governor Jimmy Carter signed the law.[31]

At the end of 1974, polls showed that two-thirds of Americans supported the death penalty. By November 1975, 376 people had been sentenced to death under the new state laws.[32] The majority of these were in the South. By 1976, thirty-five states and Congress had enacted new laws reinstating the death penalty, laws that contained a variety of provisions intended to avoid the constitutional shortcomings of the statutes struck down in *Furman*.

In *Furman*, Brennan and Marshall had quoted from a 1958 opinion of Earl Warren (deciding that loss of citizenship was unconstitutional punishment for an Army private who in 1944 had deserted in Morocco but surrendered the next day) that the interpretation of the "cruel and unusual punishment" clause "must draw its meaning from evolving standards of decency that mark the progress of a maturing society." [33] The "evolving standards of decency" test was also quoted by Chief Justice Burger, writing for the four *Furman* dissenters. Burger said that the determination of what constitutes cruel and unusual punishment is "a moral judgment" and its "applicability must change as the basic mores of society change." [34] The dissenters, however, insisted that the question whether those mores had changed enough to rule out death sentences was a judgment for state legislatures, not the Court. Legislatures, Burger said, will respond to "changes in social attitudes and moral values." [35] The outburst of legislative activity restoring the death penalty after *Furman*, along with public opinion polls, made clear that those standards had not evolved in favor of abolition.

Gregg v. Georgia

The question of the constitutionality of capital punishment soon returned to the Supreme Court. In 1975, the Court began sifting through the many petitions for certiorari from death row inmates sentenced under post-*Furman* state statutes, looking for a group of cases appropriate for evaluation of the constitutionality of the new state laws. Ultimately, the Court took five cases, one each from Florida, Georgia, Louisiana, North Carolina, and Texas. In 1976, in *Gregg v. Georgia*, the lead case, the Court reinstated the death penalty, concluding, by a 7–2 vote, that death sentences need not violate the Constitution's prohibition against "cruel and unusual punishment." [36] While sparing more than six hundred inmates then on death row, the Court's decision in *Furman* had returned the question of continuing the death penalty to state and federal legislatures, and, in the process, reinvigorated executions in the United States.

The path to *Gregg* and its companion cases was tortuous. In October 1974, the Court took a death penalty case from North Carolina, which, like sixteen other states, had enacted a law making death sentences mandatory for certain crimes.[37] Unlike 1972 in *Furman*, when Nixon's Justice Department had remained silent, Robert Bork, serving as Gerald Ford's solicitor general, filed a lengthy brief supporting the constitutionality of capital punishment and asserting a federal interest in upholding the death penalty. Then, on New Year's Eve, William Douglas, who had been in *Furman*'s five-vote majority, suffered a stroke. Expecting that the other justices might be evenly divided, the Court postponed argument until April 21, 1975, when Douglas could attend. Douglas came to the argument in a wheelchair, but he returned to hospital the next day and missed the conference. The remaining justices deadlocked 4–4 and set the case over for reargument the next term.

William Douglas would not be there: on November 12, 1975, in failing health, he resigned. Ford chose John Paul Stevens to succeed him. Five death penalty cases were before the Court when Stevens took his seat—holding the deciding vote. No one knew what to expect.

The Burger Court in 1977. Left to right: John Paul Stevens, Lewis F. Powell, Jr., Harry A. Blackmun, William H. Rehnquist, Thurgood Marshall, William J. Brennan, Jr., Warren E. Burger, Potter Stewart, Byron R. White.

All five of these death row inmates had been convicted of murder. Four of the five were white; the Court had been careful not to take cases predominantly with black convicts.[38] Burger wanted the Court to take the most brutal cases, and in the Texas case he got his wish: [39] Jerry Lane Jurek, a twenty-two-year-old man, had been convicted of strangling a ten-year-old girl to death and drowning her while committing rape.[40]

On April 2, 1976, the justices met in conference to decide all five cases. Three months later, two days before the nation's July 4 bicentennial celebration, the Court announced its decisions. By this time, more than 450 inmates were on death row.[41] At issue were the two mandatory death penalty statutes from North Carolina and Louisiana and three discretionary laws from Georgia, Florida, and Texas. The Louisiana and North Carolina laws made death mandatory for certain convictions regardless of the circumstances. The North Carolina statute demanded death for a much wider list of crimes than Louisiana. The discretionary laws from Georgia, Florida, and Texas all provided bifurcated trials in capital cases. Each of these state laws specified a different set of aggravating and mitigating circumstances relevant to the jury's sentencing decision.

The Court's decision to reinstate the death penalty wasn't close. With only Brennan and Marshall dissenting, the Court ruled that the death penalty is not inherently cruel or unusual, and by a vote of 7–2 it upheld the death penalty statutes of Georgia, Florida, and Texas, which allowed juries some discretion in applying the penalty. But, by a vote of 5–4— with Stewart, Powell, and Stevens joining Brennan and Marshall—the Court struck down the mandatory death penalty laws of Louisiana and North Carolina. Together, these cases induced twenty-four separate opinions.

Death penalty abolitionists had thought they could count on at least four votes for striking down all of the death penalty laws: Brennan, Marshall, Stewart, and White, who had rejected the death penalty in *Furman*. So they thought they needed only the vote of the Court's newest member, John Paul Stevens. But at the justices' conference, it became clear that there were only two justices for halting executions in America: Brennan and Marshall. Both said they would never waver from their view that the death penalty is always unconstitutional cruel and unusual punishment.

Burger and Rehnquist voted to uphold all the state laws. White— having voted against imposition of the death penalty in *Furman*—now also voted to uphold all five statutes, taking comfort that mandatory death penalties would not be imposed infrequently. Stewart emphasized that, in 1972 when *Furman* was decided, he had thought the death penalty to be unconstitutional only because of the "sporadic and discriminatory way" in which executions were carried out. Thirty-five states' subsequent enactment of death penalty statutes had demonstrated to him that "capital punishment is not incompatible with evolving standards of decency."[42] Stewart nevertheless felt that the mandatory statutes of Louisiana and North Carolina would likely produce "jury irrationality," and he voted to strike them down. Powell was initially skeptical only about North Carolina's laws, which he regarded as overly broad. He described the Louisiana statute as "one of the best," but he worried that it did not bifurcate trials for separate determinations of guilt and sentence. He said that if "a procedural type of analysis is the appropriate type of analysis under *Furman*," Georgia, Florida, and Texas had "devised careful systems with standards and procedures designed to minimize, if not eliminate, *Furman*'s concerns." Like Powell, Stevens also interpreted *Furman* as demanding only "a procedural analysis study of the total picture." He, however, regarded the North Carolina system as a "monster," and Louisiana's mandatory death penalty as "lawless."

Burger initially had assigned all five cases to White, hoping to get a majority to uphold all five statutes, even though it was clear that the justices had voted 5–4 at conference to strike down North Carolina's statute. When that gambit failed, Burger tried to reassign all the opinions to Stewart. Ultimately Stewart, Powell, and Stevens cobbled together plurality opinions addressing each of the five cases.[43] Their plurality opinions became the controlling analysis. They rejected the claim that the Constitution precludes the imposition and execution of death sentences in all circumstances.[44] Instead, in *Gregg*, which became the lead opinion, they elaborated the safeguards the Constitution requires for death sentences to be imposed. Then, they incorporated that analysis by reference to *Gregg* in each of the four other cases. In *Gregg*, the three justices made clear that unbridled jury discretion produces arbitrary results. They concluded, however, that a bifurcated trial with individualized consideration of both aggravating and mitigating circumstances is acceptable. In this, they had the concurring votes of Burger, White, Rehnquist, and Blackmun with only Brennan and Marshall dissenting.

In striking down the mandatory statutes, Stewart, Powell, and Stevens rejected mandatory death sentences as "unduly harsh and unworkably rigid." According to these three justices, Louisiana's and North Carolina's failure to permit juries to consider the particular circumstances of each case rendered their laws unconstitutional. The two death penalty opponents, Brennan and Marshall, concurred, maintaining their view that the death penalty is always unconstitutional. Burger, Blackmun, White, and Rehnquist dissented, the latter two at length.

When all was said, mandatory death sentences for specific crimes—with no jury sentencing discretion—were prohibited, and, in light of *Furman*, which was not overruled by *Gregg*, so was unfettered jury discretion.[45] The three-justice plurality described *Furman* as having decided *"only* that, in order to minimize the risk that the death penalty would be imposed on a capriciously selected group of offenders, the decision to impose it had to be guided by standards so that the sentencing authority would focus on the particularized circumstances of the crime and the defendant."[46] Individualized determinations are constitutionally required. Bifurcated trials—with separate jury determinations of guilt and a sentence of death—are constitutional so long as the jury in its sentencing hearing considers both "aggravating" and "mitigating" circumstances in an attempt to limit death sentences only to those murderers who "deserve to die." Because not all first-degree murders may produce death sentences, this means that something special about the murder or the murderer is necessary to justify capital punishment. The Stewart-Powell-Stevens plurality read *Furman* to mandate that "where discretion is afforded a sentencing body on a matter so grave as the determination of whether a human life should be taken or spared, that discretion must be suitably directed and limited so as to minimize the risk of wholly arbitrary and capricious action."[47] In its effort to make imposition of death sentences less random, the Court in *Gregg* accepted the regulatory task of "guiding" jury discretion—the very guidance that a majority, just a few years earlier in *McGautha*, had concluded to be "beyond present human ability."

The Burger Court's split decisions in *Gregg* ultimately facilitated the execution of almost half the six hundred people then on death row. *Gregg* and its companion cases transformed the future of the death penalty in America. The Supreme Court had now firmly entered the death penalty business—a business it soon wanted to shed.

After *Gregg*

At 8:07 on Monday morning, January 17, 1977, in a dank cannery warehouse near the Utah State Prison in Danner, Gary Mark Gilmore was pronounced dead. Four bullets had been pumped into a white cloth circle that the prison doctor had pinned above Gilmore's heart onto his black T-shirt. Blood pooled onto Gilmore's lap, staining his white pants, covering his shackles and his red, white, and blue tennis shoes. He was slumped forward, at least as forward as he could be, constrained by the leather straps anchoring his head, waist, and arms to the dark green chair where he had been sat. The stench of gunpowder was pervasive.

Reporters and photographers view the chair where Gary Gilmore sat when he was executed by firing squad at the Utah State Prison on January 17, 1977.

Five riflemen had pushed their gun barrels through slits cut into a dark blue curtain about twenty-five feet from Gilmore's chair. They were all excellent shots: all had hit the cloth target. Their bullets clustered within about a half-inch radius. Gilmore couldn't have seen the men who shot him even if they had not been hidden by the curtain; his head was covered by a loose-fitting black hood. After the execution, the riflemen, who had not looked at Gilmore before shooting him, went to a nearby coffee shop for breakfast. Gary Gilmore was the first person executed in the United States in nearly a decade.[48]

Gilmore had been impatient for his execution, which was rare. After *Gregg*, delays of a decade or more between sentencing and execution became common.

After the Court had validated the restoration of capital punishment, it shifted to the processes for making and reviewing sentences of death. The only two justices who were in the majority in both *Furman* and *Gregg*, White and Stewart, remained especially important, along with Powell and Stevens, who with Stewart had co-authored the important plurality opinions in *Gregg* and its companion cases. The difficulty was that these justices had quite different objectives. White never wavered in his view that for the death penalty to be an effective deterrent, it should be imposed more frequently and more expeditiously. Stewart and Stevens, on the other hand, generally regarded fewer death sentences as better.[49] This hardly was a recipe for consistency or coherence.

The Supreme Court decided about thirty more death penalty cases before Warren Burger stepped down. These decisions generally fell into three categories. The first two—which dealt with questions of who could be executed and for what crimes—have been comparatively successful, at least in the sense of producing clear results and being reasonably coherent. The Court, for example, has determined that persons of limited mental capacity cannot be sentenced to death, although decisions have varied over time about just how limited that capacity must be.[50] And the Court has found the death penalty to be unconstitutional for juveniles, again with differing conclusions regarding the requisite minimum age to be eligible to be executed.[51]

In 1977, by a 7–2 vote, the Court—reflecting concerns about racial discrimination voiced by Justice Douglas in *Furman*—concluded that death is an unconstitutional, disproportionately excessive, cruel, and unusual penalty for the rape of an adult woman (even when committed in conjunction with an armed robbery and kidnapping).[52] The case, *Coker v. Georgia*, was again from Georgia, which was the only state then imposing death sentences for rape of an adult.[53] When the death penalty was imposed for rape, it was typically imposed for the rape of white women by black men. In the four decades before *Furman*, fifty-eight of the sixty-one people executed for rape in Georgia fit this pattern; nationwide 89 percent of those executed for rape did.[54] After *Furman*, Georgia juries had imposed death sentences for only four of forty-two rape convictions.[55]

Seven women's rights organizations, including the National Organization for Women, filed friend-of-the-court briefs opposing the death penalty. They worried that prosecutors would not bring charges and that juries would acquit accused rapists when they thought the penalty too severe. (The NOW brief, by Ruth Bader Ginsburg, also argued that imposing a death sentence for rape reflected an archaic view of women as a man's possession becoming "damaged goods" if she were raped.)

At oral argument, David Kendall, who was representing Coker, detailed the brutality of this rape, which had been committed after Coker, who was serving a life sentence, had escaped from prison. Justice Powell was especially troubled at the thought of simply sending Coker back to prison. When Kendall answered "imprisonment" to Powell's question about what punishment would be appropriate for Coker's crimes, Powell muttered, "the same way [society] was protected on the first go-around."[56]

Justice Stewart, however, would not accept capital punishment as a penalty for rape. "The rapist might be encouraged to kill," he said, "since the penalty would be the same."[57] At the conference following oral argument, Stewart insisted that death was a "disproportionate" penalty for rape and emphasized that Georgia was an outlier, "almost unique," he said, given "contemporary mores." Surprisingly, White (who ultimately wrote the majority opinion striking down the Georgia statute) agreed with Stewart that death was a "disproportionate" penalty and said the benefits to society from death sentences for rape are "negligible."[58] Although the Court remained silent about potential racial discrimination, the justices were certainly influenced by the overwhelming disparity in sentencing blacks to death for raping white women. Only Burger and Rehnquist dissented.[59]

A year later, in an Ohio case, the Court decided that death was cruel and unusual punishment for participating in a robbery in which another robber murders someone.[60] Sandra Lockett, who had been sentenced to death, had driven the getaway car in an armed robbery that resulted in an unexpected murder.[61] Rather than ruling the death penalty always unconstitutionally disproportionate for such a crime, as it subsequently would, the Court struck down the Ohio statute for unduly restricting the kinds of mitigating factors that the jury could consider in sentencing. The statute did not, for example, allow testimony about Lockett's limited role in the robbery or that the robber who actually shot the victim had been sentenced to life imprisonment. The Court's opinion by Chief Justice Burger stated:

> There is no perfect procedure for deciding in which case governmental authority should be used to impose death. But a statute that prevents the sentences in all capital cases from giving independent mitigating weight to aspects of the defendant's character and record and to circumstances of the offense proffered in mitigation creates the risk that the death penalty will be imposed in spite of factors which may call for a less severe penalty. When the choice is between life and death, that risk is unacceptable and incompatible with the commands of the Eighth and Fourteenth Amendments.[62]

As a result of *Lockett*, any and all mitigating evidence must be allowed to be presented to a jury considering whether to impose a penalty of death. Justice Rehnquist dissented, depicting the Court's death penalty decisions as unprincipled. He described the Court as having "gone from pillar to post with the result that the sort of reasonable predictability upon which legislatures, trial courts, and appellate courts must of necessity rely has been all but completely sacrificed."[63] Columbia law professor James Liebman, who has written extensively on the death penalty, says that the *Lockett* case turned "every capital sentencing judge or jury into a miniature constitutional court . . . with a new responsibility for determining whether the punishment of death was appropriate under federal constitutional law by assuring that death was proportionate to the amount of aggravation remaining after being discounted by available mitigation."[64] *Lockett*, of course, also implied that every such determination might be reviewed by the Supreme Court, which has the final say over federal constitutional questions.

In 1983, the Burger Court reached a similar judgment about aggravating factors: states may permit sentencing juries to hear all sorts of aggravating evidence.[65] The Court did, however, impose some modest limits on aggravating factors, such as "heinousness," as being unduly vague.[66]

By then, the Court had become frustrated by long delays between death sentences and execution and by its role as the final arbiter of death sentences in America. The Court's divisions had become bitter, dissents more angry. A majority of the Court was determined to cut back its role in reviewing the flood of death penalty appeals and to shorten the time from death sentences to executions.[67] Burger, Powell, and Rehnquist had all publicly deplored delays in executions while defendants exhausted their appeals. In 1981, complaining that only one inmate, having pursued his appeals, had been executed since *Gregg*, Rehnquist said, "The existence of the death penalty in this country is virtually an illusion" in which "virtually nothing happens except endlessly drawn-out legal proceedings."[68] White, unsurprisingly given his view that executions needed to be frequent to serve as an effective deterrent, agreed. So did Sandra Day O'Connor, who in 1981 had filled Potter Stewart's seat.[69]

In 1983 the Court voted 6–3 to overturn a federal appellate court's stay of execution of a condemned Louisiana man, in a case that raised issues similar to another case from Texas then before the Court. William Brennan said the decision "belies our boast to be a civilized society." Harry Blackmun accused the majority of a "rush to judgment."[70]

That year, making clear its intention to limit its death penalty traffic, the Court awarded great deference to the judgments of state courts— a path that became a Burger Court favorite, and not just in criminal cases.[71] After 1983, the Court generally limited its docket to resolving issues that would have broad application; it refused to hear nearly all death penalty cases, and, in essence, substituted state jury determinations and state appellate review of death sentences for federal oversight.[72] Blackmun and Powell would later describe death penalty cases as having "haunted and debilitated" the Court.[73]

Lethal Injections

In 1977, an Oklahoma medical examiner, Jay Chapman, proposed that executions be carried out by lethal injection of three drugs: a barbiturate to anesthetize the inmate, a paralyzing agent, which stops the inmate from breathing, and potassium chloride, which stops the heart. Oklahoma adopted this procedure that year, and similar legislation was adopted by many other states. In 1982, Texas became the first state to deploy such injections when it executed Charles Brooks, who had been convicted of murdering a Fort Worth mechanic. Between 1977 and 2009, 936 of the 1,107 convicts executed in the United States were killed by such lethal injections.[74]

In 1985, death row inmates from Oklahoma and Texas brought to the Burger Court an unusual challenge to lethal injections. The inmates claimed that, although it had approved these drugs for other purposes, the Food and Drug Administration (FDA) had not approved the use of these drugs for use in human executions, nor had the FDA concluded that the drugs were "safe and effective" for this purpose. This "unapproved use of an approved drug," they claimed, violated a federal law that required the FDA to evaluate drug safety and efficacy. The inmates won in the appellate court, but the Supreme Court unanimously reversed. Justice Rehnquist's opinion for the Court concluded that the FDA's decision not to take any enforcement action against this unauthorized use of the drugs was immune from judicial review.[75]

The Supreme Court's subsequent death penalty litigation has been well analyzed elsewhere, so we will not review it here. But one case decided in 1987, soon after William Rehnquist replaced Warren Burger as chief justice, warrants attention.

McCleskey v. Kemp has been properly described as "the most important capital case in a decade."[76] Warren McCleskey, a black man, had been sentenced to death by a Georgia jury for shooting and killing a white police officer, who had responded to an alarm from a store McCleskey and three companions were robbing.[77] McCleskey's appeal challenged the constitutionality of racially based disparities in capital punishment. His advocates presented to the Court a comprehensive study, which demonstrated that the murderer of a white, rather than black, person was 4.3 times more likely to be sentenced to death.[78] Prosecutors in Georgia, where McCleskey had been sentenced, sought the death penalty in 70 percent of cases where the defendant was black and the victim white, but in only 32 percent of cases where both the defendant and victim were white. Overall, in 87 percent (108 of 128) of the Georgia cases where the sentence was death, the victims were white.[79]

The federal Court of Appeals rejected the relevance of this evidence on the ground that McCleskey had not proved that "the race of McCleskey's victim in any way motivated the jury to impose the death sentence in his case." [80] His Supreme Court brief argued that "evidence of racial discrimination that would amply suffice if the stakes were a job promotion or the selection of a jury, should not be disregarded when the stakes are life and death." [81] But to no avail.

Lewis Powell, in the opinion for the five-vote majority (which included Rehnquist, White, O'Connor, and Antonin Scalia, whom Ronald Reagan had appointed to fill Rehnquist's seat when he was elevated to Chief Justice), acknowledged that jury death sentences are "difficult to explain" and contain a "risk of racial prejudice." He also conceded that the statistical discrepancies "correlate [death sentences] with race." [82] Powell nevertheless distinguished employment discrimination and jury selection cases, saying that the evidence "does not demonstrate a constitutionally significant risk of racial bias affecting the Georgia capital sentencing process." [83] McCleskey, according to the majority, had to prove that he was purposefully discriminated against by the jury based on race—a virtually impossible requirement to show that without such discrimination he would not have been sentenced to death. [84] A contrary decision, Powell said, would subject "our entire criminal justice system—indeed every state institution—to constitutional attack as racist." "McCleskey's arguments," he said, "are best presented to the legislative bodies." [85]

Powell was convinced that accepting McCleskey's argument would undermine the "guided" jury discretion, based on hearing both aggravating and mitigating circumstances, at the heart of the Court's decisions in *Furman* and *Gregg*, and their progeny. He saw no principled way to limit *McCleskey's* challenge to death sentences, so no statistical showing could move him. Nor was Powell willing to subject prosecutors' decisions to seek death sentences to judicial review. [86]

Justices Brennan and Marshall, of course, dissented, but in this watershed case Brennan did so at length, emphasizing the impact of race on death sentences and reciting Georgia's long sordid history of racial prejudice. "Considering the race of a defendant or victim in deciding if the death penalty should be imposed," Brennan wrote, "is completely at odds with [the] concern that an individual be evaluated as a unique human being." [87] Surprisingly, given his view that death sentences were a legislative prerogative, Harry Blackmun agreed and described the evidence as establishing "a constitutionally intolerable level of racially based discrimination leading to the imposition of [McCleskey's] death sentence." [88] John

Paul Stevens agreed and responded to Powell's concern that deciding for McCleskey would upend the entire criminal justice system by suggesting that the Court could limit its decision to a relatively small category of capital cases.

Writing in *The Washington Post* a week after the *McCleskey* decision, conservative columnist George Will applauded the Court for avoiding "chaos throughout the criminal justice system." "Arguments against capital punishment on constitutional (as distinct from moral) grounds," he said, "have driven themselves into an intellectual cul-de-sac." The death penalty, he concluded, was now "immune to constitutional challenge."[89]

Warren McCleskey was executed by Georgia's electric chair at 3:00 a.m. on September 26, 1991.[90] He was the 155th person executed after the Supreme Court's decision in *Gregg*.[91] As Columbia's James Liebman has observed: "The Court blinked. It surveyed death sentencing outcomes, saw the pattern Justice Douglas had seen in *Furman*, granted that the Eighth Amendment does not tolerate the pattern, and held the pattern tolerable."[92] The Court had refused to remedy systemic discrimination even when its consequence is a death sentence. Years later, after he had retired from the Court, when asked about votes of his that he would now change, Lewis Powell answered *"McCleskey."*[93]

Will the Death Penalty Fall Again?

No one believes that *Gregg* and its progeny actually remedied the infirmities with the imposition of death sentences that led the Court to invalidate the death penalty a few years earlier in *Furman*. One cannot find any serious analyst of our nation's death penalty who believes that the Burger Court's efforts in *Furman, Gregg,* and subsequent cases to rid death sentences of their arbitrariness—of their struck-by-lightning character—succeeded in reliably separating out those who "deserve to die" from those who do not. After struggling for nearly a decade trying to ensure that sentences of death are imposed less randomly, the Court in the 1980s essentially retreated, leaving death sentence determinations in the hands of state actors: juries, judges, and legislators.

After *Gregg*, the Court remained attentive to public opinion, especially as reflected by the public's legislative representatives. For the rest of the twentieth century, the public mood remained punitive. In January 1992, just before the New Hampshire primary during his campaign for the presidency, Bill Clinton, then Arkansas governor, denied the clemency appeal of convicted murderer Ricky Ray Rector. After murdering a white policeman, Rector, an African American who had always suffered from mental problems, shot himself in the head, destroying the front part of his brain. The day of his execution, Rector "was howling and barking like a dog, dancing, singing, and laughing inappropriately."[94] Nevertheless, with great fanfare, Clinton flew back to Arkansas to personally oversee Rector's execution. That night, as he had every other night, Ricky Ray Rector put his dessert aside to eat at bedtime. He obviously did not understand that he would not be coming back for his pie. A 1986 Burger Court decision prohibiting the execution of "insane" prisoners did not save Rector.[95]

Political gain, obviously, could then still be harvested from supporting executions with panache, demonstrating to the public a politician's unyielding toughness on crime. Elected governors, Republicans and Democrats alike, feared that clemency of death row inmates would be portrayed as weakness by political adversaries. Less obviously, many state court judges are also elected or subject to recall by the electorate and are subject to similar political pressures. Consider California. From 1976 to 1986—in the decade following *Gregg*, after the state had restored its death penalty—the California Supreme Court reversed death penalty sentences in 42 percent of its cases. Then, in 1986, responding to this "leniency," the voters removed from office the three state court justices who had voted consistently to reverse death sentences. During the next decade (1986–1996), the new court reversed death sentences in less than 4 percent of its cases.[96]

Nor are state prosecutors free from electoral pressures. District attorneys and state attorneys general are frequently elected officials and, if appointed, often harbor political ambitions. Prosecutors enjoy absolute immunity from liability for their decisions, mistakes, or overzealousness (as Chapters 3 and 12 describe). As with other elected officials, the political costs of being "soft" on crime are often high, while being tough yields political rewards.

Gary Gilmore's execution marked a turning point in our nation's approach to capital punishment. Throughout the 1960s and into the 1970s, debate raged in the academic literature over whether the death penalty serves as an effective deterrent. The truth is that we still do not know. But, over time, deterrence came to be quite beside the point: retribution provided all the justification death penalty proponents needed. The idea of rehabilitating convicts—not just murderers, but any convicts—had become an archaic artifact of an earlier, softer, presumably more naive time.

Thirty-two states and the federal government retain the death penalty. From 1976 through 1982, only six of the more than one thousand inmates on death row were executed. The Burger Court's determination not to review death penalty cases had some of the effect in increasing executions that a majority of the Court desired; between 1983 and 1990, 117 prisoners were executed—twenty times as many as during the previous seven years—but by 1990 2,237 convicts had been sent to death row after *Gregg*.[97] Between 1990 and 2010, the states put to death 1,101 people. In 2013, more than 3,100 inmates were on death row, but, in no year since *Gregg*—including the peak year of 1989, when ninety-eight of the 3,600 people then facing death were executed—has more than 3 percent of death row inmates been executed. The average is about 1.5 percent.[98] Since 2010, there have been fewer than fifty executions a year.[99] More than twice as many inmates left death row by having their sentences or convictions overturned as by execution.

Death sentences devour enormous resources—millions of dollars more than other cases. One California study estimated that, from 1978 to 2011, the state spent $4 billion more on death penalty cases than it would have spent if the sentences had been life imprisonment without parole.[100] As the most visible and widely reported aspect of the U.S. criminal justice system, death penalty controversies exert an outsized influence on public perceptions. They get great attention from the media, public interest lawyers, law professors, state courts, and the bar. In the meanwhile, resurrection of the death penalty made the harsh sentence of life imprisonment with no possibility of parole seem merciful.[101] And, as Chapter 3 describes, its struggle with death penalty cases played an important role in the Burger Court's determination to limit the availability of federal court review for all state prisoners.

During recent years, attitudes toward death sentences seem to be shifting. Excessive costs, long delays, and gross miscarriages of justice are diminishing the public's enthusiasm for death sentences. DNA exonerations of death row inmates have played a crucial role in this transformation. Governors of several states have imposed moratoriums on executions and even advocated their abolition. Most notable was Illinois governor George Ryan, who, in 2000—after learning that seventeen death-sentenced inmates had been exonerated in the previous twenty-five years—commuted the death sentences of all of Illinois' death row inmates. For the first time since the 1960s, state legislatures have repealed their death penalty statutes.[102] In 2011, Illinois abolished the death penalty, soon followed by Connecticut and Maryland. California came close to abolishing death sentences by initiative in 2013. (At the end of that year, eighteen states, mostly in the North and Midwest, did not permit sentences of death.) In 2014, executions in the United States hit a two-decade low of thirty-five and death sentences were at the lowest level in forty years. Only seven states carried out executions, with 80 percent of those in just three states: Missouri, Texas, and Florida.[103]

The conclusions of three Burger Court justices, who confronted death penalty laws and usually voted to uphold executions, confirm the ongoing arbitrariness of death sentences. After his retirement, Lewis Powell said he had voted the wrong way in *Furman*, as well as *McCleskey*, and wished he had always voted with the defendant in capital cases. He said, "I have come to think that capital punishment should be abolished."[104]

Harry Blackmun, who had expressed serious reservations with the death penalty all along, but voted with the majority in *Gregg*, finally dissented in 1987 in *McCleskey*, finding the "level of racially based discrimination" to be "constitutionally intolerable."[105] Seven years later, in February 1994, Blackmun dissented from the Court's refusal to hear the death sentence appeal of a man who had been convicted of killing a customer while robbing a bar. Blackmun famously wrote, "From this day forward, I no longer shall tinker with the machinery of death."[106] By way of explanation, he added:

> For more than 20 years, I have endeavored—indeed I have struggled—along with a majority of this Court, to develop procedural and substantive rules that would lend more than the mere appearance of fairness to the death penalty endeavor. . . . Rather than continue to coddle the Court's delusion that the desired level of fairness has been achieved . . .

I feel morally and intellectually obligated simply to concede that the death penalty experiment has failed. . . . No combination of procedural rules or substantive regulations ever can save the death penalty from its inherent constitutional deficiencies.[107]

Two months later, Justice Blackmun announced that he was retiring from the Court.

Having voted with the majority in *Gregg,* John Paul Stevens over time also came to express great qualms about the death penalty. Like Harry Blackmun, he dissented in *McCleskey.* Stevens also dissented from permitting victim impact statements in capital cases because they encourage jurors to decide in favor of death based on emotions rather than reason.[108] In 2002, he voted with the majority that executing mentally handicapped people is unconstitutional.[109] Then, in 2008, two years before he retired, Justice Stevens—in a concurring opinion, when out of respect for the Court's precedents, he voted to uphold a death sentence—expressed great concern about the very real potential for executing an innocent person, suggested that potential discrimination and the risks of error are especially high in capital cases, and said that the death penalty is always unconstitutional cruel and unusual punishment.[110]

Notably, these three justices did not come to reject the death penalty out of moral revulsion. Instead, after participating in hundreds of death penalty appeals over two or more decades, they finally accepted Thurgood Marshall's view in *Furman*: if the average citizen knew all the facts regarding death sentences, he would find it "shocking to his conscience and sense of justice." [111] After the Court decided *Gregg* and its companion cases in 1976, however, this view has never commanded a majority of justices while they served. Nor does it command a majority of today's Supreme Court.[112]

In July 2014, for the first time in four decades, a federal judge held a state's death penalty to be unconstitutional cruel and unusual punishment. Federal district court judge Cormac J. Carney, an appointee of George W. Bush sitting in conservative Orange County, California, said that lengthy delays and the uncertainty of execution made California's death penalty "a system in which arbitrary factors, rather than legitimate ones, like the nature of the crime or the date of the death sentence, determine whether an individual will actually be executed." The "random few" who will be executed, he said, "will have languished so long on Death Row that their execution will serve no retributive or deterrent purpose and will be arbitrary." [113] Judge Carney pointed out that of the more than nine hundred people who have been sentenced to death in California since 1978, only thirteen have been executed, and said that "for every one inmate executed in California, seven have died on death row, most from natural causes." He could have said that being executed in California was a lot like being struck by lightning.

The Burger Court's struggles with the death penalty corroborate the critical links between Supreme Court decisions and the politics and public attitudes outside its chambers. Our nation's punitive turn altered not only death penalty law, but, as the next two chapters make clear, also molded criminal law and procedure more broadly.

CHAPTER 2

Taming the Trilogy

66 Y ou have the right to remain silent. Anything you say can and will be used against you in a court of law. You have the right to an attorney. If you cannot afford an attorney, one will be appointed for you."

We all know that. The Warren Court in *Miranda v. Arizona*, an extraordinarily controversial 5–4 decision, insisted that the Fifth Amendment right not to incriminate oneself and the Sixth Amendment right to counsel require police to inform suspects in custody of these rights.[1] If the police fail to do so, any confession by the suspect cannot be used against him at trial. We have heard those words spoken in movies and on virtually every television crime show for half a century. Thanks to the worldwide popularity of shows like *Law & Order*, these are no doubt the best known U.S. constitutional commands worldwide. Americans take comfort in our knowledge that we have these rights, rights that people arrested in many other countries do not enjoy.

The Warren Court handed down the *Miranda* requirements in 1966 just as crime was escalating and beginning to command the attention of the American people. To Warren Court critics, *Miranda* was the most outrageous of a series of cases that bolstered the rights of criminal defendants, even guilty defendants. *Miranda* was the third of a trilogy— including *Gideon v. Wainwright*, which provided indigents with the right to a lawyer in federal and state courts,[2] and *Mapp v. Ohio*, which affirmed that both federal and state trials must exclude evidence illegally obtained by the police[3]—that came to symbolize a Supreme Court soft on crime.

As we have said, Warren Burger took his seat at the center of the

Supreme Court bench determined to roll back these Warren Court precedents and to restore primacy to the forces of law and order. The Court's case-by-case adjudication, however, produced some detours along its way to a much more conservative position. Some contemporaneous observers mistook these for major turns, but when the Burger Court did, on occasion, expand the rights of criminal defendants, these decisions typically proved to be short detours. Ultimately, the Court constricted greatly the rights that the Warren Court had granted criminal defendants. This was exactly what Richard Nixon intended.

Most observers had expected the Burger Court to overrule the major criminal procedure decisions of the Warren Court, but it did not. Instead, the Court eviscerated them. We start with *Miranda*, which not only enjoys special stature as a symbol of our constitutional rights, but also has frequently been described as the "centerpiece of the Warren Court's revolution in criminal procedure."[4] The *Miranda* warnings were a major target of the Warren Court's critics.

Minimizing *Miranda*

Before *Miranda*, confessions were excluded from evidence at criminal trials only if a defendant could show that his confession was "involuntary" or "coerced." But, except for a handful of instances when the suspect is brutally beaten, case-by-case determination of whether a confession is "voluntary" is fraught with difficulty.[5] After reviewing many decisions, Michigan criminal law professor Yale Kamisar described the "voluntariness" test as "too amorphous, too perplexing, too subjective and too time-consuming to administer effectively."[6]

By requiring the specific *Miranda* warnings, the Warren Court wanted to standardize police practices. The Court also wanted to protect unsophisticated, uninformed suspects—especially blacks arrested by white police in the South—from abusive police interrogations and to empower anyone in police custody to request and receive legal counsel. The horror of Bull Connor, Birmingham's commissioner of public safety, turning fire hoses and attack dogs on peaceful black protesters in the spring of 1963 remained fresh when Ernesto Miranda's confession came to the Court. But—even though the *Miranda* warnings conformed to

FBI procedure—the Court's decision to regulate police conduct was extremely controversial.[7]

The *Miranda* Court itself was closely divided. Four justices dissented, including Byron White, who wrote a spirited dissent (joined by Harlan and Stewart). White characterized much of the majority opinion as "irrational."[8] "The proposition that the privilege against self-incrimination forbids in-custody interrogation without the warnings specified in the majority opinion and without a clear waiver of counsel," he said, "has no significant support in the history of the privilege or in the language of the Fifth Amendment."[9] Warning that the *Miranda* warnings would "necessarily weaken the ability of the criminal law" to provide security to the American people, White wrote, "In some unknown number of cases, the Court's rule will return a killer, a rapist or other criminal to the streets . . . to repeat his crime whenever it pleases him."[10] White's *Miranda* dissent gave great credence to complaints that the Warren Court was "soft" on crime.

Nearly three years later, on April 1, 1969, William Rehnquist, recently appointed by Richard Nixon as assistant attorney general, sent a memorandum to John Dean, then associate deputy attorney general, urging the president to appoint a national commission to determine whether "the overriding public interest in law enforcement requires a constitutional amendment."[11] Complaining about *Miranda*, Rehnquist said, "The Court is now committed to the proposition that relevant, uncoerced statements of the defendant will not be admissible unless an elaborate set of warnings be given, which is very likely to have the effect of preventing a defendant from making any statement at all." Rehnquist added: "By believing that the poor, disadvantaged criminal defendant should be made just as aware of incriminating himself as the rich, well-rounded criminal defendant, [the Warren Court] has undoubtedly put an additional hurdle in the way of convicting the guilty."[12]

Many court watchers predicted that after Rehnquist and the three other Nixon appointees joined White and Stewart on the Supreme Court, *Miranda* would soon become a dead letter. Instead the Burger Court just badly wounded it.

In 1968, as part of a broad response to rising crime, Congress enacted a law to overrule *Miranda* and restore the "voluntariness" standard—a far milder response than that urged by some influential senators, who wanted to take away the Supreme Court's ability to hear cases involving confessions.[13] Surprisingly, in 2000, after languishing unenforced for decades, the law reversing *Miranda* was determined to be unconstitutional in a 7–2 decision authored by Rehnquist, who was then chief justice. By then, Rehnquist no longer feared *Miranda*'s impact on law and order; it had become toothless. The recitation of *Miranda* rights had become so conventional that in reaffirming the requirement, Rehnquist said, "*Miranda* has become embedded in routine police practice to the point where the warnings have become part of our national culture."[14] What he didn't say is that the Burger and Rehnquist Courts had so eviscerated *Miranda* that even William Rehnquist, one of its most avid critics, could affirm its ongoing constitutional status.

Despite widespread fears that the *Miranda* warnings would hinder police, their cultural significance is now more important than constraints they actually place on law enforcement. *Miranda*'s strongest supporters now describe the warnings as a "hollow ritual," and insist that "little is left of *Miranda*'s vaunted safeguards and what little is left is not worth saving."[15] As Michigan's Kamisar has said, "a majority of the Court is unwilling to overrule *Miranda* . . . however, a majority is also unwilling to take *Miranda* seriously."[16]

The Burger Court began weakening *Miranda* by allowing a defendant's confession obtained without any *Miranda* warnings to be used to impeach his testimony if he takes the stand in his own defense.[17] Then, rejecting *Miranda*'s broad view that warnings are required whenever "an individual is taken into custody or otherwise deprived of his freedom by the authorities in any significant way,"[18] the Court limited the "custody" requirement and allowed unfettered police questioning in a variety of circumstances, including when a suspect is brought to the police station for questioning or is detained for a traffic violation.[19]

In 1984, in a hotly contested 5–4 decision, the Court created an important public safety exception to the *Miranda* requirements.[20] Today, the public safety exception is routinely used in questioning suspects of terrorism. The Burger Court further diminished *Miranda*'s reach by permitting prosecutors to use at trial evidence other than an illegal confession that has been obtained without giving the *Miranda* warnings.[21] Police are now routinely trained how to obtain such evidence.[22]

The Burger Court also made it remarkably easy for a suspect to waive his rights to remain silent and have legal counsel present, making a hash of the *Miranda* Court's insistence that such waivers could occur only "knowingly and intelligently." In 1979, the Court determined that there is no need for any express written or oral waiver of a defendant's *Miranda* rights.[23] Justice Brennan, then the only remaining member of the *Miranda* majority, dissented, arguing futilely that "only the most explicit waiver of rights can be considered knowingly and freely given."[24] Soon after William Rehnquist became chief justice, the Court upheld an oral confession after the defendant had previously asked for legal counsel,[25] extending a Burger Court decision that allowed into evidence a confession obtained when the police had failed to tell a defendant, who had not requested an attorney, that a friend had obtained a lawyer who was trying to reach the suspect before he confessed.[26] In both cases, the confession waived the defendant's rights.

Police officers attempting to secure confessions now commonly exaggerate the incriminating evidence they claim to have and threaten that suspects will face much harsher charges if they refuse to tell the police their side of the story. After reading hundreds of court decisions, Rutgers law professor George Thomas concluded: "Once the prosecutor proves that the warnings were given in a language that the suspect understands, the courts find waiver in almost every case. *Miranda* waiver is extraordinarily easy to show."[27] In a detailed review (and defense) of the Burger Court's "lax waiver standards," William Stuntz, a leading criminal law scholar, said that the courts "have applied *Miranda* in a way that tolerates both a great deal of ignorance and mistake on suspects' part and also a great deal of deceptive conduct by the police."[28]

Police officers now have little difficulty working around *Miranda* and getting suspects to talk.[29] Over time, *Miranda* has had only a negligible effect on confession rates.[30] In 1988, shortly after Warren Burger stepped down, a comprehensive report of the American Bar Association concluded that the *Miranda* decision posed no serious problems for law enforcement[31]—a sound assessment for which the Court deserves substantial credit. No one today expresses the fears for law enforcement that Byron White predicted in his *Miranda* dissent and William Rehnquist conveyed in his 1969 memo.

Eviscerating the Exclusionary Rule

Some of the Warren Court's decisions concerning the Fourth Amendment's protections against illegal searches and seizures were nearly as controversial as *Miranda*. There are two issues here: the scope of the Fourth Amendment's prohibition of illegal searches and seizures and the rule that excludes illegally seized evidence from use at trial. We will say little about the former, except to note that many searches that would have been illegal without a court-issued warrant when Earl Warren left the Supreme Court are lawful today.

During the four decades from 1970 until 2010, the Supreme Court decided more than 150 Fourth Amendment cases. Over time—as the "War on Drugs" and then the "Global War on Terrorism" came to the fore—the Court narrowed the instances when police searches violate the Fourth Amendment.[32] In 1973, for example, the Burger Court concluded that a search is constitutionally valid whenever an individual consents to it, even if the person who consents did not know and was not informed that he could refuse the police request to search.[33] The Court also significantly expanded the ability of police to search automobiles they legally stop based only on a "reasonable suspicion," leaving Americans today with little protection against automobile searches.

Importantly, the Burger Court created a "special needs" exception to justify warrantless searches.[34] This occurred toward the end of Burger's term in a 1985 case, *New Jersey v. T.L.O.*[35] T.L.O., a fourteen-year-old high school student, challenged a search of her purse by school officials after a teacher had seen her and a friend smoking cigarettes in the school bathroom contrary to school rules. The purse search revealed some marijuana, plastic bags, a substantial amount of money, and a list of students who owed her money.[36] School officials then notified the police, and T.L.O. was subsequently charged in juvenile court with delinquency for selling marijuana. Justice White, in an opinion for the Court upholding the search's legality, emphasized the recent increases in school disorder and the flexibility needed by school officials to maintain order and discipline. He concluded that the search had been based on a "reasonable suspicion" that T.L.O. had violated school rules and said that "the school setting requires some easing of the restrictions to which searches by public authorities are ordinarily subject."[37]

Justice Blackmun wrote a concurrence, justifying the search on the school officials' "special need for an immediate response to behavior," and on "exceptional circumstances . . . in which special needs, beyond the special need for law enforcement, make the warrant and probable cause requirement impracticable."[38] Blackmun's invocation of "special needs" swung open a very big door. In the following decade, the Court frequently quoted Blackmun—for example, to uphold warrantless searches of a public employee's office, a probationer's home, and of a regulated business; to justify drug tests of public employees and high school students; and to uphold stops and inspections of automobiles at "sobriety checkpoints."[39]

Warren Burger's main target, however, was not the warrant requirement of the Fourth Amendment, but rather the "exclusionary rule" used to enforce it. The exclusionary rule prohibits the admission in a criminal trial of evidence obtained from a search that is illegal under the Fourth Amendment. The rule has a long history, having been applied to federal trials by the Supreme Court at least since 1914.[40] The Warren Court's major expansion of the exclusionary rule came in 1961 in *Mapp v. Ohio*, the first of its famous criminal procedure trilogy, when it nationalized the rule by excluding from state criminal trials evidence obtained by the police through illegal searches. Because the great bulk of criminal cases are brought in state courts, this was a major extension—even though freeing Dollree Mapp, who had been convicted of possessing obscene material after police had illegally ransacked her home, gave little cause for alarm.

Debate ensued over whether, as Burger claimed, the exclusionary rule is just one of many possible judge-made remedies for Fourth Amendment violation, civil damages, for example, being an alternative. Or whether, as Potter Stewart insisted, the exclusion of evidence is a necessary adjunct to the right to be free from illegal searches. Stewart said "searches conducted outside the judicial process without prior approval of judge or magistrate are *per se* unreasonable under the Fourth Amendment— subject only to a few specifically established and well-delineated exceptions."[41] He had little truck with criticisms like Burger's. Attacks on the exclusionary rule, Stewart said, are "misdirected" because the "critics sometimes fail to acknowledge that, in many instances, the same extremely relevant evidence would not have been obtained had the police officer complied with the commands of the [F]ourth [A]mendment in the first place."[42]

Before becoming chief justice, Warren Burger had expressed contempt for the exclusionary rule in a 1964 law review article entitled "Who Will Watch the Watchmen?," which (along with his Ripon College commencement address) brought him favorable attention from Richard Nixon and his advisers. In that article, Burger said that the exclusion of illegally seized evidence at trial is neither required nor justified by the Constitution; it is, he said, an inappropriate remedy to deter constitutional violations by police and other officials. Once he got to the Supreme Court, he set about to eliminate it.

As with *Miranda*, the Burger Court failed to overrule *Mapp*, but the Court so circumscribed the exclusionary rule as to render it virtually impotent. The Court's attack on the exclusionary rule took two tacks. The first involved new limitations on its applicability. The second—which was indirect but ultimately more important—restricted inmates' ability to appeal their convictions by expanding the doctrines of "waiver" and "harmless error" and by restricting convicts' opportunities to have their claims heard by federal courts in habeas corpus proceedings (see Chapter 3).[43]

The most important Burger Court decision limiting the scope of the exclusionary rule involved the admissibility of a large quantity of illegal Quaaludes found in Alberto Leon's Burbank, California, home, when police executed an invalid search warrant that they had thought to be valid. In a 6–3 opinion for the Court in *United States v. Leon*, overturning the exclusion of the drug evidence at Leon's trial, Justice White announced a number of propositions concerning the exclusionary rule, all of which have endured.[44] First, he rejected implications of earlier decisions, including *Mapp*, that the exclusionary rule is a necessary corollary to the Fourth Amendment; instead, his opinion characterized the rule as a judicially created remedy intended to deter police misconduct. Second, White said that application of the exclusionary rule turns on weighing its costs and benefits—a balancing that has since become the hallmark of exclusionary rule decisions. In *Leon*, White emphasized the exclusionary rule's costs, pointing out that illegally seized evidence is "inherently trustworthy" and that its exclusion imposes "substantial social costs" by impeding "the criminal justice system's truth-finding function." White also said that by allowing some guilty defendants to go free, the exclusionary rule "may well generate disrespect for the law." On the benefits' side, White made clear that the majority did not regard the exclusionary rule as an effective deterrent to misconduct by the police or by judges or magistrates. So, finding that the rule's costs outweighed its benefits, the Court created a new exception to the exclusionary rule when the police have acted "reasonably" and in "good faith"—an exception that soon became entrenched in constitutional law.[45] The Burger Court had successfully shifted the courts' focus away from the illegally searched individual's constitutional rights to the culpability of the police conduct.

The Court further narrowed the exclusionary rule's scope by cutting back on the evidence that would be excluded when the rule applies. It permitted the admission of evidence that would "inevitably" have been discovered absent the violation of the defendant's constitutional rights.[46] Consistent with its practice for a failure to give *Miranda* warnings, the Court also allowed the admission of illegally seized evidence to impeach the testimony of the defendant at trial.[47] The Burger Court also determined that the exclusionary rule has no application in contexts outside the criminal trial, allowing the admission of illegally seized evidence, for example, in civil tax and deportation cases.[48] Lower courts extended these rulings to eliminate the exclusionary rule in numerous other circumstances, such as parole, supervision, and sentencing hearings.[49]

After Burger stepped down, the even more conservative Courts that followed have applied *Leon*'s cost-benefit calculus to further narrow the exclusionary rule. Writing for the Court in 2009 in a 5–4 decision rejecting the exclusion of illegally seized evidence from an "unreasonable" search, Chief Justice John Roberts applied *Leon*'s balancing test to conclude that police misconduct must now be "deliberate, reckless, or grossly negligent" to justify the exclusion of evidence unconstitutionally obtained.[50] Today, the police hardly ever lose.

As Carol Steiker, a Harvard criminal law professor, observed: "When the strands [of Burger Court decisions] are considered together, the web of exceptions to the Fourth Amendment exclusionary rule . . . represents a complete reworking of the exclusionary rule regime that existed during the 1960s."[51] Again, the Burger Court succeeded in sharply constricting the Warren Court's constitutional protection of criminal defendants' constitutional rights without overruling the Warren Court's key decision.

Muting Gideon's Trumpet

The least controversial of the Warren Court's criminal procedure trilogy was *Gideon v. Wainwright*, a 1963 case that guaranteed legal counsel to criminal defendants charged by a state with a serious crime.[52] Clarence Earl Gideon, a poor, uneducated ex-convict, was accused of a minor burglary of the Bay Harbor Pool Room in Panama City, Florida. At his trial, Gideon requested counsel, but was told by the trial judge that Florida appointed attorneys for indigent defendants only in capital cases. Despite Gideon's best efforts to represent himself, he was convicted and sentenced to the maximum five years. From prison, Gideon filed a handwritten petition for review of his conviction by the Supreme Court, which appointed Abe Fortas to represent him. The Court—in an opinion that Earl Warren would later identify as one of the three most important issued by his Court—decided that a poor defendant charged with a serious crime was entitled in both federal and state courts to representation by a court-appointed lawyer. Writing for a unanimous Court, Justice Black said that "lawyers in criminal courts are necessities, not luxuries." The "noble ideal" that "every defendant stands equal before the law," he wrote, "cannot be realized if the poor man charged with crime has to face his accusers without a lawyer to assist him."[53]

After serving two years in prison, Gideon was retried, represented this time by an experienced Panama City trial attorney. After less than an hour's deliberation, the jury acquitted Gideon. His story was eloquently told by *New York Times* reporter Anthony Lewis in a bestselling book, *Gideon's Trumpet*. The book inspired a 1980 TV movie by the same name with Henry Fonda portraying Clarence Gideon and an award-winning 2013 HBO documentary *Gideon's Army*.[54]

The *Gideon* decision requires states to provide lawyers for poor defendants either by appointing private counsel or establishing public defender offices. Now most of the twelve million people arrested each year are represented by one of the nation's fifteen thousand public defenders. Unlike its decisions in *Miranda* and *Mapp*, the Warren Court's *Gideon* decision did not provoke a backlash: the public believes that everyone charged with a serious crime is entitled to a lawyer.[55] Nevertheless, despite its general support of the Sixth Amendment right to counsel, the Burger Court first expanded then limited the circumstances where the right exists.[56]

Criminal defendants, armed with the unanimous view of both the Warren and Burger Courts that legal representation is critical to our nation's system of criminal justice, believe that they are entitled to *effective* counsel, counsel like Clarence Gideon ultimately got.[57] Speaking in 1970 for a 6–3 majority, which included Burger, Justice White said that "defendants facing felony charges are entitled to the effective assistance of competent counsel." He elaborated: "It has long been recognized that the right to counsel is the right to the effective assistance of counsel."[58] But, despite White's insistence, there is no genuine right to competent or effective counsel. A criminal defendant is guaranteed a trial companion, who is a licensed lawyer, but not effective advocacy.

The Court has never abandoned lip service to the "crucial role" of effective counsel; it routinely acknowledges that "counsel's skill and knowledge is necessary to accord defendants the 'ample opportunity to meet the case of the prosecution' to which they are entitled."[59] But in 1984 in *Strickland v. Washington*, the Court set a very low bar for evaluating whether the constitutional right to effective counsel has been fulfilled. Speaking for a seven-justice majority, Justice O'Connor said that the "benchmark for judging any claim of ineffectiveness must be whether counsel's conduct so undermined the proper functioning of the adversarial process that the trial cannot be relied on as having produced a just result."[60] A defendant must show that his attorney performed poorly *and* that the attorney's poor performance was bad enough to produce an unjust result. A convict must demonstrate a "reasonable probability" that absent counsel's "unprofessional errors," the outcome would have been different. The Burger Court was not about to set guilty defendants free just because their lawyers were incompetent.

David Washington was the wrong person to bring this issue to the Supreme Court. He was surely guilty, having been sentenced to death by a Florida jury for what O'Connor described as an especially heinous, atrocious, gruesome, and cruel ten-day crime spree, including "three brutal stabbing murders, torture, kidnapping, severe assaults, attempted murders, attempted extortion, and theft."[61] Washington had confessed to the three murders, the last two against advice of his counsel, an experienced criminal lawyer who had been appointed by the state of Florida to represent him. After pleading guilty, Washington was sentenced to death by the trial judge. His complaint before the Court was that his lawyer had not presented psychiatric or character evidence on his behalf at his sentencing hearing. Unsurprisingly, given the facts, the justices found it difficult to believe that any lawyer—no matter how talented, industrious, and effective—could have spared Washington his death sentence.

Justices Marshall and Brennan dissented, as they always did, to reiterate their view that the death penalty is always unconstitutional. Marshall also attacked—as an abdication of essential judicial oversight—the majority's malleable requirement that counsel must "act like a reasonably competent attorney" and its introduction of a presumption that this requirement has been fulfilled. Marshall also complained about the Court's requirement that the defendant must show prejudice, a likely different outcome. Having served as an effective defense lawyer himself, he observed that "seemingly impregnable cases can sometimes be dismantled by good defense counsel." [62] Marshall pointed out that the best evidence for the defendant may not appear in the trial record precisely because of counsel's incompetence, making it often difficult, if not impossible, for an appellate court to assess whether the outcome of a trial was affected by the lawyer's incompetence. But despite Marshall's concerns, the Court held fast to a requirement of prejudice, and it applied that requirement to many other instances of "harmless error" in criminal trials.

David Washington was executed on July 13, 1984. But the requirements of *Strickland v. Washington* survived. The case is among the most cited in Supreme Court history, having been relied on by federal and state courts in thousands of cases, making it extremely rare for a court to overturn a conviction or sentence because counsel was ineffective. Writing a decade after the Supreme Court decided *Washington*, Stephen Bright, a prominent advocate for death penalty inmates (in an article entitled "Counsel for the Poor: The Death Sentence Not for the Worst Crime but for the Worst Lawyer"), describes numerous cases where defendants were convicted and sentenced to death having had grossly ineffective and inadequate counsel. Bright reports convictions upheld where the attorneys were intoxicated or dozing, and he quotes a Texas trial judge in a capital case saying, "the Constitution does not say that the lawyer has to be awake." [63] The American Bar Association issued a report describing many death penalty cases where attorneys had little experience, paid little attention, failed to investigate or make obvious requests to the court, and did not provide even a modicum of professional assistance at any time. [64]

No one now doubts that *Gideon*'s promise of effective legal representation for all criminal defendants—as Anthony Lewis put it: "The dream of a vast, diverse country in which every [person] charged with crime will be capably defended, no matter what his economic circumstances"[65]—has gone unfulfilled. States are simply unwilling to commit sufficient resources to guarantee adequate representation. *Washington*'s requirements that a defendant must both overcome a presumption that his counsel was effective and show the likelihood of a different outcome at trial in essence gave the Supreme Court's blessing to this deplorable state of affairs.

Surprisingly, today's even more conservative Supreme Court has signaled concern with some of *Washington*'s consequences. In 2010, the Court reversed the conviction of Jose Padilla, a lawful U.S. resident and Vietnam War veteran, who pled guilty to transporting marijuana after his attorney advised him erroneously that he "did not have to worry" that such a conviction would result in his deportation. Applying *Strickland v. Washington*, the Court, in an opinion by Justice Stevens, said that the failure to warn Padilla of the risks—indeed the virtual certainty—of his deportation was ineffective assistance of counsel that voided his conviction.[66] Then, in 2012, the Court decided two more cases reversing guilty pleas because of ineffective assistance of counsel.[67]

The Burger Court's constriction of the scope, consequences, and import of the *Miranda, Mapp*, and *Gideon* trilogy demonstrates the error in taking comfort from the Court's failure to overrule these cases. But these constraints were not its greatest blows against the rights of criminal defendants. Those came in its decisions about plea bargaining and concerning the writ of habeas corpus.

CHAPTER 3

Closing the Federal Courthouse Doors

The Burger Court did not share the Warren Court's distrust of state decision makers and state processes. In Chapter 1, we described how the Court—fatigued and bitterly divided over burgeoning requests to review convicts' challenges to sentences of death—decided essentially to leave these questions to the states. As Chapter 2 conveys, Warren Burger and his colleagues were committed to limiting the federal constitutional rights that the Warren Court had granted criminal defendants charged with violating state criminal laws. In addition to cutting back directly on the import of those rights, the Burger Court again concluded that, where state crimes are at issue, state, not federal, officials and courts will have the primary responsibility for assessing whether a criminal defendant's federal constitutional rights have been violated. This occurred principally in two legal contexts: challenges to exercises of discretion by prosecutors and efforts to obtain review of state court convictions in federal court through writs of habeas corpus.

Unshackling Prosecutors

Plea bargaining was unheard of until the mid-nineteenth century, and as late as the 1950s some appellate judges considered it unconstitutional.[1] But today, criminal trials, whether in state or federal courts, are rare. As the scope and complexity of criminal law has expanded, with an increased potential for overlapping criminal violations, prosecutors' decisions about which crimes to charge and which pleas to accept determine the fate of the vast majority of the people arrested by the police. Roughly 95 percent of all felony cases are now resolved through guilty pleas.[2] As William Stuntz has complained: "Criminal codes . . . cover everything and decide nothing, [they] serve only to delegate power to district attorneys' offices and police departments."[3]

"We were told they were 'strict constructionists.' "

In one of its last decisions before Earl Warren retired, the Supreme Court invalidated the guilty plea of a twenty-seven-year-old black man, Edward Boykin, who had been charged with five counts of armed robbery, a crime then punishable in Alabama from ten years in prison to death. When Boykin entered his plea, the Alabama judge asked no questions and the defendant remained silent. The jury, which was charged with determining Boykin's sentence following his guilty plea, sentenced him to death on each of the five armed robbery charges. The Supreme Court reversed, saying that a valid guilty plea demands "an affirmative showing that it was intelligent and voluntary."[4] No such showing had occurred in Boykin's case.

Boykin had been represented by an attorney who did not raise the question of the voluntariness of his plea in the state courts or in the lower federal courts. Demonstrating a much more limited view of attorneys' waivers of defendants' constitutional rights than the Burger Court subsequently would, the Warren Court concluded that "presuming waiver from a silent record is impermissible." Writing for a 7–2 majority, Justice Douglas said: "A plea of guilty is more than an admission of conduct; it is a conviction. Ignorance, incomprehension, coercion, terror, inducements, subtle or blatant threats might be a perfect cover-up of unconstitutionality."[5] But it would not be long before the Burger Court took a very different view of an attorney's silence and greatly expanded the occasions when such silence waives a defendant's constitutional rights.[6]

The Burger Court also embraced plea bargaining, viewing prosecutors' inducements to a defendant to accept a guilty plea not only as constitutional, but as an "essential" and "highly desirable" part of the criminal process.[7] Writing for a unanimous Court in a 1970 case upholding a guilty plea, Byron White said that, while the Court was not deciding that "the methods of taking guilty pleas presently employed in this country are necessarily valid in all respects," as long as the prosecutor had not threatened "physical harm" or used "mental coercion overbearing the will of the defendant," a prosecutor's suggestion or promise of leniency, coupled with the possibility of a higher penalty at trial, is perfectly valid.[8]

As the number of criminal cases grew and the volume and costs of criminal trials escalated during the 1970s (due, at least in part, to the Warren Court's expansion of defendants' constitutional rights), the prevalence of plea bargaining surged. Overcharging by prosecutors became commonplace, both as a negotiating tactic and to secure longer sentences.[9] This practice was explicitly countenanced by the Court in a little known and rarely cited 1978 case, *Bordenkircher v. Hayes.*[10]

At age seventeen, in 1961 Paul Hayes had been convicted of illegally detaining a female "for the purpose of having carnal knowledge of her." One of the participants in this activity was sentenced to life imprisonment for rape, but, presumably because his role was minor, Hayes served just over five years in the state reformatory, which he likened to a college, where you "just walk around the campus." Almost a decade later in 1970 he was convicted of robbery and, even though sentenced to five years in prison, he was immediately released on probation. While on probation in November 1972, Hayes stole a blank check from a local Lexington, Kentucky, business, filled it in for $88.30 payable to the Pic-Pac grocery, forged a signature, and cashed it. The following January he was indicted for "uttering a false check," a crime punishable by two to ten years' imprisonment.

The local prosecutor, Glen Bagby, offered Hayes a five-year prison term if he pled guilty, but Bagby said if Hayes did not plead and "save the court the inconvenience and necessity of a trial," he would charge Hayes under Kentucky's "three-strikes" habitual criminal law, which mandated life imprisonment for persons convicted of three felonies.[11] Hayes rejected the deal, saying that he did not believe the habitual criminal statute was meant for someone like him. He had seen "six-time losers" in the reformatory who had not been charged as "habitual criminals." Bagby then brought the habitual criminal charges, and Hayes was convicted and sentenced to life in state prison. Hayes's attorney then challenged his life sentence, arguing that Hayes was the victim of "vindictive prosecution" and claiming that Bagby had sought life imprisonment only because Hayes had exercised his constitutional right to a trial.

Hayes lost in the state appellate courts and in the federal district court, but the federal appeals court found for him. In a unanimous opinion for a three-judge court, Wade McCree (who would soon become the nation's second African American solicitor general) distinguished between "concessions relating to prosecution under an existing indictment" and threats to seek harsher charges under a new indictment if the defendant goes to trial.[12] According to McCree, if Bagby had originally indicted Hayes under Kentucky's three-strikes law and then offered to lower the charge to forgery, the plea negotiations would have been acceptable, but bringing a new harsher indictment because Hayes insisted on a trial was not permitted. In the tango of plea negotiations, the appellate court made important consequences turn on which foot the prosecutor puts on the dance floor first.[13]

Paul Hayes's case split the Supreme Court, even though neither the majority nor the four dissenters had any intention of introducing genuine judicial oversight of plea bargaining into the criminal process. The majority, in an opinion by Potter Stewart (joined by Burger, White, Rehnquist, and Stevens), denied Hayes relief, emphasizing the critical importance of plea bargaining in our nation's system of criminal justice. Stewart distinguished earlier cases where, after a full trial, prosecutors had reindicted defendants who had asserted their constitutional rights. In such cases, he said, prosecutors who brought the subsequent more serious charges were "retaliating against the accused for lawfully attacking his conviction." Here, Stewart insisted, the plea bargaining process, including the "fear of the possibility of a greater penalty upon conviction after a trial," creates a "mutuality of advantage to defendants and prosecutors alike." It is difficult, however, to see any advantage in these negotiations for Paul Hayes. "In our system," Stewart said, "the decision whether or not to prosecute and what charge to file or bring before a grand jury, generally rests entirely in [the prosecutor's] discretion," notwithstanding the potential that this "breadth of discretion" brings for "both individual and institutional abuse."[14]

The *Hayes* case greatly troubled Lewis Powell. He originally cast a tentative vote with the majority at the conference. Powell was not troubled by prosecutors threatening harsher sentences whenever defendants insisted on going to trial, and he agreed with Stewart that "the very concept of plea bargaining is pressure." In his notes, Powell said that "the already overloaded system would collapse if a significantly larger percentage of defendants elected jury trials."[15] However, Powell's law clerk, Nancy Bregstein, urged him to find for Hayes on narrow grounds because, as she put it, "the prosecutor's actions and motives in this case affront even my relatively conservative sense of justice."[16] No one needed

Victor Hugo to know that a life sentence in this case was a miscarriage of justice. Ultimately, that injustice proved more than Powell could bear, and he dissented, indicating that, while he agreed with much of the majority opinion, including its approval of broad prosecutorial discretion, he could not abide the result in this case. Powell said that "persons convicted of rape and murder often are not punished so severely," and he pointed out that Bagby's original offer of five years' imprisonment "hardly could be characterized as a generous offer." [17] So, even though he questioned its logic, Powell would have accepted Judge McCree's narrow ruling.

Justice Blackmun (joined by Brennan and Marshall) also dissented and urged the Court to accept Judge McCree's distinction between appropriately bargaining down from an initially harsh indictment and inappropriately seeking a second harsher indictment after a defendant has rejected a plea and demanded trial. Blackmun conceded that such a rule might make "little difference," since it "merely would prompt the aggressive prosecutor to bring the greater charge initially in every case and only thereafter to bargain." But he nevertheless thought that such a requirement might inspire greater public oversight of prosecutors' conduct and would retain at least some scope for judicial oversight of overcharging by prosecutors. As Blackmun correctly observed: "The Court's holding gives plea bargaining full sway despite vindictiveness." [18]

The Court's abdication of any judicial oversight over plea bargaining in *Hayes* may be its most consequential criminal law decision. It blindfolded criminal justice to prosecutorial abuses. A year earlier, in *Imbler v. Pachtman*, the Burger Court had extended absolute immunity from liability to prosecutors. [19] In combination, prosecutors since *Hayes* have enjoyed essentially unfettered discretion over the criminal charges they file and the sentences they request.

The *Hayes* decision came at a critical time for the country. As we have said, ever since the late 1960s politicians at every level of government had made "law and order" a rallying cry. Democrats had by then become as tough or tougher than Republicans, who had first spotted and seized the law and order issue. Federal and state legislators added more prohibitions on conduct to our criminal laws. Mandatory minimum sentences and three-strikes laws were adopted throughout the land. Long prison sentences, even for relatively minor crimes, especially drug crimes, became routine. Prosecutors knew the public would reward them for being tough on criminals and that they would pay no price for being too punitive.

The number of prosecutors, however, failed to rise commensurately with the nation's punitive turn. Between the mid-1970s and early 1990s, state felony prosecutions doubled, but the total number of prosecutors increased by less than 20 percent, from 17,000 to 20,000.[20] Judicial resources also failed to keep pace. (Only prison spending was adequately funded.) Taking criminal defendants to trial is far more costly than securing guilty pleas. When the Supreme Court heard the *Hayes* case, about 80 percent of felony convictions resulted from guilty pleas. Subsequently the number of guilty pleas expanded: to 90 percent by the late 1980s, 95 percent by 2000.[21] Despite the burgeoning state and federal criminal codes, trial rates fell by three fourths.[22] In *Hayes*, the Burger Court sent a clear signal to prosecutors that neither their plea bargaining tactics nor the consequences would face serious judicial scrutiny.

Beginning in the 1970s, district attorneys, many of whom crave higher office, turned up the heat on criminal defendants, insisting on pleas to more serious crimes and longer prison sentences. Many of the expanded constitutional rights that the Warren Court had provided criminal defendants, such as the exclusion of illegally obtained evidence or of confessions obtained without *Miranda* warnings, can be exercised only at trial. In the plea bargaining process, defendants can count on only their attorneys to protect them, and, like prosecutors, public defenders faced expanding caseloads.[23]

Two years after *Hayes*, a case came to the Court that offered another path to judicial supervision of criminal sentences, one that would encourage judges to review sentences based on the culpability of the offender and the harm to the victim. In *Rummel v. Estelle*, however, the Court, by a 5–4 vote, upheld the life sentence of William James Rummel, who in 1973 had been convicted by a Texas jury of the felony of obtaining money under false pretenses.[24] Rummel had accepted and kept $120.75 that he had been paid to repair an air conditioner, which he never repaired. He had previously pled guilty in 1969 to passing a forged check for $28.36, for which he had been sentenced to four years in prison. Five years before that, Rummel had been sentenced to three years' imprisonment for fraudulently charging $80 of goods to a credit card. The prosecutor in 1973 charged and convicted Rummel under Texas's three-strikes "habitual offender" statute, which provided a mandatory life sentence for three felony convictions. After the state courts upheld his sentence, Rummel challenged it in federal court as unconstitutional cruel, grossly disproportionate punishment.

In his majority opinion, William Rehnquist distinguished prior Supreme Court cases (described in Chapter 1) that had found the imposition of sentences "grossly disproportionate to the severity of the crime" to violate the constitutional prohibition of cruel and unusual punishment. Rehnquist also distinguished the Court's recent opinion in *Coker v. Georgia* (striking down the death penalty as unconstitutionally disproportionate for the rape of an adult woman) and the *Gregg* decision on the ground that death sentences are different: "the unique nature of the death penalty for purposes of Eighth Amendment analysis," Rehnquist said, "has been repeated time and time again in our opinions."[25] The "point at which a recidivist will be deemed to have demonstrated the necessary propensities and the amount of time that the recidivist will be isolated from society," Rehnquist said, "are matters largely within the discretion of the punishing jurisdiction."[26]

Powell wrote a strong dissent (joined by Brennan, Marshall, and Stevens) arguing that Rummel's punishment was unconstitutional. He rejected the notion that only capital cases engender a requirement that sentences not be "grossly disproportionate" to the severity of the crime. To minimize the "risk of constitutionalizing the personal predilections of federal judges," Powell suggested that courts look to three "objective" factors: (1) the nature of the offense, (2) the sentences imposed for the same crime in other jurisdictions, and (3) the sentences imposed on other criminals in the same jurisdiction.[27] But Powell couldn't garner a fifth vote.[28]

Then, in 1983, the dissenters in *Rummel* convinced Blackmun to join them in a 5–4 majority to strike down as an unconstitutional cruel and unusual punishment a South Dakota life sentence that allowed no possibility of parole under that state's recidivist statute.[29] Jerry Helm had been sentenced to life imprisonment without parole after being convicted in 1979 of issuing a "no account" check for $100, his sixth South Dakota conviction since 1964 of a nonviolent felony, all of which occurred when he had been drinking. Without his prior convictions, Helm's maximum sentence would have been five years in prison and a $5,000 fine. Powell's opinion was a ringing endorsement of "the constitutional principle of proportionality," the history of which he traced to the Magna Carta and the English Bill of Rights.[30] He said that the principle of proportional punishment had been "recognized explicitly" by the Supreme Court for "almost a century." Powell insisted that there was no difference between sentences of death and imprisonment relevant to a proportionality inquiry. Powell then elaborated the three "objective factors" that courts should use in evaluating claims of grossly disproportionate sentences, the same three that he had urged to no avail in his *Rummel* dissent. The decision in *Solem v. Helm* looked like it might be a turning point, but it soon proved a dead end.

Chief Justice Burger (joined by White, Rehnquist, and O'Connor) penned a blistering dissent. Claiming that the case was governed by *Rummel*, he said that the majority "blithely discards any concept of stare decisis [respect for precedent], trespasses gravely on the authority of the states, and distorts the concept of proportionality by tearing it from its moorings in capital cases."[31] By comparison with Jerry Helm, Burger said, "Rummel was a relatively 'model citizen."[32] He described the majority opinion as "nothing more than a bald substitution of individual subjective moral values for those of the legislature." And he worried that the decision "will flood the courts with cases in which . . . arbitrary lines must be drawn."[33]

Blackmun, the only justice who was in the majority of both *Rummel* and *Helm*, was silent. At conference, he said only that this case was different from *Rummel*, presumably because Rummel would be eligible for parole in twelve years and Helm had no possibility of parole. Responding to Powell's early drafts of the majority opinion, Blackmun asked that Powell omit one paragraph. Blackmun said that he might "write a few words in separate concurrence, but this will depend on what the forthcoming dissent has to say."[34] Ultimately, Blackmun decided not to write. The "Minnesota twins," as Blackmun and Burger were known, because they both came from that state and had long been close friends, had gone their separate ways.

On November 8, 1933, Harry Blackmun (left) was the best man at the marriage of his childhood friend, Warren Burger, to Elvera Stromberg. The maid of honor was Ella Caroline Anderson.

Ultimately, however, the Burger and Rehnquist position eventually prevailed. In 1991, the Rehnquist Court, in another 5–4 decision, upheld Michigan's mandatory life sentence without any possibility of parole for a conviction of possession of more than 650 grams of cocaine.[35] Without explicitly overruling *Helm*, the Court eviscerated it. In upholding a life sentence for a first-time nonviolent offender—a sentence more severe than imposed by any other state or the federal government—the Court eliminated *Helm*'s comparative approach to the reasonableness of criminal sentencing, and it reaffirmed *Rummel*'s effort to bar challenges to noncapital sentences as excessive. White, Marshall, Stevens, and Blackmun dissented.

The failed effort to inject into the criminal process any serious judicial review of the reasonableness or proportionality of sentences, coupled with the Burger Court's refusal to oversee or limit prosecutors' conduct, left prosecutors firmly in control of criminal sentencing. By refusing to review lifetime sentences where state legislatures imposed them, even for three relatively minor violations, the Court essentially blessed mass incarceration.[36] The Supreme Court determined that federal courts should defer to state legislatures, essentially ratifying the political rewards to state and federal legislators of pandering to a fearful public. Because the states enacted excessively harsh sentences in redundant and overlapping criminal statutes, the real discretion resides in the hands of prosecutors.[37]

The Court was a crucial participant in validating this transformation of our nation's system of criminal justice. The Burger Court made it easy for prosecutors to obtain guilty pleas, even without an attorney present. The Court also made it difficult to win a claim of ineffective assistance of counsel, just as the stakes for having effective and competent counsel and the costs of attorney incompetence ballooned. As William Stuntz, reflecting on *Hayes* and its aftermath, observed:

> The *real* law, the rules that determine who goes to prison and for how long, is not written in code books or case reports. Prosecutors like Bagby define it by the decisions they make when ordering off the menus their states' legislatures have given them. The behavior that will lead to a stay in the local house of corrections varies from courthouse to courthouse, and from prosecutor to prosecutor. So do the sentences that attach to most crimes.[38]

Shrinking the "Great Writ"

As we have said, the Warren Court, in cases like *Mapp, Miranda*, and *Gideon*, extended constitutional rights under the Fourth, Fifth, and Sixth Amendments to criminal defendants facing state criminal charges. To fully understand how much the Burger Court cut back the effects of these landmark rulings, we need to look at the remedy that the Warren Court relied on to enforce those rights: the writ of habeas corpus.[39] Habeas corpus allows those in the "custody" of the federal or state governments to challenge their confinement in federal court. The Constitution acknowledges the importance of habeas corpus by providing that "The Privilege of the Writ of Habeas Corpus shall not be suspended, unless when in Cases of Rebellion or Invasion the public Safety may require it."[40] Abraham Lincoln famously invoked this clause to suspend habeas corpus during the Civil War. Following the war, the 1867 Habeas Corpus Act gave federal courts power to grant habeas writs "in all cases where any person may be restrained of his or her liberty in violation of the constitution, or any treaty or law of the United States," thereby, for the first time, providing federal courts jurisdiction to hear habeas petitions of state prisoners.[41]

Like the great legal historian William Blackstone, the Warren Court viewed the habeas corpus writ as perhaps the most important writ of constitutional law.[42] The Court's expansion of federal habeas review reflected, in part, its concerns over racial prejudice. The Court feared—rightly in the era of Jim Crow—that in many instances black defendants could not secure a fair trial in Southern state courts. Here, the Court had historical support: the Court's reliance on the habeas writ had been of great importance in nineteenth-century disputes between slave owners and abolitionists.[43] Through its habeas decisions, the Warren Court enlisted the lower federal courts to oversee claims concerning state violations of criminal defendants' constitutional rights.

In three key cases, the Warren Court granted federal district courts enormous latitude to conduct evidentiary hearings to review the constitutionality of state court convictions.[44] The first two of these, issued on March 18, 1963, the same day the Court decided *Gideon*, expanded habeas corpus review in federal courts to situations where convicted prisoners had bypassed state appellate courts and come to federal court instead and to circumstances where the prisoner had not received a "full and fair hearing" of his constitutional claims in federal court.[45]

Charles Noia had been confined in New York state prison for nearly two decades. Along with two others, Noia had confessed under duress to participating in a robbery in which the victim had been killed and had been sentenced to life imprisonment. Noia's co-defendants, Frank Bonino and Santo Carminito, had been freed nearly a decade earlier because the confessions—which were the only evidence against any of the three—had been unconstitutionally coerced. Unlike Bonino and Carminito, Noia had not appealed his conviction in the state courts, claiming that he could not afford the costs of doing so and that he feared a retrial and second conviction might result in a death sentence. The lower federal court denied Noia's habeas petition on the ground that the habeas statute then in effect required applicants to have "exhausted the remedies available in the courts of the state."[46] In *Fay v. Noia*, the Supreme Court disagreed.[47]

Writing for a 6–3 majority, Justice Brennan said that "Noia's failure to appeal cannot under the circumstances be deemed an intelligent and knowing waiver of his right to appeal such as to justify the withholding of federal habeas relief."[48] After describing in detail the history and importance of the habeas writ, he said, "state procedural rules plainly must yield to this overriding federal policy."[49] *Fay v. Noia* allowed federal district courts to overlook virtually all of a convict's state procedural defaults by creating a standard under which a federal district court judge "may in his discretion deny relief to an applicant who had deliberately bypassed the orderly procedures of the state courts."[50] By deciding that Noia's decision not to appeal out of fear of a death sentence and to spare his family the appeal's expenses was not a "merely tactical" decision to avoid state courts, and therefore not "deliberate bypass," the Warren Court in *Noia* opened federal district courts to a large number of habeas petitioners who might have otherwise been barred by procedural defaults.

The second habeas decision announced that day, *Townsend v. Sain*,[51] expanded the instances when a federal district court is required to grant a habeas petitioner a hearing and make an independent determination of the validity of a convict's constitutional claims. Charles Townsend had been sentenced to death, based primarily on his confession, which he claimed had been unconstitutionally coerced. The state court had concluded that his confession was voluntary, and the lower federal courts had denied Townsend a new federal hearing. The Supreme Court reversed, in a 5–4 decision by Chief Justice Warren, which announced expansive federal review. "When the facts are in dispute," Warren said, "the federal court in habeas corpus must hold an evidentiary hearing if the habeas applicant did not receive a full and fair evidentiary hearing in state court."[52] To make unmistakable just how important a federal judicial hearing was, he added: "The opportunity for redress, which presupposes the opportunity to be heard, to argue and present evidence, must never be totally foreclosed."[53] In a third decision later that spring, the Warren Court expanded federal prisoners' rights to a second federal habeas hearing even after one has already been held.[54]

The Warren Court's habeas decisions greatly expanded the occasions where federal district courts had to review decisions of state courts at the request of a prisoner who alleged a federal constitutional violation. Vindicating those constitutional rights was the Court's priority; the guilt or innocence of the inmate was beside the point. In 1964, the year following these three decisions, habeas corpus petitions in federal courts swelled from 1,903 to 3,531.[55] A decade earlier, in 1953, there had been 541 such petitions.[56] Five years later, in 1969, state prisoners filed 7,359 petitions for habeas corpus in federal district courts, double the number of 1964.[57]

To the great dismay of state prosecutors, judges, and legislators, the Warren Court's habeas decisions allowed convicted criminals great leeway to relitigate their state confinement in federal court. The writ of habeas corpus and its remedy—the release of the prisoner whenever a retrial is impractical—became the routine way for convicted criminals to pursue their newly expanded federal constitutional rights. This was the state of habeas law when Warren Burger replaced Earl Warren. By the time Burger stepped down, the law of habeas corpus would be thoroughly transformed.

In 1973, once all four Nixon appointees had arrived, the Burger Court began dismantling the Warren Court habeas precedents. The new justices were extremely reluctant to free guilty convicts, and they believed that state court determinations deserve finality. For example, without even hearing oral argument, the Court, in a short opinion, trimmed *Townsend*'s requirement of a fresh federal court evidentiary hearing.[58] The federal district court had concluded—contrary to the state court—that two confessions used at trial were "involuntary," and said that the state had the burden to show they were voluntary. The federal appellate court agreed and ordered the release of a man convicted in state court of the premeditated murder of his wife. The Burger Court reversed, concluding, without any explanation, that the federal court must give a "presumption of correctness" to the state court's finding that the convict's confessions had been "voluntary." The majority was comprised of Nixon's four appointees plus Byron White, who had dissented in *Townsend*.[59]

Three years later, the Burger Court barred habeas relief in two cases where it deemed the convicts' constitutional objections to have been waived by their attorneys' failure to raise constitutional issues in the state court trials.[60] In one of these cases, the defendant was tried while dressed in his prison uniform, which all the justices agreed was a violation of his due process rights to a fair trial. In the other, African Americans had been excluded from the grand jury that brought the criminal charges, also a constitutional violation. In both cases, the Court said that the failure of the defendants' attorneys to object in a timely manner meant that the defendant had "knowingly, voluntarily and intelligently" waived his rights.[61] Justice Brennan dissented in both cases, complaining that these waiver decisions greatly weakened the "deliberate bypass" requirement of *Fay v. Noia*.[62] (Marshall joined Brennan in dissent in one of the cases, but did not participate in the other.)

Two months later—reflecting its antipathy to the exclusionary rule—the Court went much further in a murder case, foreclosing habeas review completely for an entire class of constitutional violations—the failure to exclude illegally seized evidence.[63] In this case, *Stone v. Powell*, Potter Stewart voted with the four Nixon appointees and Gerald Ford's recent appointee, John Paul Stevens, to form a 6–3 majority.[64] White, who had voted with the majority in the two earlier cases, joined Brennan and Marshall in dissent. White's vote had become very difficult to predict in habeas cases.

Around midnight on February 17, 1968, Lloyd Powell got into a fight over his theft of a bottle of wine with the manager of the Bonanza Liquor Store in San Bernardino, California. Ultimately, Powell pulled out a gun and shot and killed the store manager's wife. At about 10:00 a.m. the next day, Powell, who looked suspicious to police in Henderson, Nevada, a suburb of Las Vegas, was arrested for violating that city's vagrancy prohibition. The police then searched him and found a .38-caliber revolver with six fired cartridges in the cylinder. The gun was subsequently determined to be the one that had killed the store manager's wife. Powell was convicted of second-degree murder based on eyewitness testimony plus the testimony of the Henderson arresting officer describing his search and discovery of the gun. Powell's attorney objected, claiming that the policeman's testimony should have been excluded from evidence because the vagrancy statute was unconstitutionally vague, and, consequently, Powell's arrest and the search were illegal. The California courts rejected Powell's claim, as did the federal district court hearing his writ of habeas corpus, but the federal Court of Appeals reversed, concluding that Powell's arrest was indeed illegal and admitting the gun into evidence was not a harmless error.

Lloyd Powell's case came to the Supreme Court in 1976 along with that of David Rice, a member of an offshoot of the Black Panthers who had been convicted, along with two others, in Nebraska state court, of murdering a police officer by exploding a booby-trapped suitcase. The lower federal courts had ordered Rice released because the evidence of explosives leading to his conviction had been illegally seized.

Justice Powell, in his opinion for the Court, announced four days after the Court had reinstated the death penalty in *Gregg*, described the question as "whether state prisoners—who have been afforded the opportunity for full and fair consideration of their reliance on the exclusionary rule . . . by the state courts . . . may invoke their claim again on federal habeas corpus review."[65] He answered that question with a resounding "no." Powell's law clerk had questioned whether Rice's case was a good case for cutting back on habeas relief, worrying that it threatened "to eliminate all deterrence against Fourth Amendment violations in the very type of case where it is most needed, the investigation of a politically radical group concerning its involvement in a very sensationalist crime."[66] But his clerk's reluctance gave Powell no pause. In his earliest notes on these cases, he said that habeas corpus "was never intended to spring the guilty." A different result, he added, would release "a dangerous criminal who [had] raised these issues in state courts." The Burger Court firmly rejected the Warren Court's insistence that a "State court cannot have the last say when it, though on fair consideration and what procedurally may be deemed fairness, may have misconceived a federal constitutional right."[67]

The Burger Court was determined to close the habeas window that the Warren Court had thrown open.[68] *Stone v. Powell* unmistakably marked a major retreat from the expansive habeas opportunities that the Warren Court had provided state prisoners. Three years earlier, in a concurring opinion upholding the constitutionality of an automobile search, Lewis Powell (joined by Burger and Rehnquist) had expressed "grave doubts" about the Warren Court's habeas decisions. He described federal habeas corpus review as disregarding "the necessity of finality in criminal trials," heightening the "friction between our federal and state systems of justice," and undermining the "constitutional balance upon which the doctrine of federalism is founded."[69] William Rehnquist, while serving as assistant attorney general, had urged Congress to eliminate federal habeas opportunities when the convicts' claims of constitutional violations had been rejected by state courts.[70] During the Senate's consideration of Rehnquist's nomination to the Supreme Court, Maine Democratic senator Edmund Muskie described Rehnquist as having "suggested the most far-reaching revision in over 100 years of the availability of [the habeas] writ in federal courts."[71]

No one doubted that Lloyd Powell and David Rice were guilty, and the Court refused to set them free, which when a retrial is impractical (which it would be here if the key evidence were excluded) is the remedy for the violations of their constitutional rights. Justice Powell's opinion emphasized that doing so would frustrate the overriding goal of criminal justice: to convict the guilty and free the innocent. Habeas relief sought, he wrote, to protect the constitutional rights of the innocent.[72] Habeas would no longer be available in federal courts for state court failures to apply the exclusionary rule. The Warren Court's reliance on federal district court habeas proceedings to vindicate violations of defendants' constitutional rights—without regard to the convicts' guilt or innocence—had long been subject to harsh criticism.[73] It was now clear that a majority of the Burger Court held a very different view of the proper role for habeas corpus.

In demonstrating much greater deference to state courts, *Stone v. Powell* also reflected the Burger Court's desire for efficacy and finality in the criminal process. A majority of the justices had concluded that the Warren Court's worries that defendants could not receive fair trials in state courts was passé: "Despite . . . the unsympathetic attitude to federal constitutional claims of some state judges in years past," Powell wrote, "we are unwilling to assume that there now exists a general lack of appropriate sensitivity to constitutional rights in the appellate and trial courts of the several States."[74] The time when the Supreme Court would view decisions of state courts with suspicion of racial bias had ended; fairness of state adjudications from now on would be taken for granted.[75]

When Sandra Day O'Connor, a former Arizona state senator and state court judge, replaced Potter Stewart in 1981, the Court had another committed opponent of federal habeas review of state court decisions. Writing in the *William and Mary Law Review* shortly before Ronald Reagan appointed her, O'Connor urged continuation of "the recent trend in the United States Supreme Court shifting to the state courts some added responsibility for determinations of federal constitutional questions in state criminal cases."[76] She added: "State judges in assuming office take an oath to support the federal as well as the state constitution. State judges in fact rise to the occasion when given the responsibility and opportunity to do so."[77] In 1982, a habeas petition allowed O'Connor to demonstrate her belief in parity between state and federal judges. Writing for a plurality of the Court in *Rose v. Lundy*, she expressed her strong views about the centrality of state court judgments to the criminal law.[78]

Sandra Day O'Connor and Chief Justice Burger in the White House with President and Mrs. Reagan, July 1981. O'Connor was in Washington to prepare for her Senate confirmation hearing.

Noah Lundy had been convicted in a Tennessee court of rape and "crimes against nature" and had been sentenced to life imprisonment. He claimed, and the federal district and appellate courts agreed, that he had been denied a constitutionally fair trial because of prosecutorial misconduct. The federal district court concluded that Lundy "did not receive a fair trial, his Sixth Amendment rights were violated, and the jury [was] poisoned by the prosecutorial misconduct."[79] Lundy, however, like many prisoners, had filed the federal and state court documents on his own behalf without a lawyer, and he had failed to present five of his ten claims of prosecutorial misconduct to the state appellate courts. The Supreme Court sent the case back to state court, concluding that in order to be heard by a federal court, a convict's claims must first be "totally exhausted" by appeals in state court. This requirement, Justice O'Connor said, would "encourage state prisoners to seek full relief first from state courts, thus giving those courts the first opportunity to review *all* claims of constitutional error."[80] Even prisoners who file habeas petitions without an attorney, O'Connor said, "should be able to master this straightforward exhaustion requirement."[81] Justice O'Connor's opinion was not sufficiently harsh for William Rehnquist, who wrote to her saying, "I am somewhat disappointed that your opinion did not place any more stringent requirements on the availability of habeas corpus to state prisoners than it did."[82]

The Warren Court extended the guarantees of the Bill of Rights, especially of the Fourth, Fifth, and Sixth Amendments, to people charged with state crimes. The Burger Court made sure—with rare exceptions for well-represented and clearly innocent defendants—that the fulfillment of those rights would have to be found in state, not federal, courts.

The Burger Court's restrictive requirements for a successful habeas corpus petition have persevered and been expanded. In 1991 in *Coleman v. Thompson*, despite an inmate's plausible claim of innocence, the Supreme Court—with Rehnquist now serving as chief justice—finally interred *Fay v. Noia*.[83] Roger Keith Coleman, who had been sentenced to death for the rape and murder of his sister-in-law, had inadvertently filed his appeal with the Virginia Supreme Court three days late. Writing for the Court, Justice O'Connor began: "This case is about federalism . . . the respect that federal courts owe the states and the states' procedural rules when reviewing the claim of state prisoners in federal habeas corpus."[84] The state's interest in finality, she said, trumped Coleman's interest in obtaining federal review of the constitutionality of his conviction and death sentence.[85]

The restrictive attitudes toward federal habeas corpus of the Burger and Rehnquist Courts were endorsed by Congress in 1996 when Congress passed and Bill Clinton signed the Antiterrorism and Effective Death Penalty Act (AEDPA). This law, enacted in the aftermath of the 1995 Oklahoma City bombing, codified much of the Court's restrictive habeas law and, in some instances, introduced even more stringent constraints on inmates seeking habeas review of constitutional claims in federal court.[86] Some academics have characterized AEDPA as little more than a "pungent political statement."[87] But that law was not merely symbolic: despite lip service to vindicating the rights of the innocent, it has had a substantial additional chilling effect on federal habeas corpus opportunities.

For the Warren Court, a violation of criminal defendants' constitutional rights was paramount. In the Burger Court, a realistic likelihood that the defendant was innocent became a necessary condition for vindicating such violations. Even then, the Burger Court made it easy for prisoners or their defense lawyers inadvertently to waive their rights to challenge constitutional violations. Taking these restrictions even further, the Rehnquist Court and Congress in AEDPA amplified the importance of complying with state procedural rules. Now an inattentive attorney's foot fault or a technical mistake by a prisoner without a lawyer may deprive even an innocent person of any opportunity to obtain a hearing in federal court. The Burger Court began in the 1970s to close federal courthouses to state prisoners' habeas claims; in the 1990s, Congress essentially locked them. Prisoners—even innocent prisoners—convicted without a constitutional trial and looking for vindication of their constitutional rights would now have to rely nearly exclusively on appellate courts in the state that convicted them.

Not Soft on Crime Anymore

The Warren Court's goal in its controversial criminal procedure cases, as in many other contexts, was to promote equality—to ensure that the poor and uneducated have a chance in defending themselves against criminal charges similar to that of the rich and sophisticated. In *Miranda* itself, Earl Warren worried about the impact of police interrogation on "an indigent Mexican defendant" and on "an indigent Los Angeles Negro who had dropped out of school in the sixth grade."[88] Warren and his colleagues were determined to ensure equal justice to blacks and whites, to rich and poor, and to see that the constitutional rights of criminal defendants are not violated with impunity by state or federal officials. The Warren Court was perfectly willing, in the service of these goals, to enlist federal district courts to review and supervise states' decisions concerning criminal justice. It flung wide open federal courthouses to prisoners' claims of constitutional violations.

The Burger Court refused to embrace either the constitutional criminal law of the Warren Court or its remedies for enforcing federal constitutional rights. Burger's Court abandoned the Warren Court's quest for equal criminal justice. Instead, in the chambers of the Supreme Court, as in the nation at large, protecting the public and punishing the guilty came to the fore. As the memory of Bull Connor faded, suspicions of racial prejudice and police misconduct waned. The Burger Court was far more willing than its predecessor to rely on the good faith of law enforcement officers and state prosecutors and to rely on the fairness of state adjudications. So, without overruling its predecessors' major criminal procedure cases, the Burger Court drastically narrowed their import.

Warren Burger's tenure as chief justice has earned little praise, and the accolades he has received have usually concentrated on his efforts to make the nation's judicial system more efficient. His concern for judicial efficiency, coupled with his and his colleagues' reluctance to free convicts in order to protect their constitutional rights, led the Court to shrink opportunities for federal review of criminal defendants' constitutional claims. The Burger Court diminished the practical import of the Warren Court's expansion of criminal defendants' rights under the Fourth, Fifth, and Sixth Amendments. It allowed state prosecutors to bully, threaten, and cajole guilty pleas from those the police arrest. It greatly broadened the likelihood of binding attorney waivers of their clients' constitutional claims. It restricted state prisoners' ability to have their cases heard in federal courthouses. Together, these changes freed the nation from any worries that the Supreme Court was in the business of freeing guilty criminals.

One needs no tour of our nation's prisons to witness the country's turn away from the Warren Court's goal of equal criminal justice. In the

United States, criminal law and procedure have always been inextricably linked with issues of race. Fears and instances of racial discrimination were at the forefront of the Warren Court's criminal law jurisprudence. Sad to say, many of those fears have been realized. Our criminal justice system fails to fulfill the Constitution's promise of equal protection of the laws. Incarceration rates vary dramatically by race. We imprison vastly more African Americans and Hispanics than whites, in the process destroying families for generations and neighborhoods for decades.[89] Death sentences and drug law enforcement offer two prominent instances where criminal law disproportionately turns on race. Many excellent books and articles have been written about this subject.[90] Some even insist that our nation's punitive turn was inspired and advanced by racial animus.[91] We cannot assess such claims here. Instead, we now turn to the Burger Court's direct struggles with issues of race, beginning with its role in public school education. Criminal law would not be the only time that equality took a backseat to other values in Warren Burger's Supreme Court.

—————— PART TWO ——————

Race

The Supreme Court's decision in May 1954 in *Brown v. Board of Education* is widely heralded as the most important decision of the twentieth century.[1] And the unanimity of the Court in overruling the 1896 decision in *Plessy v. Ferguson*, which had upheld official segregation laws as long as the separate facilities are "equal," is frequently touted as Earl Warren's greatest political achievement. *Brown* itself was a case only about schools, emphasizing the importance and foundational nature of education, but over time it—along with the Civil Rights Act of 1964, enacted a decade later—became a bar against all official government-sponsored segregation. A year after *Brown*, the Court, for example, in a one-sentence opinion affirmed a lower court decision holding segregated public beaches and bathhouses unconstitutional.[2] The Court also banned segregated public golf courses.[3] A much more controversial sign that the regime of official segregation was ending came in the *Loving v. Virginia* case in 1967, when the Court unanimously struck down a Virginia statute making it a crime for any white person to "intermarry with a colored person." Earl Warren's opinion—again for a unanimous Court—made clear that no "legitimate" purpose was served by the statute, which he described as "designed to maintain white supremacy."[4] *Brown*'s legacy, therefore, is as a catalyst for revolutionary changes in race relations in America.

Today, black Americans serve in the highest levels of government, business, and education, but race perseveres as an "American dilemma."[5] A half century after *Brown*, our nation still suffers dramatic racial disparities of wealth, income, education, employment, health, and incarceration. Despite all the progress that has occurred, blacks and whites in America are still largely segregated, dramatically unequal.

Why and how this has happened is a challenge beyond our aspirations here, but there is no doubt that the Court's decisions when Warren Burger was chief justice of the United States played a pivotal role in shaping our nation's destiny. The Burger Court had choices of enormous consequence to make with respect to race, choices that still matter greatly today. What is the real meaning of *Brown*? The answer to that question is more complicated than it might appear—indeed, the Supreme Court is still in the process of answering it. Did *Brown* mean that the government could not stamp one race with a badge of inferiority? If so, how might such humiliation be defined? Is a policy that has a subordinating effect on blacks or other minorities unconstitutional in the absence of proof that the effect was intended? Or, to the contrary, did *Brown* mean that the government couldn't classify people on the basis of race? If so, what limits, if any, might this imply for affirmative action, which assumes as a starting premise that the government may take account of race for benign purposes? Can there be such a thing as a benign racial classification? The Burger Court wrestled with these questions. The American legal and political systems wrestle with them still—as recent Supreme Court decisions demonstrate.

We begin, as the Court did, with public schools.

CHAPTER 4

Still Separate, Still Unequal

L egal scholars revere the Supreme Court's decision in *Brown v. Board of Education* as the most important decision of the twentieth century. Here, for example, is how J. Harvie Wilkinson, a former law clerk to Justice Powell and now a distinguished federal appellate court judge, eloquently makes the claim:

> *Brown* may be the most important political, social, and legal event in America's twentieth-century history. Its greatness lay in the enormity of injustice it condemned, in the entrenched sentiment it challenged, in the immensity of how it both created and overthrew.[1]

What we remember about *Brown* today is how it sought to transform the legal status of race in America, to end Jim Crow, to lift blacks out of the subordination to which they had been relegated, especially in the South. We revel in our civil rights successes; some even proclaim a post-racial society. We have long forgotten—if we ever knew—the difficulties the Court had in reaching its judgment that public schools segregated by race are demeaning to blacks and inevitably unequal. And, as time passes, only a dwindling few recall the extraordinary resistance of Southern politicians and their voters to the Court's order to desegregate the public schools.

Now, more than half a century later, *Brown*'s promise of children of all races sitting side by side being educated by well-functioning public schools is unfortunately mostly a mirage. Decisions by the Burger Court bear much responsibility for that. Today's Supreme Court has abandoned the quest. The enormous injustice to African American schoolchildren that *Brown* sought to redress persists.

Brown v. Board of Education

In 1951 and 1952, five cases challenging segregated public schools came to the Supreme Court: two from the South, Clarendon County, South Carolina, and Prince Edward County, Virginia; two from the border states of Delaware and Kansas; and one from the District of Columbia. After oral argument in the fall of 1952, the Court was split. Only four justices clearly viewed segregated public schools as unconstitutional; two almost certainly did not; and the remaining three were not sure.[2] Then the chief justice, Fred Vinson (the most recent chief justice to be appointed by a Democrat), who had served since 1946, died from a sudden heart attack in September 1953. Dwight Eisenhower, in a decision he would regret, chose Earl Warren, who had been elected governor of California three times, to replace Vinson as chief justice. In the conference following the reargument of *Brown* in December 1953, Warren made clear his view that "the separate but equal doctrine rests on the basic premise that the Negro race is inferior," a premise that he insisted violated the intent of the Thirteenth, Fourteenth, and Fifteenth Amendments adopted following the Civil War "to make equal those who once were slaves."[3]

Much has been written about how Earl Warren moved a Court so divided to unanimity, and we will not retell that tale here.[4] Justices Felix Frankfurter and Robert Jackson regarded segregated schools as wrong, but not necessarily illegal. Jackson's law clerk, William Rehnquist (whom Richard Nixon appointed to the Burger Court nearly two decades later) described the *Brown* decision in a memorandum to the justice as "palpably at variance with precedent and probably with legislative history" and different from a long-discredited Supreme Court jurisprudence "only in the kinds of litigants it favors and the kinds of special claims it protects."[5] Stanley Reed of Kentucky, who said at conference that the "states should be left to work out the problems for themselves" and had urged that "separate but equal schools must be allowed" in the South, was the last to sign on.[6] Each of these potential dissenters subjugated their personal views to the national interest, demonstrating the kind of concern and respect for the Court that we hardly ever see from justices today. Warren knew that the Court's decision could take hold only if it spoke with one voice, without dissent. He managed a formidable political feat, but his eleven-page opinion for a unanimous Court, issued on May 17, 1954, was hardly the final word.

The *Brown* decision deliberately ducked deciding on a desegregation remedy; that issue was delayed until April 1955, when the Court heard more than thirteen hours of argument. Thurgood Marshall, arguing on behalf of the black schoolchildren, urged that desegregation occur promptly when school opened in September 1956.[7] But the Court in *Brown II* prescribed no deadline, leaving space for southern resistance. The Court instructed federal district court judges, charged with enforcing *Brown*, that they should weigh the interest "in admission to public schools as soon as practicable on a nondiscriminatory basis" against "the public interest" in "systematic and effective" desegregation, which should occur "with all deliberate speed."[8]

Justice Black had warned his colleagues that enforcing desegregation in the South would be as tough as enforcing Prohibition had been in New York City.[9] He was right. But the Court failed to foresee just how intransigent the problem of school segregation would be, and it acceded to the solicitor general's request that the reluctance of the South to integrate be "met with understanding and good will"—a concession that the South would not reciprocate.[10]

The South Resists

Most whites in the South viewed integrating their public schools as an ominous challenge to their way of life. For more than a decade after *Brown*, southern politicians treated "deliberate speed" as an invitation to massive resistance. Defiance was pervasive, but the techniques varied.

On September 4, 1957, defying a federal court order, Governor Orval Faubus of Arkansas deployed the state's National Guard to block nine black children from entering Little Rock's all-white Central High School, where a screaming mob had assembled to keep the black children out.[11] A reluctant President Eisenhower, no fan of *Brown*, federalized the National Guard and on September 25 sent the 101st Airborne to Little Rock.[12] The soldiers escorted the children into the school building, but that was hardly the end of the ordeal.[13] The school board turned to the federal courts to force the black students' withdrawal. In 1958, in the famous case of *Cooper v. Aaron*, with a decision signed by each of the nine justices individually, the Supreme Court ordered integration to proceed.[14] "The constitutional rights" of the black children, the Court said, "are not to be sacrificed or yielded to the violence and disorder which have followed upon the actions of the governor and legislature."[15] The governor and legislature responded by closing all Little Rock high schools for the school year.

By this time, massive resistance to *Brown* had taken hold throughout the South. In Virginia, resistance played out in different forms across the state. In January 1959, after the Virginia Supreme Court had denied local governments the ability to close public schools, the legislature repealed the state's compulsory attendance law, allowing localities discretion whether to provide public schools. Some schools remained closed for years as white parents sent their children to hastily organized private schools, often supported by public funds. A decade after *Brown*, Prince Edward County, Virginia, one of the original *Brown* defendants—in defiance of a federal court of appeals order—was providing only private all-white schools subsidized by tax credits and tuition grants. The Prince Edward board of supervisors explained that it would not follow "a court decree which requires the admission of white and colored children to all of the schools of the county without regard to race or color."[16] In response, the Court in 1964 for the first time empowered the federal district court to require a local government to levy taxes "to operate and maintain without racial discrimination a public school system." Justice Black ended his opinion for the Court: "The time for mere 'deliberate speed' has run out."[17]

In May 1968, a month after the assassination of Martin Luther King, the Warren Court's patience finally came to an end. In *Green v. County School Board of New Kent County*, a case from rural Virginia, the justices unanimously ruled that delays were "no longer tolerable" and ordered the local school board "realistically to convert promptly to a system without a 'white' school and a 'Negro' school, but just schools."[18] The significance of this decision, with an opinion by Justice Brennan, was to place on local school boards an affirmative obligation to provide a "unitary nonracial system of public education."[19] The Supreme Court would no longer countenance Southern resistance to *Brown*.[20] But how the Court would enforce the constitutional obligation to desegregate public schools remained very much an open question as Warren Burger took his seat as chief justice.[21]

Desegregation in the Burger Court

The first school desegregation case to reach the Burger Court—the most important case of Burger's first term—is often ignored.[22] It, however, exposes the political machinations of the Nixon administration concerning school desegregation and reveals how Chief Justice Burger behaved inside the Court. To abbreviate a complex negotiation, Nixon, in order to obtain a key vote from Mississippi senator John Stennis on a nuclear arms agreement, had his Department of Justice permit a delay until after the start of the 1969 school year of desegregation in thirty-three Mississippi school districts. In a short unanimous opinion issued in October 1969, the Court reiterated its intolerance of further delays and ordered immediate desegregation, in the middle of the school year, despite potential disruptions.[23]

Inside the Court, Burger himself had lain low until it was unmistakably clear how all eight of the other justices were voting. He then attempted to retain for himself the right to write the opinion for the Court.[24] The other justices, however, refused to allow Burger either to absolve the Nixon administration of responsibility for the delay or to disguise the fact that the Court's decision was a sharp rebuke to Nixon. The decision produced headlines around the country dramatizing a conflict between the Court and the president.[25] An angry Richard Nixon ultimately responded by enforcing the Court's order, avoiding a confrontation with the Court that had been urged by some of his advisers committed to a political "southern strategy" to transform the South from Democratic to Republican.[26] Nixon then promised to wipe out school segregation "root and branch," but he explicitly disapproved of busing schoolchildren as a segregation remedy.[27]

In 1970, the Burger Court seemed fully committed to prompt desegregation of public schools.[28] The justices did not have a long wait before this commitment was tested. In an effort to achieve cost savings, Charlotte, North Carolina, the largest city between Atlanta and Richmond, with a population of about 250,000, in 1960 had merged its public school system with the surrounding more rural Mecklenburg County schools, which served an additional 100,000 residents in an area totaling 550 square miles. By 1965, when the *Swann v. Charlotte-Mecklenburg Board of Education* litigation commenced, about 2 percent of the school district's black students attended schools with whites, and the vast majority of these were in one school with just seven white students.[29] No one disputed that the Charlotte-Mecklenburg school system failed to be the unitary integrated system required by the Court's decision in *Green*. The case raised two hotly contested issues that would long bedevil disputes over school segregation remedies: (1) the use of numerical goals based on race and (2) busing schoolchildren to integrate schools.

The federal district court in North Carolina ordered the school board to accept a plan to desegregate all of its schools, making "efforts" to "reach a 71–29 ratio in the various schools." The court required that "pupils of all grades [should] be assigned in such a way that as nearly as practicable the various schools at various grade levels have about the same proportion of black and white students," to reflect the ratio of white to black pupils in the school system (which was 71 percent white, 29 percent black).[30] The district court also ordered the school system to bus both elementary and high school students from their homes to school to implement the desegregation plan. Under this order, bus rides for elementary school students would average about seven miles and never exceed thirty-five minutes.[31] The federal court of appeals accepted the district court's orders for secondary schools, but demanded reconsideration of its plan for busing elementary school students, who it said would face an "unreasonable burden."

One of the briefs filed in the Supreme Court was on behalf of Richmond and Norfolk, Virginia, supporting Charlotte-Mecklenburg's opposition to the desegregation plan. The brief was signed by the Virginia attorney general, but its principal author was Lewis Powell, a senior partner at a white-shoe Richmond law firm, who had presided over the American Bar Association and served for two decades on the Richmond and Virginia school boards.[32] The brief foreshadowed Powell's positions when he joined the Court a couple of years later. It expressed fears that busing would accelerate white flight to the suburbs and undermine high-quality neighborhood schools, diminishing the quality of education for whites.[33] The brief also pointed out that the integration ordered by the district court in *Swann* would diminish white support for taxes and bonds to finance public schools, a political response to *Brown* that had already occurred in Virginia. Powell was fully prepared to give up on *Green*'s demand for integrated schools "now" and instead to wait until residential segregation ended.[34] As his biographer, John Calvin Jeffries, Jr., puts it, Powell wanted the Court to limit *Brown* to removing the "stigma of legal apartheid" in the South. Lewis Powell would soon play a crucial role in school desegregation, advancing his views as a Supreme Court justice.

But, for now, the Court was unpersuaded. After oral argument in October 1970, a clear majority existed to uphold the district court's order; only Burger and Black were reluctant to do so. Rather than dissent, however, Burger again ultimately voted with the majority and grabbed the opinion for himself in an effort to control its reach. Complaints from other justices required Burger to produce seven drafts of his opinion before it was issued the following April. Contrary to the views of seven of his colleagues, Burger's initial draft refused to affirm the district court's orders, treated the district court's suggested white-black ratio as an invalid "requirement," accepted the maintenance of single-race schools, and would have limited busing based on the scope of past discriminatory actions of the school board, the age and health of the students, and whether the time and distance of travel would "impinge on the educational process."[35] These were obviously his own views. His final opinion, for a unanimous Court, upheld the district court's 71–29 ratio as "a starting point in the process of shaping a remedy, rather than an inflexible requirement."[36] Burger's opinion, however, said that if the lower court's order had contained a "fixed mathematical racial balance reflecting the pupil constituency of the system" or if it had required "any particular degree of racial balance or mixing," the Court "would be obliged to reverse." Conceding that district court judges should "be concerned with the elimination of one-race schools," the opinion also said that "the existence of some small number of one-race, or virtually one-race, schools within a district is not in and of itself the mark of a system that still practices segregation by law."[37]

The Court's opinion in *Swann*—for the first time—explicitly approved busing as a desegregation remedy. That is what made it a landmark. "Desegregation," Burger's opinion said, "cannot be limited to the walk-in school," but, Burger continued, busing is inapt "when the time or distance of travel is so great as to either risk the health of the children or significantly impinge on the educational process." Burger insisted that limits on travel time should be lower for younger students.[38]

The Court was split over *Brown*'s reach when segregated schools resulted because of residential segregation, rather than law. Burger wanted to say that *Brown* was inapplicable to the former de facto segregation, confining its scope to cases where the segregation was de jure (legally compelled). Burger's original draft asserted that *Brown* was limited to cases where segregation was enforced by "government action," and it "does not and cannot embrace all the residential problems, employment patterns, location of public housing, or other factors beyond the jurisdiction of school authorities that may indeed contribute to some disproportionate racial content ratios in some schools."[39] Through three drafts, Burger clung to his view that the Court had no power to order busing as a remedy for de facto segregation.[40] However, Justice Douglas, with the support of a majority of his colleagues, vigorously argued the contrary, pointing out that residential segregation had itself long enjoyed governmental support and legal protections, such as enforcement of racial barriers in private agreements and local zoning practices.[41] *Swann* failed to address this dispute. Burger's final opinion dropped his earlier assertions and explicitly saved for later the question of *Brown*'s scope when "school segregation is a consequence of other types of state action, without any discriminatory action by the school authorities."[42]

When the Court's *Swann* decision was issued on April 20, 1971, *Newsweek* described it as "by far the most momentous Court pronouncement on school segregation since the landmark *Brown* decision of 1954."[43] Dramatic it was, but not really a historic landmark; it would soon be eroded. Disagreements over busing, the use of numerical goals or requirements, and the application of *Brown* to segregated schools outside the South would divide the justices in the years ahead. Their desire for unanimity—for speaking with one voice in such a contentious, highly visible, southern school desegregation case—allowed Burger to fashion an opinion that opened the door to subsequent retreat.

Just four months after the Court announced *Swann*, speaking alone in his capacity as the supervising justice for the Fourth Circuit in a case from Winston-Salem, North Carolina, Burger wrote that "nothing could be plainer, or so I had thought, than *Swann*'s disapproval of the 71%–29% racial composition . . . in assignment of pupils." He deliberately ignored *Swann*'s approval of such a ratio as "a starting point in the process of shaping a remedy." [44] Burger's *Winston-Salem* opinion also emphasized *Swann*'s limits on busing, repeating its language concerning the time and distance of travel. [45]

The Supreme Court upheld the use of busing to desegregate the public schools in Charlotte and Mecklenburg County, North Carolina, but white parents kept their children home. This empty bus made its rounds on September 9, 1971.

Given the expanse of the Charlotte-Mecklenburg school district, white flight to the suburbs to avoid the Court's decision was impractical, so the city ultimately complied. A decade later, Charlotte-Mecklenburg had nine black school board members, and Charlotte had elected its first black mayor. [46] But such progress was neither pervasive nor irreversible. The Court's desegregation cases then moved outside the South, most importantly to Denver, then Detroit—with all four Nixon appointees in place. [47]

The Denver case, along with contemporaneous litigation from San Antonio and Detroit, became watersheds in desegregation of our nation's schools. From *Brown* in 1954 until *Green* fourteen years later, the Court had played the role of cautious bystander as the South resisted desegregation. Then, having lost all patience, the Court in 1968 ordered prompt desegregation, endorsed the goal of racially balanced schools, and, three years later in *Swann*, ordered extensive busing to achieve that balance— acting unanimously.

From 1964 until *Swann*, the Court had enjoyed strong support from the president and a congressional majority. But once the Court embraced busing as the prime remedy for segregated schools, it lost the backing of both. President Nixon called for a moratorium on busing and urged congressional action to restrict busing if a constitutional amendment was impractical.[48] In May 1972—a year after the *Swann* decision—running a strong antibusing campaign, Alabama's segregationist governor George Wallace won the Democratic presidential primary in Michigan. After Wallace's victory, Nixon directed his aides to "hit the busing issue . . . in a strong, unequivocal way."[49] The House of Representatives enacted antibusing legislation, but in October 1972, after three attempts to break a filibuster failed in the Senate, the bill was shelved. By the time the Denver case reached the Court, the president and a majority of Congress and the public were all clearly hostile to busing. So, as it turned out, were Richard Nixon's four appointees to the Court. None would play a more crucial role than Lewis Powell.

The Denver decision, *Keyes v. School District No. 1*, announced on June 21, 1973, was a victory for desegregation, but one that would soon prove illusory.[50] Denver's laws explicitly barred segregated schools, but its school board, in one area of the city at least, had manipulated school locations and student placement to segregate white students from blacks and Latinos and to assure higher quality schools for the whites. In other parts of the city, schools were also segregated, but there was no evidence that this had resulted from deliberate actions of school or other officials. Nevertheless, writing for the majority, Justice Brennan held that the school board's actions constituted de jure segregation for all of Denver. Although it did not order busing, the Court's opinion meant that busing students throughout the Denver school district would be required. Having initially voted with the dissenters, which allowed Justice Douglas to assign the opinion to Brennan, Burger concurred with the result in one sentence, but he did not join Brennan's opinion. Rehnquist dissented.[51] Justice Powell wrote a long opinion concurring with the majority that the case should be sent back to the district court, but disagreeing with much of Brennan's opinion. This technically made the vote 7–1, obscuring just how ruptured the Court had become.

Powell's files reveal the great care he took in crafting his concurring opinion. Powell, a southern conservative, struggling, as he confided, to put aside his "confederate emotions," agreed with William Douglas that there should be no difference whether segregation was de jure or de facto. He called the distinction a "constitutional phony"—a distinction that would require desegregation only in the South. With segregated schools common throughout the land, Powell viewed it irrelevant whether they were sanctioned by law or emerged from the locations of people's residences. He also thought it foolish—and in some fundamental sense discriminatory—to limit our nation's redress of separate and unequal minority schools to the South. In 1973, when *Keyes* was decided, a majority of justices shared this view. Harry Blackmun agreed and said that the "*de facto–de jure* distinction must eventually give way," but he ultimately joined Brennan's opinion. So the *Keyes* case never addressed that issue, nor would any other case, principally because Lewis Powell would not accept busing as a remedy for segregation.[52]

Powell's *Keyes* opinion echoed positions he had taken in his *Swann* brief. He expressed "profound misgivings" with "large-scale or long-distance transportation of students in . . . metropolitan school districts."[53] In his private exchanges with his clerks, Powell was more candid. He said *Swann*'s affirmance of the district court's busing plan in Charlotte was "unfortunate," and predicted that "in the end [busing] will be a disservice to education and particularly the younger children who are bused so extensively."[54] "Present and future generations of children," he said, "are being penalized—in terms of being bused away from their neighborhoods—in a highly punitive manner for the 'sins' of their forebears."[55]

Powell insisted that *Swann* permitted flexibility and consideration of other "values and interests." The values that Powell held most dear exalted neighborhood schools and abhorred any sacrifice of quality education by whites in pursuit of desegregation.[56] Powell knew, of course, that residential segregation was ubiquitous and extremely resistant to change, but his commitment to neighborhood schools was steadfast. Although he never said so publicly, Powell was convinced that busing white students to black schools would diminish the white students' educational opportunities. He was sure that school integration orders like those in *Swann* would escalate white flight and lead to a decline in educational quality.

The Court's conference to grant certiorari in *Keyes* had been the first conference for both Lewis Powell and William Rehnquist. As Nixon's southern appointee, Powell knew that his first important school desegregation opinion would surely attract media scrutiny. He was determined to write a forceful opinion in *Keyes*, but he worried about how it would be viewed by the "eastern media," so he endeavored to ensure that what he wrote was "scholarly, restrained, and carefully crafted." For this task, he was fortunate to have J. Harvie Wilkinson III as his law clerk. Wilkinson was a close family friend of Powell's, a clear thinker, and an elegant writer, who would go on to have a distinguished career as an author, law professor, and federal appellate judge. And Wilkinson shared Powell's views about the case. He and Powell exchanged several memos and drafts, and when the opinion was nearly final, Powell circulated the draft to his other two clerks, Larry Hammond and William Kelly. Both were considerably less in accord with Powell's views and made suggestions—particularly concerning Powell's reading of *Swann*—that ultimately strengthened Powell's opinion. His *Keyes* opinion, along with his two decades of experience on the school boards of Richmond and Virginia, made Powell the most important vote and voice of the Burger Court in cases involving race and education.

Moving Dollars Instead of People?

In an extremely important case from San Antonio, *San Antonio Independent School District v. Rodriguez*, argued the same day as *Keyes*, Lewis Powell again played a starring role.[57] In *Keyes*, Powell insisted that the "allocation of resources within the school district must be made with scrupulous fairness among all schools."[58] In a memo to Jay Wilkinson six months before the *Keyes* opinion was announced, Powell said that "the socioeconomic status of children (white or black) is the single most relevant factor in determining the success in schools."[59] And, in a subsequent memo, Powell wrote, "I personally doubt that mixing the races in the schools will have any significant effect on elevating the learning ability or the ultimate quality of the education. Socioeconomic backgrounds are far, far more relevant than race or racial mixing."[60]

Nevertheless, Powell, with Hammond's help, was simultaneously writing the opinion for a 5–4 majority in a momentous decision to be issued that April—a decision that would close the federal courthouse to constitutional claims of socioeconomic disadvantage in education and degrade the impact of a school's resources on its educational quality. In a memo to Powell, Hammond described it as one of the most important cases of recent years.[61] Indeed it was—a case that would have far greater and more lasting significance for the education of blacks, other minorities, and poor whites than *Keyes*.

The case began in 1968—while the Warren Court was still in place—when a group of mostly Mexican American parents from the poor Edgewood school district of San Antonio decided to challenge the inequities in Texas's system of school finance. They prevailed before a three-judge district court, which ruled in 1971 that the disparity in school resources suffered by poor and minority school districts violated the Constitution.

The residents of Edgewood, a residential neighborhood near the center of San Antonio, paid the highest property tax rates in the area. But because property values were low, the district's per-pupil spending was only 60 percent of that in Alamo Heights, the most affluent San Antonio school district, even after taking into account the money for public education from state coffers.[62] Property in Alamo Heights—with its five thousand students, compared to Edgewood's 22,000—had an average value more than eight times that of Edgewood, and its overwhelmingly white residents paid significantly lower property tax rates than those in Edgewood.[63] Alamo Heights also had much greater ability to issue school finance bonds at substantially lower interest costs. In a similar case, the California Supreme Court found that such disadvantages violated both the state and federal constitutions.[64]

The San Antonio case, which Powell described as novel and complex, divided the Court. After much coaxing of Potter Stewart, Powell ultimately garnered a five-vote majority to reject the Edgewood parents' challenge. In joining Powell, Stewart became a crucial ally of the four

Nixon appointees in school cases. White and Marshall wrote strong dissenting opinions. White (joined by Brennan and Douglas) emphasized that there was simply no way for parents in poor districts like Edgewood to levy property taxes sufficient to finance an education even close to that provided by districts like Alamo Heights. Marshall stated his position simply: "The right of every American to an equal start in life, so far as the provision of a state service as important as education is concerned, is far too vital to permit state discrimination on grounds as tenuous as those presented by this record."[65]

Writing for the majority, Powell acknowledged the importance of education. But the plaintiffs had argued that education was a fundamental constitutional right, and here Powell said no. Both the Warren and Burger Courts would go beyond the Constitution's text to find "fundamental" rights to marry, to use birth control, to terminate a pregnancy, to travel. But Powell drew the line here. His opinion dismissed as irrelevant the statements from the *Brown* decision ascribing unique importance to education.

Previous Supreme Court decisions had shown special solicitude for the poor in contexts as varied as criminal defense, waivers of fees for voting, and divorce proceedings, but the *Rodriguez* majority insisted that the poor have no claim to special constitutional concern. Powell acknowledged that the Edgewood school district was 90 percent Mexican American and 6 percent black, but neither he nor his colleagues treated this case as about race or minorities; they ignored correlations between low property values and minority status.[66]

Powell was flummoxed about the potential scope of a Court order to remedy the financial disparities, but his rejection of the parents' claim rested on his zeal for local autonomy in K–12 education. Ignoring the Edgewood parents' extraordinary financial efforts and economic disadvantages and indifferent to their inability to fund high-quality neighborhood schools, a tone-deaf Powell described "local control" as providing "the freedom to devote more money to the education of one's children," as well as the ability to innovate, experiment, and compete for "educational excellence."[67] This was a freedom the Edgewood parents lacked, a competition Edgewood was sure to lose. Greater state financing, Powell claimed, would enhance the state's and diminish the locality's influence over education policies—a prospect that dismayed him. The fact that some families—mostly higher income white families—resided in school districts with significantly higher residential values and far greater ability to attract valuable commercial and industrial property, Powell said, did not result from "purposeful discrimination" or "hurried, ill-conceived legislation." Texas school financing was, according to Powell, "an enlightened approach to a problem for which there is no perfect solution."[68]

Parents like those in Edgewood, whose children were consigned to public schools with limited resources, would thereafter find no relief in federal courts. The Burger Court had consigned their children's plight to state legislatures and state courts.

It is easy to view the *Rodriguez* case as an admirable, if unremarkable, exercise of judicial restraint and to underestimate its importance. Many have; the case is not mentioned, for example, in John Jeffries's comprehensive biography of Lewis Powell, nor in Jay Wilkinson's estimable book *From Brown to Bakke* (even though he was clerking for Powell when *Rodriguez* was before the Court). Nor is it mentioned in Bob Woodward and Scott Armstrong's *The Brethren*, a detailed examination of the Burger Court during this period.

But the five votes cast against Demetio Rodriguez and the Edgewood parents momentously influenced the future of public education in America. By ratifying and entrenching school financing based principally on local property values, the Court's decision in *Rodriguez* guaranteed that the resources of public schools would remain grossly unequal throughout the land—turning predominantly on the value of parents' residences. And by restricting the constitutional consequences of being poor, demanding only a minimal justification from states and localities to discriminate based on socioeconomic status, *Rodriguez* eviscerated the most promising alternative avenue for claims based on racial discrimination. Finally, by consigning the right of public education to the constitutional dustbin, the Court constricted the minimal requirements of our Constitution's guarantee of liberty and justice for all.

After *Rodriguez*, schools in America would remain starkly unequal. One would have to look elsewhere than public school funding to find a national commitment to equal opportunity for all. In addition, *Rodriguez*'s emphasis on the primacy of local school districts did not augur well for cases that were coming to the Court from Richmond and Detroit challenging racial discrimination among schools in neighboring school districts. The Court's next encounter with school desegregation would ensure that our nation's public schools would also remain largely segregated.

Stopping at the School District Line

Along with *Keyes* and *Rodriguez*, a third crucial school case came to the Court during its 1972 term. This was a case from Richmond that had first been heard by a federal district court judge in Virginia, Robert R. Merhige, Jr., a transplant to Richmond from Brooklyn and a longtime friend of Lewis Powell's despite their large substantive and stylistic differences. Before taking the bench, Merhige had been a charismatic trial lawyer who had handled criminal and divorce cases below both the dignity and price threshold of Powell's silk-stocking law firm.[69] In 1971, Judge Merhige ordered school busing in Richmond. Angry residents then burned a cottage he owned, shot his dog, and threatened his life. During the following months, white flight to the suburbs from Richmond raised the city's share of black schoolchildren in the metropolitan area's public schools from 63 to 69 percent. Richmond was busing children across neighborhoods in what was becoming a single-race city.

Seeing no other path to a unified integrated school system, Judge Merhige in January 1972 (on the Monday following Lewis Powell taking his seat in the Supreme Court) ordered consolidation of the Richmond school district with those of the two counties—Henrico and Chesterfield—that surrounded the city. Both Henrico and Chesterfield had overwhelmingly white residents, more affluent than Richmond's inner-city blacks. Reaching this unprecedented ruling, Merhige issued a carefully crafted 325-page opinion, loaded with factual findings justifying his order. He related the long history of de jure segregation and the resistance to *Brown* intended to deny black schoolchildren their constitutional rights to integrated public schools by all three local jurisdictions, supported by the Virginia state government. Finding no other efficacious alternative, Merhige ordered cross-district busing of white suburban and black inner-city children. Such busing, he said, would produce integrated schools ranging from 17 to 40 percent black. Judge Merhige found that neither the school district's boundaries nor the counties' control over them had any educational justification, but served instead to encourage residential segregation and defeat school integration.[70]

The federal court of appeals (which today sits in the Lewis F. Powell, Jr., U.S. Courthouse in Richmond) disagreed. It upheld busing within Richmond's city limits (in accordance with *Swann*) but vacated Merhige's order of busing between Richmond and its surrounding suburban counties.[71]

When the case came to the Supreme Court, Powell (who had closely followed his hometown developments) disqualified himself because of his long service on the Richmond and Virginia school boards. The remaining eight justices split 4–4.[72] Justices Blackmun and Stewart concluded that by crossing the city limits, Merhige had gone too far. Stewart reportedly told his clerks that he had gone along with busing in Charlotte and Denver, but Richmond "is where I get off."[73] Along with Burger and Rehnquist, Stewart and Blackmun voted to uphold the appellate court's decision to halt busing at the county line. Douglas, Brennan, White, and Marshall voted to ratify Merhige's order. So, as is the rule in cases where the Court splits evenly, the appeals court was upheld without setting a Supreme Court precedent. The Richmond school case ended with one sentence: "The judgment is affirmed by an equally divided Court."[74]

But Robert Merhige was not the only federal judge who concluded that combining city and adjacent suburban school districts was the only way to achieve integrated schools. After taking forty-one days of testimony over a four-month period, federal district judge Stephen Roth reached the same conclusion in Detroit.[75]

Despite its role as a pre–World War II haven for both blacks and whites seeking well-paying industrial jobs, no city, north or south, had a worse race relations history than Detroit. Blacks and whites had fought there over jobs, political power, policing, residential segregation, and public schools.[76] The Detroit Tigers were the next-to-last major league baseball team to field African American players. After minor race riots in 1966, a major riot in July 1967 spurred Lyndon Johnson to send 2,700 Army paratroopers to fortify Detroit's police and Michigan's National Guard. More than seven thousand rioters were arrested and thirty-three blacks and ten whites died in the violence.[77] As we have noted, in 1972, Alabama's George Wallace won the Michigan Democratic primary, carrying white districts in and around Detroit.

A year earlier, in 1971, Judge Roth had found that the Detroit school board had used a variety of techniques—including boundary changes, attendance zones, and school siting decisions—to segregate its schools. Judge Roth also found that Michigan's state government had taken actions that helped cause and maintain segregated schools in Detroit.[78] Detroit's 133 public schools then served 133,000 students, nearly all black. The surrounding suburban schools were virtually all white. Inner-city Detroit was becoming America's poorest large city, while the surrounding suburbs prospered. So, like Judge Merhige, Judge Roth ordered consolidation of school districts and busing between the city and its suburbs. Roth's decision was upheld by the Sixth Circuit Court of Appeals (which now sits in the Potter Stewart Courthouse in Cincinnati).[79] On November 19, 1973—over the objections of Justices Brennan, Douglas, and Marshall, who feared the worst—the Burger Court agreed to hear the case.

The Detroit case, *Milliken v. Bradley*, presented legal issues identical to those in Richmond.[80] After *Milliken* was heard in February 1974, the eight justices who had participated in the Richmond case split the same way. Lewis Powell held the deciding vote. Anyone who had read his *Swann* brief or his *Keyes* opinion could harbor no doubt about how he would choose.

Powell hoped that Burger would assign this opinion to him, but Burger, once again, kept this important opinion for himself. And, not for the first time, the other justices in the majority, especially Powell and Stewart, were not happy with what he wrote.[81] Powell was most upset with Burger's efforts to pin the decision on what he described as Judge Roth's insistence on achieving "racial balance." Roth had not done this, and, in any event, Powell thought it quite beside the point. Stewart agreed. Rehnquist, on the other hand, was content for the Court to disavow any suggestion that racial balance in schools might be constitutionally required. Powell and Stewart had a struggle on their hands. Burger's opinion was not issued until July 27, 1974, a time when the Court normally would have been recessed for the summer, but the Court had stayed in session that year to deal with the controversy over the release of Nixon's Watergate tapes (discussed in Chapter 13). This gave Powell enough time to shape Burger's opinion to reflect his views.

Powell wanted the Court to endorse the argument advanced by

Nixon's solicitor general, Robert Bork, that any desegregation remedy must be limited to the scope of the constitutional violation. In this case—if one ignored the actions of the state of Michigan—that would restrict any remedy to the city of Detroit and let the suburbs off the hook. After months of trying, Powell finally managed to get Burger to revise his opinion to make this point. Stewart wrote a separate concurrence to emphasize it.

Lewis Powell remained firmly opposed to busing, which he continued to believe wasted money and would lead to lower quality schools. In his *Swann* brief and his *Keyes* opinion, he also had worried that busing would stimulate white flight, but in *Milliken* that prospect didn't trouble him. Powell was genuinely concerned about the practical difficulties of judicially ordered consolidations of school districts, and he advocated fervently to retain local control over schools. He managed to rewrite large chunks of Burger's opinion, and although given *Swann*, rejecting busing as a desegregation remedy was not possible, Powell essentially got what he wanted: emphasis on the importance of local control of schools and the elision of any state responsibility for segregation in Detroit.

Along with Blackmun, Stewart was worried about the loss of public and congressional confidence in the Court because of its busing orders. He had good reason to worry. Antibusing sentiment, along with proposed legislation to halt it, had firm majorities in both the House and Senate, with Richard Nixon leading the charge.[82] In June 1974, as the final touches were being applied to the *Milliken* opinion, Boston's district court judge Arthur Garrity incited further antibusing sentiment when, to remedy a deliberate pattern of segregation by the Boston School Committee, he ordered eighteen thousand Boston students to be bused to different schools. Nearly half of these students, 8,500, were white. Of those, about eight hundred were to be bused to a school located in a black Roxbury ghetto. An even greater number of black students were to be bused into a South Boston Irish working-class neighborhood. That April, two months before Judge Garrity's order, three thousand antibusing whites gathered in the Boston Common to protest, achieving national attention that the justices could not have missed. (Busing in Boston subsequently resulted in years of violence and a sizable diminution of students enrolled in the Boston public schools.[83])

Potter Stewart wrote a concurring opinion in *Milliken* denying that the Court was answering any "questions of substantive constitutional law."[84] The dissenters, on the other hand, knew exactly what was at stake. Douglas's dissent was brief and conclusory. "Today's decision," he said, "given *Rodriguez*, means that there is no violation of the Equal Protection Clause though the schools are segregated by race and though the Black schools are not only 'separate' but 'inferior.' "[85]

Thurgood Marshall's dissent (which infuriated Powell), joined by all three of the other dissenters, was a long, anguished cry of despair on behalf of the Detroit schoolchildren. Now, two decades after arguing *Brown*, Marshall saw the Court transforming that victory into defeat: a "giant step backwards," an "emasculation of our constitutional guarantee of equal protection of the laws." "We deal here," Marshall wrote, "with the right of all of our children, whatever their race, to an equal start in life and to an equal opportunity to reach their full potential as citizens. Those children who have been denied that right in the past deserve better than to see fences thrown up to deny them that right in the future." "Today's holding, I fear," he said, "is more a reflection of a perceived public mood that we have gone far enough in enforcing the Constitution's guarantee of equal justice than it is the product of neutral principles of law."[86]

Unlike the death penalty, which had befuddled him, Byron White knew exactly what he thought about the desegregation of schools. He had witnessed resistance to desegregation up close in Mississippi when he served as John Kennedy's deputy attorney general and, after that, he never wavered in his support for school integration.[87] White's dissent in *Milliken* (which the other three dissenters also joined) emphasized the culpability of Michigan's state government and its responsibility to ensure desegregated schools. Judge Roth had explicitly found that state authorities had "taken actions with the purpose of segregation" that "created or aggravated segregation in the schools."[88] But this inconvenient fact was ignored in Burger's majority opinion. White observed that any remedy confined to the city of Detroit would leave many of its schools 75 to 90 percent black, and he concluded that only a metropolitan solution could satisfy *Brown* in such a residentially segregated metropolitan area. White also pointed out that the city-suburban plan adopted by Judge Roth would be "physically easier and more practicable and feasible than desegregation efforts limited to . . . the city of Detroit." Judge Roth's plan, White said, would require only 350 new buses compared to 900 for a Detroit-only plan. White insisted that the majority's "talismanic invocation of the desirability of local control over education" offered neither an educational nor constitutional justification for denying black students the rights promised by *Brown*.[89]

Two aging justices, William J. Brennan, Jr. (left), and Thurgood Marshall, walk down an empty Supreme Court corridor, 1979.

No one can deny that, in combination with *Rodriguez*, the Burger Court's decision in *Milliken* doomed to failure the Warren Court's effort to ensure integrated schools of equal quality. Harvard legal historian Michael Klarman correctly describes *Milliken* as the most important school desegregation case since *Brown*.[90] After *Milliken*, flight to the suburbs by those whites who could afford it was guaranteed to accelerate, and it did. Intra-district busing remained the law of the land and was effective in places, such as Charlotte, North Carolina, where city and suburban schools were in the same school district. Success elsewhere, however, was limited. Public opposition to busing for desegregation produced violent outbursts in a number of cities, including Boston and Louisville. Antipathy between working-class whites and poor blacks spread and intensified. But *Rodriguez* precluded them from joining together to advance federal constitutional claims for improving their schools based on socioeconomic disadvantages. After *Rodriguez* and *Milliken*, one needed to look elsewhere than the public schools for *Brown's* legacy: from the mid-1970s forward, both desegregation and quality education depended on elected politicians—mainly serving state and local governments.

Then Things Got Worse

Justice Marshall's prediction in his *Milliken* dissent that the Burger Court's decision would "allow our great metropolitan areas to be divided up each into two cities—one white, the other black" came to fruition. He might have added, "one well-to-do, the other poor." Well into the 1980s, federal district courts continued to order single-district busing, and schools became more desegregated, mostly in the South, in rural areas, and in cities where city and suburban schools were in the same school district. Elsewhere, increased integration sometimes occurred in the context of "neighborhood" schools, often on the boundaries of minority communities. Most northern and midwestern metropolitan areas, however, are fragmented into many separate school districts, and *Milliken* ensured that these would not be consolidated. Then, beginning in the 1990s, dissatisfied parents challenged the continuation of court-ordered desegregation plans even where local school boards wanted the plans to remain in effect. With the explicit blessing of George H. W. Bush's Justice Department and William Rehnquist's Supreme Court, lower courts began terminating court-supervised desegregation orders and declaring school districts to be "unitary."[91] The school district of the city of Denver, for example, was declared unitary in September 1995.[92] After that, resegregation took hold.[93]

Population growth, along with immigration, especially by Latinos, has tended to turn both city neighborhoods and integrated schools back into all-minority schools. White families with young children migrated first to the suburbs and then the exurbs, seeking good, usually nearly all-white, public schools.[94] By 1998, the levels of integration in the South were back to where they had been in 1970—albeit dramatically higher than when *Brown* was decided in 1954 (when only 0.001 percent of black students attended majority white schools in the South)—and they have continued to decline. Because of the persistence of residential segregation (and the Court's refusal to consider it), school segregation in the North now surpasses that in southern states.[95] In Denver, the public schools today "are plagued by patterns of segregation and low achievement, the very patterns that prompted the *Keyes* litigation."[96]

From today's perspective, the slow crawl toward integrated schools during the three decades following *Brown* looks like full-steam-ahead progress. The Burger Court's constraints on remedying school segregation have been extended. *Milliken v. Bradley* in 1974 halted the prospects for school desegregation in virtually all of America's major metropolitan areas. By the 1990s, the Supreme Court had lost any taste for requiring constitutionally compelled desegregation anywhere. And in 2007, by a 5–4 vote, the Court created new hurdles for school districts even where local political leaders vote *voluntarily* to promote school integration.[97] Now the vast majority of America's public schools remain segregated by race.

Less widely noticed, but at least equally important, was the Burger Court's decision in *Rodriguez*, which ratified the dramatically unequal ability of families who live in poor districts to finance their children's public schools—a burden that falls especially heavily on black and other minority families. Given the opposition to busing that followed *Swann*, the Court's refusal in *Rodriguez* to affirm a constitutional right to more equal school financing was of great importance. Courts in a number of states have endeavored to redress somewhat under their state constitutions the inequities that the Burger Court blessed at the national level in *Rodriguez* and federal money for K–12 education has increased, but large disparities in school finances abound.

In October 2014, Janet L. Yellen, chair of the Board of Governors of the Federal Reserve, in a speech reviewing recent trends in inequality of wealth and income in the United States, identified four "building blocks" of economic opportunity in America. Two of these building blocks involve educational opportunities—for higher education and elementary and secondary schooling. With regard to the latter, Yellen emphasized the role that public funding plays for "families below the top." "Public funding for education," she said, "is [a] way governments can help offset the advantages some households have in resources available for children. . . . The United States," she continued, "is one of the few advanced economies in which public education spending is often lower for students in lower-income households than for students in higher income households. . . . A major reason the United States is different is that we are one of the few advanced nations that funds primary and secondary public education mainly through subnational taxation. Half of U.S. public school funding comes from local property taxes, a much higher share than in other advanced countries, and thus the inequalities in housing wealth and income I have described enhance the ability of more affluent school districts to spend more on public schools."[98] An economist, Yellen had no reason to know about the *Rodriguez* decision; otherwise, she might have mentioned it.

Speaking for a unanimous Court in *Brown* more than half a century ago, Earl Warren famously said: "We conclude that in the field of public education the doctrine of 'separate but equal' has no place."[99] In contrast to its determination to reduce the rights granted by the Warren Court to criminal defendants, the Burger Court had no mission to limit the impact of *Brown*. But throughout today's America, public schools remain starkly separate and grossly unequal. Warren Burger's Supreme Court must take much of the responsibility for that. The Burger Court—and the nation—fared only a little better in higher education.

CHAPTER 5

Seeking a Higher Education

In the fall of 1973, a new and different kind of case reached the Burger Court. Marco DeFunis, a disappointed applicant to the University of Washington's law school, had sued the university, claiming that his rejection resulted from unconstitutional discrimination on the basis of his race. DeFunis was white and, pointing to black applicants who had been admitted with lower scores and grades than his, claimed that he was the victim of "reverse discrimination."

Admission to the law school was highly competitive; in 1970, when DeFunis first applied, there were more than 1,500 applications for 150 places. At the time, the school placed its minority applicants (defined as those who were "black, Chicano, American Indian, or Filipino") in a separate pool and evaluated them apart from the white applicants, giving less weight to their scores and grades. The school's published guide for applicants explained that its admissions process took racial and ethnic background into account "as one factor in our general attempt to convert formal credentials into realistic predictions" about an applicant's ability to make "significant contributions" not only to the law school, but to "the community at large." In 1971, when it rejected DeFunis's application for the second time, the law school admitted thirty-seven minority applicants, of whom eighteen enrolled.[1] None of the thirty-seven would have been admitted under the law school's criteria for nonminority applicants, Washington's attorney general, Slade Gordon (later a senator), subsequently conceded when he defended the program before the Supreme Court.

At the state trial of DeFunis's case, the university's president, Charles Odegaard, explained the reasons for the two-track admissions system: "More and more it became evident to us that just an open door seemed insufficient to deal with what was emerging as the greatest internal problem of the United States of America, a problem which obviously could not be resolved without some kind of contribution being made not only by the [K–12] schools, but obviously . . . the University of Washington."[2] Unmoved, the state trial court ruled against the university and ordered the law school to admit DeFunis. Race, the judge said, could not be considered—any race, for any reason—when it came to distributing government benefits.

After admitting DeFunis, the university appealed. As DeFunis neared completion of his second year, the state Supreme Court reversed the trial court and ruled for the university, foreshadowing many of the arguments with which the country would soon become familiar. Eighteen years after *Brown*, "minority groups are still grossly underrepresented in law schools," the Washington justices observed, adding: "If the law school is forbidden from taking affirmative action, this underrepresentation may be perpetuated indefinitely."[3]

Significantly, the state court rejected the university's argument that official actions to advantage minorities should be judged by a more forgiving constitutional standard than actions that favor whites at minorities' expense. Strict judicial scrutiny should apply equally to both, the court said, and the government in either instance should have to demonstrate a "compelling interest." The Washington Supreme Court concluded that the law school's admission policy met this test. "The shortage of minority attorneys—and consequently minority prosecutors, judges and public officials—constitutes an undeniably compelling state interest," the court said, adding: "If minorities are to live within the rule of law, they must enjoy equal representation within the legal system."[4]

Despite the ruling against him, DeFunis was allowed to stay in law school. Justice Douglas, acting in his capacity as circuit justice, granted him a stay of the state high court's judgment, pending final disposition of the case by the U.S. Supreme Court. By the time the justices heard his case in the spring of 1974, Marco DeFunis was approaching the end of his third year of law school and was certain to earn his degree no matter what the Court decided. Thus, by a vote of 5 to 4, the Supreme Court dismissed the case as moot.

That was the end of the *DeFunis* case, but only the beginning of a prolonged struggle over affirmative action in higher education that continues to this day. Mootness provided a relief valve this time, because a finding that a case no longer presents a live controversy strips a federal court of jurisdiction to decide it. But the Burger Court justices knew that they were simply deferring an inevitable confrontation with the competing equities that affirmative action entailed—and with the passions that it stirred.

Even the decision to dismiss the case as moot was contentious. Four justices—Douglas, Brennan, White, and Marshall—wanted to proceed to the merits. Powell was uncertain. His law clerks urged him to vote for mootness. One clerk, John Jeffries, described the case in a memo to the justice as "a veritable can of worms, full of legal questions of first impression with ramifications for related areas, many of which are as yet unforeseen."[5] Powell ultimately agreed to join Potter Stewart's short—and unsigned—opinion describing the basis for mootness and saying nothing about the merits of the case.[6] But a lengthy, rambling, and confusing dissenting opinion by Justice Douglas opened a window on the turmoil inside the Court. Douglas acknowledged that minorities were disadvantaged by current admission standards. He described the standardized Law School Admission Test (the LSAT) as culturally biased and called for its elimination. But he also said that Marco DeFunis "had a constitutional right to have his application considered on its individual merits in a racially neutral manner."

Douglas declared his intention to vote against consideration of race or ethnicity in admissions. Preferential admissions programs, he claimed, stigmatized blacks with a "stamp of inferiority."[7] Almost at that very moment, a young black man named Clarence Thomas was preparing to graduate from Yale Law School, to which he had been admitted under that school's affirmative action policy. Nearly thirty years later, as a Supreme Court justice, he would dissent from the Court's upholding of another law school's affirmative action policy and repeat Douglas's point in deeply personal terms.[8]

His *DeFunis* dissent was William O. Douglas's last word on affirmative action. He suffered a massive stroke later that year and retired the following November, after a record-setting thirty-six years on the Supreme Court. For the Burger Court's next encounter with affirmative action, his successor, John Paul Stevens, would be on the bench. The Court was changing, and so was the country.

When the *DeFunis* case came to the Court, efforts by colleges and universities to admit qualified African American applicants were a recent phenomenon. To fully understand the stakes in the battle over affirmative action in higher education that was just beginning to unfold in the Burger Court and throughout the country, one needs to consider the struggle, still recent at the time, of African Americans to overcome outright bans on their admission to colleges and universities. Only a decade earlier, blood had been spilled and federal troops deployed in the fight simply to allow them into the classroom of state universities. Once again, the South was the battleground.

Meredith at Ole Miss

The most violent episode that stood as a backdrop to the Burger Court's deliberations over race and higher education involved struggles to keep a black man out of the University of Mississippi.

James Meredith was a twenty-eight-year-old, nine-year veteran of the Air Force. After having been admitted to Ole Miss, but turned away once the university's officials learned he was black, he attended all-black Jackson State College, but he continued to press to be allowed to matriculate at the University of Mississippi. Meredith's effort to attend Ole Miss was rebuffed by the local federal district judge, but in September 1962, the United States Court of Appeals for the Fifth Circuit (the southern appellate court most sympathetic to claims of racial discrimination) ordered Meredith admitted to the University of Mississippi.

On September 30, he registered for classes, and that day President Kennedy addressed the nation. Speaking particularly to the people of Mississippi, Kennedy said that "observance of the law" is "the eternal safeguard of liberty" and its defiance is "the surest road to tyranny." The president said that he "deeply regret[ted]" that federal action was necessary to secure Meredith's enrollment, but that "all other avenues and alternatives, including persuasion and conciliation, had been tried and exhausted."⁹ If the president was optimistic that his words might avert violence, he was soon disappointed.

Mississippi was the most black, the most rural, and the most violently intransigent southern state. With the vocal support of Governor Ross Barnett, a large mob of students and outsiders attacked the university's administration building and the dormitory that was to house Meredith. Hundreds of marshals with tear gas were no match for the mob. Six marshals were shot and more than a hundred were injured. Two bystanders, including a foreign journalist, were killed before 2,500 federal troops arrived, five and a half hours after the violence had broken out.¹⁰

The University of Mississippi accepted Meredith's credits from Jackson State, so he stayed at Ole Miss for only one year. Federal marshals accompanied him the entire time, standing outside the doors when Meredith was in class.¹¹ He claimed that he was more heavily guarded than the president—and he was probably right.¹² He graduated with a degree in political science on August 18, 1963, ten days before Martin Luther King gave his "I Have a Dream" speech to a quarter million people on the Washington Mall.

George Wallace Stands in the Schoolhouse Door

While the University of Mississippi had been made to relent, the University of Alabama was still resisting. Two months before Meredith graduated, in one of the epochal moments of the civil rights era, Alabama's segregationist governor George Wallace stood in the doorway of the university's Foster Auditorium in a theatrical bid to block the admission of two African-American students, James Alexander Hood and Vivian Juanita Malone. Wallace was fulfilling a promise he had made in his gubernatorial inaugural speech to "stand in the schoolhouse door" if necessary to prevent integration of any school in Alabama—the same inaugural speech in which he famously proclaimed "segregation now, segregation tomorrow and segregation forever."¹³

Hood and Malone were following in the footsteps of Autherine Juanita Lucy, a shy, unassuming daughter of a southwest Alabama cotton farmer, who seven years earlier had been ordered admitted to the university by a federal judge and eventually by the United States Supreme

Court itself.[14] Despite years of successful litigation, however, Lucy was allowed to attend only three classes before her victory unraveled in the face of mob violence and university intransigence.

As Lucy awaited her court-ordered admission, racial tensions escalated in Alabama. On December 1, 1955, Rosa Parks famously refused to move to the back of a Montgomery city bus, inspiring the Montgomery bus boycott and galvanizing the nation's attention to civil rights, while also raising the temperature of white racism in the South. The following weekend, twenty-six-year-old Reverend Martin Luther King, Jr., told a packed Montgomery Baptist Church, "There comes a time when people get tired of being trampled by the iron feet of oppression. There comes a time, my friends, when people get tired of being thrown across the abyss of humiliation where they experience the bleakness of nagging despair. . . . And we are determined here in Montgomery—to work and fight until justice runs down like water, and righteousness like a mighty stream." [15]

During the days before and immediately after Autherine Lucy registered for classes eight weeks later, crosses were burned nightly on the university's campus in Tuscaloosa and on the grounds of the local black high school. A bomb exploded that day at Martin Luther King's home in Montgomery. Lucy was informed that the university's board of trustees had denied her a dormitory room and had prohibited her from eating in the university cafeteria. Despite these obstacles, she attended three classes on Friday, February 3, 1956.[16]

Over the weekend, mobs of white racists, including students and outsiders, rallied in Tuscaloosa. When Lucy returned to class the following Monday, she confronted hundreds of whites throwing eggs, gravel, and rotten produce at her. By the end of her second class, the mob had swelled to thousands. Lucy escaped the campus lying hidden across the backseat of a local police car. That night the university's board of trustees voted unanimously "to exclude Autherine Lucy until further notice from attending the University of Alabama." [17] One student rejoiced: "It took her four years and the Supreme Court to get her in, and it took us only four days to get rid of her." [18]

Represented by Thurgood Marshall, Lucy returned to federal court and once again prevailed, winning an order for her reinstatement. But in what proved to be a strategic blunder, Marshall charged on Lucy's behalf that the university's board of trustees had conspired with the mob to bar her from attending the university. That night the board permanently expelled Lucy "for making . . . baseless, outrageous and unfounded charges of misconduct on the part of . . . university officials."[19]

The next day, the court determined that this expulsion did not violate its order of readmittance—some say because the judge feared for Lucy's safety. Marshall tried one last maneuver by publicly withdrawing his conspiracy charges, but Lucy's efforts to attend the University of Alabama were finished. Mob violence had prevailed.

In the seven years that followed, other blacks applied to the University of Alabama, but none were admitted. The university worked with local police and private detectives to obtain any basis, no matter how slim, for denying admission to black applicants. When that proved impossible, the university substituted economic pressure, physical intimidation, and interminable bureaucratic delays. Hundreds of blacks were turned away, more than two hundred in 1962–1963 alone.[20]

But in 1963 Malone and Hood (along with Dave "Mack" McGlathery, who sought admission to the university's Huntsville campus) stepped forward to try once more. They were black students with impeccable credentials and stiff spines, and that spring an Alabama federal district judge ordered all of them admitted, expressly forbidding Governor Wallace from interfering with their enrollment.[21]

The Kennedy administration was far better prepared for the Alabama showdown than it had been the previous year in Mississippi. Along with preparations to use federal troops if necessary and to federalize Alabama's National Guard, FBI agents were sent into Tuscaloosa to harass and, when possible, remove members of the Ku Klux Klan.[22]

Shortly after 10:00 a.m. on June 11, with national television cameras rolling, a sweating Nicholas Katzenbach, deputy attorney general, approached Wallace and said, "I have come here to ask you now for unequivocal assurance that you will permit these students who, after all, merely want an education at the great university—" Wallace interrupted Katzenbach, and told him, "We don't need your speech." Wallace then gave his own speech. Wallace's five-minute oration vigorously denounced the "central" government, valorized the rights and sovereignty of the states, and made clear that he wanted to avoid violence, saying, "I stand before you today in place of thousands of Alabamans whose presence would have confronted you had I been derelict and neglected to fulfill the responsibilities of my office." Wallace then made clear that he had no intention to move. Katzenbach turned away and, accompanied by a protective force, took Vivian Malone and James Hood to their dormitories.

They slept that night under the protection of the then-federalized Alabama National Guard under the command of the tall, silver-haired General Henry V. Graham, whose daughter, also a student at the university, had been assigned to the same dorm as Vivian. The general slept on a sofa in the lobby.[23] It had taken armed force to admit black students to the University of Alabama, but this time, unlike Autherine Lucy, they were there to stay.

The Aftermath

George Wallace's doorway stunt made him the public face of white, racist determination to keep blacks out of public education and catapulted him onto the national stage. It was a turning point in American politics. The following year, in 1964, he ran for the Democratic presidential nomination, and received a surprisingly large number of votes in states such as Maryland and Wisconsin. He ran again in 1968, this time as an independent, and won 10 million votes, nearly thirteen percent of the total, carrying five southern states, and garnering forty-six electoral votes. That year Wallace ended the long history of Democrats carrying the "solid south" and sent Richard Nixon to the White House. In his final run in 1972, again as a Democrat, Wallace won primaries in North Carolina, Maryland, Michigan, Florida, and Tennessee, but he was crippled in Maryland by an assassin's bullet and had to end his campaign. Culpepper Clark, who served as dean of the University of Alabama's College of Communication and later authored an outstanding history of African Americans' efforts to gain admission there, described Wallace's widespread appeal:

> Racism was the muscle and sinew of white anger but it was so interlarded with traditional suspicions of power and privilege that race itself could not be separated from other themes of the powerless: localism versus federalism, the working many versus the monied few, south-

erners versus Yankees, farmers versus bankers, average citizen versus pointy-headed intellectual, individual ballot versus bloc voter, little/ big, light/dark, white/black, and so on.[24]

George Wallace gave populist voice to these tensions and, in doing so, proved to have broad, popular appeal—and not just in the South.

James Hood and Vivian Malone's entry to the University of Alabama marked a turning point in John F. Kennedy's presidency. The night they slept in the dorms in Montgomery, he addressed the nation, condemning racial segregation and announcing, for the first time, his intention to press for new, effective civil rights legislation. Kennedy congratulated the students of the university on the peaceful reception of Hood and Malone, and went on to link civil rights to the worldwide struggle with communism, observing that "when Americans are sent to Vietnam or West Berlin, we do not ask for whites only." Kennedy then said:

> One hundred years of delay have passed since President Lincoln freed the slaves, yet their heirs, their grandsons, are not fully free. They are not yet freed from the bonds of injustice. They are not yet freed from social and economic oppression. . . .
>
> We face, therefore, a moral crisis as a country and as a people. It cannot be met by repressive police action. It cannot be left to increased demonstrations in the streets. It cannot be quieted by token moves or talk. It is a time to act in the Congress, in your State and local legislative body and, above all, in all of our daily lives.[25]

Only a few hours after Kennedy spoke, Medgar Evers, a World War II veteran and the most prominent black civil rights advocate in Mississippi, was assassinated in front of his family's home in Jackson.[26] Less than six months after Evers's assassination, Kennedy himself was assassinated. The legislation he had proposed the night that the University of Alabama had been desegregated became the Civil Rights Act of 1964, but if he had hoped the law would calm the national turmoil over race, education, and concentrated poverty, he would have been disappointed.

Over the next four years, riots by largely poor and frustrated African Americans erupted in hundreds of American cities, resulting in thousands of injuries, burned buildings and neighborhoods, and over a hundred deaths, the most widespread coming in the wake of the assassination in April 1968 of Martin Luther King, Jr.[27] Three months later, Robert F. Kennedy was shot dead in Los Angeles after winning the California Democratic presidential primary. The riots that spring and summer set 140 American cities ablaze; more than twenty thousand rioters were arrested. That November Richard Nixon was elected president.

Turnabout

In 1954, when *Brown* was decided, only 4.9 percent of college undergraduates were African American. By 1965, through federal court orders enforced by federal troops, public colleges and universities in the South had reluctantly admitted a handful of blacks. Nationally, the needle had not moved: the number was exactly the same as a decade earlier, 4.9 percent.[28] And many of these students were enrolled in the traditionally black colleges. Into the 1960s, many colleges and universities, including elite Ivy League schools, made little effort to expand their black enrollments. In 1960, Princeton had one black in its freshman class of 826; Yale had five of one thousand; Harvard twelve of 1,212.[29]

After Martin Luther King's death and the riots that followed, black college students became more vocal and militant in their demands. By the time the 1970 freshman class was admitted, colleges and universities had begun to engage in various "affirmative actions" to recruit black students: these included recruitment visits by students and faculty to black schools, the addition of African Americans to admission committees, and "looser test score interpretations," especially with regard to the Scholastic Aptitude Test (SAT).[30] In 1970 Princeton enrolled 103 blacks in its freshman class, Harvard ninety-eight, and Yale eighty-three.[31] Although the universities had rejected formal quotas for black admissions, "numerical targets" and goals had, by then, gained acceptance. Harvard's admissions officers, for example, had "privately accepted that a 'critical mass' of black students would be needed to provide one another with moral and social support."[32]

Public colleges and universities outside the South were also taking voluntary affirmative actions to increase their small numbers of black students. The universities of Indiana, Illinois, and Michigan, for example, all introduced special admissions programs mostly for black disadvantaged applicants. Illinois admitted 250 African Americans to its 1969 freshman class of 5,630.[33] Before long, such programs expanded to include other minorities: Native Americans, Puerto Ricans, Mexican Americans, and Asian Americans.[34]

Professional schools, especially in law and medicine, also attempted to increase their black enrollments. In 1963, the Law School Admission Council introduced a new program to help African American students obtain admission to law schools. The program included free Law School Admission Tests, targeted recruitment events, and waivers of application fees.[35] The American Association of Medical Colleges in 1969 recommended that 12 percent of first-year medical students should be black in the class admitted in 1975. The next year the association said that this 12 percent should include not only African Americans, but also Mexican Americans, Puerto Ricans, and American Indians.[36] By 1970, two-thirds of all medical schools and half of all law schools had affirmative admissions programs, and all ninety medical schools that responded to a 1974 survey said they had some program to increase their number of minority students.[37] In 1977, the Educational Testing Service indicated that if law schools eliminated racial preferences, the percentage of blacks in first-year classes would drop from 5.3 percent to between 1 and 2 percent.[38]

As at the University of Washington Law School, colleges, universities, and professional schools throughout the country were admitting African Americans whose grades and standardized test scores often fell below those of the whites in their class. According to one estimate, half the approximately three thousand minority students who entered the nation's law schools in 1970 enjoyed some preference.[39] Even with this affirmative action, in 1970, of the approximately eight hundred minority students attending American medical schools, nearly 80 percent were enrolled at Howard University in the District of Columbia and Meharry Medical School in Nashville, the nation's two predominantly black medical schools.[40]

At the most elite colleges preferences for African Americans were in the same ballpark as had long been reserved for legacies and athletes. At Harvard in 1971, for example, legacies and athletes were admitted at rates 2.3 and 2.1 times higher than other whites; blacks were admitted at a rate 1.2 times higher than nonblacks. Controlling for their academic scores, African Americans were admitted at a rate slightly higher than legacies and slightly lower than athletes.[41] Jerome Karabel, who has written the definitive analysis of the transformation of admissions policies at elite universities, concluded that "the most profound and far-reaching impact of the black struggle for racial justice was to delegitimize long-standing admissions practices that favored the privileged."[42] He added: "Groups that had traditionally been discriminated against—Jews, graduates of public high schools, and scholarship applicants—came to be treated in a far more evenhanded fashion." "Paradoxically, then," he wrote, "the black struggle for inclusion . . . contributed to the emergence of admissions policies at Harvard, Yale, and Princeton that were far more meritocratic in 1970 than in 1960."[43] But that is not the way many white applicants and their supporters saw it.

Giving black or other minority applicants a leg up implies that a white applicant, who does not enjoy the same preference, has been disfavored. Once the nation turned seriously to the task of remedying its long history of racial segregation and subordination of African Americans, it became inevitable that some whites would cry foul, arguing that they now were being discriminated against on account of their race.[44] Harvard sociologist Nathan Glazer called it "affirmative discrimination"; his Harvard Law School colleague John Hart Ely labeled it "reverse racial discrimination."[45] The legal claim is that taking race into account in order to integrate public schools, universities, workplaces, or housing is equivalent under the Constitution to taking race into account to segregate or otherwise subordinate blacks. The assertion is that the Constitution—as interpreted by the Supreme Court in *Brown*—requires society, or at least society's major institutions, to be "colorblind."

Allan Bakke in the Burger Court

That was the issue before the Supreme Court in the *DeFunis* case and, soon enough, it was back again at the Court's door. Allan Bakke, a former Marine and Vietnam War veteran—the middle-class son of a mailman and a schoolteacher—decided late that he wanted to be a doctor. After a four-year stint in the Marines, he took an engineering job at a California NASA research center. During the six years he worked there, he took science courses at San Jose State and Stanford to fulfill medical school prerequisites that he had missed while an engineering undergraduate at the University of Minnesota. He also volunteered in the emergency room at a local hospital. In 1972, at age thirty-two, he applied for admission to eleven medical schools. That year, and again in 1973, he was rejected everywhere he applied.[46]

Medical school admissions committees told Bakke that his age was an important barrier to admission, that "an older applicant would have to be unusually highly qualified if he is to be seriously considered."[47] But Allan Bakke, then a father of two, living comfortably in Los Altos, California, forty miles south of San Francisco, was undaunted.

Bakke's rejection from the new University of California Davis Medical School in Sacramento especially galled him because UCD had reserved sixteen of its one hundred first-year places for "economically and/or educationally disadvantaged" minorities, whose applications were placed in a separate pool and evaluated by a different admissions subcommittee than whites.[48] Bakke's ire was stoked by Peter Storandt, a thirty-year-old assistant to George Lowery, the medical school's associate dean and chair of its admissions committee. Storandt, in July 1973 after Bakke's first rejection, told him about Marco DeFunis's lawsuit against the University of Washington and suggested that Bakke challenge the medical school's admissions program in court if he was rejected again the following year—advice Bakke soon took.[49]

UCD Medical School had established its minority set-aside and separate admissions process in 1970, four years after the school opened, in response to its difficulty in attracting and admitting minorities. There was a substantial disparity in the scores and grade-point averages of the whites and minorities that the school admitted in 1973 and 1974. Allan Bakke's scores were on the high side for the white pool and much higher than the minority averages.[50] Echoing William Douglas's view of the Law School Admission Test, medical school administrators regarded the standardized medical school admissions test as biased against minorities.[51] In its Supreme Court brief, the school argued that its minority admissions program was necessary to "enhance diversity in the student body and the profession, eliminate historic barriers for medical careers for disadvantaged racial and minority groups, and increase aspiration for such careers on the part of members of these groups."[52]

The UCD medical school rejected Bakke's second application for admission on April 1, 1974. On June 20, just two months after the Supreme Court had ducked the reverse discrimination issue in *DeFunis*, Bakke sued in California state court for admission to the medical school, alleging that he was "the victim of racial discrimination" because of the medical school's "16% racial quota." The trial court agreed but did not order Bakke admitted. Instead, the judge ordered UCD to reconsider Bakke's application without regard to his or any other applicant's race. In March 1975, the court enjoined UCD from considering the race of any applicant in its admissions process.[53]

The university appealed the decision to the California Supreme Court, which, in a 6–1 decision, agreed with the trial court that UCD's admissions policy was an illegal quota that violated Bakke's rights under the Equal Protection Clause of the Fourteenth Amendment. The California court barred UCD from taking race into account in its admissions decisions. Despite its uncertainty about whether Bakke would have gained admission to the medical school if its minority admissions program did not exist—George Lowery, who had interviewed Bakke in the admissions process, had given him quite a critical evaluation—the California Supreme Court ordered the medical school to admit Bakke.[54] However, William Rehnquist, who had replaced William Douglas as circuit justice for the Ninth Circuit, stayed the court's order to admit Bakke pending the Supreme Court's disposition of UCD's petition for certiorari.

Despite its obvious importance, the justices split over whether the Court should take the *Bakke* case. The Court's liberals, William Brennan and Thurgood Marshall, voted "no" out of fear that the manner in which the medical school considered minority applications might ring the death knell for affirmative action in university admissions. Warren Burger and Harry Blackmun also wanted to dodge this case and voted against taking it. But the remaining five justices—Stewart, White, Powell, Rehnquist, and Stevens—voted in February 1977 to hear the case in the Court's next term. A monumental struggle over the future of affirmative action in university admissions then commenced in the Court's chambers.

Court watchers needed no crystal ball to predict how at least four of the justices would vote. The two liberals, Brennan and Marshall, were going to side with the university and vote to uphold affirmative action for minorities in virtually any form. On the other side, Burger and Rehnquist viewed any preference based on race as unconstitutional. Potter

Stewart agreed with Burger and Rehnquist that the Equal Protection Clause forbids taking race into account even to favor blacks or other minorities. Byron White, as he had in other cases involving race, sided with Brennan and Marshall. The outcome turned on how the three remaining justices—Blackmun, Powell, and Stevens—would vote.

They had no shortage of help. In addition to the parties' briefs, nearly sixty briefs were filed as friends of the court on behalf of more than 160 organizations and individuals—including one by Marco DeFunis on behalf of the Young Americans for Freedom—setting a new Court record.[55] The lawyer for one of those *amici*, the United States, however, had a great deal of trouble formulating an argument. Usually, but not always, when filing a brief as an *amicus*, rather than for the government as a party, in controversial Supreme Court cases, the solicitor general offers the Justice Department's best analytic and dispassionate analysis of the legal issues before the Court. Because the Court frequently heeds the government's argument, the solicitor general has sometimes been called the "tenth justice."[56] But dispassionate legal analysis insulated from political pressures was not possible in the *Bakke* case.[57]

Jimmy Carter had been in the White House for just a month when the Supreme Court agreed to hear the *Bakke* case. His solicitor general, Wade McCree, was only the second African American to hold that position (Thurgood Marshall having been the first). Political forces within and outside the Carter administration endeavored mightily to shape the solicitor general's argument to conform to their views. Numerous leaks to the press made the brief-writing process especially contentious and chaotic. When all was said and done, the Carter administration's brief, filed in September 1977, satisfied no one. The attorney general, Griffin Bell, said that it "supported neither Bakke nor the university."[58] It argued for reversing the California Supreme Court and urged upholding the UCD admissions process, but said that further factual determinations were necessary to know whether Bakke should be admitted.[59] This time the solicitor general's brief had little impact in the justices' chambers.

At the oral argument on October 12, 1977, Archibald Cox (a Harvard professor, former solicitor general, and former special prosecutor of Richard Nixon), representing UCD, repeated arguments he had made in his *DeFunis* brief, insisting that the sixteen places the medical school set aside for minorities was a "goal" not a "quota." "For generations," Cox said, "racial discrimination in the U.S. isolated certain minorities [and] condemned them to inferior education. . . . There is no racially blind method of selection which will enroll today more than a trickle of minority students in the nation's colleges and professions." Wade McCree, the solicitor general, spoke next, urging the Court to uphold affirmative action. Bakke's lawyer, Reynold Colvin, who had never argued before the Court, made an impassioned plea for Bakke's admission, but spent an inordinate amount of his time on the facts. He seemed confused about what he wanted the Court to say about the law and was largely ineffective.

At the conference shortly after the argument, the positions of eight justices became clear. Harry Blackmun hadn't been there, having recently undergone prostate surgery at the Mayo Clinic. To their great dismay, his colleagues would have to wait until May to learn where he stood.

The newest justice, John Paul Stevens, wanted the Court to postpone again any determination of the constitutionality of preferential admissions. Instead, he concluded that the UCD medical school's admissions process violated Title VI of the 1964 Civil Rights Act, which prohibits racial discrimination in any program receiving federal funding—as all medical schools do. Stevens embraced the maxim that the Court should avoid deciding a case on constitutional grounds when a statutory basis is available, but his approach raised a number of important new legal issues, such as whether Title VI could be enforced by a private litigant like Allan Bakke or only by the federal government itself. Over the objection of several justices, the Court ordered additional briefs on the Title VI issue, which the parties had previously ignored. The briefs were filed, but they changed no one's vote.

Stevens wanted to avoid either entrenching affirmative action in a constitutional decision (which Brennan, Marshall, and White wanted) or constitutionally prohibiting any preference for minorities based on race (which Burger, Stewart, and Rehnquist urged). Lewis Powell was sympathetic to but unpersuaded by Stevens's Title VI approach. Powell did not believe the Court could avoid the constitutional issue for the second time in three years.

In fact, Lewis Powell had developed his position months before, during the summer of 1977. He was convinced that racial preferences in university and professional school admissions were necessary to provide meaningful opportunities for blacks and certain other minorities; he saw no other avenue. He believed that prohibiting all affirmative action would be "a disaster for the country," so he rejected his conservative colleagues' view that the Constitution required state institutions always to be "color-blind." But Powell did not agree with Brennan, Marshall, and White that all affirmative action programs were constitutional, and he was not prepared to endorse the medical school's approach. As his biographer John Jeffries has said, "Faced with two intellectually coherent, morally defensible, and diametrically opposed positions, Powell chose neither."[60]

Powell confronted two challenges: writing a convincing and reasonably coherent opinion and persuading his colleagues to join him. He ultimately succeeded in the former, but not the latter. It wasn't for lack of trying.

After winning a lottery with his co-clerks, Bob Comfort, a Harvard Law graduate, chose the *Bakke* case. On August 29, 1977, he gave Powell a seventy-one-page memo, which he described as both "too long and too short." Comfort's memo contained the legal structure of a detailed memorandum that Powell circulated to his colleagues in November and formed the basis of the opinion he published the following June.

Given the 3-1-4 split at the October conference, if Harry Blackmun voted with the foursome of Burger, Stewart, Rehnquist, and Stevens, there would be five votes to prohibit affirmative action, and, given past practices, Burger would likely have assigned the majority opinion to himself. While awaiting Blackmun's vote—which he did not announce until May 1—Burger suggested that the justices circulate memorandums describing their views of the case. Powell's November memo was one of many that the justices circulated between October 1977 and May 1978. As it turned out, Blackmun, after agonizing for months, finally agreed with Brennan, Marshall, and White that the Court should uphold UCD's admissions process.[61] Thus, the Court was split 4-1-4 with Lewis Powell in the driver's seat. Recognizing this, Burger and Brennan agreed together to assign the Court's opinion to Powell. As Burger said in a May 2 memo to the conference: "There being four definitive decisions tending one way, four another, Lewis' position can be joined in part by some or all of each 'four group.'"[62]

On June 28, 1978, in a packed courtroom, Lewis Powell announced the judgment of the Court. Powell observed, "Perhaps no case in modern memory has received as much media coverage and scholarly commentary." He announced that no opinion was joined in its entirety by five justices. Then he explained how the Court had divided, indicating that Allan Bakke, at age thirty-eight, would be admitted to medical school and that "the way is open to Davis to adopt the type of admissions program proved to be successful at so many of our universities."[63] Justices Stevens, Brennan, Marshall, and Blackmun then described their own positions.

The medical school's policy of setting aside a specific number of places for minority candidates and considering nonwhite applicants separately from whites was found illegal (by a five-vote majority of Powell, Burger, Rehnquist, Stewart, and Stevens). In reaching this conclusion, Powell said that the Equal Protection Clause required the "most exacting judicial examination" of any racial classification, even one beneficial to blacks, and insisted that such a classification could be justified only by a "compelling state interest," which must be implemented by the "least intrusive means."[64] This became the high hurdle that any classification based on race would thereafter face. The medical school's admissions procedures flunked the last of these tests. But the Court reversed the California Supreme Court's decision barring the university from considering race in its admissions decisions (by a different five-vote majority of Powell, Brennan, Marshall, White, and Blackmun).

The portion of Powell's opinion describing *how*—consistently with the Constitution—universities might take race into account in their admissions decisions failed to garner any of his colleagues' votes despite his months of efforts. Powell's opinion here was a metamorphosis of the legal rights at stake. Everyone thought that the rights being contested—rights of blacks and other minorities to get special beneficial consideration in admissions—were intended to compensate minorities for deprivations long suffered throughout our nation's history. Powell instead treated the right to take race into account in admissions decisions as a component of a university's First Amendment rights to academic freedom and to attain a diverse student body. Powell's opinion provided a roadmap for admissions officials. The "assignment of a fixed number" of places to minorities, he said, is not "a necessary means toward . . . achieving the educational diversity valued by the First Amendment."[65] Quotas are out. But universities can use an applicant's race or ethnic status as a "plus" to achieve "beneficial educational pluralism" so long as the university treats "each applicant as an individual in the admissions process."[66]

Powell used an example (which had been advanced by Archibald Cox in his *DeFunis* brief and his oral argument in *Bakke*) of an Idaho farm boy in his discussion of potentially diverse applicants.[67] As a roadmap for a constitutionally acceptable university admissions practice, Powell attached Harvard's description of its process as an appendix to his opinion. That document said that Harvard seeks "variety" in its admissions and extends special consideration to disadvantaged applicants, including "blacks and Chicanos and other minority students." Lewis Powell, in essence, delegated constitutionally acceptable decisions over affirmative action in higher education to the officers and admissions committees of the nation's colleges and universities. In doing so, he defined the interests at stake—racial diversity within the context of academic freedom—as those of the university rather than its minority applicants, a distinction that would grow in significance over time.

The Supreme Court published five additional opinions in *Bakke*. Justice Brennan's opinion (joined by White, Marshall, and Blackmun) said that the UCD admissions program was constitutional and also valid under Title VI because race may be taken into account "to redress the continuing effects of past discrimination."[68] Justice Stevens's short opinion (joined by Burger, Stewart, and Rehnquist) argued that the UCD system was barred by Title VI. Justice White wrote separately, insisting that Title VI could not be enforced in a lawsuit by a private citizen.

Thurgood Marshall wrote a lengthy, impassioned opinion tracing the nation's long history of racial discrimination and detailing how the disadvantages of blacks with regard to life expectancy, infant mortality, income, poverty, unemployment, and minimal representation in the legal and medical professions deprived them of any "meaningful equality." "The position of the Negro today in America," Marshall said, "is the tragic but inevitable consequence of centuries of unequal treatment." "I do not believe," he continued, "that anyone can truly look into America's past and still find that a remedy for that past is impermissible."[69]

Justice Blackmun added a brief opinion of his own, stating his view that the medical school's admissions program was constitutionally permissible, while insisting, "I yield to no one in my earnest hope that the time will come when an 'affirmative action' program is unnecessary." He added, "I would hope that we could reach this stage within a decade at the most." "In order to get beyond racism," Blackmun wrote, "we must first take account of race. There is no other way. And in order to treat some persons equally, we must treat them differently. We cannot—we dare not—let the Equal Protection Clause perpetuate racial supremacy."[70]

The *Bakke* decision made headline news throughout the country— with newspapers emphasizing the aspect of the decision most congenial to their readership.[71] Writing in *The Wall Street Journal*, Robert Bork— whom Ronald Reagan would nominate nine years later to take the seat of retiring Justice Lewis Powell—described everyone who supported the Davis admissions process, including the justices, as "hard-core racists of reverse discrimination."[72] Anthony Lewis, the former *New York Times* Supreme Court correspondent, had quite a different take. In a column entitled "A Solomonic Decision," Lewis wrote, "I have seen great moments there, but nothing to match the drama as five members of the Court explained their positions in homely terms."[73] Their opinions, he continued, "underline the unique quality of what the American Supreme Court does often and did in this case: grapple with the fundamentals of a society."[74]

The preface of an otherwise excellent book on the *Bakke* case by Howard Ball, a political scientist at the University of Vermont, describes Lewis Powell as having forged a "fragile consensus" that linked "the opposing views of two groups of Justices."[75] But, in truth, Powell failed to achieve any consensus: he could not get even one additional vote for his position. However, Powell's solitary view of what constitutes constitutionally valid affirmative action in university admissions hardly proved fragile. No one knew it then, but Lewis Powell's singular opinion in *Bakke* has had a profound and long lasting impact on the nation's institutions of higher learning, on employment practices, and on race relations throughout America. When he retired, Powell said that *Bakke* was his "most important opinion."[76] He was surely right: the *Bakke* case was one of the Burger Court's most important as well. But it would be twenty-five years before Lewis Powell's view garnered the five votes necessary for a Supreme Court majority—and that majority's consensus would prove fragile indeed.

Bakke Barely Survives

Following *Bakke*, the Court considered many cases involving disputes over affirmative action in employment and government contracting (see

Chapter 11), but twenty-five years passed before the Supreme Court again tackled a controversy over racial preferences in admission to colleges and professional schools.

Michigan, as it had been with school desegregation in *Milliken*, was the source of the controversy. This dispute involved the University of Michigan, the state's flagship university, located in Ann Arbor, just thirty-five miles from Detroit. The university's history of educating blacks was disturbing. It had enrolled its first two black students in 1868, just after the Civil War, but between then and the end of World War II, the university typically admitted fewer than twenty African American students a year.[77] By 1966 about four hundred students of 32,000 were African American. In the early 1970s, responding to student protests, the university set a goal of 10 percent black students, which it reached in 1976. Reacting to racial tensions and the "prejudice, discrimination, bigotry and racism" that still existed on campus, the university's president, James Duderstadt, announced in 1990 what he called the "Michigan Mandate," a program to expand minority admissions and faculty hiring. By 1997, minorities comprised nearly a quarter of the university's enrollment: 10 percent were Asian, 8 percent African American, and 6 percent Hispanic.

As minority admissions grew, white applicants became increasingly resentful of the university's affirmative action programs.[78] After a state court compelled the university to release publicly its confidential admissions policy, lawsuits followed, challenging both the undergraduate and law school's admissions policies.[79]

The Supreme Court decided the cases in June 2003. By a vote of 6–3, the Court struck down the undergraduate program. After discussing at length Justice Powell's *Bakke* opinion, Chief Justice Rehnquist's opinion for the Court said that because it automatically granted every "underrepresented minority" applicant a specific number of bonus points (amounting to one fifth of those necessary for admission), the University of Michigan's undergraduate admissions program failed to provide the "individualized consideration" of each applicant's file that Powell had demanded in *Bakke*.[80] That, the majority concluded, violated both the Constitution's Equal Protection Clause and Title VI of the Civil Rights Act.

The University of Michigan Law School, on the other hand, conducted an individualized consideration of each applicant's file, and it passed constitutional muster. Writing for a 5–4 majority in *Grutter v.*

Bollinger, Justice Sandra Day O'Connor reviewed in detail the various opinions in *Bakke,* observing that in the twenty-five years "since this Court's splintered decision in *Bakke,* Justice Powell's opinion . . . has served as the touchstone for constitutional analysis of race-conscious admissions policies."[81] Then, without deciding whether Powell's opinion should be considered "binding," O'Connor endorsed "Justice Powell's view that student body diversity . . . can justify the use of race in university admissions."[82] Quotas, O'Connor said, are out, as are "separate admissions tracks" for minorities, but the "Law School's goal of attaining a critical mass of underrepresented minority students does not transform its program into a quota." The Court upheld the law school's use of race in a "truly individualized . . . flexible, nonmechanical way" that does not make "an applicant's race or ethnicity the defining feature of his or her application."[83] The law school, Justice O'Connor said, is not required to exhaust "every conceivable race-neutral alternative" or "to choose between maintaining a reputation for excellence or fulfilling a commitment to provide educational opportunities to members of all racial groups." But, she added, "race-conscious admissions" must have "a termination point." "We expect," she said, "that 25 years from now, the use of racial preferences will no longer be necessary."[84]

Having influenced university admissions for twenty-five years, Justice Powell's solitary opinion in *Bakke* finally won a Supreme Court majority in 2003, and the Court appeared to have granted it a second twenty-five-year extension as the law of the land. But O'Connor's timetable seems optimistic: taking race into account in university admissions is now threatened by the current Supreme Court and the ballot box.

Justice O'Connor retired in January 2006, succeeded by the exceptionally conservative Samuel A. Alito, Jr. This change allowed the Roberts Court to train its sights on affirmative action without waiting anything close to twenty-five years. The first cases to reach the Court involved the flagship Austin campus of the University of Texas, which achieves most of its diversity under a state law requiring it to offer admission to the top 10 percent of graduating seniors from every high school in the state. This unique "Top Ten Percent Plan" produces racial diversity only because so many Texas high schools remain segregated by race or ethnicity. The plan fills about 80 percent of the places available to the entering class, and it was not challenged. Rather, in 2012 and again in 2016, the Court wrestled with the *Grutter*-like way the University of Texas has filled the remaining twenty percent of the class: by individualized consideration of applicants in which race and ethnicity were factors.[85] These cases were brought to the courts by the Project on Fair Representation, a one-man advocacy organization supported by conservative donors eager to fund litigation striving to eliminate racial considerations in university admissions and voting-rights enforcement.[86] (It also sponsored the litigation that led to the Supreme Court eviscerating the Voting Rights Act of 1965 in *Shelby County v. Holder*, decided in 2013.[87]) Expecting that the Texas case, given the 10 percent plan, would not fully achieve its goals, the Project on Fair Representation also challenged other universities' admissions policies—starting with Harvard (Justice Powell's model program) and the University of North Carolina at Chapel Hill.[88]

The Court's decision in *Grutter* upholding the University of Michigan Law School's admission plan produced a backlash in the state. In 2006, the state's voters, by a 58 percent majority, approved a referendum amending that state's constitution to prohibit any discrimination or preferential treatment based on race or sex in public education, including by colleges and universities, or in government contracting or public employment. In April 2014, the Supreme Court, by a 6–2 vote, upheld the referendum.[89]

Florida and California have adopted similar state constitutional provisions. Along with Michigan, all these states have experienced a significant drop in black and Hispanic enrollment at their most selective colleges and universities.[90] More states where public referendums can amend the state's constitution may follow. Affirmative action in public college admissions hangs on—but just barely.

A Dispute over Values

Issues of race in higher education admissions—as in elementary and secondary education—brought contests over fundamental American values to the Supreme Court. In disputes over integrating public schools, local autonomy and local finance prevailed, despite ongoing residential racial segregation and the large funding disparities produced by reliance on local property taxes. As Chapter 4 described, efforts to create integrated elementary and high schools that provide equality of opportunity for all our nation's children foundered at school district lines.

When questions concerning the nation's commitment to equality of opportunity turned to public colleges, universities, and professional schools, they bumped headlong into opposing forces grounded in claims of meritocracy—claims that forgot or ignored long-standing disadvantages based on race. Many of the universities now committed to affirmative action had their own histories of segregation that they were trying to overcome and had long maintained admissions preferences for legacies and athletes.[91] Half a century ago, President Lyndon Johnson, a Texan, told the mostly black students and faculty at Howard University that:

> you do not take a person who, for years, has been hobbled by chains and liberate him, bring him up to the starting line of a race and then say, "you are free to compete with all the others," and still justly believe you have been completely fair. . . . We seek not just freedom but opportunity. We seek not just legal equity . . . but equality as a fact and equality as a result.[92]

But that equality continues to elude us. In a comprehensive recent examination of higher education in America, William Bowen, former president of Princeton University, and his colleagues wrote: "Racial disparities . . . remain, in our view, by far the most daunting of the challenges in achieving equity in American higher education—and real opportunity in American society."[93] "It is historically indefensible and morally wrong to think of race as 'just another' dimension of disadvantage," they said, "or 'just another' dimension of diversity."[94]

In a careful, but quite depressing, analysis, Princeton economist Alan Krueger (who served as chairman of President Barack Obama's Council of Economic Advisers) and two colleagues investigated whether the racial gap in SAT scores in admissions applications was likely to disappear in twenty-five years after *Grutter*, as Justice O'Connor had predicted. They concluded that this was unlikely. "Maintaining a critical mass of African American students at the most selective institutions," Krueger and his colleagues said, "would require policies at the elementary and secondary levels or changes in parenting practices that deliver unprecedented success in narrowing the test score gap in the next quarter century."[95]

About a month before the Supreme Court announced its *Fisher* decision, Columbia University president Lee Bollinger, who had been a defendant in the University of Michigan cases when serving there as president, argued that universities need to engage in efforts to enroll more children from low-income families—but not as a substitute for endeavoring to fulfill "higher education's historic commitment to racial diversity." "For those of us whose job it is to preserve and enhance the quality of higher education," he said, "the new insistence on choosing either socioeconomic or racial diversity makes no more sense than deciding that we can dispense with exposing our students to Alexis de Tocqueville's *Democracy in America* because they've already read Adam Smith's *Wealth of Nations*. To view them in the alternative is willfully and unnecessarily to impoverish the educational mission." [96]

That same day, *The New York Times* published a front-page article detailing the difficulties for colleges in enrolling students of "low socioeconomic status." In addition to the task of identifying and recruiting qualified students, there is the problem of money. As a Michigan State University dean explained, "It's really expensive once they enroll because they need more financial aid." [97] Nevertheless, where race or ethnicity cannot be considered in admissions, there may be no practical alternative to affirmative action based on socioeconomic status. It would be disastrous if U.S. colleges and universities were once again to be the bastions of privilege they were during most of twentieth century.

The Burger Court's failure to achieve anything approaching a consensus concerning the role of race in admissions to higher education is hardly surprising—given the deep divisions in our society about how to fairly allocate the limited number of seats at competitive universities. Would the issue be less contested today had the Court spoken more clearly and with one voice? Not likely. As we have seen with *Brown*, a Supreme Court decision is fixed on paper, but our nation's attitudes and its politics change. American politics in the decades after *Bakke* would hardly have left such a tempting target alone. By transforming the rights at stake into a university's right to have a diverse student body, *Bakke* essentially disabled minority applicants from advancing any legal claim (in the absence of intentional discrimination, of course). However, it simultaneously allowed disappointed white applicants to claim that their rejection was illegal because it was based on race. In its halting and divided way, the Burger

Court made sure not to slam the door on minorities' opportunities when the nation's colleges and universities voluntarily undertook to provide them, but it bestowed on future courts a basis for eliminating affirmative action altogether. The days of affirmative action at colleges and universities are numbered. John Roberts's Supreme Court seems inclined to make that number a small one.

PART THREE

Social Transformation

The late 1960s and early 1970s were a time of social transformation in America. The signs and symbols were everywhere. The "Summer of Love" in 1967 drew tens of thousands of young people, many following Timothy Leary's advice to "turn on, tune in, and drop out," to San Francisco's Haight-Ashbury neighborhood. On the other side of the country, as many as half a million people converged on Max Yasgur's dairy farm in upstate Bethel, New York, for the muddy, drug-infused, weekend-long rock concert that came to be known as Woodstock.

Films, stage productions, books, and magazines that would have faced instant suppression as obscene not many years earlier were entering mainstream culture. The Pill was changing sex lives and attitudes. So many couples were living together without benefit of marriage that census takers invented the acronym POSSLQ, for persons of opposite sex sharing living quarters. (The census form itself, for the first time in 1970, offered "partner" as a category for a person sharing the rent with another unrelated adult.) Abortion, a word scarcely uttered in polite company before the 1960s, and illegal in every state as the result of a public morals crusade nearly a century earlier, became the focus of reform efforts by the legal and medical professions even before the cause was taken up by a new generation of feminists.

The relationship between men and women was changing outside the bedroom as well as within it. Title VII of the Civil Rights Act of 1964 had prohibited employers from discriminating against women. But as a practical matter, even as women were entering the paid workforce in growing numbers, little had changed for them in the average workplace by the end of the decade. On August 26, 1970, the fiftieth anniversary of the day women got the right to vote under the Nineteenth Amendment, tens of thousands of women left home and office in response to the feminist leader Betty Friedan's call for a "strike for equality," aimed at protesting the unfilled promises of the franchise.

Congress approved the Equal Rights Amendment in 1972 and sent it out for a ratification effort that ultimately fell three states short, victim of a cultural backlash and a new "pro-family" movement that depicted the ERA and the forces behind it as threats to the established order—which of course they were. That was, after all, the point.

Well under the radar, another social revolution was taking shape. On June 28, 1969—five days after Warren Burger took the oath of office as chief justice—patrons of a gay bar in New York City called the Stonewall Inn resisted a police raid with a barrage of rocks and bottles. The Stonewall riot marked the coming out not only of individuals, but of a movement that soon was making its own claims on the Constitution.

A new form of religious activism became visible. As the mainstream Protestant denominations were shrinking, evangelicals entered the public square. Reaction to the women's movement and gay rights movement; the fight over the ERA; the continued effort to maintain a place for religion in the public schools and to retain religious schools' tax exemptions in spite of racially discriminatory policies, all propelled a vigorous Religious Right into politics.

In law as in life, the status quo was under attack. The pressures generated as a new order struggled to be born turned into court cases; that was the American way. And soon enough, the cases were at the Supreme Court's door.

The Court that Warren Burger joined at the age of sixty-one was not young. Three of its members—Hugo Black, John Marshall Harlan, and William Douglas—had been born in the previous century. Thurgood Marshall was sixty. Only Potter Stewart and Byron White were in their fifties—relatively young by Supreme Court standards, but old enough to have come of age in a much different pre–World War II America. Of the next four justices to join the Court, William Rehnquist was the youngest, at forty-seven. Harry Blackmun was sixty-one, Lewis Powell was sixty-four, and John Paul Stevens was fifty-five.

How would the Burger Court respond to the oncoming social tide? On what resources, what knowledge, what networks would these men draw when confronting claims to the right to abortion, to constitutional equality between the sexes, to the right of gay men and lesbians to conduct their private lives free of criminal sanction? What would eight conventional Protestants and the Court's sole Catholic, the liberal William J. Brennan Jr., make of demands by minority religions for exceptions from the obligations that applied to all, or by mainstream denominations for a more prominent place at the table?

CHAPTER 6

Privacy at a Price

Ask almost anyone outside of a law school which group of Supreme Court justices decided *Roe v. Wade* and chances are very high that the answer will be the Warren Court. Ask next what the vote was, and the likely answer is 5–4. In fact, *Roe v. Wade*,[1] decided January 22, 1973, was a decision of the Burger Court, with the chief justice in the majority. The margin was a comfortable 7–2, with the majority including five of the Court's six Republican-appointed justices. Three of Richard Nixon's four appointees were in the majority; the fourth, William Rehnquist, was joined in dissent by a Democratic appointee, Byron White.

In giving constitutional protection to a woman's decision to terminate a pregnancy, *Roe v. Wade* and a decision in a companion case[2] overturned criminal laws in Texas and, by extension, in the forty-three other states where abortion was either still a crime or remained tightly regulated under a new generation of "reform" statutes. *Roe* was clearly one of the Burger Court's most consequential decisions, but more than that, it became one of the most widely recognized Supreme Court decisions of all time. In a poll conducted in 2009, 84 percent of people who said they could think of any Supreme Court decision at all named *Roe v. Wade* (*Brown v. Board of Education* came in second, at 9 percent).[3]

Yet for all its fame, *Roe* remains profoundly misunderstood, probably more so than any other Burger Court decision. The passing decades and the continuing controversy surrounding abortion make it hard to recapture the context in which the case reached the Court or to imagine how an issue that looms so large on the political landscape today could have appeared well short of transformative—and far from politically polarizing—to the nine men who faced it.

There are many accounts of how *Roe v. Wade* made its way to the Supreme Court: how two recent law school graduates, Sarah Weddington and Linda Coffee, recruited Norma McCorvey, a twenty-two-year-old unmarried Texas woman pregnant with her third child, as the anonymous "Jane Roe" plaintiff in a constitutional challenge to the state's mid-nineteenth-century criminal abortion law.[4] We won't recount that story here. Instead, this chapter has a two-fold purpose. The first is to frame the case not as we see it today but, as nearly as possible, as members of the Burger Court saw it. The second is to depict how the Court, having quite unwittingly launched a revolution, drew back from its implications.

Roe v. Wade is often described as having recognized a "right" to abortion, a right that Justice Harry Blackmun's majority opinion indeed deemed "fundamental." But as we shall see, what the Court bestowed was a negative right: not a right *to* anything but a right *against* something, the right not to be prosecuted for performing an abortion or obtaining one. The Court decided *Roe* during the same term it ruled in *San Antonio v. Rodriguez* that the Equal Protection Clause places no obligation on the government to alleviate the consequences of poverty by equalizing the resources available to local school districts (discussed in Chapter 4). In fact, the two cases were argued a day apart in October 1972. Granted, *Rodriguez* was an equal protection case, while *Roe* rested on the right to privacy grounded in the constitutional guarantee of due process. The Court's rejection of the notion that the Constitution contained "positive rights" was explicit in *Rodriguez*, while it was implicit in *Roe*, waiting to be fleshed out when the question presented itself. Nonetheless, these two crucially important decisions of the Burger Court offer the same lesson in historical contingency: if there ever might have been a Supreme Court majority for placing affirmative obligations on the government to solve problems not of its direct making, that moment passed after Richard Nixon finished filling the vacancies that good fortune had bestowed on him. *Roe v. Wade* recognized a right to privacy, but it was privacy at a price. Poor women were—as they still are—on their own.

The Road to *Roe*

Roe v. Wade was neither the only nor necessarily the most promising challenge to the many state laws that made abortion a crime. It simply got to the Supreme Court first, with more than a dozen other cases not far behind. One closely watched case had become moot after the New York legislature legalized abortion in 1970.[5] The federal district court in a Connecticut case, *Abele v. Markle*,[6] also known as "Women versus Connecticut" for the 858 women whom a group of female students at Yale Law School had recruited as plaintiffs, invalidated that state's law while *Roe v. Wade* was pending at the Supreme Court.

The rapidly expanding lawsuits derived their energy from the recently galvanized women's movement. They sought to build on the Supreme Court's 1965 decision in *Griswold v. Connecticut*,[7] which struck down an archaic law that made it a crime for a doctor to prescribe birth control and for anyone, even a married couple, to use it. The often-married Justice William O. Douglas, addressing his majority opinion to the rights of husbands and wives, declared that couples within marriage enjoyed "a right of privacy older than the Bill of Rights." Seven years later, in *Eisenstadt v. Baird*,[8] the Court extended the right to unmarried people. Justice Brennan wrote for the Court that "If the right of privacy means anything, it is the right of the *individual*, married or single, to be free from unwarranted governmental intrusion into matters so fundamentally affecting a person as the decision whether to bear or beget a child." Brennan's choice of words was no accident; *Roe v. Wade* was already briefed and awaiting the Court's decision.

Although all states had once banned abortion, many under laws dating back a century, it was not until the 1960s, the decade of the Pill and the sexual revolution, that a reform movement emerged. The impetus came from doctors who were alarmed at the number of illegal abortions—an estimated half million or more a year, with the precise number never known—and the risks that the back alley posed to women's health and lives.[9] In 1960, a leading public health physician, Dr. Mary Steichen Calderone, medical director of Planned Parenthood, published an academic article entitled "Illegal Abortion as a Public Health Problem."[10] The article was a call to reform, based on a robust notion of professional obligation and social justice. Calderone stressed the impact that the regime of criminal abortion laws had on poor women, those most likely to be exploited and placed in peril, compared with those who could use cash and connections to terminate a pregnancy in relative safety. Calderone called on her profession to substitute "concrete help and sympathetic understanding" for the "frightening hush-hush" and "closed doors" that attended the entire subject. By the mid-1960s, the American Medical Association, which had helped lead the charge for criminalization nearly a century earlier, began to reconsider its position. The American Public Health Association voted in 1968 to support legalized abortion. The American Medical Association followed in 1970.

At the same time, the legal profession was reexamining the abortion issue. The American Law Institute (ALI), a prestigious group of judges, legal academics, and leading practitioners, offered a new approach to abortion regulation as part of a "model penal code" that it was proposing for adoption by the states. During the 1960s, twelve states adopted the ALI model, which legalized abortion for women whose doctors certified that they met certain qualifying indications, including a health-threatening condition of their own or a serious fetal anomaly. (It was Georgia's ALI-style law, under which a woman had to satisfy five doctors that she met one of the required conditions, that the Supreme Court struck down in the companion case to *Roe, Doe v. Bolton.*)

The women's movement came rather late to the abortion reform movement, focusing instead during much of the 1960s on expanding opportunities for women in employment and education and on persuading Congress to approve the Equal Rights Amendment and send it to the states for ratification. Betty Friedan, who in 1966 had founded the National Organization for Women, was the first to publicly place abortion at the core of the women's rights agenda. In 1969, she gave a speech to a group of (mostly male) doctors who had gathered in Chicago to organize what would eventually become the National Abortion Rights Action League (NARAL).[11] Making the connection between economic opportunities for women and the ability of women to control their reproductive lives, Friedan told the doctors that their cause "is now mine."[12] In Friedan's highly publicized "strike for equality" on August 26, 1970, women in cities across the country took to the streets to demand access to abortion and to publicly funded child care as well as equality in education and employment. The right to be working mothers and the right to choose against motherhood were now both subsumed under the feminist banner.

Women and men gather for a lunch-hour rally in New York's City Hall Park on August 26, 1970, to support the women's movement and mark the fiftieth anniversay of women's suffrage.

Another prominent woman, Phyllis Schlafly, soon drew a very different message from the connection between abortion and women's rights. A Republican Party activist and early leader of the pro-family movement that was to reshape domestic politics in the 1970s, Schlafly characterized the women's movement as antifamily and "pro-abortion," and warned that the Equal Rights Amendment would embed a right to abortion in the Constitution. As Schlafly's nationwide STOP ERA movement gained visibility and traction, leading feminists retreated strategically from the claim that a right to abortion was inherent in women's equality.[13]

Congress sent the Equal Rights Amendment to the states in March 1972, a fact of which the justices were certainly aware, as demonstrated by explicit references to the ERA in their internal discussions about what level of judicial scrutiny should apply to discrimination on the basis of sex (see Chapter 7). In those early years of the ratification effort, the justices

seemed to share the widespread expectation that the ERA would win ratification. In any event, it is far from clear that the debate over the amendment's potential implication for abortion was even visible to the Court.
The ERA played no role in the deliberations in *Roe.* A few of the briefs
filed in the case did contain strongly worded feminist arguments—even
one analogizing undesired pregnancy to slavery[14]—but the Court seems
not to have heard the voices presenting such arguments. Perhaps they
came from too far afield, too far outside the justices' understanding of
how the world worked. It would be years—after the fight for the ERA
and the Burger Court itself had entered the history books—before any
Supreme Court opinion drew a link between reproductive rights and
women's equality.[15]

The voices that the Burger Court justices undoubtedly did hear were
those of their professional peers: the doctors, the lawyers, members of the
liberal Protestant clergy,[16] and, in increasing numbers, fellow judges who
found that the enforcement of nineteenth-century notions of morality
through the criminal law was inconsistent with a twentieth-century Constitution. (Although "Jane Roe" was technically the appellant in *Roe v.
Wade*, the lower court had actually ruled in her favor, on the ground that
the Texas law, which permitted only those abortions necessary to save a
pregnant woman's life, was unduly broad and vague in failing to inform
doctors how they were to weigh the imminence of the emergency. But the
federal district court failed to issue an injunction to bar the state from
enforcing its unconstitutional law, thus leading the plaintiffs' lawyers to
appeal; the state appealed from the underlying judgment.)[17]

In the years leading up to *Roe*, editorials in leading newspapers joined
the call for abortion reform. Only rarely were editorials framed in terms
of a constitutional right, or the Constitution at all. The themes commonly struck were those of women's health and safety and the ability of
doctors to use their best judgment without fearing prosecution. Women's
autonomy as independent actors, outside the doctor-patient relationship,
was rarely mentioned; the assumption was that doctors knew best in providing this particular medical service, as they did with others.[18]

Beyond their own social and professional networks, the justices also
had to be aware that the public strongly favored decriminalizing abortion. A Gallup Poll in June 1972 asked people whether they agreed or disagreed with the statement: "The decision to have an abortion should be

made solely by a woman and her physician." Agreement with this statement, which reflected the medical lens through which abortion was generally viewed, came from majorities across the demographic spectrum: men (63 percent), women (64 percent), Protestants (65 percent), Catholics (56 percent), college graduates (74 percent), Democrats (59 percent), Republicans (68 percent). George Gallup's article reporting these finds was published in *The Washington Post*.[19] It was brought to the Court's attention by a brief filed by Planned Parenthood, and Harry Blackmun kept a copy of the original article in his case file.[20]

Clearly, *Roe v. Wade*—or the decision in whatever other case might have been first in the Supreme Court's queue—was the product of strong historical forces that were sweeping away old concepts of the appropriate role of the state in enforcing codes of personal behavior in matters of sex and reproduction. That isn't to say—as some persist in arguing—that reform would have marched unimpeded across the country if only the Supreme Court had stayed its hand or ruled less decisively. Alone among religious faiths at the time, but politically sophisticated and powerfully organized, the Catholic Church was determined to use the political process to stop legalization. In 1972, the Church succeeded in persuading the New York legislature to repeal the legalization measure of two years earlier; only the veto by Governor Nelson A. Rockefeller kept abortion legal in New York. The United States Catholic Conference's Family Life Division had set up the National Right to Life Committee in 1968 and set dozens of local committees to work mobilizing against reform legislation in the states. Reform measures were defeated in twenty state legislatures in the spring of 1971, with none being enacted anywhere in the country. A voter referendum in Michigan that had been expected to succeed in repealing the state's criminal abortion law failed in 1972.[21]

The question remains how visible any of what we might call pre-*Roe* backlash—directed not at judicial decisions but at political developments—was to the justices. It's possible that, just as the justices couldn't hear the feminist voices in support of reform, neither could they hear the organized Catholic voices of opposition—and, as the Gallup Poll indicated, a majority of individual Catholics favored decriminalization. Although *Roe v. Wade* is often depicted today as a bolt sent down from the blue by an activist Court, the justices had every reason to suppose that they were embracing a broad national consensus—and, indeed, the post-*Roe* polling as well as the earlier surveys indicate that they were correct. In the immediate aftermath of the decision, support for the legalization of abortion appeared to increase. A poll taken by NBC News on election day in November 1974 showed strong support for continuing to keep abortion legal: one third of the public thought the Supreme Court had struck the right balance in permitting abortion to be restricted only in the third trimester of pregnancy; one third thought the Court had gone too far; and one third thought the Court should have gone further in permitting abortion late in pregnancy.[22]

Reaching Consensus

As the justices prepared to hear the *Roe* argument in the fall of 1971, they didn't appear to consider it a case of surpassing importance, or even as one of the most important cases on the docket at the time. The argument was set for December, but shortly before the start of the term on the first Monday in October, two of the most senior justices, Hugo Black and John Harlan, abruptly retired for reasons of health. Since it was likely to be several months before their successors would be chosen, confirmed, and seated, the question was whether to let the scheduled arguments go ahead or whether to remove some cases from the calendar to await a full nine-member Court. On the advice of a committee that included Blackmun and Stewart, the justices held some cases back, but they let the argument in *Roe v. Wade* and *Doe v. Bolton* take place as originally scheduled on December 13.

The discussion in conference after the arguments revealed a clear consensus to strike down the Texas statute at issue in *Roe*. The fate of Georgia's American Law Institute–model reform law in *Doe* was less certain. Nor was it clear on what constitutional basis the Court might rule in either case. Burger assigned both cases to Blackmun, who proceeded on the assumption that the Georgia case would produce the primary opinion. In *Roe*, Blackmun was prepared to agree with the District Court that the life-saving exception in the Texas law was too vague to meet constitutional standards under the Due Process Clause of the Fourteenth Amendment. On May 18, 1972, he circulated a seventeen-page draft opinion resting on vagueness. "I think that this would be all that is necessary for disposition of the case," he told his colleagues in a cover letter.[23] The draft struck a tentative, even apologetic tone. "We are literally showered with briefs—with physicians and paramedical and other knowledgeable people on both sides—but this case, as it comes to us, does not require the resolution of those issues," Blackmun wrote in the draft opinion. (In fact, only fifteen friend-of-the-court briefs were filed in *Roe*. That may have seemed like a big number at the time, but in major Supreme Court cases today, one hundred or more briefs are not uncommon.) The draft opinion continued:

> Our holding today does not imply that a State has no legitimate interest in the subject of abortions or that abortion procedures may not be subjected to control by the State. The nub of the matter is the appropriateness of the control when criminal sanctions are imposed. We do not accept the argument of the appellants and of some of the *amici* that a pregnant woman has an unlimited right to do with her body as she pleases.[24]

The Court's liberals found the draft unsatisfactory, nor were they enthusiastic about the twenty-one-page draft that Blackmun circulated a few days later in *Doe v. Bolton*. Blackmun proposed to strike down the Georgia statute by extrapolating to the abortion context from the privacy holdings in the contraception cases *Griswold v. Connecticut* and *Eisenstadt v. Baird*. He also invoked other decisions in which the Court had protected an individual's private choices against state intrusion, including *Loving v. Virginia*,[25] the 1967 decision by which the Court invalidated state laws that made interracial marriage a crime.

However, Blackmun wrote, unlike the plaintiffs in the earlier cases, "The pregnant woman cannot be isolated in her privacy" because "she carries an embryo and, later, a fetus." The question of abortion was therefore "inherently different from marital intimacy, or bedroom possession of obscene material, or marriage, or the right to procreate, or private education" because "the heart of the matter is that somewhere, either forthwith at conception, or at 'quickening,' or at birth, or at some other point in between, another being becomes involved and the privacy the woman possessed has become dual rather than sole." Blackmun continued:

The woman's right of privacy must be measured accordingly. It is not for us of the judiciary, especially at this point in the development of man's knowledge, to speculate or to specify when life begins. On this question there is no consensus even among those trained in the respective disciplines of medicine, or philosophy, or theology. . . . Except to note that the State's interest grows stronger as the woman approaches term, we need not delineate that interest with greater detail in order to recognize that it is a "compelling" state interest. As such it may constitutionally be asserted when the State does so with appropriate regard for fundamental individual rights.[26]

The bones of the opinion that was to become *Roe v. Wade* are visible, barely, in these inconclusive sentences. To his colleagues, it was unclear exactly where Blackmun's analysis was heading. He had proposed several months earlier, after the two new justices, Lewis Powell and William Rehnquist, took their seats, that the cases be reargued to a full Court. He now renewed the request, writing to his colleagues on May 31 that "I believe, on an issue so sensitive and so emotional as this one, the country deserves the conclusion of a nine-man, not a seven-man court, whatever the ultimate decision may be."[27] This time, his colleagues agreed. With no guarantee that he would retain the opinion assignment after the new argument in October, Blackmun continued to work on the cases during the summer recess.

Harry Blackmun never knew why his childhood friend Warren Burger had given him the assignment in the abortion cases. Before becoming a federal appeals court judge, Blackmun had been general counsel of the Mayo Clinic in Rochester, Minnesota. A longtime client of the Minneapolis law firm where Blackmun had been a partner, Mayo was a major medical research and clinical center. Blackmun was fascinated by medicine and had considered a career as a doctor. At Mayo, he sometimes accompanied the doctors on their rounds. Since the justices saw the abortion issue as one of public health policy, perhaps Blackmun was a natural choice for the assignment. Or perhaps Burger intuited what most of the others did not: that the issue inevitably raised questions of public morality and social policy. Best to give the cases to his reliable friend who could be counted on to keep them at a low simmer, without adding any unnecessary ingredients that might cause them to boil over.

Blackmun spent a week that summer back at Mayo, going through a stack of articles on the history and practice of abortion that the librarians there had compiled for him. This information, beginning with practices in ancient Persia, Greece, and Rome, and running through the recently adopted positions of leading medical groups, was to occupy nearly twenty pages of Blackmun's final opinion. Blackmun seemed to be assuring himself, and eventual readers, that abortion was part of human history, and that efforts to make it a crime were, as the opinion eventually read, "not of ancient or even of common-law origin" but dated only to "the latter half of the 19th century." [28] At that time, Blackmun went on to observe, abortion was "hazardous" to a woman and "placed her life in serious jeopardy," whereas early abortion was now as safe or even safer than normal childbirth. [29] The Mayo research, Blackmun said in notes he made to himself after returning to Washington, gave him "an awareness of medical history I have not had before." [30]

The reargument took place on October 11. Preparing for the justices' conference two days later, Blackmun polished the draft opinions on which he had continued to work, preparing to circulate them in a bid to keep the assignment. The notes he made on what he planned to say at the conference show that he was of two minds on how the public was likely to receive a decision to strike down every state's abortion law. On the one hand, he wrote in pencil on a legal pad, "it is not a happy assignment—will be excoriated." But on the other hand, he suggested that any ensuing turmoil would be short-lived. He listed four points under the heading of "Mandate"—the formal order that puts a decision into effect:

1. A majority of state statutes go down the drain.
2. It will be an unsettled period for a while.
3. But most state legislatures will meet in '73.
4. Any point in withholding the mandate? To 4/1. [31]

The suggestion in Point 4 was that a delay of a few months in putting the decision into effect would permit the states, and the public, to settle down. Blackmun could not possibly have imagined that some state legislatures would devote the ensuing decades to limiting the impact of *Roe v. Wade*.

Six weeks later, Blackmun circulated a new draft opinion in *Roe*, much expanded at fifty pages, and structured much as the final opinion would be. "In short, the unborn have never been recognized in the law as persons in the whole sense," Blackmun wrote, adding: "As a consequence, we do not agree that by adopting one theory of life Texas may override the rights of the pregnant woman that are at stake." [32] Nearly identical sentences would appear in *Roe.*

There would be one major difference, however. In the draft, Blackmun wrote that the state's interest in protecting potential human life became "compelling" at the end of the first trimester, the first twelve weeks of pregnancy. During the first trimester, the state "must do no more than to leave the abortion decision to the best medical judgment of the pregnant woman's attending physician," he wrote. But during the final six months of pregnancy, the state was free to restrict abortion "to stated reasonable therapeutic categories that are articulated with sufficient clarity so that a physician is able to predict what conditions fall within the stated classifications." In his cover note to his colleagues, Blackmun observed: "This is arbitrary, but perhaps any other selected point, such as quickening or viability, is equally arbitrary." [33]

The following week, Blackmun received a hand-delivered letter from Lewis Powell, one of the two new Nixon appointees to the Court. It had been no surprise when the other new justice, the very conservative William Rehnquist, voted in dissent after the reargument. But Powell's views were unknown, and his strong support for overturning the Texas and Georgia laws came as a pleasant surprise to the Court's liberals. Now he was urging Blackmun to go further, to set viability—the point at which a fetus can live outside the womb, at the time about twenty-eight weeks—as the point at which the state's interest in protecting potential life becomes "compelling" and abortion can be prohibited except to preserve a woman's life or health.

Powell told Blackmun that he had recently read Judge Jon O. Newman's opinion in *Abele v. Markle,* the "Women versus Connecticut" case that struck down Connecticut's abortion law. The state's appeal was pending at the Court. In his opinion, Judge Newman had selected viability as the cut-off point, observing that "the state interest in protecting the life of a fetus capable of living outside the uterus could be shown to be more generally accepted and, therefore, of more weight in the constitutional sense than the interest in preventing the abortion of a fetus that is not viable." Wouldn't viability "be more defensible in logic and biologically than perhaps any other single time," Powell wanted to know.[34]

Blackmun replied that while he had "no particular commitment" to one point or another, he preferred the end of the first trimester because it was likely to be more acceptable to the other justices.[35] When he asked the others for their views, Brennan and Douglas both said they preferred to stay with the end of the first trimester. But Thurgood Marshall made a forceful argument for viability. "Given the difficulties which many women may have in believing that they are pregnant and in deciding to seek an abortion," Marshall wrote to Blackmun, with copies to the other justices, "I fear that the earlier date may not in practice serve the interests of those women, which your opinion does seek to serve." Marshall proposed that during the several months between the end of the first trimester and viability, states be permitted to impose restrictions on abortion "directed at health and safety alone."[36]

This was the approach that Blackmun took as the drafts neared final form in late December: the state could impose no restrictions during the first trimester and could regulate during the second trimester only in the interest of the pregnant woman's health. During the third trimester, when the fetus was viable and the state's interest had become compelling, abortion could be prohibited unless necessary to preserve a woman's life or health. *Roe v. Wade* was now the main opinion, based on "this right of privacy," derived from the Court's precedents and "broad enough to encompass a woman's decision whether or not to terminate her pregnancy." The privacy right "is not unqualified" and "cannot be said to be absolute," Blackmun emphasized. As to the argument that "the woman's right is absolute and that she is entitled to terminate her pregnancy at whatever time, in whatever way, and for whatever reason she alone chooses," Blackmun said bluntly: "With this we do not agree."

Close to the end of the opinion, Blackmun summarized: "The decision vindicates the right of the physician to administer medical treatment according to his professional judgment up to the points where important state interests provide compelling justifications for intervention. Up to those points, the abortion decision in all its aspects is inherently, and primarily, a medical decision, and basic responsibility for it must rest with the physician."[37]

Several weeks earlier, reviewing a previous draft, one of Powell's law clerks, Larry Hammond, had brought that paragraph to his justice's attention. "HAB has placed considerable emphasis on the role of the physician and the free exercise of his professional judgment," the law clerk wrote in a memo to Powell, pointing to Blackmun's assertion that "responsibility for that decision must rest with the physician." Hammond asked Powell: "Doesn't it seem that this language overstates the doctor's role and undercuts the woman's personal interest in the decision? All medical decisions are the product of an agreement between patient and doctor. I see no reason, therefore, not to add a clause to this sentence indicating that the abortion decision must rest 'with the physician *and his patient.*' " The law clerk urged Powell to take up the matter with Blackmun.[38] There is no evidence in either justice's papers that Powell acted on the advice. In any event, aside from a slight grammatical modification, the paragraph went into the final opinion unchanged.

As Blackmun prepared to announce the decision to the world—the public summary that an opinion's author gives from the bench is referred to at the Court as a "hand-down"—Burger urged him to include a sentence declaring that the Court was not authorizing "abortion on demand." This phrase had appeared nowhere in the opinion, but was gaining some political currency outside the Court. Blackmun disregarded the advice.[39] Much of the early news coverage nonetheless did stress the limitations the Court placed on the new right it was declaring. News accounts incorrectly portrayed the abortion right as limited to the first trimester. The public health orientation of the opinion also figured prominently in the early articles. But the notion of a "right to privacy" soon proved irresistible, providing a public frame for viewing the abortion issue from the woman's perspective and away from the doctor's. *Roe v. Wade* became something the Burger Court neither intended nor even necessarily understood: a symbol of women's empowerment and, as such, a lightning rod, and in the hands of Republican Party operatives smart enough to understand the possibilities, a tool of political realignment.[40]

Building the Backlash

What many people today assume to have been an overnight political backlash to *Roe* actually took years to develop. Support for legalized abortion—as for the Equal Rights Amendment—was notably stronger among Republicans than Democrats. John Paul Stevens, nominated to the Supreme Court by President Gerald Ford in December 1975 to replace Douglas, received no questions about abortion during his Senate confirmation hearing, evidence that nearly three years after *Roe*, abortion was not a prominent issue in national politics.[41]

The Republican Party maintained a big-tent position on abortion until its 1980 convention, when Ronald Reagan won the presidential nomination. That convention for the first time adopted a platform that called for the appointment of federal judges who would vote to overturn *Roe*: "judges at all levels of the judiciary who respect traditional family values and the sanctity of innocent human life." The backlash against *Roe* and the Court that decided it had become a dominant factor in American politics.[42]

The realignment of the major political parties over the abortion issue was not fully visible until more than seven years had passed since *Roe*. The seeds that took so long to sprout had, in fact, been planted even before the Supreme Court ruled. Beginning in the early 1970s, Republican strategists had seen the possibility of using opposition to abortion to lure an important bloc of voters away from its traditional home in the Democratic Party. The target was the ethnic, largely Catholic population of the urban Northeast. Nixon had paid little attention to abortion during his political career, his moderate views mirroring those of the Republican mainstream. But he readily took the advice of Pat Buchanan and Kevin Phillips during his 1972 reelection campaign to embrace the opposition. At the same time, Republicans painted the Democratic nominee, Senator George McGovern, whose moderate position on abortion differed little from Nixon's previous position, as a dangerous radical at war with traditional values.

Roe v. Wade was still to come and played no role in these developments; had there been no Supreme Court decision, abortion would, from all the pre-*Roe* evidence, still have become caught up by the evolving culture wars that would eventually sink the Equal Rights Amendment. It was the fight over the ERA that drew conservative evangelicals into the fray. Having previously viewed abortion as a Catholic issue, the evangelical churches had hung back and some had even adopted mild reform positions in the early 1970s.[43] But, persuaded that the ERA was a threat to the traditional family and to social and legislative arrangements that protected women in their roles as wives and mothers, evangelicals were open to a "pro-family" alliance with Catholics, for whom the motivation was opposition to abortion. From this marriage of convenience, a powerful social movement was born.

Among the briefs filed in the Court in *Roe* had been briefs from the National Right to Life Committee and other antiabortion organizations. While these groups argued forcefully for the rights of the unborn, their arguments were not reflected in the opinions of the two dissenting justices, White and Rehnquist. The dissenters' objection to the majority opinion was not moral but jurisprudential. Rehnquist, acknowledging that "society's views on abortion are changing," meaning at that time that abortion had become acceptable, argued in his dissenting opinion that the fact that a majority of states had banned abortion when the Fourteenth Amendment, with its Due Process Clause, was adopted in 1868 showed that the amendment's drafters "did not intend to have the 14th Amendment withdraw from the States the power to legislate with respect to this matter."[44] Until the Court's membership changed, there was little prospect that the pro-life forces could make progress there. So they turned their attention elsewhere: to overturning *Roe* by a constitutional amendment, a daunting prospect that never got off the ground, and to the state legislatures.

Back to the Court

The years following *Roe* saw a steady stream of cases arriving at the Supreme Court that challenged restrictions imposed by state and local governments on access to abortion. The first, in 1976, was *Planned Parenthood of Central Missouri v. Danforth.*[45] By a 6–3 vote, the Court invalidated the Missouri legislature's requirement that a married woman receive her husband's consent to an abortion. "We are not unaware of the deep and proper concern and interest that a devoted and protective husband has in his wife's pregnancy and in the growth and development of the fetus she is carrying," Justice Blackmun wrote for the majority. However, he added, "we cannot hold that the State has the constitutional authority to give the spouse unilaterally the ability to prohibit the wife from terminating her pregnancy when the State itself lacks that right."

The Missouri statute also required that a girl under the age of eighteen receive the consent of one parent before obtaining an abortion. The Court in the *Danforth* decision invalidated this provision as well, Blackmun writing: "Constitutional rights do not mature and come into being magically only when one attains the state-defined age of majority." But here the vote was 5–4. John Paul Stevens, the only justice to have joined the Court since *Roe*, agreed with the majority on the spousal consent requirement, but voted to uphold parental consent for minors. On the spousal consent provision, the two dissenters in *Roe*, Justices White and Rehnquist, were joined now by Chief Justice Burger; his attachment to the *Roe* majority, tenuous from the outset, was obviously now strained nearly—although not yet completely—to the breaking point. White wrote for the dissenters: "This law represents a judgment by the State that a mother's interest in avoiding the burdens of childrearing do not outweigh or snuff out the father's interest in participating in bringing up his own child."

The Court was far from finished with the parental consent issue. It would continue for years to wrestle with the rights of minors in the abortion context,[46] eventually concluding that a state could require parental *notification* (not consent) as long as the girl had the alternative of going before a judge to obtain a "judicial bypass" of the notice requirement. This remains the law today; judges are supposed to determine whether a minor is sufficiently "mature" to make her own decision or, if not, whether terminating the pregnancy is in her best interest. The question of the husband's involvement would reemerge years later, in the 1992 decision *Planned Parenthood v. Casey*.[47] The Court ruled then by a vote of 5–4 that the state could not require a married woman to notify her husband in advance of an abortion.

This book is not the place for a comprehensive survey of the Supreme Court's jurisprudence regarding abortion. However, one decision bears discussion before we turn to the question of whether the government is constitutionally obliged to pay for abortions for poor women. This was *Akron v. Akron Center for Reproductive Health*,[48] decided on June 15, 1983. Five years earlier, the Ohio city had adopted a seventeen-part ordinance regulating the practice of abortion. It contained provisions similar to those that were cropping up around the country as antiabortion forces gained political leverage while the abortion rights movement, considering *Roe v. Wade* a decisive victory, remained largely disengaged.

Among the Akron ordinance's most important provisions were a twenty-four-hour waiting period; a requirement that all abortions after the first trimester be performed in a hospital; and an "informed consent" requirement. This last provision required the doctor to tell the woman that a fetus is a human being from the "moment of conception"; to describe fetal development; and to characterize the abortion itself as a "major surgical procedure." In his majority opinion invalidating these provisions, Justice Powell took particular aim at the consent requirement. He said it required the doctor to give a "dubious" description of an abortion and to recite a "parade of horribles" that was "designed not to inform the woman's consent, but rather to persuade her to withhold it altogether." The opinion also invalidated the waiting period and the hospitalization requirement, calling the latter "a heavy, and unnecessary, burden on women's access to a relatively inexpensive, otherwise accessible, and safe abortion procedure." The Akron ordinance "unreasonably infringes upon a woman's constitutional right to obtain an abortion," Powell concluded.

The decision had considerable practical importance. Twenty-one states, for example, had second-trimester hospitalization requirements, now invalidated. Powell's language in his majority opinion was unusually sharp. He began by noting that although a decade had passed since *Roe*, cases continued to reach the Court arguing that "we erred in interpreting the Constitution." He didn't hide his impatience. The Court "repeatedly and consistently has accepted and applied the basic principle that a woman has a fundamental right to make the highly personal choice whether or not to terminate her pregnancy," Powell wrote. *Roe v. Wade* remained a controlling precedent, and the doctrine of stare decisis—to stand by a precedent—"demands respect in a society governed by the rule of law."

The source of the majority's distress was clear enough—a threat to *Roe* not only from outside the Court, but from within it. The vote was 6–3, and the newest justice had joined White and Rehnquist in dissent. In fact, Justice Sandra Day O'Connor was the author of the dissenting opinion. The vigorous attack on the right to abortion that had begun to shape American politics was bearing fruit.

The two post-*Roe* justices, O'Connor and Stevens, arrived at the Court less than six years apart: December 1975 for Stevens and September 1981 for O'Connor. But what a difference those years had made. While abortion was a nonissue in the nomination and confirmation of Stevens, it had become the dominant issue as the Reagan administration shepherded the first female Supreme Court nominee through Senate confirmation.

In choosing Sandra O'Connor to succeed Potter Stewart, who retired in July 1981 at the relatively young age of sixty-six after twenty-three years on the Court, Reagan moved at the first opportunity to fulfill a campaign promise to put a woman on the Supreme Court. (He would go on to appoint Antonin Scalia and Anthony M. Kennedy, and to name William Rehnquist to succeed Warren Burger as chief justice.) Aside from gender, O'Connor was an unusual selection. Unlike anyone on the Supreme Court that she joined—or anyone since—O'Connor had had a successful career in electoral politics before becoming a judge. She had been majority leader of the Arizona State Senate, the first woman in the country to hold so high a position in a state legislature. At the time of her nomination, she was a judge on Arizona's intermediate appellate court, a rather modest judicial position. But she had a few important Supreme Court connections. She and Rehnquist had been classmates and friends at Stanford Law School (he graduated first in the class, and she was third) and she had met and favorably impressed Warren Burger on several occasions.

The abortion wars had reached Arizona, and O'Connor, a moderate Republican known for seeking consensus, had taken what looked to be a mildly pro-choice position. In 1970, well before the issue was hotly contested in the state, she had voted for a Senate bill that would have legalized abortion. In the year following *Roe*, she voted against a measure that would have prohibited some hospitals in the state from performing abortions. Arizona's antiabortion leadership remembered those votes and opposed her Supreme Court nomination; Dr. John Willke, chairman of the National Right to Life Committee, testified against her at her Senate confirmation hearing, the first Supreme Court confirmation hearing ever televised.

Chief Justice Burger escorts the new Justice O'Connor down
the court's front steps, September 25, 1981.

At the hearing, O'Connor was primed for questions on her abortion
views and, like the good politician she was, she gave away little. As expected, the adversarial questions came not from Democrats but from
conservative Republicans who sought assurance that the new president
was carrying out the party platform's injunction to name judges and justices who would overturn *Roe v. Wade.* Answering questions from Senator Jeremiah Denton, an Alabama Republican and former prisoner of war
in Vietnam who had placed opposition to abortion at the center of his political career, O'Connor said that abortion was "simply offensive to me."

She continued: "It is something that is repugnant to me, and something in which I would not engage. Obviously, there are others who do
not share these beliefs, and I recognize that. I am over the hill. I am not

going to be pregnant anymore, so it is perhaps easy for me to speak." O'Connor, fifty-one years old, was the mother of three sons, whom she had introduced to the members of the Judiciary Committee. Despite their doubts, the conservative Republicans couldn't maintain their opposition to a star-quality nominee who quickly captured the television-watching public's fancy. The Senate confirmed O'Connor by a vote of 99–0.[49]

The *Akron* case was O'Connor's first opportunity to cast a Supreme Court vote on abortion. The Reagan administration had entered the case to argue in support of the ordinance, underscoring the significance of the case among the numerous other abortion cases the Court had heard and decided during the preceding decade. Her vote, and the fact that her two senior colleagues, whose position in dissent was a foregone conclusion, had evidently invited her to speak for them, came as a shock to women's rights groups that had cheered the appointment of a woman to the Court.

While O'Connor's opinion did not repudiate the notion that the Constitution offered some protection for a woman's choice to terminate a pregnancy—"even assuming that there is a fundamental right to terminate pregnancy in some situations" is how she put it—the new justice's disagreement with the way the Court had decided the issue in *Roe v. Wade* was profound. "I believe that the State's interest in protecting potential human life exists throughout the pregnancy," she wrote; there was "no justification in law or logic" for the trimester framework that precluded the state from asserting that interest until the final months of pregnancy. Indeed, she said, medical advances since *Roe* were already making it possible to save more premature babies, thus moving the effective date of fetal viability "ever back toward conception." The trimester framework, she wrote, was "clearly on a collision course with itself," "a completely unworkable method of accommodating the conflicting personal rights and compelling state interests that are involved in the abortion context."[50]

O'Connor proposed an alternative analysis, adopting the approach urged by Rex E. Lee, the Reagan administration's solicitor general, who had presented the administration's position when the Court heard the *Akron* case on November 30, 1982. The state should be permitted to vindicate its interest in potential life by limiting access to abortion, O'Connor wrote, as long as the restrictions were not "unduly burdensome," in the sense of imposing "absolute obstacles or severe limitations." Applying her "undue burden" standard to the case at hand, O'Connor concluded that because the Akron provisions did not either "infringe substantially or heavily burden" a woman's ability to terminate a pregnancy, they were constitutional.

In *Planned Parenthood v. Casey*, nine contentious years later, Sandra O'Connor's undue burden standard became the law of the land, reformulating *Roe* without directly overruling it. With its vigorous invocation of stare decisis, the *Casey* decision appeared, when it was issued in June 1992, to have achieved a constitutional settlement of the abortion issue. But in the decades since, it has proven to be anything but that. The question of which burdens are "undue" and which obstacles are "substantial" remains deeply contested.

Privacy at a Price

Not so, however, with the other major abortion question the Burger Court faced: whether a government program that subsidizes poor people's medical care, including the expenses of pregnancy and childbirth, can exclude abortion. The Court's unambiguously affirmative answer, combined with a political climate increasingly hostile to both social welfare programs and abortion, eventually served to drive the issue of public subsidies for abortion out of the arena of public discussion. But that was not always the case, and it is worth revisiting the justices' encounter with the question: their answer lay at the core of how the Burger Court understood the Constitution's guarantee of equal protection.

The public funding debate emerged soon after the Court decided *Roe*, and a trio of cases reached the justices during the 1976 term. One was a statutory case from Pennsylvania, raising the question whether the federal Medicaid law required states participating in the Medicaid program to pay for elective abortions—those not deemed medically necessary. The answer, in *Beal v. Doe*, was no, although Justice Powell's opinion for the 6–3 majority (Justices Brennan, Marshall, and Blackmun dissenting) emphasized that states remained free to pick up the cost of these "nontherapeutic" abortions if they so desired.[51]

The second case, *Poelker v. Doe*, upheld, by the same 6–3 vote, a policy barring abortions in the two public hospitals in St. Louis, Missouri.[52] (The policy made an exception for women whose pregnancy posed a threat to life or a grave threat to health.) The city's mayor, who proposed the policy, had been elected to office on an antiabortion platform. "The Constitution does not forbid a state or city, pursuant to democratic processes, from expressing a preference for normal childbirth as St. Louis does here," the Court's short unsigned opinion read.

Most significantly, the third case, *Maher v. Roe*,[53] addressed the basic constitutional question. At issue was a Connecticut welfare regulation that provided Medicaid coverage for only those abortions deemed "medically necessary." The state subsidized all other expenses incurred by poor women for pregnancy and childbirth. The federal district court had declared the abortion exclusion to violate the constitutional guarantee of equal protection. Writing for the three-judge district court panel, Judge Jon O. Newman observed that "abortion and childbirth, when stripped of the sensitive moral arguments surrounding the abortion controversy, are simply two alternative medical methods of dealing with pregnancy."[54]

For Judge Newman, who two years earlier had written the opinion in the "Women versus Connecticut" case that invalidated the state's abortion law, the issue was straightforward. "The Constitution does not require the state to pay for any medical services at all," he began his analysis. But given the fundamental nature of the right to an abortion, he continued, the state needed a "compelling" reason to choose to pay only for childbirth and for medically necessary abortions, a policy that he said "weights the choice of the pregnant mother against choosing to exercise her constitutionally protected right to an elected abortion."

The state's argument that it had a financial interest in refusing to cover elective abortions was "wholly chimerical," Judge Newman said, because "abortion is the least expensive medical response to a pregnancy." The "only other possible state interest," he continued, was that the state was refusing to spend public money on a purpose it found "morally objectionable." He concluded: "To sanction such a justification would be to permit discrimination against those seeking to exercise a constitutional right on the basis that the state simply does not approve of the exercise of that right."

What appeared straightforward to Judge Newman, a former law clerk to Chief Justice Earl Warren, seemed equally straightforward to the Burger Court majority—but in the opposite direction. "We think the district court misconceived the nature and scope of the fundamental right recognized in *Roe*," Lewis Powell wrote for the six-member majority in *Maher v. Roe*, overturning Judge Newman's decision.

In preparing for the justices' conference following the January 11, 1977, argument, Powell had made extensive notes, writing out his thoughts on a yellow pad in complete sentences as if drafting an opinion. "The refusal to fund does indeed *burden* the exercise of the right," he wrote. "But failure to provide funds to enable citizens to exercise rights has not heretofore been unconstitutional." The examples he gave to prove this point were the right to travel, the right to associate, and speech itself.

"The source of deprivation—indigency—is not action of state," Powell continued. The state policy imposed "no prohibition and criminal penalty as in *Roe*." His conclusion was that the Constitution didn't speak at all to the distinction the state had made. It was a matter, he wrote, "for *Congress*."

At conference, it was clear that there was a majority for Powell's view. The Court "can't carry *Roe* this far," Burger said. John Paul Stevens, who had not been present for *Roe*, observed that while the equal protection analysis was "close," *Roe* itself had not been an equal protection case. While Stevens obviously disliked the regulation, he concluded that there was no constitutional basis on which to invalidate it. He was clearly uncomfortable. We "can't trust legislatures to fund" without being required to, he said. He concluded his remarks with more hope than certainty: "We can't assume legislatures will fail to act responsibly."

Voting to affirm Judge Newman's opinion, Justice Brennan said the case was an "easy" one. "This burden on a fundamental right is clearly unconstitutional," he told his fellow justices. If the Court upheld it, "we might as well overrule *Roe* and *Doe*." Thurgood Marshall and Harry Blackmun agreed. Only Potter Stewart wrestled visibly with the case, withholding his vote on the first round. But as the discussion proceeded, he joined the clear majority to reverse. The equal protection argument, Stewart said, was "very close and difficult." He continued: "The government does have large discretion in dispensing largess. But this case doesn't involve those considerations" because it is "cheaper to provide abortions and prevent the welfare rolls being increased." The state's ordinary financial interest was thus not involved. Powell's notes suggest that after a lengthy rumination, Stewart basically gave up. "The state's interest in preferring life over abortion is enough," he announced, adding, as if to soften the impact of his own conclusion, that the "state does pay whenever a doctor finds medical necessity."[55]

Burger assigned the *Maher* case to Powell, whose eventual opinion, issued with the other two cases on June 20, 1977, deviated little from his initial response. At the start of his analysis, Powell observed that the case "involves no discrimination against a suspect class." Here he cited his own majority opinion's rejection four years earlier in *San Antonio v. Rodriguez*[56] of the notion that "financial need alone identifies a suspect class for purposes of equal protection analysis."

Thus dispensing with the need to consider the poverty-driven claim at the heart of the case, Powell went on to discuss how this case fit with the Court's abortion precedents. Connecticut's regulation "does not impinge upon the fundamental right recognized in *Roe*," Powell wrote, adding that in upholding the funding exclusion, "our conclusion signals no retreat from *Roe* or the cases applying it." There is, he said, a "basic difference between direct state interference with a protected activity and state encouragement of an alternative activity consonant with legislative policy." Powell continued, explaining that the state law struck down in *Roe* "was a stark example of impermissible interference with the pregnant woman's decision to terminate her pregnancy." However, "*Roe* did not declare an unqualified 'constitutional right to an abortion,' as the District Court seemed to think. Rather, the right protects the woman from unduly burdensome interference with her freedom to decide whether to terminate her pregnancy. It implies no limitation on the authority of a State to make a value judgment favoring childbirth over abortion, and to implement that judgment by the allocation of public funds."[57]

Justice Brennan, in a dissenting opinion that Marshall and Blackmun also signed, said the majority's analysis displayed "a distressing insensitivity to the plight of impoverished pregnant women." The state regulation, he continued, "clearly operates to coerce indigent pregnant women to bear children they would not otherwise choose to have, and just as clearly, this coercion can only operate upon the poor, who are uniquely the victims of this form of financial pressure."[58]

Harry Blackmun also wrote a dissenting opinion, which he attached to the St. Louis hospital case (*Poelker v. Doe*) while addressing all three financing decisions. "The Court today, by its decisions in these cases, allows the States, and such municipalities as choose to do so, to accomplish indirectly what the Court in *Roe v. Wade* and *Doe v. Bolton*—by a substantial majority and with some emphasis, I had thought—said they could not do directly," Blackmun began. Four paragraphs later, he concluded with what were to become among his best-known lines:

> There is another world "out there," the existence of which the Court, I suspect, either chooses to ignore or fears to recognize. And so the cancer of poverty will continue to grow. This is a sad day for those who regard the Constitution as a force that would serve justice to all even-handedly and, in so doing, would better the lot of the poorest among us.[59]

Blackmun had circulated a draft of his dissenting opinion— unchanged in the final published version—to his colleagues a few weeks earlier. After reading it, Lewis Powell scrawled across the top: "Wow!" And the bottom of the first page, he wrote: "Is this a *legal* opinion?!" [60] Not too many years earlier, the concerns Blackmun expressed might well have formed the basis for an opinion of the Court. But now that the Burger Court had come into its own, such thoughts could lead in only one direction: to a dissenting opinion.

On the Federal Stage

Not only the states, but Congress, too, had acted quickly to keep public funds from subsidizing abortion. Beginning in September 1976—before the Supreme Court ruled in the trio of state cases—Congress appended to the annual appropriation bill for the Department of Health, Education, and Welfare what became known as the Hyde Amendment. Named for Henry J. Hyde, a Republican from Illinois and the leader of the anti-abortion forces in the House, the measure withheld the federal share of Medicaid money from abortions for poor women with certain exceptions that changed annually, according to the strength of Hyde's coalition. Sometimes, Congress refused to pay for terminating any pregnancy that didn't threaten a woman's life. Sometimes there were exceptions for pregnancy resulting from rape or incest. In any event, abortions, whether or not deemed medically necessary, were not to be subsidized with federal money. In this, the Hyde Amendment was notably more severe than the Connecticut regulation upheld in *Maher v. Roe*, which applied only to abortions that were not certified by a doctor as medically necessary.

In January 1980, the federal district court in New York ruled the Hyde Amendment unconstitutional. By paying for all other medically necessary services for poor women but carving out medically necessary abortions, the court ruled, Congress violated the constitutional guarantee of equal protection.[61]

Given the *Maher* precedent, the prospect that the Supreme Court would agree with the district court and strike down the Hyde Amendment looked remote unless any justice or justices concluded that the refusal to fund even medically necessary abortions made a difference of constitutional dimension. The Court that confronted the new case, *Harris v. McRae*,[62] was unchanged. At the justices' conference on April 25, 1980, four days following the argument, only John Paul Stevens seemed to be finding his way toward a different position. As the most junior justice, Stevens spoke last. This was a "difficult case," he said; he didn't see it as controlled by the decision in *Maher*, which he had joined and still viewed as correctly decided. For one thing, the new case presented none of the federalism concerns that were in the background of the state cases. Here, he said, the governmental interest was a "federal interest in fetal life, not a state interest" and "by denying funds for abortion, more federal funds will be spent for birth." Stevens observed that "a substantial additional cost will result from Hyde," in other words, that any claim to protecting the federal treasury would be inaccurate. Stevens continued: "Under *Roe v. Wade*, a state could not impose a fine on a woman who aborts. Nor can a state impose the risk of poor health or death as a penalty for getting pregnant."[63]

Stevens was particularly offended by the fact that the Hyde Amendment had never been debated as separate legislation. "We make federal policy by holding a revenue bill hostage—reprehensible!" It was, he said, "a perversion of the spending power."[64] He was not the only one to think so. "If I were in Congress I would have voted *against* the Hyde Amendment," Powell wrote in a note to himself as he was preparing for conference. But the notes of *Maher*'s author make clear that he viewed the funding decision, whatever the details, as a matter for the legislatures and not the courts.[65]

The vote was 5–4 to reverse the district court's decision. Burger assigned the opinion to Potter Stewart. As Stewart was working on his opinion, he received a memo from Powell urging him not to be unduly concerned with any asserted difference between abortions deemed medically necessary and those that were merely elective. Powell cited testimony in the record of another abortion case that, he said, "makes clear that doctors tend to be persuaded easily that there is some 'medical necessity.' " As many as half of all abortions were labeled "necessary," Powell continued, while the overall mortality rate for pregnant women was only 2 per 10,000. Powell then offered this rather eyebrow-raising observation: "One could guess that two out of every 10,000 pregnant women die from automobile accidents, slipping in bathtubs, or in quarrels with their husbands or lovers."[66]

Whatever effect Powell's intervention might have had on Stewart's thinking, Stewart showed no hesitation in carrying out the conference's conclusion. The Court had made clear in *Maher*, his opinion asserted, that "although government may not place obstacles in the path of a woman's exercise of her freedom of choice, it need not remove those not of its own creation." Stewart added that "to hold otherwise would mark a drastic change in our understanding of the Constitution." He explained:

> The financial constraints that restrict an indigent woman's ability to enjoy the full range of constitutionally protected freedom of choice are the product not of governmental restrictions on access to abortions, but rather of her indigency. Although Congress has opted to subsidize medically necessary services generally, but not certain medically necessary abortions, the fact remains that the Hyde Amendment leaves an indigent woman with at least the same range of choice in deciding whether to obtain a medically necessary abortion as she would have had if Congress had chosen to subsidize no health care costs at all.[67]

This was Warren Burger's Constitution in the raw. The public health concerns for the perils faced by poor women unable to obtain a safe, legal abortion, expressed two decades earlier by Dr. Mary Calderone, remained unabated. Earlier in the drafting process, Stewart's law clerk, Saul Goodman, had tried to inject a mild note of compassion into the draft opinion while still remaining true to his justice's analysis. "This is not to say that the situation of an indigent woman who is unable to afford a medically necessary abortion is any less tragic because it results from her own indigency, rather than from governmental restrictions," the law clerk wrote. He continued:

> Her options, in the absence of public assistance, appear limited to either (1) foregoing the medically necessary abortion and thus suffering the adverse health consequences arising from her pregnancy, or (2) obtaining an abortion through less expensive, and often unsafe, procedures. That our elected representatives have not chosen to remedy this situation through public assistance is sure to cause her hardship.
>
> But the sad fact remains that the relief sought by the appellees is not to be found in the Constitution.[68]

Upon receiving this offering from his law clerk, Justice Potter Stewart made his reaction indisputably clear. Over those two paragraphs, he made a big **X**.

CHAPTER 7

The Rocky Road to Sex Equality

As the justices were considering a woman's right to terminate a pregnancy, a new claim concerning pregnancy arrived at the court. The new appeal, filed in the fall of 1972 as the work on *Roe v. Wade* neared completion, challenged the forced maternity leave policies that were then common to public school systems around the country. Many school districts required pregnant teachers to leave the classroom months before their due date, unpaid and often with no guarantee that they could reclaim their jobs, and new mothers were often required to stay home for many months after giving birth, also without pay.

To twenty-first-century ears, such policies sound preposterous. But they reflected widely held assumptions that had long gone unchallenged: that children should be spared the sight of a visibly pregnant woman in front of a classroom; that pregnant women were too delicate for the workplace; and—deepest of all even when unexpressed—that a mother's place was at home.

Unsurprisingly, the women's movement had begun to challenge both these attitudes and the employment policies that resulted from them. And unsurprisingly, the justices of the Burger Court had trouble grasping the argument that the women were making. The plaintiffs and their lawyers were claiming sex discrimination, but what did "discrimination" mean in this context? After all, only women could become pregnant. In the life cycle of the human species, pregnancy was a unique event. There was no male equivalent. How could treating pregnancy as unique then amount to discrimination on the basis of sex?

Or could it? Perhaps the law should consider pregnancy as one of numerous temporarily disabling conditions, common to one sex or another or both, to be treated according to the general rules that applied to such conditions. But wasn't pregnancy something special, to which special rules ought to apply, special accommodations be made? This was the deep question the new case posed: in the search for constitutional equality, what is the relevance of difference? It was a question that the nine men of the Burger Court could neither ignore nor fully answer.

We use the justices' struggle with the case of the pregnant teachers to frame the complex narrative of how the Burger Court built a jurisprudence of sex equality—a body of law that, while erasing many of the formal distinctions that federal and state laws made between men and women, nonetheless fell short of full equality within the meaning of the Fourteenth Amendment's guarantee of equal protection. To give the Court its due, Warren Burger and his Court really did create something new, a more expansive definition of sex equality than the country had ever known. The Warren Court, for all its activism and broad vision of constitutional rights, had been deaf to the claim that the Constitution's guarantee of equal protection had anything to do with women. The Constitution, Professor Ruth Bader Ginsburg wrote in an article published before she became a federal judge, "was thought an empty cupboard for sex equality claims." [1]

The story of how the Burger Court, to a surprising degree at Ruth Ginsburg's urging, came to incorporate women into the constitutional firmament—a story of promises fulfilled and unfulfilled, of the path the justices traveled, and the points at which they could go no further—illustrates how a particular Supreme Court responded to a changing America. And one court's story may have much to tell us about how any court navigates a profound social revolution.

No court operates and no law develops in a vacuum. At the Burger Court's inception, women were entering the workplace in ever increasing numbers. Under the umbrella of a reinvigorated feminist movement, women were organizing politically and turning to the courts to give substance to the rights that Congress, through the Equal Pay Act of 1963 and the Civil Rights Act of 1964, had recently bestowed. Previously closed doors to higher education and the professions were opening. New realities were slowly but steadily erasing some of the social differences between men and women. The men of the Burger court—all of whom had wives, many of whom had daughters—responded to these winds of change. How could they not? But, as the saga of the pregnant teachers illustrates, there were limits.

It was hardly surprising to find the Court wrestling with the relevance, in constitutional terms, of the difference between male and female biology. Feminists themselves were deeply divided over how the law should treat pregnancy and motherhood, over whether it violated or honored core principles of equal protection to acknowledge and accommodate difference.[2] In its way, the question proved more challenging for the Court than the issue of abortion, which, as we have seen, raised no question of equal protection in the justices' minds. (That would come years later, after the arrival of female justices and after the Court had a robust sex discrimination jurisprudence to call upon.[3])

In the fall of 1973, the beginning of the term after *Roe v. Wade*, we find Justice Harry Blackmun struggling even with how to categorize the pregnant teachers' claim as he prepared for the argument in the case the court had agreed to decide, *Cleveland Board of Education v. LaFleur*.[4] The policy at issue in the Cleveland case was a particularly extreme variant of the common mandatory-leave policies. Pregnant teachers had to go on unpaid leave no later than five months before their due date, with no guarantee of reemployment. After the child's birth, the mother had priority in seeking a new assignment—not necessarily her old job—but could not return in any capacity until the start of the semester that followed the child's three-month birthday. A woman who—like the two plaintiffs in the case—gave birth in midsummer consequently would be out of the workplace for ten months or more, regardless of her willingness and ability to return to the classroom. Of course a man who suffered a heart attack or other condition requiring an extended medical leave would, by contrast, be expected to return to work as soon as a doctor attested to his fitness.

In notes he made as he prepared to hear the case, Blackmun wrote:

> It is easy to say initially that any regulation which relates to pregnancy is automatically and per se sex discriminatory. I am not at all certain that this is necessarily so. Actually, what the regulation does is to draw distinctions between classes of women, that is, those who are pregnant and those who are not pregnant, rather than between male and female.

It is somewhat similar to an Army regulation requiring that enlisted men be shaved and not wear beards or mustaches. Such a regulation discriminates between one class of men and another class of men, and not as between men and women.

To the typed version of his notes that his secretary prepared, Blackmun added by hand: "Not sex related."[5]

Pregnancy—and the glaringly disparate treatment of pregnant teachers—not sex-related? Blackmun's colleagues fared little better in their efforts to grasp the issue. To Lewis Powell, the old Richmond, Virginia, school board chairman, the case was confounding. Referring to the early date at which pregnant Cleveland schoolteachers were required to leave the classroom, Powell wrote on his law clerk's memo analyzing the issues: "The time periods are unduly conservative but it is a little absurd to say that the *Constitution* forbids a school board to enforce maternity leaves by teachers."[6]

The notion that the Constitution had anything at all to say about government policies that treated men and women differently would, as Ruth Ginsburg's article suggested, indeed have been considered absurd not very many years earlier. But "changes pervasively affecting society set the stage," her article went on to say, "and impelled a response from legislative and judicial chambers."[7] Indeed, by 1973, the constitutional landscape was changing. In November 1971, just weeks before Lewis Powell took his seat on the Supreme Court, the court had issued the first decision ever to find that a difference in how the government treated men and women amounted to unconstitutional sex discrimination.

The case was *Reed v. Reed*,[8] "a very simple little case," as Harry Blackmun described it in his pre-argument notes to himself in October 1971.[9] The case challenged an Idaho probate law that gave an absolute preference to a man over a woman to administer an estate when each had the same relationship to a person who died without leaving instructions. Sally and Cecil Reed, an estranged couple whose teenaged son committed suicide, each sought to be named to administer the estate. After the father received the appointment in accordance with the state law, the mother went to court to challenge the law itself as a violation of the Fourteenth Amendment's guarantee of equal protection. She lost, and the Supreme Court agreed to hear her appeal.

One of Sally Reed's lawyers was Ruth Ginsburg, a thirty-eight-year-old professor at Columbia Law School. Through an affiliation with the American Civil Liberties Union, she was embarked on a project to construct a jurisprudence of women's rights through strategically chosen cases aimed at the Supreme Court. Although the court didn't know it at the time—and Warren Burger would remain oblivious, even after the fact—*Reed v. Reed* was Ginsburg's opening shot, the target much bigger than the Idaho probate law. Her goal was to identify laws that embodied stereotyped assumptions about the abilities and proper roles of men and women, and to employ the Constitution's guarantee of equal protection as a weapon to strike down such laws.[10]

Ruth Ginsburg didn't argue the case; that assignment fell to Sally Reed's original lawyer from Boise, Allen Derr. But she was the principal lawyer on a sixty-eight-page brief that, for the force of its rhetoric about the "subordination of women to men," and the sweep of its vision of the command of constitutional equality, came to be known in feminist circles as the "grandmother brief": every ensuing legal argument for sex equality would be its descendant. Drawing on the Supreme Court's recent cases on racial equality, Ginsburg's brief told the justices: "Legislative discrimination grounded on sex, for purposes unrelated to any biological difference between the sexes, ranks with legislative discrimination based on race, another congenital, unalterable trait of birth, and merits no greater judicial deference." The brief stressed the "pervasive social, cultural and legal roots of sex-based discrimination," declaring that "American women have been stigmatized historically as an inferior class and are today subject to pervasive discrimination," which on their own they lacked the political power to combat effectively. The Supreme Court's intervention was overdue and essential, Ginsburg told the Court: "Absent firm constitutional foundation for equal treatment of men and women by the law, women seeking to be judged on their individual merits will continue to encounter law-sanctioned obstacles."[11]

This was strong stuff, and the justices' reaction was probably best captured by Harry Blackmun's note to himself. The brief was "mildly offensive and arrogant," he said. But significantly, he added: "of course, it has the better side of the case and is not to be avoided."[12]

The court was unanimous in holding the Idaho law unconstitutional. Burger assigned the case to himself and dispatched it in a dozen paragraphs. He noted that the Idaho Supreme Court had upheld the statutory preference for men in the interest of avoiding the need for a hearing to choose between male and female contenders. While this interest was "not without some legitimacy," Burger wrote:

> To give a mandatory preference to members of either sex over members of the other, merely to accomplish the elimination of hearings on the merits, is to make the very kind of arbitrary legislative choice forbidden by the Equal Protection Clause of the Fourteenth Amendment; and whatever may be said as to the positive values of avoiding intrafamily controversy, the choice in this context may not lawfully be mandated solely on the basis of sex.[13]

In other words, even though the Idaho law was not completely irrational, it was still unconstitutional. This was a highly consequential move, although the court didn't bother to explain or even identify it. A long line of precedents, most in the area of economic regulation, made it clear that courts would generally defer to categorical distinctions made by the government between one group and another. As long as the distinction had a rational explanation, it wouldn't violate the Equal Protection Clause. The only exception was for distinctions based on what the precedents identified as one of a small number of "suspect classifications": race, national origin, and alienage. A law that drew distinctions on the basis of any of these characteristics needed a "compelling" justification; a merely rational explanation wouldn't suffice. In Equal Protection terms, this form of judicial analysis was known as "strict scrutiny." In practical terms, any form of "heightened scrutiny" turned the tables, requiring the government to justify the challenged law rather than, as would ordinarily be the case, placing the burden on the plaintiff to prove how the law violated the Constitution.

In her brief, Ruth Ginsburg had argued that distinctions based on sex were just as suspect as the classifications deemed entitled to strict scrutiny. Burger's opinion didn't even acknowledge the argument. The chief justice simply quoted, without further explanation, a line from a corporate tax case from 1920: "A classification 'must be reasonable, not arbitrary, and must rest upon some ground of difference having a fair and substantial relation to the object of the legislation, so that all persons similarly circumstanced shall be treated alike.' "[14] Burger seemed to be bending over backward not to create new law.

But yet he did. Mere rationality—administrative convenience—hadn't sufficed to save the Idaho law. The Burger Court had stepped unanimously off a familiar path and onto a new one, propelled, surely, by the justices' perception of events in the wider world. Justices with chambers in the front of the Supreme Court Building could look out their windows across First Street and see the Capitol, where on October 12, 1971, barely six weeks before the court announced its decision in *Reed*, the House of Representatives had approved the Equal Rights Amendment by a wide margin and sent it on to the Senate. American women were on the move, and so was the Constitution.

The "very simple little case" did not go unnoticed. *The New York Times* put its account of the decision on the front page of the November 23 paper under the headline "Court, for First Time, Overrules a State Law That Favors Men." Fred P. Graham, the newspaper's Supreme Court correspondent, wrote that "for the first time since the 14th Amendment went into effect in 1868, declaring that no state may 'deny to any person within its jurisdiction the equal protection of the laws,' the Supreme Court held that women had been denied equal legal rights." Writing in the *Harvard Law Review*, Gerald Gunther, one of the country's leading constitutional scholars, called *Reed* one of the "truly startling and intriguing developments" of the Supreme Court term.[15]

The Pedestal or the Cage?

A next step was inevitable, and it came quickly. In the summer of 1972, with the Equal Rights Amendment having received final approval by the Senate and been sent out to the states for ratification, a new appeal reached the court. *Frontiero v. Richardson*[16] challenged a law that differentiated, for the purpose of dependent benefits, between the wives and husbands of members of the armed forces. While any wife of a soldier could qualify as a dependent and thus entitle the family to enhanced medical and housing benefits, a man was considered a dependent only if he relied on his soldier wife for more than half his support. In effect, a man who married got a pay increase, while a woman who married did not. The law was challenged by an Air Force lieutenant, Sharron Frontiero, whose husband, a full-time student, received veterans benefits and thus didn't depend on her financially. Consequently, benefits that a serviceman and his wife would have received automatically were denied to Lieutenant Frontiero and her husband. After losing in federal district court, Frontiero appealed to the Supreme Court. Ruth Ginsburg argued as a friend of the court on behalf of the Women's Rights Project of the American Civil Liberties Union.

It was her first Supreme Court argument. The case was "kin to *Reed v. Reed*," she told the justices, in that "the legislative judgment in both derives from the same stereotype," namely that a man was "the independent partner in a marital unit" while women were "dependent, sheltered from breadwinning experience." While Ginsburg maintained that the court's decision in *Reed* was sufficient to invalidate the military law, she urged the justices to go further and use this case to declare that sex was a suspect classification, one that under strict judicial scrutiny could only be justified as serving a "compelling" governmental interest. This was, of course, the question the Court had so recently ducked in *Reed*. Had the court taken up the invitation, it would have achieved, by judicial decision, the goal of the Equal Rights Amendment.

The question was close, and the Burger court was almost ready—but not quite. At the conference after argument, all except Burger and Rehnquist agreed that the statute drew an unconstitutional distinction between men and women and thus had to fall.[17] But while there was broad agreement on the outcome of the case, the justices knew that what would really matter was the analysis.

Brennan quickly circulated an eight-page draft opinion that avoided the question of the level of scrutiny by calling the case "virtually identical to *Reed*." The government was relying on administrative convenience, and under *Reed* that wasn't good enough. But along with his uncontroversial draft, Brennan opened another door and invited his colleagues to walk through it with him. "I do feel, however," he wrote to the other justices, "that this case would provide an appropriate vehicle for us to recognize sex as a 'suspect criterion.' " He added: "I'd have no difficulty in writing the opinion along those lines."[18]

Accepting his own invitation, Brennan circulated a new draft in February 1973, arguing that "since sex, like race and national origin, is an immutable characteristic determined solely by the accident of birth, the imposition of special disabilities upon the members of a particular sex because of their sex would seem to violate 'the basic concept of our system that legal burdens should bear some relationship to individual responsibility.' " (The internal quotation was from a case decided the previous year on the rights of illegitimate children.) Consequently, Brennan proposed to say: "With these considerations in mind, we hold today that classifications based upon sex, like classifications based upon race, alienage, or national origin, are inherently suspect and must therefore be subjected to strict judicial scrutiny." The draft asserted that there was "at least implicit support for such an approach in our unanimous decision only last Term in *Reed v. Reed.*" [19]

Lewis Powell, upon receiving the draft, wrote by hand on the first page: "I cannot join." To Brennan, Powell wrote:

> I joined your opinion in its original draft on the authority of *Reed v. Reed.* This is as far as we need go in the case now before us. If and when it becomes necessary to consider whether sex is a suspect classification, I will find the issue a difficult one. Women certainly have not been treated as being fungible with men (thank God!). Yet, the reasons for different treatment have in no way resembled the purposeful and invidious discrimination directed against blacks and aliens. Nor may it be said any longer that, as a class, women are a discrete minority barred from effective participation in the political process. [20]

Powell explained himself further to his law clerk, William Kelly. "As you know, I feel quite strongly that the court is acting unnecessarily and unwisely. It is this sort of action which subjects the court to criticism which even its friends have difficulty in rebutting. I sincerely think that our democratic institutions are weakened—and the ultimate position of the court in our system also weakened—by unnecessary action of this kind." Powell had drafted, and asked his clerk's help in editing, a "concurrence in the judgment," striking down the military benefits statute on the basis of *Reed* alone. [21]

Burger, initially in dissent at conference along with Rehnquist, had changed his mind as to the ultimate judgment. But in response to Brennan's expanded draft, he sent a note to his colleagues:

I have watched the "shuttlecock" memos on the subject of *Reed v. Reed* and the "suspect" classification problem.

Some may construe *Reed* as supporting the "suspect" view but I do not. The author of *Reed* [Burger himself] never remotely contemplated such a broad concept but then a lot of people sire offspring unintended![22]

Brennan persisted in his adherence to strict scrutiny, publishing his draft as a plurality opinion that was joined only by Justices Douglas, White, and Marshall. In declining to go along, Powell noted that not only was *Reed* sufficient to resolve the case in favor of the plaintiff, but that the question of whether sex was a suspect classification would be resolved by the Equal Rights Amendment, then awaiting ratification and widely expected to succeed. "If this Amendment is duly adopted, it will represent the will of the people accomplished in the manner prescribed by the Constitution," Powell wrote in his concurring opinion. He added: "this reaching out to pre-empt by judicial action a major political decision which is currently in process of resolution does not reflect appropriate respect for duly prescribed legislative processes."

Powell concluded: "There are times when this court, under our system, cannot avoid a constitutional decision on issues which normally should be resolved by the elected representatives of the people. But democratic institutions are weakened, and confidence in the restraint of the court is impaired, when we appear unnecessarily to decide sensitive issues of broad social and political importance at the very time they are under consideration within the prescribed constitutional processes."[23] Burger and Blackmun signed onto Powell's opinion. Stewart wrote a one-sentence *Reed* concurrence of his own. Only Rehnquist remained in dissent.

The court issued the *Frontiero* decision on May 14, 1973. During the same term, not even four months earlier, the court had decided *Roe v. Wade*. It is fascinating to compare Lewis Powell's unwavering support for the majority opinion in *Roe* with his acute and simultaneous anxiety in *Frontiero* about the consequences for the court of deciding sensitive issues with which the political system was already fully engaged. What might account for the sharp distinction he drew between the two cases when, from today's perspective, the abortion case would seem by far the more sensitive, offering the greater reason for the court to stay its hand?

Clearly, Powell (along with Burger, Blackmun, and Stewart, all members of the *Roe* majority who joined him in declining to sign Brennan's *Frontiero* opinion) saw the two cases as unconnected. That at the heart of the right to abortion lay an inevitable claim about women's autonomy was a message that these men were not yet ready to hear. That was not the claim they thought they had vindicated, nor had they intended to. To be sure, in *Roe v. Wade* they had joined together to fashion a new constitutional right—but it was a right evidently without significant consequences for the constitutional status of the women who would exercise it.[24]

For Powell himself, there may have been cultural reasons for his relative comfort with the abortion issue in contrast to his reluctance to aid the Supreme Court in creating a robust jurisprudence of sex equality. He was the Supreme Court's only southerner, and the South, with its relatively small Catholic population, had been the region most receptive to the early efforts at abortion reform along the lines of the American Law Institute model. (Recall that *Roe's* companion case, *Doe v. Bolton*, was a challenge to Georgia's modern reform statute.) Abortion was seen as a public health issue, not as the location of cultural and political conflict, because such conflict was simply absent; two days after the court's decisions in *Roe* and *Doe*, the *Atlanta Constitution* praised the outcome as "realistic and appropriate."

But for a gentleman of the Old South, which Lewis Powell, born in 1907, certainly was, women's role in society was another matter. To rid the statute books of irrational distinctions, as in *Reed v. Reed*, was one thing. But to expand the meaning of the Equal Protection Clause itself to make it nearly impossible for the government to justify treating men and women differently—even when women were the intended beneficiaries of the law's differential solicitude—was something else entirely. Lewis Powell was not about to enlist the Supreme Court in the feminists' social revolution.

Feminist lawyers were acutely disappointed by the court's failure to accord strict scrutiny to sex discriminations claims. The court never did take that step, and the Equal Rights Amendment never became part of the Constitution. In fact, by the time the Court issued *Frontiero*, momentum behind the proposed amendment, which thirty state legislatures had ratified in 1972 and early 1973, was slowing fatally. Only three states would vote to ratify in 1974, one in 1975, none at all in 1976, and a final ratification (Indiana) in 1977. ERA supporters managed to persuade Congress to extend the original 1978 ratification deadline until 1982, to no avail. A last-ditch battle in Illinois, the only northern state not to ratify, ended in failure.[25]

Not coincidentally, Illinois was the home base of Phyllis Schlafly, the Republican activist whose nationwide STOP ERA organization effectively tapped into the fears of social conservatives by portraying the amendment as a profound threat to the natural order of male-female relationships. Schlafly aimed her message not only at religious fundamentalists but at women themselves, warning not only of unisex bathrooms and a female military draft, but of the disappearance of the privileged status that—or so the argument went—protected women in their traditional roles as homemakers and mothers. Where Ruth Ginsburg saw a cage, Phyllis Schlafly saw a pedestal: women were the beneficiaries, not the victims, of policies that protected women's traditional roles as the natural order of things. What the feminists wanted, Schlafly argued forcefully and not without justification, was nothing less than a social revolution; to support the Equal Rights Amendment, she warned, was to follow the feminists off a cliff, from a place of safety into the unknown. Schlafly's message resonated with her target audience. While her STOP ERA can't claim sole credit for the ERA's defeat—the Constitution's requirement for ratification of a proposed amendment by three quarters of the states has proved a daunting barrier throughout U.S. history— Schlafly's counter-movement helped shape the constitutional discourse of equality in profound and lasting ways.[26]

At the time of *Frontiero* these developments lay ahead. Given Lewis Powell's reluctance to move to strict scrutiny when he assumed that the ERA would carry the day, it's worth considering the fate of Brennan's plurality opinion had the justices been able to predict the amendment's defeat. Would Brennan have been able to marshal a majority by arguing that a gap existed in equal protection doctrine that only the Supreme Court could fill? Or would the Court have drawn the opposite lesson, foreshadowed by Powell's comments: that the Court should not impose constitutional change on a public that had, after having been presented with the choice, rejected it? And who, exactly, comprised the rejecting public: residents of those states that refused to push the Equal Rights

Amendment over the finish line? What might the justices have made of that? Not implausibly, they might have acted precisely as they did, as we shall see: insist on formal equality but stop short when it came to ensuring equality of social roles in the face of the biological facts of pregnancy and motherhood.

Between 1974 and 1979, Ruth Ginsburg argued five more Supreme Court cases and worked on more than two dozen others before her litigation career ended with her appointment by President Jimmy Carter to the United States Court of Appeals for the District of Columbia Circuit in April 1980. Her litigation project proceeded incrementally, with cases that for the most part followed the *Frontiero* model in challenging government benefit programs that often for benign reasons incorporated stereotyped assumptions about the respective roles of women and men in the economy and of mothers and fathers in the home.[27] Stereotypes burdened members of both sexes, she reasoned, and government did women no favors by extending them special privileges, such as exemption from jury duty, that marked them as less than fully capable citizens. Years later, as an eighty-one-year-old Supreme Court justice, Ruth Ginsburg looked back on the goal of those early years and on the strategy she used to convey her message to her audience of nine. Reflecting on her twelve minutes of argument time in *Frontiero*, she told an interviewer from the women's high-fashion magazine *Elle*:

> I felt a sense of empowerment because I knew so much more about the case, the issue, than they did. So I relied on myself as a kind of a teacher to get them to think about gender. Because most men of that age, they could understand race discrimination, but sex discrimination? They thought of themselves as good fathers and as good husbands, and if women are treated differently, the different treatment is benignly in women's favor. To get them to understand that this supposed pedestal was all too often a cage for women—that was my mission in all the cases in the 70s. To get them to understand that these so-called protections for women were limiting their opportunities.[28]

There is scant evidence that members of the Burger Court ever fully grasped that big picture, even as they handed Ruth Ginsburg one victory after another. Try as they might—and most of them did try—the justices couldn't figure out how to make the essential difference between men and women—women's ability to conceive and bear a child—fit within the court's maturing sex equality jurisprudence. Men in the workplace of course suffered illness, accidents, and other conditions requiring medical attention and temporary absence. But pregnancy was, in the minds of the justices, simply different. Potter Stewart, who received the assignment to write for the majority in the pregnant schoolteacher case, made this note to himself on his law clerk's early draft of an opinion: "Pregnancy is different from illness or injury not in degree but in kind." [29]

A Difference in Kind

The challenge to Cleveland's pregnancy policy, along with a challenge to a somewhat more flexible policy in Chesterfield County, Virginia that the Supreme Court agreed to hear at the same time,[30] had been litigated in the lower federal courts as equal protection cases. Ruling in favor of the two Cleveland plaintiffs, Jo Carol LaFleur and Ann Elizabeth Nelson, the United States Court of Appeals for the Sixth Circuit cited the recently decided *Reed v. Reed* and concluded that "Here, too, we deal with a rule which is inherently based upon a classification by sex." [31] Noting that "under no construction of this record can we conclude that the medical evidence presented supports the extended periods of mandatory maternity leave required by the rule both before and after birth of the child," the appeals court went on to say: "Male teachers are not subject to pregnancy, but they are subject to many types of illnesses and disabilities. This record indicates clearly that pregnant women teachers have been singled out for unconstitutionally unequal restrictions upon their employment."

Unconstitutionally unequal restrictions. That was the nub of the argument. To reject the school board's appeal and affirm the Sixth Circuit on equal protection grounds, the justices would have to start from the assumption, as the appeals court did, that pregnancy was just another one of many "illnesses and disabilities." But that was not an assumption that the justices shared. Lewis Powell wrote a note on his law clerk's preargument memo: "The Board regulation in *these* cases may be unreasonable—but we could still hold that pregnancy is *sui generis* and may be treated differently."[32]

The argument took place on October 15, 1973, and found Powell still struggling. In notes he made to aid his preparation for the October 19 conference at which the justices would cast their votes, he wrote: "I am not persuaded that this is a sex classification rather than a disability one. . . . Here, the women are not prohibited from teaching. They are required to take a leave of absence on a scheduled basis on account of a condition peculiar to women—pregnancy. Men suffer no comparable type disabilities." A large majority of public school teachers, he noted, were women, many of them of childbearing age. "In terms of the problems presented to the school authorities pregnancy is *sui generis*. . . . The certainty and the magnitude of the 'replacement teacher' problem is of a different dimension from that of any other type disability."[33]

In these preliminary notes, Powell even came up with a justification for mandatory pregnancy leave that appeared to be of his own devising, not suggested in the briefs or lower court opinions. "It is at least arguable," he wrote to himself, "that some pregnant teachers lose a measure of their intellectual rigor and acuity, especially if they are nervous and apprehensive about themselves and the approaching birth. Certainly, such a teacher—with new and additional family plans and problems ahead—may lack the same degree of wholehearted concentration on her school responsibilities as her sisters without comparable anxieties and distractions."

And yet, remarkably, by the time it came to vote two days later, Powell had changed his mind. Along with Justices Douglas, Brennan, Stewart, White, Marshall, and Blackmun, he voted to affirm the lower court's finding of unconstitutionality. But Powell's notes from the conference make clear that affirmance did not mean agreement with the appeals court's rationale. Quite the opposite. Justice after justice in the emergent majority declared his view that the problem with the policy was anything but sex discrimination. Requiring pregnant teachers to leave the classroom five months in advance of their due date and to stay home for three months or more after birth was arbitrary, perhaps a violation of due process, several justices said. But "pregnancy is different in kind from other disabilities and may be treated separately," Potter Stewart observed.

"The right to procreate is a special interest and so this is different from most cases," said Byron White, who expressed his agreement "with Potter that this is not a sex classification." Harry Blackmun, the most tentative member of the majority, reiterated his preliminary view that the case was "not sex related" and worried aloud that if the Court concerned itself with erasing lines that might be described as arbitrary, the "next case we will receive is [a challenge to] compulsory retirement at age 65."[34]

The Burger Court's reluctance to confront, or even acknowledge, the sex discrimination argument is striking, given that the argument was so readily at hand, not only in the lower court's opinion but in friend-of-the-court briefs filed on the teachers' behalf. A brief filed by the Nixon administration's solicitor general, Robert Bork, used language that today sounds anachronistic, observing of the plaintiffs at one point that "neither lady wished to resign or take an unpaid leave of absence." But the brief was up to the minute in its understanding of precisely how, in its words, "the challenged pregnancy and maternity regulations work as sex discrimination in violation of the Equal Protection Clause." Pregnancy was unique, but it was not uniquely disabling, the brief explained:

> The suggestion has been advanced that, because there are no pregnant men, and therefore no "similarly situated" males, pregnancy rules cannot be deemed to discriminate on the basis of sex; that, at worst, they work as discrimination as between two classes of women, those who are pregnant and those who are not. In our view, this is a *non sequitur. . . .* On the contrary, precisely because pregnancy is a condition unique to women, treating the pregnant less favorably is, at least presumptively, a discrimination based on sex. The upshot is that women, who alone are subject to pregnancy, are denied equal employment opportunity by any rule which treats pregnancy as a disqualification for work.[35]

Ruth Bader Ginsburg signed a brief filed on the teachers' behalf by a coalition that included the American Civil Liberties Union, the American Federation of Teachers, and the National Organization for Women Legal Defense and Education Fund. (Marilyn Hall Patel, who signed the NOW-LDF brief, later served as chief federal district judge for the Northern District of California; she, like Ginsburg, was named to the federal bench in 1980 by President Carter.) Although Ginsburg was only one of nine lawyers on the brief, the language was unmistakably hers. The challenged policies, the brief asserted:

> reflect arbitrary notions of a woman's place wholly at odds with contemporary legislative and judicial recognition that individual potential must not be restrained, or equal opportunity limited, by law-sanctioned stereotypical prejudgments. Operating on the basis of characteristics assumed to typify pregnant women, and in total disregard of individual capacities and qualifications, the regulations violate the equal protection clause of the fourteenth amendment to the United States Constitution. . . .
>
> Until very recent years, jurists have regarded any discrimination in the treatment of pregnant women as "benignly in their favor." But in fact refusal to permit capable, healthy pregnant women to continue working drastically curtails women's economic opportunities. . . .
>
> Concern for the health of a pregnant woman hardly justifies an iron rule dealing with all pregnancies in an identical, dehumanizing fashion. . . . Sex discrimination exists when all or a defined class of women (or men) are subjected to disadvantaged treatment based on stereotypical assumptions that operate to foreclose opportunity based on individual merit.[36]

While reaching the justices' eyes and ears, these arguments failed to engage their hearts and minds. With only Burger and Rehnquist dissenting, the vote was 7–2 to declare the policies unconstitutional. Potter Stewart's dry fifteen-page opinion avoided the equal protection issue by finding the Cleveland policy "wholly arbitrary and irrational" in violation of the guarantee of due process of law. The problem wasn't discrimination—a concept the opinion never mentioned—but rather the establishment by the government of a "conclusive presumption that every pregnant teacher who reaches the fifth or sixth month of pregnancy is physically incapable of continuing."

Stewart went on: "There is no individualized determination by the teacher's doctor—or the school board's—as to any particular teacher's ability to continue at her job. The rules contain an irrebuttable presumption of physical incompetency, and that presumption applies even when the medical evidence as to an individual woman's physical status might be wholly to the contrary." [37]

The concept of an "irrebuttable presumption" offered the troubled court a safe harbor. Just the previous term, in *Vlandis v. Kline*, [38] the court had declared that "permanent irrebuttable presumptions have long been disfavored under the Due Process Clauses of the Fifth and Fourteenth Amendments." The question in the earlier case was the validity of a Connecticut law regarding the tuition charged by the state university system to students who could not prove that they had lived in Connecticut for at least a year before applying for admission. Such students were deemed to be out-of-state residents for the duration of their attendance, and were charged a higher tuition even if they subsequently moved to Connecticut and established legal residency. The state permitted no set of facts to rebut the presumption of out-of-state residency. Stewart wrote the majority opinion finding the law unconstitutional on the ground of due process.

In his majority opinion in the Cleveland case, Stewart noted that even assuming that "there are some women who would be physically unable to work past the particular cutoff dates embodied in the challenged rules, it is evident that there are large numbers of teachers who are fully capable of continuing to work for longer." He concluded: "While it might be easier for the school boards to conclusively presume that all pregnant women are unfit to teach past the fourth or fifth month, or even the first month, of pregnancy, administrative convenience alone is insufficient to make valid what otherwise is a violation of due process of law." [39]

Potter Stewart's opinion in *Cleveland Board of Education v. LaFleur* was joined by Justices Brennan, Marshall, White, and Blackmun. Douglas appended a statement concurring in the result, without further explanation. Powell also concurred only in the result. For all his struggles with the case, he had fought his way through to a surprising conclusion: "it seems to me that equal protection analysis is the appropriate frame of reference."

Powell explained that he found the "irrebuttable presumption" analysis of *Vlandis v. Kline*, which he had joined, to be a poor fit for this case. "The constitutional difficulty is not that the boards attempted to deal with this problem by classification. Rather, it is that the boards chose irrational classifications," those that were "either counterproductive or irrationally overinclusive." He concluded: "Accordingly, in my opinion these regulations are invalid under rational-basis standards of equal protection review."[40]

In a footnote, Powell made clear that he was neither reopening the strict scrutiny debate of the previous term's *Frontiero* case nor necessarily even saying anything about sex discrimination. "I do not reach the question whether sex-based classifications invoke strict judicial scrutiny," he wrote, "or whether these regulations involve sex classifications at all. Whether the challenged aspects of the regulations constitute sex classifications or disability classifications, they must at least rationally serve some legitimate articulated or obvious state interest. While there are indeed some legitimate state interests at stake here, it has not been shown that they are rationally furthered by the challenged portions of these regulations."[41]

The court issued its decision in the pregnant teachers case on January 21, 1974—one year minus one day after handing down the decision in *Roe v. Wade*. Both cases concerned the same essential attribute of women's lives. But in neither opinion did the Burger Court put women front and center. The question of whether discrimination on the basis of pregnancy amounted to discrimination on the basis of sex remained to be decided.

In fact, a case raising precisely that question was on the court's docket, already accepted and set for argument by the time the Cleveland decision came down. The justices were obviously aware of it, since they had voted more than a month earlier to hear it. But since by that time it was clear that the pregnant teachers case would not be decided on equal protection grounds, no member of the court evidently even saw a need to refer to it.

The new case, *Geduldig v. Aiello*,[42] was an appeal by the state of California from a federal district court's ruling that by excluding coverage for pregnancy, the state's disability insurance program for private employees violated female employees' constitutional right to equal protection. For an employee who contributed the required amount into the state-run fund, the program made weekly payments to make up for lost wages due to a temporary disability stemming from "mental or physical illness and mental or physical injury." Pregnancy, however, was explicitly excluded from the definition of disability.

In defense of the exclusion, the state had argued that it would simply cost too much to cover pregnancy. The district court rejected that rationale. Since the program was financed by employee contributions, the court noted that any "increased costs could be accommodated quite easily by making reasonable changes in the contribution rate, the maximum benefits allowable, and the other variables affecting the solvency of the program." In any event, the court said, "by excluding all pregnancy-related disabilities on the grounds that these claims will be large, the state denies pregnant women benefits on the basis of generalities and stereotypes contrary to the requirements of the equal protection clause." Achieving the state's "salutary purposes," the court concluded, "does not require that the disability insurance program embody an element of discrimination that denies pregnant women equal treatment."[43]

That was straightforward enough but, not surprisingly, the justices who couldn't see sex discrimination in the pregnant teachers case were no more able to find it in California's pregnancy exclusion. Harry Blackmun, in notes to himself before the March 26, 1974, argument, observed that while "one has to concede that pregnancy is restricted to women," other conditions "are more likely to occur in one sex rather than in the other or in one race rather than in another." He mentioned hernia, hemophilia, and sickle-cell anemia, among others. "Thus, one can say that an exclusion of pregnancy is sex discriminatory. Similarly, he could say that an exclusion of any one of these named diseases would be sex discriminatory. But where do we stop if we come into that kind of accounting?"

Blackmun's musing continued: "It is easy to carry this kind of thing to a great extreme. If we start carving out any particular physical condition or disease, then we inevitably run into a mathematical factor that affects the sexes or the races differently. I think we would never come to an end in this kind of analysis."

His conclusion: "Although I am not entirely at rest on this issue, I am inclined to think that on the equal protection approach, pregnancy, despite its application only to women, is not a sex classification."[44]

When the justices met in conference three days after the argument, it was immediately apparent that Blackmun wasn't alone in his reluctance to affirm the district court. There were also votes to reverse from Burger, White, Powell, Rehnquist, and Stewart, who remarked that it was an "easy case" because there were "rational reasons to exclude normal pregnancy." Powell spoke at length. What the plaintiffs really wanted, he said, "is in reality a maternity benefit program." Pregnancy "is not the type of involuntary disability resulting from illness or accident that programs like this are designed to meet."

He continued (according to his own notes from the conference): "There is no sex discrimination. Women participate fully in the California program and indeed are its principal beneficiaries." The issue was essentially one for the legislature, not the courts, he concluded.[45]

Potter Stewart's majority opinion, issued on June 17, 1974, closely tracked the tenor of the conference discussion. The judgment the Court had avoided in the pregnant teachers case now came home with devastating directness. All the state needed was a rational reason for the pregnancy exclusion, Stewart said, and it had provided one: including pregnancy would mean that either the rate for employee contributions to the plan would go up, or benefits for all would go down. "There is nothing in the Constitution, however, that requires the State to subordinate or compromise its legitimate interests solely to create a more comprehensive social insurance program than it already has," Stewart wrote for the 6–3 majority. The state's justification has "an objective and wholly noninvidious basis."[46]

In dissent, Justice Brennan, joined by Douglas and Marshall, said that while the statute limited women's ability to receive benefits for "a gender-linked disability peculiar to women"—namely, pregnancy— the state placed no equivalent limit on men's right to collect for "all disabilities suffered, including those that affect only or primarily their sex." He listed prostatectomies, circumcision, hemophilia, and gout. "In effect, one set of rules is applied to females and another to males. Such dissimilar treatment of men and women, on the basis of physical characteristics inextricably linked to one sex, inevitably constitutes sex discrimination."[47]

Stewart responded to the dissent in a long footnote. The California program, he said, "does not exclude anyone from benefit eligibility because of gender but merely removes one physical condition—pregnancy—from the list of compensable disabilities." Stewart said there was no indication that the pregnancy exclusion was a pretext for discrimination. "The program divides potential recipients into two groups—pregnant women and nonpregnant persons. While the first group is exclusively female, and second includes members of both sexes. The fiscal and actuarial benefits of the program thus accrue to members of both sexes."[48] As Stewart had been saying all along, pregnancy was different.

And the Court kept saying it. Two years later, the justices looked again at the exclusion of pregnancy from a medical disability plan. At issue was a plan run by the General Electric Company, which paid 60 percent of the ordinary weekly earnings, up to a maximum of twenty-six weeks, of employees who were unable to work due to accident or sickness. Disability due to pregnancy—whether a miscarriage, a normal delivery, or a complication requiring treatment—was excluded.

The question in *General Electric Company v. Gilbert*[49] was not the Fourteenth Amendment equal protection issue of *Geduldig*, since this was a private sector rather than a government program, but rather whether the pregnancy exclusion violated the federal law prohibiting employment discrimination. Seven female G.E. employees, supported by their union, brought a class-action lawsuit in federal district court in Virginia under that law, Title VII of the Civil Rights Act of 1964, which makes it an unlawful employment practice "to discriminate against any individual with respect to his compensation, terms, conditions, or privileges of employment, because of such individual's race, color, religion, sex, or national origin."

After the plaintiffs won in district court, and while the case was on appeal to the United States Court of Appeals for the Fourth Circuit, the Supreme Court decided *Geduldig v. Aiello*. What was the relationship between the constitutional holding of that case and the statutory prohibition against sex discrimination on the job? None, was the answer the Fourth Circuit gave in affirming the women's victory; the statute was designed to combat sex discrimination on the job, and the statute governed. Five other federal appeals courts ruled the same way in cases that had been filed against similar pregnancy exclusions in benefit plans all over the country. There was no dispute among the lower courts that the exclusions violated Title VII even if they didn't violate the equal protection guarantee itself.

Solicitor General Robert Bork, now serving in the administration of President Ford, filed a brief for the United States urging the justices to affirm the lower court. "As the six courts of appeals which have addressed the issue have unanimously stated," the brief said, the decision in *Geduldig* "does not require or even suggest" that Title VII's prohibition of sex discrimination "should be interpreted to permit exclusion of pregnancy coverage from otherwise comprehensive employee disability insurance plans." The brief continued that, to the contrary, "to subject only women employees to a substantial risk of total loss of income because of temporary medical disability" was "necessarily a discrimination on the basis of sex." [50]

This was not how the justices saw the issue. Far from being irrelevant, Justice Rehnquist wrote for the 6–3 majority, "*Geduldig* is precisely in point in its holding that an exclusion of pregnancy from a disability-benefits plan providing general coverage is not a gender-based discrimination at all." [51]

Justices Brennan, Marshall, and Stevens dissented. Stevens had been named to the Court by President Ford a year earlier, in December 1975, to replace Douglas. An experienced federal appeals court judge, Stevens was already displaying the pragmatic, commonsense approach that would mark his subsequent decades on the Supreme Court. Not having participated in any of the earlier cases, he came to the issue fresh, unencumbered by having staked out a position, and he tried in vain to persuade his colleagues to wipe the slate clean. "Of course," he observed, "when it enacted Title VII of the Civil Rights Act of 1964, Congress could not possibly have relied on language which this Court was to use a decade later in the *Geduldig* opinion. We are, therefore, presented with a fresh, and rather simple, question of statutory construction." Noting that the G.E. policy "places the risk of absence caused by pregnancy in a class by itself," he said that "by definition, such a rule discriminates on account of sex; for it is the capacity to become pregnant which primarily differentiates the female from the male." Stevens concluded that "the language of the statute plainly requires the result which the Courts of Appeals have reached unanimously." [52]

The decision received widespread attention, coming as it did at a moment of intensifying struggle over women's rights. A front-page *New York Times* article called the ruling "a major setback for the women's rights movement." Noting that pregnancy coverage was an issue in many workplaces, the article observed that "companies that have not had such plans, but have been under pressure to adopt them, now need not do so." [53] Ruth Ginsburg, summarizing the Court's performance several years later, noted that the pregnant teachers had won their case while the pregnant California and General Electric employees had lost theirs. She observed sardonically: "Perhaps the *able* pregnant woman seeking only to do a day's work for a day's pay is a sympathetic figure before the Court, while the woman *disabled* by pregnancy is suspect. (Is she really sick or recovering from childbirth, or is she malingering so that she may stay 'where she belongs'—at home with baby?)"[54]

By the date of the *General Electric* decision, December 7, 1976, momentum toward ratification of the Equal Rights Amendment had slowed to a crawl. But Congress was still responsive to feminist voices. It responded to the Court's ruling by amending Title VII, adding to it the Pregnancy Discrimination Act, which made explicit that discrimination on the basis of pregnancy and childbirth was, in fact, sex discrimination. The new law provided that "women affected by pregnancy, childbirth or related medical conditions shall be treated the same for all employment-related purposes, including receipt of benefits under fringe benefit programs, as other persons not so affected but similar in their ability or inability to work." In other words, what mattered was ability or disability, not pregnancy as such. In one sentence, the drafters of the Pregnancy Discrimination Act cut through the fog that had settled over the men of the Burger Court. The Senate committee report on the new law used a phrase that might have helped the justices but that had eluded them during their years of struggle with what to do about pregnant women in the workplace: "functional comparability to other conditions."[55] In simpler words: can she do the job?

High Stakes in a Silly Case

The *Frontiero* case during the Court's 1972 term had presented but failed to resolve the question of how courts should evaluate a claim of unconstitutional sex discrimination. Justice Brennan had been unable to find five votes for the "strict scrutiny" standard, which would have required the government to justify any distinction of law between men and women as serving a "compelling state interest" by the narrowest means possible. *Reed v. Reed*, the Burger Court's initial sex discrimination decision, had suggested somewhat equivocally that courts must apply a standard of review more searching than the mere "rational basis" that applies to ordinary economic regulations. By the start of the Court's 1976 term, the question had been left hanging for more than three years. It was to be answered in the most unlikely of cases: a challenge, brought by a young man in search of a beer and the owner of a bar who wanted to sell him one, to an Oklahoma law that permitted women to buy 3.2 percent beer starting at age 18 but required men to wait for that privilege until they turned twenty-one. The plaintiffs argued that the age differential amounted to unconstitutional discrimination on the basis of sex.

"This is the silly case from Oklahoma" is how Lewis Powell began a memo he dictated in preparation for the October 1976 argument in the case, *Craig v. Boren*.[56] Silly it might have appeared, but as Ruth Bader Ginsburg told the Court in a friend-of-the-court brief on the plaintiffs' behalf, it was a little case—"at first glance a sport"—that raised a big question. What did it take to justify such a distinction—indeed, any distinction—between men and women? What, finally, should be the standard of review?

In its successful defense of its law in federal district court, Oklahoma had presented statistical evidence showing that young men were more likely than young women to drive after drinking. The state defended the law as a highway safety measure. But beware of "overbroad generalizations," Ruth Ginsburg warned the Court in her brief, filed for the American Civil Liberties Union's Women's Rights Project. "This legislation places all 18–20 year old males in one pigeonhole, all 18–20 year old females in another, in conformity with familiar notions about 'the way women (or men) are.' . . . Such overbroad generalization as a rationalization for line-drawing by gender cannot be tolerated under the Constitution."

Further, Ginsburg argued that such laws "serve only to shore up artificial barriers to full realization by men and women of their human potential, and to retard progress toward equal opportunity, free from gender-based discrimination. Ultimately harmful to women by casting the weight of the state on the side of traditional notions concerning women's behavior and her relation to man, such laws have no place in a nation preparing to celebrate a 200-year commitment to equal justice under law."[57]

Of course, equal justice for women had not been part of the Founders' vision for the new country in 1776; it took nearly 150 years for women even to get the right to vote. No matter: Ginsburg was pushing on an open door, arguing strategically for "heightened scrutiny" rather than the "strict scrutiny" the Court had rejected three years earlier. The justices quickly decided that the lower court had to be reversed and the law had to fall. The only issue was by what standard.

One initial complication was whether this was still a live case. Curtis Craig, the young man who wanted his beer, had recently turned twenty-one, so the law no longer stood in his way. After some debate, the justices decided that the saloon owner herself had standing to assert the rights of her young customers, and the case proceeded on that basis. Chief Justice Burger voted at conference to dismiss the case for lack of standing.[58] This left Brennan as the senior justice in the majority, and he assigned the opinion to himself. Here was an opportunity to press for as searching a standard of review as his colleagues would support—not strict scrutiny, granted, but as close as Brennan could come by means of a careful, and strategic, choice of words.[59]

The words Brennan chose were these: "To withstand constitutional challenge, previous cases establish that classifications by gender must serve important governmental objectives and must be substantially related to achievement of those objectives."[60] Brennan's opinion referred repeatedly to *Reed v. Reed* but didn't cite it directly because he couldn't; *Reed* itself had not expressed the standard in such robust terms. The repeated references were too much for *Reed*'s author. Warren Burger wrote to Brennan after receiving the draft of the opinion that while he had considered joining it, "you read into *Reed v. Reed* what is not there." Burger added almost plaintively: "*Reed* was the innocuous matter of who was to probate an estate. As written, I cannot possibly join."[61] More unintended offspring.

The Burger Court—minus Burger himself and minus Rehnquist, who also dissented[62]—had at last come to rest on a "middle tier" standard of review for sex discrimination. It was an outcome that, while not fulfilling Brennan's fondest hopes, was still a triumph for the liberal warrior. He persuaded two justices who were not fully on board, Powell and Stevens, to give him their votes in full concurrence despite their misgivings.

Powell filed a rather opaque concurring opinion, offering his preferred articulation of a standard in the words that Burger had used five years earlier in *Reed v. Reed*: "this gender-based classification does not bear a fair and substantial relation to the object of the legislation." In a footnote, Powell added that while he "would not welcome a further subdividing of equal protection analysis, candor compels the recognition that the relatively deferential 'rational basis' standard of review normally applied takes on a sharper focus when we address a gender-based classification." [63] Justice Stevens, in his concurring opinion, made an argument that he would make often in future years: "There is only one Equal Protection Clause. It requires every State to govern impartially. It does not direct the courts to apply one standard of review in some cases and a different standard in other cases." [64] It was a battle he wouldn't win. There were now three tiers of equal protection scrutiny.

Coda: Whose ERA?

Had the Equal Rights Amendment been ratified, sex, like race, would have been a suspect classification, and sex discrimination, like racial discrimination, would have been judged by strict scrutiny. In the ensuing years, "intermediate scrutiny" inched closer to strict scrutiny, but the two have never completely converged. The Supreme Court's most recent word on the subject came in 1996, a decade after Warren Burger left the bench. With only Justice Antonin Scalia dissenting, the Supreme Court ruled by a vote of 7–1 in *United States v. Virginia*[65] that the state-supported Virginia Military Institute's male-only admissions policy was unconstitutional. Official classifications on the basis of sex, the Court said, must meet an "exceedingly persuasive justification" and "must not rely on overbroad generalizations about the different talents, capacities, or preferences of males and females." If the phrase "exceedingly persuasive justification" was not quite strict scrutiny, it was hard to tell the difference. And if the voice in the majority opinion sounded familiar, that's because it was. The opinion's author was Justice Ruth Bader Ginsburg.

Scholars refer to the "de facto ERA" to describe the constitutional settlement that emerged from the struggle during the 1970s over women's place in a rapidly changing society.[66] Framed by the effort to ratify the amendment, the contest was inevitably about constitutional meaning. But the Court itself wielded neither monopoly nor leadership over the evolution of meaning. Rather, in its wary and partial responses, the Burger Court provided a backdrop against which the contest played out. The result was a new body of law, surely—but whose? Not William Brennan's and not Ruth Ginsburg's either. It was, perhaps, Phyllis Schlafly's ERA that the Burger Court enacted.

By never embracing strict scrutiny and never requiring a "compelling" justification for government policies that treat men and women differently, the Burger Court left room for the other branches to legislate and implement. The result was a continuing conversation, one that continues to this day. Schlafly had warned, for example, that ratifying the Equal Rights Amendment would make women vulnerable to the military draft. The draft ended in 1973 and registration for the draft was discontinued in 1975. Following the Soviet invasion of Afghanistan in 1980, President Carter decided to reinstitute registration to enable the military to maintain an active list of young people who might be called up for service if that proved necessary. Carter asked Congress to appropriate money to reactivate the Selective Service System and to authorize the immediate registration and theoretical conscription of young men— and women.

Although the president made it clear that there were no actual plans to draft members of either sex, there was no way to separate draft registration and the draft itself in the public mind. The congressional backlash was immediate. Congress appropriated only enough money to register men, and not the additional $8.5 million required to expand registration to include women. And Congress refused to amend the Military Selective Service Act to authorize registering and drafting women.

Nine years earlier, when the draft was still in effect, a group of young men had filed a federal lawsuit claiming that the male-only draft, by placing solely on men the burden of military service, amounted to unconstitutional sex discrimination against males. With the end of the draft, the lawsuit had lain dormant, but the new registration program revived it. On July 18, 1980, a three-judge federal district court panel in Philadelphia, applying the intermediate scrutiny standard of *Craig v. Boren*, ruled for the plaintiffs and enjoined the government from starting the registration process, due to begin in three days.[67] The Supreme Court issued a stay of the decision and agreed to hear the government's appeal.[68]

The briefs filed with the Court as the March 1981 argument date approached fully reflected the culture wars then raging. Ruth Bader Ginsburg had already become a federal judge, but two feminist lawyers who had worked closely with her, Wendy Webster Williams and Judith L. Lichtman, filed a brief for a coalition of women's organizations. It was impossible not to hear Ruth Ginsburg's voice as the women stated their argument:

> The exclusion of women from registration is based solely on archaic notions of women's role in society which this Court has explicitly rejected as a valid foundation for legislative classifications. It echoes the stereotypic notions about women's proper place in society that in the past promoted "protective" labor laws and the exclusion of women from juries and the legal profession. Until women assume their equal share of societal obligations, they will retain their inferior status.[69]

Phyllis Schlafly, meanwhile, organized a group of sixteen young women from around the country to make the opposite argument. "The threat to 'family life' which was feared by Congress and by the witnesses who testified against expanding the draft to include women is not a mere imprecise generalization," the brief asserted, adding: "Only women can become pregnant and bear children. Even slight uncertainty as to when and how she will be required to fulfill a draft obligation can seriously affect a woman's plans in this regard." The brief continued:

> These concerns cannot readily be dismissed as the "outmoded baggage of sexual stereotypes." Few would question the value that the family unit provides to our national life, both in peacetime and in war. To dismiss Congressional attempts to ensure a continuation of the benefits of the family unit as "sexual stereotyping" misses the point, for it is vitally important to the national resolve to minimize strains on that unit. The historical exemption of women from the draft has ensured a certainty to the family unit that would not otherwise be there.[70]

When the Court ruled 6–3 that male-only draft registration did not violate the Constitution, Phyllis Schlafly was exultant. "We thank God the Equal Rights Amendment is not in the Constitution," she said, "or else the Supreme Court would have been compelled to hold that women must be drafted any time men are drafted."[71]

Justice Rehnquist's opinion for the majority held that the existing statutory ban on women serving in combat provided all the justification the government needed to exclude women from draft registration. "Men and women, because of the combat restrictions on women, are simply not similarly situated for purposes of a draft or registration for a draft," Rehnquist wrote. "The Constitution requires that Congress treat similarly situated persons similarly, not that it engage in gestures of superficial equality."[72]

The Supreme Court had finished speaking, but American society had not. In January 2013, the secretary of defense, Leon Panetta, lifted the military's ban on women serving in direct combat jobs. By that time, 280,000 women—all volunteers, as were their male fellow soldiers—had served on active duty in Iraq and Afghanistan, and some 14 percent of active-duty troops were female. Panetta's announcement was followed five months later by a further announcement from the Pentagon making clear that the most elite and physically hazardous assignments, including the Army Rangers and Navy SEALs, would now be open to women. (In August 2015, the first two women—both graduates of West Point— joined ninety-four men in graduating from the Army's grueling Ranger training school.) In December 2015, Defense Secretary Ashton B. Carter made clear that all combat roles are now open to women.

Nearly a quarter century had passed since the flare-up over draft registration. The new developments caused little public controversy. A column in the conservative publication *Human Events*, however, expressed vigorous disapproval, calling Panetta's decision an "act of political cowardice."[73] The column's author, age eighty-eight and still on message, was Phyllis Schlafly.

CHAPTER 8

Expression and Repression

On April 1, 1969, an American newspaper carried an editorial under the headline "Beyond the (Garbage) Pale." "The explicit portrayal on the stage of sexual intercourse is the final step in the erosion of taste and subtlety in the theater," the unsigned piece began. "It reduces actors to mere exhibitionists, turns audiences into voyeurs and debases sexual relationships almost to the level of prostitution. It is difficult to see any great principle of civil liberty involved."

The editorial went on to deplore not only sexual activity on the stage, but also depictions of sex in bestselling novels and in films, particularly "the more notorious Swedish imports." The "insensate pursuit of the urge to shock" was common to them all: "Far from providing a measure of cultural emancipation, such descents into degeneracy represent caricatures of art, deserving no exemption from the laws of common decency merely because they masquerade as drama or literature."

This was not the voice of a country newspaper editor from the heartland. The editorial appeared in *The New York Times*.[1] The newspaper didn't identify the offending productions by name. It didn't need to. As most *Times* readers surely knew, the stage performance that so alarmed the newspaper's editorial board was an Off-Off-Broadway play called *Che!*, in which a nude actor depicting the Cuban guerrilla leader Ernesto "Che" Guevara was assassinated by an actor depicting Uncle Sam, dressed only in a hat. Before that dramatic finale was "a frenzy of homosexual and other unorthodox sexual acts," according to an account of the play's opening night at the Broadway Free Store Theater in the East Village.[2]

A reporter's query to a police official about whether the performance might be violating any obscenity laws elicited a shrug. "This is a problem the Supreme Court couldn't agree on, so please don't ask us to rule on what is art or how far it can go before it becomes hard-core pornography," said Deputy Inspector Joseph Fink.[3] But Inspector Fink was evidently speaking without having consulted his department's public morals squad, which two days later descended on the theater and arrested five performers, the playwright, the producer, and a member of the technical crew.

On February 25, 1970, after a five-week non–jury trial in Manhattan Criminal Court—the Broadway producer David Merrick testified as a witness for the prosecution on the play's worthlessness—the eight defendants were convicted of obscenity and public lewdness for participating in what the presiding judge of the three-judge panel called "a nadir of smut on the stage." The play, Judge Arthur H. Goldberg declared, had no "redeeming social value."[4]

In the interval between the defendants' arrest and their conviction, Warren Burger became chief justice of the United States.

When it came to the law of obscenity, the new chief justice inherited, as Inspector Fink suggested, a mess. The Warren Court, while declaring that obscenity lay outside the protection of the First Amendment, had been unable to come up with an actual definition that could be reliably and coherently applied. The justices, to their growing discomfiture, had been reduced to watching sexually explicit movies in a basement screening room and deciding on a case-by-case basis which of them met the inchoate legal test of obscenity. That test, derived from a 1957 opinion, *Roth v. United States*, which its author, Justice William Brennan, was to disavow sixteen years later, was "whether to the average person, applying contemporary community standards, the dominant theme of the material taken as a whole appeals to prurient interest."[5] The justices' frustration was captured by Justice Potter Stewart's famous concurring opinion in a 1964 case, *Jacobellis v. Ohio*, in which he confessed to being unable to come up with an intelligible definition of hard-core pornography. "But I know it when I see it, and the motion picture involved in this case [a French film called *Les Amants*] is not that."[6]

The cases kept coming, with the Court deciding thirty-four of them between 1967 and 1971.[7] From today's perspective, the Supreme Court's obsession with obscenity appears oddly out of step with mid-twentieth-century America. Surely there were issues of greater moment to occupy the country's highest court. But as the *New York Times* editorial demonstrates, on the eve of Warren Burger's investiture the obsession was scarcely the Court's alone. The liberal Establishment to which the *Times* editorial page gave voice undoubtedly had more tolerance than some other sectors of society for sexually explicit works with literary merit, such as *Ulysses* and Henry Miller's *Tropic of Capricorn*, both of which had once been banned from importation into United States. But liberals, too—including Chief Justice Earl Warren—were deeply concerned about the link between ever more explicit and crude depictions of sex and what appeared to be the inexorable coarsening of American society.

A unanimous Supreme Court decision in April 1969—one of the final decisions of the Warren Court—added to the general sense that the old barriers were breaking down. Police in Atlanta, executing a search warrant, had raided the home of a man suspected of running an illegal bookmaking operation. While searching a desk drawer, they came upon three rolls of eight-millimeter film. Using a projector and screen they found in the house, the officers viewed the sexually explicit films, obscene by any definition. The homeowner, Robert Eli Stanley, was convicted of possessing "obscene matter" in violation of Georgia law, and the Georgia Supreme Court upheld his conviction.

In an opinion by Justice Marshall, the Supreme Court overturned the state court decision in a ringing declaration of personal privacy that made front-page news throughout the country.[8] "Whatever may be the justifications for other statutes regulating obscenity," Justice Marshall wrote for the court in *Stanley v. Georgia*,[9] "we do not think they reach into the privacy of one's own home. If the First Amendment means anything, it means that a State has no business telling a man, sitting alone in his own house, what books he may read or what films he may watch. Our whole constitutional heritage rebels at the thought of giving government the power to control men's minds."

The decision led an alarmed Congress to beef up funding for a national "Commission on Obscenity and Pornography" that President Johnson had established in 1967. The commission, headed by Dean William B. Lockhart of the University of Minnesota Law School, had a commendably balanced membership, including some civil libertarians. However, President Richard Nixon later filled a vacancy by naming

Charles H. Keating, Jr., a wealthy real estate investor and well-known anti-pornography crusader who had founded an organization called Citizens for Decent Literature, which claimed 100,000 members. (Keating later went to prison for his role in the savings and loan crisis of the 1980s, in which five U.S. senators who had accepted his campaign contributions were implicated.) In 1970, over the dissent of Keating and two other commissioners, the eighteen-member panel released a final report calling for the decriminalization of pornography for consenting adults.[10]

This was not an acceptable outcome to Nixon and most other politicians. The Senate officially rejected the report and the president, two weeks before the 1970 midterm elections, announced that he "categorically" disavowed the report's "morally bankrupt conclusions and major recommendations." Calling pornography a "pollution of our civilization" that "should be outlawed in every state in the union," Nixon declared that "so long as I am in the White House, there will be no relaxation of the national effort to control and eliminate smut from our national life."[11] Nixon's attention to the smut problem proved short-lived. Kevin J. McMahon, a historian of the Nixon era, notes that of the twenty-eight times the word "obscene" appeared in Nixon's public papers, all but four occurred in the fall of 1970, while the president was campaigning for Republican candidates during the midterm elections.[12] (McMahon quotes William Safire, Nixon's speechwriter, as observing: "Pornographers do not have supporters, only customers."[13])

Burger Steps In

Nixon's chief justice could not turn off the subject quite so easily. For one thing, Burger was actually, rather than just opportunistically, troubled by the pervasiveness of obscenity. In June 1972, while the Court was debating the future of obscenity law in what would become the landmark case of *Miller v. California*,[14] Burger wrote to William Brennan, his chief adversary: "I confess I do not see it as a threat to genuine First Amendment values to have commercial porno-peddlers feel some unease. . . . In short, a little 'chill' will do some of the 'pornos' no great harm and it might be good for the country."[15] In *Miller*'s companion case, *Paris Adult Theatre 1 v. Slaton*, Burger would pick up on Nixon's use of the word "pollution," analogizing regulation of obscenity to government efforts "to protect the physical environment from pollution." [16]

Beyond his own policy preferences, Burger was keenly aware of the toll the obscenity issue was taking on the Supreme Court. For how much longer could the justices spend their afternoons passing judgment on one dirty movie after another? Whatever the Court thought it was doing didn't seem to be having any effect on the public welfare. It was time, Burger announced to his colleagues in the spring of 1972, to take the Court out of the obscenity business to the extent possible. The answer was "contemporary community standards." In other words, local control.

"In a society that prides itself—and properly so—in supporting pluralism and diversity," Burger wrote to the other justices, "there is no sound reason for the law to say that what is found tolerable in the portrayal of sexual activities in Los Angeles or Las Vegas must be accepted in Maine or Vermont." He continued: "In the long run this Court cannot act as an efficient Super Censor and the sooner we leave the problem to the States the better off we and the public will be." [17]

The vehicle for this change in direction was *Miller v. California*, an appeal brought by a man convicted of violating California's criminal obscenity statute by mailing unsolicited brochures advertising a film called *Marital Intercourse* along with four books: *Man-Woman, Sex Orgies Illustrated, An Illustrated History of Pornography*, and *Intercourse*. The brochures contained graphic illustrations depicting the advertised works. A restaurant manager and his mother complained to the police after receiving them in the mail.

The case was argued along with several others in January 1972, and Burger assigned the majority opinion to himself. By May, with the end of the Court's term in sight, Burger was ready to share his thoughts, although not yet a complete draft, with his colleagues. In addition to his new approach to community standards, Burger also proposed to revise the definition of obscenity. Instead of the broad-brush "utterly without redeeming social value," the chief justice offered a three-part definition. As his final *Miller* opinion would put it more than a year later, the definition was to be:

limited to works which, taken as a whole, appeal to the prurient interest in sex, which portray sexual conduct in a patently offensive way, and which, taken as a whole, do not have serious literary, artistic, political, or scientific value.[18]

Whether a particular work fit that three-part definition would be left to the judgment of state and local authorities and juries.

Burger's proposal dismayed Justice Brennan, who, like the chief justice, had concluded that it was time for the Court to make a fresh start on obscenity—but in the opposite direction, not more precise regulation but deregulation. "With all respect, the Chief Justice's proposed solution to the obscenity quagmire will, in my view, worsen an already intolerable mess," Brennan responded to Burger's memo, with copies to the other justices. Drawing on the report of the Commission on Obscenity and Pornography, Brennan proposed that while "exposure to unwilling adults and dissemination to juveniles" should continue to be deemed impermissible, obscenity intended for the eyes of consenting adults should be placed back in the First Amendment pantheon of protected speech—from which, he acknowledged ruefully, his own opinion in *Roth* back in 1957 had removed it. "I'll try in due course to circulate my views," Brennan promised.[19]

Burger vs. Brennan

Brennan's "due course" arrived a mere three weeks later, with his circulation of a fully fleshed out thirty-page memo. "I think the time has come," he began, "when the Court should admit that the standards fashioned by it to guide administration of this Nation's obscenity laws do not work, and that we must change our constitutional approach if we are to bring stability to this area of the law." The "core of our problem," he continued, "has been our inability to provide tools that effectively separate obscenity from other sexually oriented expression that has constitutional protection, so that our laws will operate only to suppress the former."[20]

Brennan was deeply mistrustful of the chief justice's plan to leave obscenity to the states, which in Brennan's view needed to be kept on a tight constitutional leash. "The law of obscenity has been fashioned by this Court—and necessarily so under our duty to enforce the Constitution," he wrote. "If that law now offends the constitutional requirement of the

Due Process Clause and the First Amendment, as I believe it does, the remedy is one this Court, expounder of the Constitution, must provide." [21]

Burger responded to Brennan's "very interesting memo" the next day. His tone was sarcastic and his annoyance was clear; he appeared to regard as disingenuous Brennan's claim to have turned around a thirty-page memo in a matter of weeks. "In the short time you have had I marvel at how you have done this job," Burger wrote. "We need more exchanges of this kind to develop our thinking." Burger characterized Brennan's proposal as "a new, uncharted swamp." In the area of obscenity, he said, "the Court has made enough false steps." [22]

Time had run out. It was mid-June, and it was unclear whether either justice's approach could attract a majority or, if not, what kind of compromise might be possible. There was no choice but to set *Miller v. California* over for reargument in the next term. The second argument, on November 7, 1972, did little to resolve the uncertainty. Burger's ultimate opinion, not issued until June 21, 1973, went through nine drafts, and the outcome was not clear until June 18, when Harry Blackmun, after having been intensely courted by Brennan all spring, finally made up his mind and provided Burger with a fifth vote. [23]

In an amusing side note, the White House tapes captured a telephone conversation between Nixon and Burger on January 2, 1973, during which the chief justice told the president that he was "struggling with this pornography thing." Burger elaborated: "I don't know how we're coming out. I'm coming out hard on it myself, whether I get the support or not." Nixon responded: "I'm a square." As the Nixon historian Kevin McMahon recounts the exchange, the two men together mocked the "utterly without redeeming social importance" standard of Brennan's *Roth* opinion:

> "Good God!" exclaimed the president. Burger responded: "One of the biggest frauds. . . . This means that if they have one of these outrageous orgies then if they mention Vietnam or the condition of the ghettoes, that redeems the whole thing." Nixon laughed, "Oh boy, isn't that something." And that was the end of it. [24]

Miller v. California was not the Supreme Court's last word on obscenity. There would be other cases, other affronts to public decency. But the Court has not retreated from *Miller*'s basic framework, neither in defining what constitutes obscenity nor in leaving it to the states to decide whether a particular work fits the definition. "We emphasize that it is not our function to propose regulatory schemes for the States," Burger wrote in his majority opinion. "Under a National Constitution, fundamental First Amendment limitations on the powers of the States do not vary from community to community, but this does not mean that there are, or should or can be, fixed, uniform national standards of precisely what appeals to the 'prurient interest' or is 'patently offensive.' These are essentially questions of fact, and our Nation is simply too big and too diverse for this Court to reasonably expect that such standards should be articulated for all 50 States in a single formulation, even assuming the prerequisite consensus exists."[25]

Miller offers the rare sight of a court confronting the outer limit of its institutional capacity and openly choosing a new direction. The direction proved to be Burger's, but it might just as easily have been Brennan's: a federalism-inflected standing-down versus a considered deregulation. Perhaps it would have amounted to the same thing. A generation after the Court's great struggle with obscenity, the public's appetite for sexually explicit content remains unabated. But the twenty-first-century media environment offers countless ways to satisfy every taste: the ultimate decentralization, and privatization as well. *Penthouse*, once at the cutting edge of sex between magazine covers, now sells only about 100,000 copies an issue, down from five million. *Playboy*'s circulation, once six million copies a month, is down to a million.[26] In 2015, the magazine announced that, given the ubiquity of photographs of nude women on the Internet, it would no longer bother to include them. Times Square was cleaned up and turned into a tourists' theme park not by prosecutors or judges, but by the economic engine of the real estate market and by customers' preference for spending their money at Madame Tussauds New York wax museum rather than on a peep show or Triple-X movie they can watch more conveniently at home.[27]

A Path Not Taken

The energy the Burger Court expended on the obscenity cases stands in striking contrast to its unwillingness—inability may be more accurate—

to engage with the emerging question of gay rights. The constitutional right to privacy recognized by the Warren Court in *Griswold v. Connecticut*,[28] the contraception case, necessarily opened the door to questions about the right to sexual privacy in other contexts. Even before the justices extended *Griswold's* right to marital privacy to unmarried persons in *Eisenstadt v. Baird*[29] in 1972, gay couples were testing the limits of the new privacy doctrine by claiming that their choice of intimate partners was also worthy of protection, even of celebration.

In 1970, Jack Baker, a student leader at the University of Minnesota, where he was a well-known gay rights activist, showed up with his male partner at the Hennepin County clerk's office to apply for a marriage license. While Minnesota's marriage law did not explicitly limit marriage to opposite-sex couples, the statute referred to "husband and wife" and "bride and groom." Not surprisingly, the clerk refused to issue the license. The couple went to court.

The men lost in the state trial court, with the Minnesota Supreme Court affirming that decision in an opinion that observed that "the institution of marriage as a union of man and woman, uniquely involving the procreation and rearing of children within a family, is as old as the book of Genesis."[30] The biblical invocation did not bode well for the plaintiffs. The court held that neither *Griswold v. Connecticut* nor *Loving v. Virginia*,[31] the 1967 decision that struck down state anti-miscegenation laws, pointed to a recognition of same-sex marriage. Of *Loving*, the Minnesota court declared that "in commonsense and in a constitutional sense, there is a clear distinction between a marital restriction based merely upon race and one based upon the fundamental difference in sex."

Jack Baker and his partner, James McConnell, promptly appealed to the U.S. Supreme Court. Under the statute that then governed the Court's jurisdiction to review federal constitutional questions decided by state courts, the case arrived as a mandatory appeal, meaning that the Court could not simply deny review as it did to thousands of cases every year.[32] While a mandatory appeal didn't oblige the justices to hear argument and issue a full opinion, it did require a disposition on the record, with such a disposition carrying weight as a precedent. If the justices chose not to hear the case, they could summarily affirm the lower court's decision, thus adopting it as a Supreme Court precedent, or they could dismiss the appeal "for want of a substantial federal question," meaning that the argument the appellants presented was so lacking in merit as to raise no constitutional issue at all; such a case was deemed not even to fall within the Court's jurisdiction.

The justices chose the latter course. On October 10, 1972, the Court decided *Baker v. Nelson* with a one-sentence order: "The appeal is dismissed for want of a substantial federal question." [33] There is no evidence that the justices had found the case even worthy of discussion. In the Blackmun chambers, for example, a law clerk prepared a memo that summarized the facts of the case in three paragraphs. Then, under the heading "Discussion," the clerk offered a one-sentence recommendation: "Dismiss for want of a substantial federal question." Blackmun accepted this recommendation without further inquiry, adding to the top of the clerk's memo his own hand-written notation, "DWQ," meaning dismiss for the want of a question. [34] A generation would pass before the Supreme Court took up the issue of same-sex marriage. On June 26, 2015, as part of its decision in *Obergefell v. Hodges* declaring a constitutional right to same-sex marriage, the Court overruled *Baker v. Nelson*, which it described as based on "assumptions defined by the world and time" of which the case—and the Supreme Court itself—had been a part. [35]

Dissenting Voices

Outside the marriage context, the issue of the rights of gay men and lesbians could not so easily be put on the shelf. If there was a right to privacy in matters relating to sex—including, by January 1973, the right to abortion—how could it be that adult men and women faced criminal prosecution for acting on their sexual desires with consenting partners of the same sex?

In 1975, two young gay men in Virginia, filing their case anonymously with the assistance of the American Civil Liberties Union, challenged the constitutionality of the state's "crimes against nature" statute that made sodomy a felony punishable by imprisonment for at least one year and as many as three. The plaintiffs themselves had not been arrested or prosecuted, so this was not a criminal appeal. Rather, they asked the federal district court in Richmond to declare that the statute violated the constitutional rights to privacy, due process, and equal protection. A divided three-judge district court panel upheld the law, sending the case, *Doe v. Commonwealth's Attorney*, on to the Supreme Court as a mandatory appeal.[36]

The majority on the district court panel expressed deference both to the state's policy choice and to the Book of Leviticus, citing the vivid biblical proscription against homosexuality as evidence of "ancestry going back to Judaic and Christian law." The court declared: "If a State determines that punishment therefore, even when committed in the home, is appropriate in the promotion of morality and decency, it is not for the courts to say that the State is not free to do so." The judges observed that they were not passing "upon the wisdom or policy of the statute," adding: "It is simply that we cannot say that the statute offends the Bill of Rights or any other of the Amendments and the wisdom or policy is a matter for the State's resolve."

The dissenter on the panel was Robert R. Merhige, Jr., no stranger to controversy; he was the federal district judge who three years earlier had ordered cross-district busing as the means to integrate the Richmond schools (see Chapter 4). Virginia's law violated the Fourteenth Amendment's guarantee of due process, he wrote. The majority, he continued, had read *Griswold* too narrowly and had failed to take into account the Supreme Court's recent abortion rulings.

> I view those cases as standing for the principle that every individual has a right to be free from unwarranted governmental intrusion into one's decisions on private matters of intimate concern. A mature individual's choice of an adult sexual partner, in the privacy of his or her own home, would appear to me to be a decision of the utmost private and intimate concern. Private consensual sex acts between adults are matters, absent evidence that they are harmful, in which the state has no legitimate interest.

Judge Merhige also cited *Stanley v. Georgia*, the 1969 case that established the right to view obscene material in the privacy of one's home. That case, Merhige wrote, "teaches us that socially condemned activity, excepting that of demonstrable external effect, is and was intended by the Constitution to be beyond the scope of state regulation when conducted within the privacy of the home."

Unlike the marriage case, *Doe v. Commonwealth's Attorney* got the Supreme Court's attention. Justices Brennan, Marshall, and Stevens voted to hear the plaintiffs' appeal. They did not, however, write an opinion to offer their view of the appeal's merits, thus giving no indication whether they thought the case had been wrongly decided or simply whether they thought the question the case raised needed the Court's answer, whatever that answer might be. The Court's decision, issued on March 29, 1976, was a one-line order: "Judgment affirmed." This was a difference, albeit a subtle one, from the one-line dismissal in *Baker v. Nelson*. In the marriage case, no member of the Court discerned a "substantial federal question." In *Doe*, by contrast, the justices expressed no doubt that the question was substantial; one plausible inference from the majority's conclusion— although not, as it turned out, the only one—was that the lower court had decided it correctly.

And *Doe v. Commonwealth's Attorney* got the public's attention as well. While *The New York Times* had reported the decision in *Baker v. Nelson* only with a one-sentence item in a roundup of Supreme Court actions,[37] the Court's rejection of the sodomy challenge was front-page news. "The ruling sharply departs from a 10-year trend in which the high court had increasingly expanded the concept of the constitutional right to privacy," the newspaper reported.[38] Part of the reason for the intensifying public attention, certainly, was that increasingly public activism meant that gay voices were beginning to be heard outside the courtroom, in politics and society generally. The claim to same-sex marriage struck many people, even within the gay community, as radical and extreme during those years. But the claim to a right to be free of criminal prosecution for one's private sexual activity had begun to resonate with other civil rights movements, although the emerging debate about gay rights in the mid-1970s was marked by controversy rather than consensus.[39]

Doe was sharply criticized in the legal academy, both for the result and for the Court's summary procedure. Addressing a convention of political scientists in Philadelphia two weeks after the ruling, Dean Louis H. Pollak of the University of Pennsylvania Law School (he was later a federal district judge) said with obvious sarcasm: "I suppose that dispensing with an opinion may be supported on the ground that explaining a decision in writing is hard and time-consuming and unrewarding labor when one is unsure of the grounds for one's decision."[40] One law review article called the decision "a devastating blow to all Americans who are concerned with the most cherished right of all civilized men—'the right to be let alone.' "[41] Another demanded:

> The Court may have summarily limited the right to privacy in a way that suggests fiat, not articulated principle, for how can the Court in a principled way sustain the constitutional right to privacy of married and unmarried people to use contraceptives or to have abortions or to use pornography in the privacy of one's home, and not sustain the rights of consenting adult homosexuals to engage in the form of sex they find natural?[42]

It was a question the Burger Court was in no rush to answer. In 1981, the justices refused to review a decision by New York's highest court invalidating the state's criminal sodomy law.[43] Two years later, the Court accepted another New York case, in which the state court had invalidated a law that prohibited loitering in a public place for the purpose of engaging in or soliciting "deviate sexual intercourse or other sexual behavior of a deviate nature."[44] But after hearing argument, the justices voted 5–4 to dismiss the case without a decision.[45] According to the unsigned majority opinion, the Court had concluded that the state court's opinion "is fairly subject to varying interpretations, leaving us uncertain as to the precise federal constitutional issue the court decided." Therefore, the opinion concluded, "we are persuaded that this case provides an inappropriate vehicle for resolving the important constitutional issues raised by the parties." Was this a strategic dodge for avoiding a decision in a case that had become too hot to handle? Quite likely, as implied by the one-paragraph dissent by Justice White that Burger, Rehnquist, and O'Connor also signed. "As I see it," White wrote, "the New York statute was invalidated on other grounds, and the merits of that decision are properly before us and should be addressed."[46]

Another failure occurred the following year. The Court had agreed to decide a case on the constitutionality of an Oklahoma law that subjected public school teachers to dismissal for speaking in favor of gay rights. The Oklahoma legislature enacted the law in 1978 at the behest of Anita Bryant, a famously homophobic entertainer of the era who was traveling the country warning of the dangers of homosexuality, especially in the schools, and urging passage of antigay legislation. The United States Court of Appeals for the Tenth Circuit invalidated the law on free speech grounds,[47] and the state appealed.

Eight justices heard argument on January 14, 1985; Justice Powell, who was recovering from surgery, was absent and would not take part in the decision. More than two months later, on March 26, the Court announced a 4–4 deadlock.[48] As a procedural matter, a tie vote affirms the lower court's decision without setting a Supreme Court precedent. As a matter of practice, the Court announces only that "the judgment is affirmed by an equally divided vote," and neither issues a further explanation nor identifies the justices who voted on each side. But the fact of the Court's division was apparent for all to see.[49] For how long could the Burger Court keep avoiding the subject of the constitutional rights of gay men and lesbians?

The country, if not the Court, was moving on. When *Doe v. Commonwealth's Attorney* was decided in 1976, thirty-six states still had criminal sodomy laws on the books. (Every state had such a law until 1961, when Illinois became the first to decriminalize private consensual homosexual acts.) Within a decade, the number had fallen to twenty-four, fewer than half the states. And even in those states, prosecutions for private homosexual acts had for years been rare to nonexistent—a challenge to gay rights advocates who were looking for a new case to bring to the Supreme Court.

The Issue Is Joined

They found a case in Atlanta. In July 1982, a police officer gave Michael Hardwick a ticket for carrying an open bottle of beer. When Hardwick failed to keep a court date, the officer went to his apartment to serve a warrant. Admitted to the apartment by a friend of Hardwick's who was staying there, the officer found Hardwick in a bedroom engaging in oral sex with another man. The officer then arrested both for sodomy. Although the local prosecutor declined to press charges, and in fact had never prosecuted anyone for private sex acts, Hardwick agreed to be a plaintiff in a test case to be brought by the American Civil Liberties Union to challenge the Georgia statute in federal court.[50]

The Federal district court promptly dismissed the case, without an opinion. Its two-sentence order simply cited the Supreme Court's summary affirmance in *Doe*, treating that nonopinion as binding precedential authority for the proposition that criminal sodomy laws were constitutional. The United States Court of Appeals for the Eleventh Circuit disagreed in a 2–1 decision.[51] The author of the majority opinion, Frank M. Johnson, Jr., and the judge who joined him, Elbert Parr Tuttle, were—like Robert Merhige, the dissenting judge in the District Court *Doe* opinion a decade earlier—judicial heroes of the civil rights movement who were accustomed to standing up for minority rights in the face of majority sentiment.

Judge Johnson wrote that the district court had interpreted the Supreme Court's *Doe* affirmance too broadly. "A summary affirmance represents an approval by the Supreme Court of the judgment below but should not be taken as an endorsement of the reasoning of the lower court," Johnson wrote. Rather, such an action by the Supreme Court should be given only "the most narrow plausible rationale." In the *Doe* case, he continued, it was plausible for the Supreme Court to have concluded that the plaintiffs, who, unlike Michael Hardwick, had not been arrested, lacked standing to challenge the Virginia sodomy statute. Since Hardwick did have standing, the Supreme Court's ruling in *Doe* was consequently "not controlling in this case."

Proceeding to the merits (the dissenting judge on the panel, Phyllis A. Kravitch, expressed no view on the merits because she regarded *Doe* as binding), Judge Johnson declared that "the Georgia sodomy statute infringes upon the fundamental constitutional rights of Michael Hardwick." Citing *Griswold v. Connecticut* and *Roe v. Wade*, Johnson said that Hardwick sought the right to engage in an activity that "is quintessentially private and lies at the heart of an intimate association beyond the proper reach of state regulation." The decision reinstated Hardwick's lawsuit and declared that the state, in order to prevail, would have to prove that "it has a compelling interest in regulating this behavior and that this statute is the most narrowly drawn means of safeguarding that interest."

The state appealed, in the name of Michael Bowers, Georgia's attorney general. There was, of course, no guarantee that the justices would agree to hear the case. In fact, the case that became *Bowers v. Hardwick*[52] came very close to reaching a dead end at the Supreme Court. When the state's petition came before the conference at the start of the 1985 term, only Justices White and Rehnquist voted to grant it. Lewis Powell was of the firm view that the Court could and should continue to avoid the issue by relying on the *Doe* summary affirmance to preclude any further action. Powell wrote out his thoughts by hand on the first page of a law clerk's memo on the case. Judge Kravitch, the dissenter on the Eleventh Circuit, was right, Powell wrote, and "we can again avoid this highly controversial issue by holding that CA-11 misread *Doe*—i.e. reiterate binding effect of affirming a three-judge court summarily." [53] He voted to deny review.

But Byron White felt so strongly about taking the case that he drafted and proposed to publish an opinion dissenting from the denial. This was not a particularly unusual move for White, and neither did it signify, at least on the surface, his view of the merits. Rather, his proposed dissent focused on the fact that two other federal appeals courts had recently ruled that *Doe v. Commonwealth's Attorney* was in fact a precedent that bound the lower courts in any case challenging state sodomy laws.[54] "Given this lack of consistency among the circuits on this important constitutional question, I would grant the petition," White wrote.

White believed that the Court should resolve any conflict that arose among the federal appeals courts, and frequently noted his dissent when his colleagues decided otherwise. So his dissent in this case, as he framed it, appeared routine. Persuaded, Brennan changed his vote from "deny" to "grant," as did Marshall. Harry Blackmun, who was attuned to the gay rights issue because of its implication for abortion rights and who understood the stakes, urged Brennan to switch back to "deny," but it was too late. Burger had also voted to grant, and the votes had been counted. For better or worse, certiorari was granted.[55]

A Swing Vote

The briefs that arrived at the Court in advance of the March 31, 1986, argument displayed the stark difference between the two sides, not only in the outcome each side sought but in how each understood what the case was about. To the state, in a brief filed by the attorney general's office, the subject was homosexuals and their sex practices. "Obviously, there is no textual support in the Constitution or laws of the United States for the proposition that sodomy is a protected activity," the state's brief maintained.[56] By the mid-1980s, the AIDS epidemic—the "gay plague," as the disease had become known—had entered public consciousness as a source of fear, even panic. The state's brief played AIDS for all it was worth. Asserting that gay sex "often" involved multiple partners and took place in public parks, restrooms, "gay baths," and "gay bars," the brief urged that "the legislature should be permitted to draw conclusions concerning the relationship of homosexual sodomy in the transmission of Acquired Immune Deficiency Syndrome (AIDS) and other diseases."[57]

By contrast, the brief for Michael Hardwick, written by a legal team headed by Laurence H. Tribe, a well-known law professor at Harvard, said very little about homosexuality as such. (Indeed, as the brief pointed out, the Georgia sodomy law also applied, at least nominally, to heterosexuals.) Rather, the case was about constitutional protection from "state control of our most private realm,"[58] about the privacy of intimate association "in a society where constitutional traditions have always placed the highest value upon the sanctity of the home against governmental intrusion or control."[59]

Tribe took account of the state's AIDS-related fear-mongering at the end of his brief. The argument was "wholly inapposite," he said, and the state should have to "explain how a threat of criminal prosecution could serve as an effective public health measure, rather than driving underground the very information that medical authorities need most by fostering fear that a visit to a doctor will mean prison for the patient."[60]

As the argument date approached and the views of the other justices appeared to solidify, Powell remained deeply conflicted about how the case should be decided. He told one of his clerks on the morning of the argument that he would probably not make up his mind until after the argument and the justices' conference that would follow.[61] But at the conference on April 2, Powell surprised everyone, perhaps even himself, by voting to uphold the Eleventh Circuit, thus giving Michael Hardwick a fifth vote. Acknowledging "mixed emotions," he told his colleagues that "sodomy in the home should be decriminalized." Harry Blackmun, for one, was so surprised that he put an exclamation point next to his notes on Powell's remarks, adding a note to his law clerks: "Clerks! Can this position hold?"[62]

With Burger, White, Rehnquist, and O'Connor in dissent, Brennan was the senior justice in the majority, giving him the power to assign the opinion. He gave the assignment to Blackmun. The assignment proved short-lived. Six days later, Powell informed his colleagues that he had changed his mind and would now vote to reverse. That placed Burger in control, and the chief justice assigned the majority opinion to White.

Powell's file contains a private letter from Burger, dated the day after the conference. Powell had observed during the conference that he regarded homosexuals much like drug addicts, suffering from a disabling "status" that could be considered much like an illness. He had invoked a 1962 decision, *Robinson v. California*,[63] in which the Warren Court, over a dissent by White, had invalidated a California law that made it a crime for a person to "be addicted to the use of narcotics." The Court held that a person's "status" or "chronic condition" could not by itself be treated as a crime.

Now, in two and a half single-spaced pages, Burger sought to win Powell's vote by persuading him that the analogy was mistaken. "Hardwick merely wishes to seek his own form of sexual gratification," Burger wrote. "Undoubtedly there are also those in society who seek gratification through incest, drug use, gambling, exhibitionism, prostitution, rape, and what not." But that was not a basis for striking down the Georgia law, Burger continued, quoting Justice Oliver Wendell Holmes: "Pretty much all law consists in forbidding men to do some things that they want to do."[64]

Burger concluded: "April 13, an unlucky day, will mark my 30th year on the Bench. This case presents for me the most far reaching issue of those 30 years. I hope you will excuse the energy with which I have stated my views, and I hope you will give them earnest consideration."

Warren Burger was just months away from announcing his retirement from the Court. The letter displays passion, to be sure. But more significantly, its rhetorical excess demonstrates how unaware Burger remained about the art of persuasion despite his decades as a judge on multimember courts. Although he and Lewis Powell had served together for more than fourteen years, Burger failed to realize that incendiary language was not the way to his colleague's heart or mind. Powell marked up the letter with handwritten objections, not for transmission to Burger—there is no evidence that he even replied—but as a way to channel his own annoyance. To Burger's list of supposedly depraved gratifications, Powell noted: "Irrelevant. The C.J. should know this." Powell drew a circle around Burger's comment that the case presented "the most far-reaching issue" of his judicial career and wrote: "Incredible statement!" At the top of the letter, Powell wrote: "There is both sense and nonsense in this letter—mostly the latter."

If Burger's intervention was not the cause of Powell's change of mind, what was? How could Powell, who never wavered in his support for the right to abortion, approach the question of gay rights with such ambivalence? The answer is that while he regarded abortion as an unfortunate but inevitable part of life, he viewed homosexuality with incomprehension and extreme discomfort. Powell's biographer and former law clerk, John Jeffries (later dean of the law school at the University of Virginia), recounts an awkward conversation that Powell initiated with one of his law clerks while *Bowers* was pending. Informing his "astonished clerk," who happened to be a gay man, that "I don't believe I've ever met a homosexual," Powell proceeded to ask a series of explicit questions about the nature of same-sex attraction.[65]

The outcome in *Bowers v. Hardwick* was a devastating blow to the gay rights movement. White's opinion, only eight pages long, was dismissive in the extreme. The majority accepted the state's argument that this was simply a case about sodomy, nothing broader or more universal. Acknowledging *Griswold, Roe*, and the other precedents the Eleventh Circuit had invoked in ruling for Hardwick, White wrote that "we think it evident that none of the rights announced in those cases bears any resemblance to the claimed constitutional right of homosexuals to engage in acts of sodomy that is asserted in this case."[66] The prohibition against sodomy has "ancient roots," White continued, noting that criminal sodomy laws were nearly universal among the states that ratified the Fourteenth Amendment, with its Due Process Clause, in 1868. "Against this background," White wrote, the claim that there existed a fundamental right to engage in homosexual sodomy "is, at best, facetious."[67]

Burger and Powell both filed short concurring opinions. "To hold that the act of homosexual sodomy is somehow protected as a fundamental right would be to cast aside millennia of moral teaching," Burger declared.[68] Powell's ambivalence was on full display in his two-paragraph concurrence. Noting that the Georgia law authorized a prison sentence of up to twenty years for a single act of sodomy, he said the law potentially violated the Eighth Amendment's prohibition against cruel and unusual punishment. But the point, as Powell had to concede, was irrelevant to Michael Hardwick's case. Observing that Hardwick "has not been tried, much less convicted and sentenced," and had not raised an Eighth Amendment question, Powell concluded lamely: "For these reasons this constitutional argument is not before us."[69]

A protest against Supreme Court's decision in *Bowers v. Hardwick*, outside the New York Hilton where Chief Justice Burger was delivering his farewell address to the American Bar Association, August 11, 1986.

Blackmun, having lost the majority opinion to White, wrote in dissent for himself and Justices Brennan, Marshall, and Stevens. (Stevens wrote an additional dissenting opinion, which Brennan and Marshall signed.) Blackmun distilled the essence of his dissent in a statement he read from the bench. "It is precisely because the issue raised by this case touches the heart of what makes individuals what they are," Blackmun read, "that we should be especially sensitive to the rights of those whose choices upset the majority." He concluded: "It seems to us in the dissent that depriving individuals of the right to choose for themselves how to conduct their intimate relationships in private poses a far greater threat to the values most deeply rooted in our Nation's history than tolerance of nonconformity could ever do."[70]

Aftermath

The Court announced the decision in *Bowers v. Hardwick* on June 30, 1986. Days earlier, on June 17, President Reagan surprised the country by announcing that Chief Justice Burger was resigning in order to "devote his full energies in the coming year to the important work of the Commission on the Bicentennial of the Constitution." The president said he was nominating William Rehnquist to be chief justice along with Antonin Scalia of the D.C. Circuit to fill Rehnquist's associate justice position.

The Court's term lasted into July in 1986, so June 30 was not Warren Burger's last day on the bench. But everyone knew by then that change was coming to the Supreme Court, change most unlikely to be favorable for the cause of gay rights. If the substitution of Rehnquist for Burger and Scalia for Rehnquist was unlikely to move the Court noticeably to the right, it certainly promised no tacking to the middle.

Blackmun ended his dissenting opinion with a nod to Supreme Court history. In 1940, the Court rejected the argument that Jehovah's Witness schoolchildren had a constitutional right to refuse, according to the tenets of their religion, to salute the flag.[71] Three years later, in *West Virginia Board of Education v. Barnette*,[72] the Court reversed itself in a landmark ruling for individual freedom. Blackmun's opinion did not spell out what happened in the interval between the two opinions, but his colleagues surely knew, even if the general public did not. As wartime fever intensified, Jehovah's Witness children who refused to stand and pledge allegiance to the flag were harassed and thrown out of school; Kingdom Halls were burned; and adult Witnesses were derided as traitors.[73] "I can only hope," Blackmun wrote, "that here, too, the Court soon will reconsider its analysis."[74] (Blackmun, who died in 1999, five years after leaving the Court, did not live to see the next chapters: the Court's repudiation of sodomy laws in 2003 and its ruling in 2015 that the Fourteenth Amendment's guarantees of due process and equal protection protect the right of same-sex couples to marry. The twenty-nine-year interval from *Bowers v. Hardwick* to *Obergefell v. Hodges* was longer than the three-year turnabout in the Jehovah's Witnesses cases, to be sure, but it was stunning nonetheless.)[75]

On Sunday, July 13, less than two weeks after the *Bowers* decision was issued, an article accompanied by a photograph of Lewis Powell appeared across the top of *The Washington Post*'s front page. "Powell Changed Vote in Sodomy Case," the headline read. The reporter, Al Kamen, credited "informed sources" with the disclosure that "the most controversial Supreme Court ruling this year," *Bowers v. Hardwick*, "was initially decided the other way until Justice Lewis F. Powell Jr. changed his mind."[76]

The article was full of detail from deep inside the Court. It reported Powell's initial vote at conference, describing it as "tentative," as well as his change of mind "within several days," before any opinions had circulated. It recounted Powell's interest in whether homosexuality might be regarded as a status offense—the *Robinson v. California* analogy that Powell had initially put forward. "The sources said Powell would vote to repeal antisodomy laws if he were a legislator"—an assertion presumably put forward by a source who wanted to make sure Powell didn't appear antigay. Powell clipped the article and put it in his *Bowers* file.

The next time Lewis Powell made news in connection with *Bowers* was more than four years later. Speaking to a student audience at New York University Law School in October 1990, the eighty-three-year-old Powell, who had retired from the Court in 1987, answered a question about *Bowers* by saying that "I think I probably made a mistake" in voting with the majority. The majority opinion, he said, "was inconsistent in a general way" with *Roe v. Wade*, and upon rereading it, "I thought the dissent had the better of the arguments."[77]

There is no way to assess the impact that Powell's expression of regret might have had on the public's understanding of *Bowers*. Certainly one plausible message was that the decision was the result of something close to happenstance: that it was not written in stone, and that future appointments to the Court could shape a different outcome.

Powell's retirement had ushered in the fierce battle over President Reagan's nomination of Robert Bork. After Bork's defeat, the vacancy went to Anthony Kennedy, a federal appeals court judge from California. While he was a much less polarizing and more mainstream figure than Bork, few people if any would have predicted when he took his seat that, fifteen years later, Justice Kennedy would write for a majority in the waning years of the Rehnquist Court that "the rationale of *Bowers* does not withstand careful analysis."[78] Even fewer might have supposed that twelve years after that, in another Kennedy opinion, the Supreme Court would declare a constitutional right to same-sex marriage.[79]

"*Bowers* was not correct when it was decided, and it is not correct today," Kennedy declared in *Lawrence v. Texas*, the 2003 sodomy case. "It ought not to remain binding precedent. *Bowers v. Hardwick* should be and now is overruled." The vote was 6–3. Sandra Day O'Connor, who had voted with the majority in *Bowers*, concurred separately; it was a step too far for her to agree to overruling the precedent. Of the four who joined Kennedy—John Paul Stevens, David H. Souter, Ruth Bader Ginsburg, and Stephen G. Breyer—only Stevens had been on the Court in 1986, and he had dissented. Kennedy explained the majority's rationale:

> The petitioners are entitled to respect for their private lives. The State cannot demean their existence or control their destiny by making their private sexual conduct a crime. Their right to liberty under the Due Process Clause gives them the full right to engage in their conduct without intervention of the government.[80]

It was June 26, 2003. The number of states with sodomy laws still on their books had shrunk to thirteen, due in part to an energized gay rights movement that had turned to state legislatures after *Bowers* for the relief denied by the Supreme Court. Enforcement of the statutes in the context of private consensual conduct was exceedingly rare. The main challenge facing gay rights litigators was finding a plaintiff with a plausible claim to standing. They found two, John Geddes Lawrence and Tyron Garner, who had been arrested by Houston police officers in Lawrence's apartment in September 1998 and convicted in Harris County criminal court of "deviate sexual intercourse."[81] The lawyer who represented the two men in their Supreme Court appeal was Paul M. Smith, a partner in a major law firm and an experienced Supreme Court advocate. During the 1980 term, years before he came out as a gay man, he had clerked on the Supreme Court for Lewis Powell.

CHAPTER 9

A Religious People's Court

66 We are a religious people whose institutions presuppose a Supreme Being," Justice William O. Douglas declared for the Vinson Court in a 1952 decision, *Zorach v. Clauson*.[1] The decision upheld a program in the New York City public schools that provided "released time" during which students could leave their classrooms to receive religious instruction off the premises. Nonparticipating students remained behind in their regular classrooms. The court rejected the argument that the program showed such favoritism toward students who sought to practice their religion (actually, it was the parents' wishes, and not necessarily the children's own desire for religious education, that mattered for enrollment) as to amount to an unconstitutional "establishment" of religion.

It was perfectly permissible, Justice Douglas wrote, for public institutions "to accommodate the religious needs of the people." While separating church and state, he said, the First Amendment's Establishment Clause did not require government to "show a callous indifference to religious groups" or to favor "those who believe in no religion over those who do believe." (Under the First Amendment's Free Exercise Clause, Justice Douglas observed, "We guarantee the freedom to worship as one chooses. We make room for as wide a variety of beliefs and creeds as the spiritual needs of man deem necessary.")

Zorach v. Clauson was ahead of its time, an outlier in a Supreme Court era that stressed separation over accommodation. The Warren Court interpreted the First Amendment's Establishment Clause to bar organized

215

prayer and Bible reading in public schools.[2] Implicit in its Establishment Clause decisions was a notion far from universally accepted, either then or now: that when it came to religion versus nonreligion, the government was barred from tipping the scale either way. Religion could claim no preferred place.[3]

By the end of the Burger years, however, a shift from separation toward accommodation was well under way, leaving the rule of neutrality between religion and nonreligion in serious question. No single religion could be preferred over others, of course, but religion itself was on the way to gaining a favored place. The change occurred in fits and starts, remaining incomplete by the time William Rehnquist—more single-mindedly committed to the project than Warren Burger was—took the reins in 1986. The Rehnquist Court, in turn, while sowing its own brand of confusion (for example, some public displays of the Ten Commandments were permissible, while others were unconstitutional, and religious claims to exemption from neutral laws were generally disallowed), handed a still more religion-friendly legacy to the Roberts Court.[4] That court in turn—with six Roman Catholic justices and, for the first time, not a single Protestant—appears well on its way to becoming the most religion-favoring Supreme Court in modern U.S. history.[5]

The religion story is not a simple one.[6] It's not surprising that no Supreme Court, no matter its orientation, can drive a straight line through the First Amendment's two religion clauses and emerge with a fully coherent and consistent doctrine on the relationship between church and state. "Congress shall make no law respecting an establishment of religion, or prohibiting the free exercise thereof." That single, spare sentence not only embraces both the Establishment and Free Exercise Clauses but binds them in an inherent tension, never to be fully resolved. When does solicitude for a Free Exercise claim veer too deeply into Establishment Clause territory? When does wariness that carving out space for religion might violate the Establishment Clause lead religious practice to be disfavored or suppressed unnecessarily? Constitutional doctrine alone provides no hard-and-fast answers to such questions. The answers come from society, from a dynamic informed by politics and energized by the claims that highly motivated individuals and groups bring before judges. For the most part, the Supreme Court—not in every term and not in every case, but over time—has been a follower and not a leader in the ever-changing relationship between church and state in America. So it was with the Burger Court.

Previous chapters have demonstrated how the court's response to the social transformations of the 1960s and 1970s shaped constitutional doctrine regarding free speech, personal privacy, and individual lifestyle choices. Likewise on questions of church and state, the court responded to changing social realities. Although it wasn't obvious from a head count of the Burger Court—eight conventional Protestants and one Catholic, William Brennan—the American religious map was in transition. The old mainstream Protestant denominations were shrinking in numbers and influence. Fundamentalist and evangelical churches were growing, their leaders embracing politics as a field of action and their lawyers turning with growing assertiveness to the courts. Demographics were also changing as a diversifying Catholic population left immigrant enclaves in the cities to build new institutions in middle-class suburbia.

As in the pre-Burger years, schools were the stage on which church-state conflicts were most likely to play out. With questions of religious observance in the public schools settled by the Warren Court as a matter of formal doctrine—although far from settled in practice in many parts of the country—the conflict often took the form of a battle for resources, with religious schools making persistent and increasingly creative claims on the public treasury even as religion itself claimed entitlement to equal access to the public square.

The Burger Court decided dozens of religion cases, many more than we can discuss here.[7] In this chapter, we focus on those decisions that have had the most lasting consequences, either directly or by opening pathways for future courts. From the beginning of the Burger Court until its end, the meaning of the religion clauses remained deeply contested. Whether the separationist or accommodationist view prevailed in any particular case was often a matter of one or two votes. Consequently, it wasn't easy for those evaluating the court's actions in this area, either at the time or in the immediate aftermath, to see the pattern that from today's perspective is clear: offered a preferred place at the constitutional table, religion emerged from the Burger Court stronger and emboldened, with new weapons at hand for the battles that lay ahead.

Entanglements

It didn't seem that way at first. The 1970 term presented parochial school aid cases from Pennsylvania and Rhode Island. The cases challenged state laws that offered financial support for the costs that private schools incurred in teaching secular subjects, either by supplementing teachers' salaries or by reimbursing the schools for teaching math, science, modern foreign languages, and physical education. (The state laws referred to "nonpublic" rather than parochial schools, but in fact nearly all private schools in the two states were religious, and nearly all of those were Catholic.) Chief Justice Burger's opinion for the court in *Lemon v. Kurtzman*[8] covered both cases and declared that both state laws violated the Establishment Clause.

Nothing about *Lemon* marked it as a landmark decision, yet it became one. And given the 8–0 vote (Thurgood Marshall did not participate), the case hardly appeared particularly controversial. Yet the test it announced became the subject of intense and lasting dispute—a fact best explained by forces external to the opinion itself, including the rapidly changing valence of religion in politics and the consequent arrival on the Supreme Court of justices committed to a decidedly more accommodationist view of the Establishment Clause. One such justice, Antonin Scalia, who arrived in the immediate aftermath of Warren Burger's retirement in 1986, expressed the Religious Right's view of *Lemon v. Kurtzman* in characteristically colorful language in a 1993 opinion: "Like some ghoul in a late-night horror movie that repeatedly sits up in its grave and shuffles abroad, after being repeatedly killed and buried, *Lemon* stalks our Establishment Clause jurisprudence once again, frightening the little children and school attorneys."[9]

What was there about Warren Burger's eighteen-page opinion that produced such invective more than two decades later? The target of Justice Scalia's wrath was what has become known as the "Lemon test," from the rule the opinion dictated for determining whether a law or other official policy would survive an Establishment Clause challenge. The test had three parts. First, "the statute must have a secular legislative purpose." Second, "its principal or primary effect must be one that neither advances nor inhibits religion." And third, "the statute must not foster 'an excessive entanglement with religion.' "[10]

Chief Justice Burger behind his desk, 1971.

Purpose, effect, and entanglement: the law or policy had to pass all three tests; fail just one, and the Establishment Clause was held to be violated. Burger derived the three-part test from what he called "the cumulative criteria developed by the Court over many years . . . gleaned from our cases." [11] The opinion found that the Rhode Island and Pennsylvania programs violated the "entanglement" prong of the Lemon test because in practice they would require repeated financial appropriations and constant surveillance by government authorities to make sure that public money was kept apart from the schools' religious mission.

The chief justice also offered another caution that in retrospect appears unusually prescient, something he called "a broader base of entanglement of yet a different character." That was the laws' "potential for political divisiveness related to religious belief and practice." [12]

Burger explained that "partisans of parochial schools" would predictably make ever greater demands as costs rose and the need for infusions of public money grew. "Candidates will be forced to declare and voters to choose," he wrote. "It would be unrealistic to ignore the fact that many people confronted with issues of this kind will find their votes aligned with their faith." It was one thing, Burger continued, to uphold, as the court had done the previous year, tax exemptions for church property: that was a benefit that all religions could share. But "here we are confronted with successive and very likely permanent annual appropriations that benefit relatively few religious groups. Political fragmentation and divisiveness on religious lines are thus likely to be intensified."[13]

The words "Roman Catholic" were never uttered, but the court's meaning was clear: this case wasn't so much about religion in general as about special pleading by the Catholic Church to open the public treasury's spigots in the service of a particular religious mission. Virtually all non-Catholic children, after all, during those years went to public school. The Court unhesitatingly drew the line.

The landscape of parochial school education was changing, and the Burger Court's attitude would change with it. Beginning in the South and spreading to other parts of the country, conservative Protestant parents began to pull their children out of public school. The initial impetus for the creation of what came to be known as Christian academies was grounded in race and spurred by desegregation orders, particularly those that required busing. The Warren Court's school prayer decisions also played a part in turning non-Catholic religious conservatives against the public schools. Many of the new schools were unaffiliated with particular churches, their enrollment driven not by membership in one denomination or another but by revulsion against the secular tide.

Numbers tell the tale.[14] In the early 1960s, there were perhaps three hundred Christian academies. By the early 1980s, there were nearly eleven thousand, enrolling more than 900,000 children, nearly one fifth of all children who attended private schools. At the same time, enrollment in Catholic religious schools was shrinking. Between the mid-1960s and the mid-1980s, Catholic schools lost nearly half their enrollment (from 5.6 million in 1965 to three million in 1983). In 1984, for the first time, there were more Christian academies than Catholic parochial schools.

These trends had powerful political implications. When private school education was predominantly Catholic, public subsidies for private schools were firmly opposed by Protestants, including fundamentalists and evangelicals. But with the rise of the Christian school movement, conservative Protestants switched sides, joining Catholics in an alliance that would have been unimaginable only a decade or two earlier. Tax relief and publicly funded vouchers for religious school tuition were shared goals that began to make inroads in legislatures and, eventually, the courts.

The commitment of the Reagan administration to the evangelical movement became unmistakable when it attempted to halt the Internal Revenue Service's efforts to ensure that tax-exempt schools not discriminate based on race. During the Nixon administration, the IRS had begun to insist that private tax-exempt schools operate on a nondiscriminatory basis, but it treated a statement of a nondiscriminatory policy as sufficient to satisfy this requirement. In 1978 Jimmy Carter's IRS issued new rules insisting that schools actually admit and treat students equally without regard to their race. Evangelical activists and supporters of the Christian academies regarded this action as an outrageous intrusion of an all-powerful government into private religious affairs. One prominent conservative, Richard Viguerie, described the IRS effort as "the spark that ignited the Religious Right's involvement in real politics." [15] Bob Jones University, which was dedicated to "fundamentalist Christian beliefs" and expelled any students who engaged in "interracial dating or marriage," and Goldsboro Christian Schools, which had been formed in resistance to the *Brown* decision and refused to admit blacks based upon its interpretation of the Bible, challenged the IRS position in the courts. Although the IRS prevailed in the courts of appeals, the Reagan Justice Department disavowed the IRS position and refused to defend it in the Supreme Court. The Burger Court then appointed William Coleman, a prominent African American attorney, to argue on behalf of the IRS view. By an 8–1 vote, the Court upheld the IRS in *Bob Jones University v. United States*.[16] Warren Burger wrote the majority decision, ratifying the IRS interpretation of the income tax law and affirming that "not all burdens on religion are unconstitutional." [17] Accepting a religious justification for maintaining racially discriminatory schools was a step too far. William Rehnquist was the sole dissenter.

Unentangled

In the immediate shadow of *Lemon*, the court held unconstitutional a New York statute providing tax credits for tuition paid by parents of children enrolled in nonpublic schools.[18] The decision left open the question of whether states could provide tax deductions for certain nonpublic school expenses, and a conflict among the federal appellate circuits developed. In the 1982 term, the court accepted *Mueller v. Allen*,[19] a case from Minnesota, to resolve the conflict.

On its face, the Minnesota law was neutral as between public and nonpublic schools. Just as rich and poor could sleep under the same Parisian bridges, parents with children in any school in Minnesota were entitled to claim limited tax deductions for tuition and, among other expenses, the cost of art, music, and athletic supplies; pencils and notebooks; and materials for shop class and home economics. The parents of Minnesota's 820,000 public schoolchildren incurred relatively few of these expenses, while the parents of some 91,000 students in private school—95 percent of which were religious schools—incurred many. No matter, Justice Rehnquist wrote for the court; whatever "attenuated financial benefit" flowed to religious schools was "ultimately controlled by the private choices of individual parents." In any event, the opinion continued, "We would be loath to adopt a rule grounding the constitutionality of a facially neutral law on annual reports reciting the extent to which various classes of private citizens claimed benefits under the law."[20]

Facial neutrality and private choice: in Rehnquist's analysis, those key features both prevented the Minnesota law from falling victim to the entanglement prong of the Lemon test and also made clear that advancing religion was not the law's primary effect. As to the remaining prong, secular purpose, Rehnquist said, the purpose of the law was clear: "An educated populace is essential to the political and economic health of any community, and a State's efforts to assist parents in meeting the rising cost of educational expenses plainly serves this secular purpose of ensuring that the State's citizenry is well educated."[21]

Justices Marshall, Brennan, Blackmun, and Stevens dissented. There was "no significant difference," the dissenters said in an opinion by Marshall, between the New York tax credit law the court had struck down a decade earlier and the Minnesota law that it now upheld. The "only factual inquiry necessary" to both cases was "whether the deduction permitted for tuition expenses primarily benefits those who send their children to religious schools," and the answer in both cases was the same.[22] "There can be little doubt," Marshall concluded, that the state's purpose was to aid religious schools. "For the first time," he wrote, "the Court has upheld financial support for religious schools without any reason at all to assume that the support will be restricted to the secular functions of those schools and will not be used to support religious instruction."[23]

The dissenting opinion read as if the four justices were aware that they had lost a pivotal battle, as indeed they had. Facial neutrality and private choice were the twin watchwords of the court's emerging Establishment Clause jurisprudence. Still to come was the "school choice" movement, a campaign fueled by libertarian hostility toward public schools and their unionized workforce; reformers who sought the freedom to experiment with new approaches; and churches eager to offer their own financially struggling but often quite successful schools as an alternative worthy of public support.

"School choice" became an important part of the Republican Party agenda. As the movement crested nearly two decades after the Minnesota decision, a case from Ohio presented the court with the question whether the Establishment Clause permitted publicly financed vouchers that parents could use to pay tuition. An Ohio law set up a pilot voucher program for the Cleveland schools, offering parents up to $2,250 per year per child to spend for tuition at schools of their choice. By the time the case, *Zelman v. Simmons-Harris*, reached the Supreme Court in 2001, the program had been in operation for five years, and 96.6 percent of the vouchers were being used at religious schools.[24]

William Rehnquist, now chief justice, wrote the majority opinion. *Mueller v. Allen* provided the answer, he said, citing his own opinion from two decades earlier; as with the Minnesota tax-deduction program, the Ohio program was "one of true private choice." In *Mueller*, he noted, the court had "found it irrelevant to the constitutional inquiry that the vast majority of beneficiaries were parents of children in religious schools."[25] Facial neutrality and private choice.

Those words, Justice David Souter wrote in dissent, were "nothing but examples of verbal formalism."[26] Joined by Justices John Paul Stevens, Ruth Bader Ginsburg, and Stephen Breyer, Souter went on to say that "every objective underlying the prohibition of religious establishment is betrayed by this scheme." [27] The decision was, he concluded, a "dramatic departure from basic Establishment Clause principle." [28] Was the angry accusation accurate? That depends on the starting point, on *which* Establishment Clause, which principle, Justice Souter had in mind. If it was only the Lemon test itself, then the answer is probably yes, the Cleveland voucher case can only be seen as a substantial departure. But *Mueller v. Allen* marked a different path, one that a future court chose to follow, one that today's Supreme Court is following still.

Religion on Display

Lemon v. Kurtzman remains the law; despite constant criticism and against all expectations, the court has never overruled it. It hasn't had to. Decades of justices have paid passing homage to the precedent as they move quickly past it to their desired destination. One such justice, ironically, was Warren Burger himself, writing for the court in a 1984 decision that a municipal Christmas holiday display that included a Nativity scene did not violate the Establishment Clause.

The case was *Lynch v. Donnelly*,[29] a colorful, seemingly rather trivial case that nonetheless caught the temper of the times and pointed the way toward future developments in Establishment Clause doctrine. It was an appeal by Mayor Dennis M. Lynch of Pawtucket, Rhode Island, from a ruling by the U.S. Court of Appeals for the First Circuit that the display the city for decades had installed in a downtown park was unconstitutional. There were colored lights, giant candy canes, reindeer and a sleigh, a Christmas tree, a big banner reading "Seasons Greetings," and the element at issue in a lawsuit brought by the American Civil Liberties Union: a city-owned life-sized Nativity scene.

Could the citizens of Pawtucket have been able to enjoy the holiday without the display's one overtly religious feature? Most likely, but as the controversy made its way to the Supreme Court, it was clear that the inclusion of the crèche had a powerful social as well as religious meaning. At trial, Mayor Lynch had observed that the effort to eliminate the scene "is a step toward establishing another religion, non-religion that it may be." Letters from Pawtucket residents introduced at trial congratulated the mayor on his effort "to keep Christ in Christmas."[30]

The author of *Lemon v. Kurtzman* could hardly ignore that precedent. But in Burger's hands, what had been a set of rules now appeared to be merely an array of options. "In the line-drawing process" that the Establishment Clause calls for, he wrote in the majority opinion in the Pawtucket crèche case, "we have often found it useful to inquire whether the challenged law or conduct has a secular purpose, whether its principal or primary effect is to advance or inhibit religion, and whether it creates an excessive entanglement of government with religion."[31]

And what was the secular purpose of a scene re-creating the birth of Jesus? "The crèche in the display depicts the historical origins of this traditional event long recognized as a National Holiday," Burger explained. "The display is sponsored by the city to celebrate the Holiday and to depict the origins of that Holiday. There are legitimate secular purposes."[32]

And the primary effect was not to advance religion, no more so than "the exhibition of literally hundreds of religious paintings in governmentally supported museums."[33]

Burger then arrived at *Lemon*'s entanglement prong. The plaintiffs had argued unsuccessfully in the appeals court that the political divisiveness the display was causing was creating entanglement between religion and government. Burger made short work of the argument. He noted that the crèche had been displayed for forty years. "A litigant cannot, by the very act of commencing a lawsuit," he wrote, "create the appearance of divisiveness and then exploit it as evidence of entanglement."[34]

While paying lip service to the Lemon test, Burger was a good deal more generous in his references to the Douglas opinion from 1952 with which this chapter began, *Zorach v. Clauson*. The Constitution "affirmatively mandates accommodation, not merely tolerance, of all religions, and forbids hostility to any," Burger wrote, citing *Zorach*.[35] And again:

> Congress has directed the President to proclaim a National Day of Prayer each year. . . . Our Presidents have repeatedly issued such Proclamations. Presidential Proclamations and messages have also issued to commemorate Jewish Heritage Week . . . and the Jewish High Holy Days. . . . One cannot look at even this brief resume without finding

that our history is pervaded by expressions of religious beliefs such as are found in *Zorach*. Equally pervasive is the evidence of accommodation of all faiths and all forms of religious expression, and hostility toward none. Through this accommodation, as Justice Douglas observed, governmental action has "followed the best of our traditions" and "respected the religious nature of our people."[36]

A religious display for a religious people: the vote was 5–4. The most important opinion in the Pawtucket case was not Burger's, but a concurring opinion by the newest justice, Sandra Day O'Connor. O'Connor was then in her third term on the court, where she would remain until early 2006, nearly twenty years after Burger's retirement. As mentioned earlier, unlike any other justice with whom she served, O'Connor had run for and won elective office; before becoming a judge on Arizona's intermediate appellate court, she was majority leader of the Arizona State Senate. Formal doctrine held little appeal for her. Rather, as she had done in her political career, she looked for workable solutions to the intractable problems that constitutional controversies presented to the court.

In her separate opinion in *Lynch v. Donnelly*, O'Connor dismissed the three-part inquiry of the Lemon test as a needless distraction. There was really only one question in the case, she wrote: "whether Pawtucket has endorsed Christianity by its display of the crèche."[37] What was crucial to the Establishment Clause inquiry, she continued, was that "a government practice not have the effect of communicating a message of government endorsement or disapproval of religion." From this perspective, the Establishment Clause was really about keeping the government from using religion to send a message of exclusion. "It is only practices having that effect, whether intentionally or unintentionally, that make religion relevant, in reality or public perception, to status in the political community."[38]

The Pawtucket display did not send a message of exclusion, O'Connor concluded. While the crèche itself was "an unarguably religious symbol," its inclusion along with Santa, the reindeer, and the candy canes was simply meant as a "celebration of the public holiday through its traditional symbols" rather than endorsing Christian beliefs.[39] O'Connor's "endorsement test" was to take its place alongside the Lemon test. She continued to employ it for the duration of her Supreme Court tenure, and because she often held the balance of power on a closely divided court, her view of what constituted endorsement more often than not became the law of the land.[40]

Justice Brennan's vigorous dissenting opinion in *Lynch v. Donnelly* was joined by Justices Marshall, Blackmun, and Stevens. The crèche, the court's only Catholic justice wrote, was "best understood as a mystical re-creation of an event that lies at the heart of the Christian faith." Brennan continued: "To suggest, as the Court does, that such a symbol is merely 'traditional' and therefore no different from Santa's house or reindeer is not only offensive to those for whom the crèche has profound significance, but insulting to those who insist for religious or personal reasons that the story of Christ is in no sense a part of 'history' nor an unavoidable element of our national 'heritage.' "[41]

In deciding the Pawtucket case, the justices had to know that this was no local dispute, but rather one with national dimensions. The case marked the Reagan administration's entry at the Supreme Court level into the culture wars surrounding the role of religion in the country's public life. The administration's solicitor general, Rex Lee, filed a brief supporting Pawtucket's mayor and received permission from the court to present oral argument. Whenever the federal government enters a Supreme Court case in which the government is not an actual party, it must identify the "interest of the United States" in the front section of the brief. The government's interest in this case was "deep and abiding," the solicitor general told the court. "The federal government has, from the earliest days of the Republic to the present, felt free to acknowledge and recognize that religion is a part of our heritage and should continue to be an element in our public life and public occasions."[42] It was a sentiment that had the Burger Court's blessing.[43]

A Model Minority

Establishment Clause cases ask whether the government has gone too far to accommodate religion. Free Exercise Clause cases ask the opposite: whether the government has gone far enough. The Burger Court plunged quickly into Free Exercise doctrine and established the court's high water mark early, in Warren Burger's second term. That case, *Wisconsin v. Yoder*,[44] decided by a vote of 6–1 on May 15, 1972, is one of the best known decisions in the modern Free Exercise canon. (Powell and Rehnquist, who had not yet joined the court when the case was argued, did not participate.) It is also one of the strangest and, in its posture of extreme deference toward believers' claim to favored treatment, one of the most problematic.

The three plaintiffs were members of the Old Order Amish community in New Glarus, Wisconsin. They pulled their children out of public school at the end of eighth grade, as they said their religion demanded, and were convicted of violating Wisconsin's compulsory education law, which requires school attendance until the age of sixteen. The state didn't require public school attendance; the Amish could have set up their own parochial high school as long as it provided a "substantially equivalent education." The Amish community refused this option, insisting that their religion prohibited exposure to secular education beyond the basics necessary to be a successful worker of the land.

As a community, the Amish were extremely reluctant to turn to the courts, and most likely would not have done so; the three fathers would have paid the $5 fine that the judge who presided over their trial assessed each man as a "symbolic penalty." But their cause resonated with a network of politically and religiously conservative individuals and groups that saw in the Amish struggle to maintain religious integrity a perfect test case with which to challenge public school hegemony and, more broadly, government's refusal to accommodate the needs of devout citizens. An organization called the National Committee for Amish Religious Freedom, led by a Lutheran minister from Michigan and including no Amish people, took up the cause. It funded the litigation, propelling the case of Jonas Yoder and his neighbors through the Wisconsin state courts.[45]

As the lawyer for the Amish, the committee recruited William Bentley Ball, a Pennsylvania lawyer who was prominent in Catholic legal circles and was known for his advocacy of state aid to parochial schools. In published articles, he had written that religiously observant families had a constitutional right to send their children to religious schools at public expense because the public schools themselves taught the doctrine of "secular humanism."

The Amish lost at trial, but won in the Wisconsin Supreme Court. The state appealed to the U.S. Supreme Court in March 1971. The litigation committee knew that it was in a long-range battle not only for the minds of the justices, but the hearts of the public. While the Supreme Court case was pending, the committee issued a press release with this headline: "U.S. Supreme Court Case: Is There Religious Freedom in America—for the Amish?"[46] The press release proceeded to lay out the case:

> The "crime" of the Amish people today is that they are dissenting from an education that is increasingly technical, secular and materialistic. . . . The larger society socializes young people in a culture that stresses competitiveness, emphasizing the materialistic, pecuniary, highly technical pursuits in a teenage atmosphere of fast cars, rock music and Hot Pants. While the Amish are taught by their elders a different set of attitudes and religious values—like slowness of pace, peace, love of hard work, democratic cooperativeness, and close-to-the-soil living.

William Bentley Ball's brief to the court likewise stressed the beauties of a culture based on obedience to parents and adherence to an old way of life.

> The Amish are emphatically in favor of education—but an "education for life" as seen in terms of their religious view as to how life should be lived and as to the single goal of life which is union with God. . . . Amish education has followed the pattern of classical *wisdom* rather than *technos*. It has emphasized the moral wisdom of producing good men, rather than the technical, which can produce the competent barbarian, the intellectual rioter, the revolutionist, and the criminal.[47]

This was quite a stretch; in fact, as Justice Douglas was to note in his solitary dissenting opinion, as many as half of Old Order Amish children defected from the faith and went out to try to make their way in the world with their truncated educations.[48] But Warren Burger was enraptured. As we have seen, the new chief justice was deeply distressed by what he saw as the moral decay of modern society. Here, indeed, was a model minority, good people doing harm to no one and seeking only to inoculate their children against the very trends that were wrecking other American families.

Burger took the case for himself. His opinion picked up the entire Amish narrative. He praised the Amish for their "excellent record as law-abiding and generally self-sufficient members of society. . . . They reject public welfare in any of its usual modern forms."[49] He added that the undisputed trial record showed that this particular Amish group "had never been known to commit crimes, that none had been known to receive public assistance, and that none were unemployed."[50] They exhibited "qualities of reliability, self-reliance, and dedication to work. . . . Indeed, the Amish communities singularly parallel and reflect many of the virtues of Jefferson's ideal of the 'sturdy yeoman' who would form the basis of what he considered as the ideal of a democratic society."[51]

As Burger framed the analysis, the Free Exercise claim had to be balanced against the state's interest in the universal application of its law; "only those interests of the highest order and those not otherwise served can overbalance legitimate claims to the free exercise of religion."[52] This was the "compelling interest test" of "strict scrutiny" that was to appear and disappear in the coming years. Burger then proceeded to do the necessary balancing. The state's compulsory education law, he concluded, was "undeniably at odds with fundamental tenets" of the Amish religion, presenting "precisely the kind of objective danger to the free exercise of religion that the First Amendment was designed to prevent."

By contrast, the state's interest in applying its law to this particular group was weak, "somewhat less substantial than requiring such attendance for children generally." What was the basis for excepting the Amish from the rules applicable to "children generally"? In Burger's view, one rationale for compulsory education laws was to prevent young children from being conscripted into the workforce. But in leaving school at fourteen, Amish children weren't sent to work in factories but remained in safety on the family farm under parental supervision. Such an arrangement, Burger noted, was "an ancient tradition."[53]

Absent from this paean to the Amish way of life, as Douglas observed in dissent, was consideration of the rights of the children involved. But "the children are not parties to this litigation," Burger wrote, adding that "this case involves the fundamental interest of parents, as contrasted with that of the State, to guide the religious future and education of their children."[54] Nor did the opinion evince any awareness of the fact that the Amish community itself had been at best a reluctant participant in the legal battle waged by others in pursuit of bigger game, although controversy over the role of the National Committee for Amish Religious Freedom had been fairly widely reported.[55]

Clearly, the *Yoder* case was an artifact of a particular moment, its extreme claim clothed in a package that the young Burger Court found irresistible.[56] It serves as a reminder of how malleable the Supreme Court's religion cases, occupying some of the most contested ground in American society, have always been: less doctrine than visceral responses and barely concealed policy judgments. The facts of *Yoder* wrenched the court into a posture of great deference to religious claims against government regulation. It was a posture that the Court couldn't sustain. But neither was it one from which the Court could fully free itself.

Correcting Course

The same Old Order Amish were before the Supreme Court again almost exactly ten years later in *United States v. Lee*.[57] An Amish employer objected to withholding and paying the quarterly Social Security and federal unemployment taxes on the salaries he paid to the Amish men who worked for him at his carpentry shop and farm in Pennsylvania. He claimed that because the Amish were obliged by their religion to provide for one another and to refrain from accepting public assistance, it would be a sin for him to pay the taxes or for his employees to accept the benefits. His lawyer, not surprisingly, based the argument on *Wisconsin v. Yoder*, and on that basis prevailed in federal district court in Pittsburgh.[58]

The Supreme Court accepted the government's direct appeal from the district court, and Burger again assigned the opinion to himself. The decision was a unanimous victory for the government. "Not all burdens on religion are unconstitutional," Burger began.[59] "To maintain an organized society that guarantees religious freedom to a great variety of faiths requires that some religious practices yield to the common good.

Religious beliefs can be accommodated, but there is a point at which accommodation would 'radically restrict the operating latitude of the legislature.' "[60] The quotation was from a Warren Court decision that refused to excuse a group of Orthodox Jewish merchants, whose religion forbade doing business on Saturday, from having to obey the Sunday-closing laws that were common at the time.[61]

Burger wrote that it would be "difficult, if not impossible" to administer a national social security or tax system if people were permitted to opt out for religious reasons. "The tax system could not function if denominations were allowed to challenge the tax system because tax payments were spent in a manner that violates their religious belief." He went further: "When followers of a particular sect enter into commercial activity as a matter of choice, the limits they accept on their own conduct as a matter of conscience and faith are not to be superimposed on the statutory schemes which are binding on others in that activity. Granting an exemption from social security taxes to an employer operates to impose the employer's religious faith on the employees."[62]

This is a striking statement read in light of the Supreme Court's 2014 *Hobby Lobby* decision, which exempted—on statutory rather than constitutional grounds—a religiously observant employer of thousands of workers in a commercial retail empire from having to provide contraception coverage as part of its employee health insurance plan.[63] The employer argued that obeying the law would make him complicit in what he regarded as the employees' sin.

In granting the exemption to Hobby Lobby, the Roberts Court had to take account of *United States v. Lee*. It did so by confining *Lee* to its specific context. "Our holding in *Lee* turned primarily on the special problems associated with a national system of taxation," Justice Samuel A. Alito Jr. wrote for the 5–4 majority.[64] The Roberts Court, which Alito joined in 2006, contains no holdovers from the time of *Lee* (let alone *Yoder*). It is a very different court, clearly in pursuit of an agenda, although by the narrowest of margins, to reanimate the Free Exercise Clause—more evidence of the contingency of the court's approach to the religion clauses.[65]

In *Lee* itself, Burger had to say something about *Yoder*, since the two cases, a decade apart, both addressed claims by the Amish and yet looked in such opposite directions. He said as little as possible, only that "unlike the situation presented in *Wisconsin v. Yoder*, it would be difficult to accommodate the comprehensive social security system with myriad exemptions flowing from a wide variety of religious beliefs." [66] This didn't satisfy Justice John Paul Stevens, who, while concurring in the judgment, characteristically took a very different view of the issues at the heart of the case. "The Court's attempt to distinguish *Yoder* is unconvincing because precisely the same religious interest is implicated in both cases," Stevens wrote, "and Wisconsin's interest in requiring its children to attend school until they reach the age of 16 is surely not inferior to the federal interest in collecting these social security taxes." [67]

Stevens had not been on the Supreme Court at the time of *Yoder*. In a tenure of thirty-four years, through the Rehnquist Court and the first five years of the Roberts Court, he was the justice most skeptical of Free Exercise claims and most likely to see an Establishment Clause problem with a law that could be seen as favoring religion. In his concurrence in *Lee*, Stevens wrote that in that case as well as in *Yoder*, the court had mistakenly given the government the burden of justifying its refusal to grant a religion-based exemption. Instead, he argued, "it is the objector who must shoulder the burden of demonstrating that there is a unique reason for allowing him a special exemption from a valid law of general applicability." [68] Stevens concluded that the court had reached the right result in *Lee*, but with the wrong reasoning. His opinion underscored a point that might otherwise have been obscured by the decision's outcome: that while the Amish lost their case, religion had not really lost its favored place in the Burger Court.

Scylla Meets Charybdis

That was clear from a case the court had decided in favor of a Jehovah's Witness less than a year earlier. Burger wrote the opinion for an 8–1 court in *Thomas v. Review Board of the Indiana Employment Security Division*,[69] decided in April 1981. The plaintiff left his job at a steel factory when his department was closed, and he was reassigned to a department that made gun turrets. He filed for unemployment insurance, claiming that his religious beliefs prevented him from performing such work. The Indiana unemployment office denied his claim, and he lost in the Indiana Supreme Court. That court held that to award benefits to a claimant who left a job voluntarily for religious reasons, while denying benefits to those who left voluntarily for all other reasons, would amount to an official religious preference in violation of the Establishment Clause.[70]

In his opinion overturning the state court decision, Burger invoked the compelling interest test from *Yoder.* "The state may justify an inroad on religious liberty by showing that it is the least restrictive means of achieving some compelling state interest," he wrote, adding that the state had offered no such interests in this case.[71] On the Establishment Clause, Burger had almost nothing to say. He simply cited a Warren Court decision, *Sherbert v. Verner,*[72] which had upheld the right of a Seventh Day Adventist to receive unemployment benefits after losing her job for refusing to work on Saturday. That the plaintiff in the earlier case had been forced to leave her job, while the plaintiff in the new case left voluntarily, made no difference.

The decision provoked a solitary dissent from William Rehnquist. The court "adds mud to the already muddied waters of First Amendment jurisprudence," Rehnquist began; *Sherbert v. Verner* was wrongly decided and *Thomas* now compounded the error.[73] "Where, as here, a State has enacted a general statute, the purpose and effect of which is to advance the State's secular goals, the Free Exercise Clause does not in my view require the State to conform that statute to the dictates of religious conscience of any group."[74]

Rehnquist said that if Indiana had actually legislated a religious exemption, such a law would "plainly" fail the Lemon test and be held to violate the Establishment Clause. And yet the Court had given the plaintiff a Free Exercise pass. The tension between the two religion clauses was obvious, but not inevitable; the problem lay in "our overly expansive interpretation of *both* Clauses," Rehnquist argued. "By broadly construing both Clauses, the Court has constantly narrowed the channel between the Scylla and Charybdis through which any state or federal action must pass in order to survive constitutional scrutiny."

Rehnquist was true to his principles, rarely finding a violation of either clause. Two years after his *Thomas* dissent, he would lead a closely divided court in narrowing the Establishment Clause in the Minnesota tax deduction case, *Mueller v. Allen*.[75] But it isn't necessary to agree with him on the merits to see the validity of his complaint—a fitting coda to this chapter.

PART FOUR

Business

On August 23, 1971—a mere two months before Richard Nixon nominated him to become a Supreme Court justice—Lewis Powell delivered a thirty-three-page "confidential" memorandum to the U.S. Chamber of Commerce, which describes itself as the "world's largest business organization." The memorandum was written at the request of Powell's longtime Richmond friend Eugene B. Sydnor, Jr., the head of the Southern Department Stores chain, after he and Powell, in Sydnor's words, "had discussed on a number of occasions the need for American businessmen . . . to wake up and tell their story and that of the free enterprise system in a clear and forceful fashion."[1] Sydnor and his business colleagues were concerned that business had not been effective in Congress or the courts and was under attack from the media and liberal college professors. Having been a president of the American Bar Association, Powell seemed to Sydnor a natural choice for this task.

In this memorandum, Powell described what he saw as the contemporary challenges to the American business and free enterprise system, and he detailed his recommendations for the Chamber to respond aggressively in the courts, in Congress, on college campuses, in think tanks, and in the media. Powell's memorandum is an extraordinary document, a bizarre hybrid—a product of his careful, analytic, lawyer's mind and an angry screed, something that sounds to today's ear more like Rush Limbaugh than Lewis Powell. The FBI failed to discover the memorandum during Powell's nomination process, so it was not available to the Senate while considering his appointment to the Court. It came to light, according to Mr. Sydnor, through an unauthorized disclosure by a member of the Chamber's staff to Jack Anderson, a widely read, Pulitzer Prize–winning muckraker, whose column, *The Washington Merry-Go-Round*, was syndicated nationally to more than one thousand newspapers with forty million readers.[2] In September and October 1972, Anderson devoted all or part of three *Washington Post* columns to Powell's memorandum.[3]

Powell's memorandum described Ralph Nader, Charles Reich, Herbert Marcuse, and others as seeking the destruction of the "American economic system." "What now concerns us," Powell said, "is quite new in the history of America. We are not dealing with sporadic or isolated attacks from a relatively few extremists or even from the minority socialist cadre. . . . The most disquieting voices joining the chorus of criticism," he continued, "come from perfectly reputable elements of society: from the college campuses, the pulpit, the media, the intellectual and literary journals, the arts and sciences, and from politicians."[4] Powell criticized the media for referring to business tax incentives "as 'tax breaks,' 'loopholes,' or 'tax benefits' *for the benefit of business.*"[5] He called for a massive response to such attacks by business interests, which he said had responded so far "by appeasement, ineptitude and ignoring the problem." Powell predicted that implementing his recommendations would require "a long road and [is] not . . . for the fainthearted." He outlined a multifaceted proposal for responses by the Chamber, including actions such as recruiting a "staff of highly qualified scholars who believe in the system" to "evaluate social science textbooks, especially in political science and sociology." He also advocated aggressive business actions in secondary education, television and other media, legislatures, and the courts.

"The judiciary," Powell said, "may be the most important instrument for social, economic, and political change." "Labor unions, civil rights groups and now the public interest law firms," he continued, "are extremely active in the judicial arena. Their success, often at businesses' expense, has not been inconsequential." He then described participation in litigation as "a vast area of opportunity for the Chamber, if it is willing to undertake the role of spokesman for American business and, in turn, if business is willing to provide the funds."[6]

Justice Potter Stewart (left) and Lewis F. Powell, Jr., not yet a justice, in St. Louis at the American Bar Association's annual meeting, August 1970.

After Jack Anderson published excerpts from Powell's memorandum, the Chamber made it available to anyone who asked. Anderson characterized Powell's memo as "so militant that it raises a question about his fitness to decide any case involving business interests."[7] This was surely excessive. But the importance of Powell's memorandum is unmistakable. Within six years, the Chamber established a litigation arm—the National Chamber Litigation Center. Following Powell's advice, the Chamber now routinely and regularly files friend-of-the-court briefs in any important cases involving business interests, and it enjoys great influence over which cases the Court decides to hear and how the cases the Court takes should be decided. Bloomberg News says that the Chamber now "may be second only to the Solicitor General's office in its influence at the Supreme Court."[8]

In the political arena, business had suffered serious legislative setbacks in the early 1970s, having been outmaneuvered by labor unions, consumer advocacy organizations, and environmentalists. Business interests were also damaged by revelations of illegal corporate contributions to Richard Nixon's 1972 reelection campaign. As we shall soon see, however, Congress's efforts to tighten business-related campaign contributions and. to limit campaign spending cratered in the Burger Court. After that, the business community became far more active, better coordinated, and much more influential in the legislative process.

Between 1976 and 1995, almost twice as many conservative Washington think tanks as liberal ones were created. They are now, with a couple of exceptions, better funded than their older liberal counterparts. The most influential of these is the Heritage Foundation, founded in 1973, which routinely takes pro-business positions. Likewise, conservative, pro-business funding of university research, particularly in areas like law and economics, increased dramatically beginning in the 1970s.[9] Lewis Powell's 1973 suggestions have become today's reality.

———

Unlike the Warren Court, the Burger Court was a pro-business Court, as were its successors, under Chief Justices Rehnquist and Roberts. The Burger Court decided hundreds of cases involving business interests, far more than we will attempt to address here. Some had enduring and momentous effects. Warren Burger's time heading the Court, for example, spanned a period of remarkable technological innovation, including the personal computer, in vitro fertilization, and recombinant DNA. In 1980, by a 5–4 vote, the Court upheld the claim of Ananda M. Chakrabarty, a biochemist, who applied for a patent on a living organism—a bacterium that he had biologically engineered to eat crude oil.[10] Of the nearly four million patents that had been awarded by that time, only one—given in 1873 to Louis Pasteur for a purified yeast—had been awarded for a viral creature.[11] Chief Justice Burger wrote the majority opinion himself. He agreed with Thomas Jefferson, the patent law's original author, who had insisted that "ingenuity should receive a liberal encouragement," and dismissed the fears of "grave risks" from genetic engineering, asserting that no matter what the law said, genetic research and development were going to press ahead. Burger said that neither the Supreme Court nor Congress could "deter the scientific mind from probing into the unknown."[12] The Court's landmark *Chakrabarty* decision opened the way to the patenting of genetically engineered corn, and soon thereafter to a patent for Harvard's "oncomouse," a genetically modified mouse used for cancer research. By allowing Chakrabarty's patent, the Burger Court played a crucial role in opening the door to patenting genetically engineered plants and animals, and in so doing, facilitated the success of the nascent biotechnology industry.[13] Controversies over patenting genetic modifications continue to be hotly contested in the Supreme Court.[14]

In 1981, in *Diamond v. Diehr* (a controversy over a computerized process for curing rubber), the Burger Court, by a 5–4 vote, ratified patents for certain aspects of computer programs.[15] That case ended the hostility of courts toward computer software patents, and was subsequently extended in the lower courts to allow software patents.[16] By allowing patents, which offer greater protection for intellectual property than copyright law, the Court "shaped intellectual property protection in an entire . . . industry."[17]

The Burger Court also decided the most famous of all copyright cases, permitting as "fair use" the private copying of television programs.[18] This case involved a titanic battle between Sony Corporation, which had created Betamax, a now archaic video taping machine, and Universal and Disney Studios, who argued that videotaping television programs violated their copyrights.[19] That case, which produced a hotly contested dispute between Justices Blackmun and Stevens and ultimately led to a rather muddled 5–4 decision, protected the economic viability of technological advances, such as DVRs, that we now take for granted. Over time, prerecorded videocassettes and DVDs came to produce greater revenues for both Universal and Disney than movie theater ticket sales, demonstrating the shortsightedness of an industry trying to halt a technological change that ultimately produced an economic bonanza.

Patents and copyright, of course, were not the only areas for contests over businesses' rights and practices. In 1972, for example, the Court upheld a defense by Major League Baseball of its long-standing exemption from the antitrust laws in response to a challenge by Curt Flood, a star outfielder for the St. Louis Cardinals, who was resisting a trade without his consent to the Philadelphia Phillies.[20] The five-vote majority opinion by Harry Blackmun—which contains a lengthy tribute to baseball history, including Blackmun's list of eighty-three of baseball's greats along with quotes from "Casey at the Bat"—questioned the ongoing basis for baseball's antitrust exemption, describing it as an "anomaly."[21] Blackmun subsequently acknowledged that some of his colleagues viewed his opinion as "beneath the dignity of the Court," but he said, "I would do it over again because I think baseball deserved it."[22] More importantly, Flood's challenge inspired the National Labor Relations Board to conclude that, notwithstanding its antitrust exemption, baseball's reserve system was subject to the nation's labor laws. In December 1975, a labor arbitrator, Peter Seitz, concluded that after a year of playing without signing a contract, players could become free agents. That ruling and Mr. Seitz's power to issue it survived challenges by baseball team owners in the federal courts.[23] Free agency transformed the sport. In 1998, President Clinton signed the Curt Flood Act, subjecting baseball's employment practices to antitrust law.

So from baseball to biotech, the Burger Court played a crucial role in the modernization of American business. This is one, but only one, reason the Burger Court has often been characterized as pro-business. We could easily devote another book to that bailiwick. Here, however, we examine only two areas. First, in Chapter 10, we describe how the Burger Court dramatically expanded the First Amendment speech rights of business corporations, both in the commercial and political contexts, an area where the Court's decisions continue to have far-reaching implications. Second, the Burger Court era—from 1969 to 1986—was a period of dramatic decline in the membership and influence of labor unions. In Chapter 11 we take up the key role that the Burger Court's labor and employment discrimination decisions played in helping to drive a wedge between unions and civil rights advocates—two key components of the Democrats' political coalition.

CHAPTER 10

Corporations Are People Too

We saw in Chapter 8 how the upheaval in societal mores, particularly the nation's newfound tolerance for profanity and sexually explicit material, influenced the Burger Court to revise the contours of the First Amendment's protections for free speech. There, the American people forced the Court to accept, and in some cases even endorse, massive shifts in public opinion and conduct. Now, in sharp contrast, we examine a pervasive expansion of First Amendment protections for speech by businesses, an expansion that emanated from inside the Court's chambers, overruled long-standing precedent, and led the Court to strike down state and federal laws. Here, the ideological commitments of the justices, rather than any public or political movement, forced a transformation of constitutional doctrine. In wreaking these changes, the Burger Court had a profound effect on our everyday life.

Creating Constitutional Protection for Advertising

If you are someone who, while watching a televised sporting event with a ten-year-old son or daughter, has awkwardly had to answer the question "What is erectile dysfunction?" you may hold the Burger Court responsible. Responsible also for the numerous commercials that send countless Americans to their doctors insisting on expensive prescription drugs, such as that little "purple pill" or one for an ailment, like "restless leg syndrome," that surely would not have come to mind without all the drug ads on television. Why, you might ask, with rising health care costs at the center of our national debate about the growth in federal spending, doesn't Congress just stop the ubiquitous prescription drug advertising? Because, you may be surprised to learn, prescription drug advertising, indeed virtually all advertising, is constitutionally protected free speech. It wasn't always so.

For nearly two centuries—until 1976—the Supreme Court had ignored or rejected efforts to extend First Amendment protections to advertisements for products—to what it called "commercial speech." In contrast, advertising concerning issues of public policy or of societal import, along with news stories and published evaluations of consumer products, had long enjoyed protection under the First Amendment. The Court viewed ordinary business advertising—advertising that does no more than solicit the purchase or sale of goods or services—as outside the scope of the First Amendment's guarantee of free speech.

Indeed, the federal and state governments had long regulated commercial advertising, generally prohibiting misleading advertisements and, in the case of certain products, such as food, cigarettes, alcohol, and automobiles, requiring disclosure of specific information, such as warnings and specified product information. Likewise, federal and state laws have long prohibited advertising in certain media of harmful products, such as cigarettes, and banned advertising of illegal products. Commercial speech has been regulated by federal and state commercial law, antitrust law, labor law, health and safety laws, and food and drug laws, to mention only a handful of prominent examples. Until the 1970s, the constitutionality of such laws was taken for granted.

In the 1942 case *Valentine v. Chrestensen*,[1] the Court made clear that the First Amendment does not protect commercial speech. F. J. Chrestensen, a Floridian, had purchased a former U.S. Navy submarine, brought it to New York, moored it at an East River pier, and sought to attract visitors who would pay an admission fee. To promote this endeavor, he attempted to distribute on New York's city streets handbills advertising visits to his vessel, but he was prohibited from doing so by a city "sanitary" ordinance forbidding distribution in the streets of "commercial and business advertising matter." After being told that the ordinance did not apply to "information or a public protest," Chrestensen revised the flip side of his handbill to protest the city's refusal to provide him wharfage facilities at a city pier. The police then told him that he could distribute the protest only, but not the double-sided handbill containing the advertising.

In a brief opinion, issued only two weeks after oral argument, the Court upheld the city. Writing for a unanimous Court, Justice Owen Roberts made clear that, absent the commercial advertising, the First Amendment would have restricted the city's ability to regulate the handbill's dissemination "in these public thoroughfares." But, Roberts said, "we are equally clear that the Constitution imposes no such restraint on government as respects purely commercial advertising."[2] Regulations of commercial activity, Justice Roberts said, "are matters for legislative judgment." Roberts's opinion conceded that difficult cases might arise raising questions about the extent to which advertisements are for the "public interest" rather than for "private profit," but in this case, he said, "the affixing of the protest against official conduct" was for the purpose of evading the ordinance. To allow that, he concluded, would allow "every merchant . . . to achieve immunity from the law's command."[3]

During the next thirty years, issues emerged that tested the boundary between public advocacy and commercial speech, most notably in the 1969 case *New York Times v. Sullivan*,[4] where the Court upheld—as *political* speech protected by the First Amendment—a newspaper advertisement soliciting funds to defend Martin Luther King against libel charges (and containing some inaccurate allegations of misconduct by the Montgomery, Alabama, police force headed by L. B. Sullivan). The fact that this solicitation was contained in an advertisement in a for-profit newspaper did not transform it into unprotected commercial speech.

The exclusion of commercial speech from the purview of the First Amendment ended in a 1976 challenge to a Virginia statute that prohibited pharmacists from advertising the prices of prescription drugs.[5] A year earlier, an opinion by Harry Blackmun heralded the coming change in the constitutional status of commercial speech. In that case, the Court, by a 7–2 vote, reversed a misdemeanor conviction—under a Virginia statute barring any publication, advertisement, lecture, or in any other manner encouraging or prompting "the procuring of abortion"—of Jeffrey Bigelow, the managing editor of a Virginia weekly newspaper.[6] Bigelow's newspaper had published an advertisement for legal, low-cost abortions in the state of New York. (The New York legislature, three years before *Roe*, had legalized abortions in the state for both in-state and out-of-state residents.) The Virginia Supreme Court had upheld Bigelow's conviction prior to the Court's decision in *Roe v. Wade*, after which the U.S. Supreme Court returned the case to the Virginia court for reconsideration. The Virginia court then reaffirmed its earlier decision, stating that a "commercial advertisement" such as this "may be constitutionally prohibited by the state," and pointing out that neither *Roe* (nor its companion case, *Doe v. Bolton*) had "mentioned the subject of abortion advertising."

In reversing Bigelow's conviction, the Court reaffirmed its previous cases that had made clear that speech protected under the First Amendment does not lose that protection simply by being contained in a paid advertisement. Blackmun was, unsurprisingly, sympathetic to an advertiser of legal abortions, and in his notes before the oral argument, he described the case as "easy," saying: "commercial speech is not *per se* more lowly than other forms." Blackmun added that he would vote to reverse and do so on a "little broader base than the absolute minimum we could get away with here." In his majority opinion, Justice Blackmun wrote that "the advertisement conveyed information of potential interest and value to a diverse audience—not only to readers possibly in need of the services offered, but also to those with a general curiosity about, or genuine interest in, the subject matter or the law of another state and its development, and to readers seeking reform in Virginia."[7] Blackmun also pointed out that "in this case, Bigelow's First Amendment interests coincided with the constitutional interests of the general public."[8] Chrestensen's submarine case was distinguished.

William Rehnquist (joined by White) dissented, emphasizing his difficulty in distinguishing Bigelow's ad from any other commercial advertising, including that in *Chrestensen*. Rehnquist regarded Virginia's law as a reasonable regulation that should be upheld in light of the state's legitimate interest in preventing "commercial exploitation of those women who elect to have an abortion." Chief Justice Burger, in a note to Blackmun of December 30, 1974, marked "personal," expressed "grave second thoughts on this case after more study and reflection" and said he was considering a vote to affirm the advertiser's conviction, but ultimately Burger put aside his doubts and joined Blackmun's opinion.

Given its link to *Roe*, including similar authorship, it was natural to read *Bigelow* as a decision more about access to information about abortions than commercial advertising. A year later, however, the *Bigelow* decision was extended far beyond its context of advertising legal abortions. Again, Blackmun wrote the majority opinion, treating *Bigelow* as a precedent for constitutional protection of "pure" commercial advertising. It was hardly the first time that a Supreme Court opinion addressing a limited dispute in one context was unexpectedly applied in quite different circumstances.

This case, *Virginia State Board of Pharmacy v. Virginia Citizens Consumer Council*, confirms the old saw that "hard cases make bad law." The challengers to a Virginia law banning the advertising of prescription prices were quite sympathetic—a woman who needed lots of prescription drugs, and two nonprofit organizations representing others similarly situated, including many elderly people who lacked the capacity to shop for cheaper drugs. The interests of consumers in knowing what prices drugstores were charging for prescription drugs and the interests of physicians in knowing what their prescriptions would cost their patients were apparent. So the Virginia statute was difficult to defend as furthering any important legitimate public purpose, other than protecting the interests of certain small business owners.[9] Making matters worse, the parties' briefs offered the Court little help, with the singular exception of a brief by Chicago law professor Philip Kurland on behalf of an association of national advertisers.[10] Then, counsel for Virginia conceded at oral argument that the case raised important First Amendment issues, a concession quickly picked up by his opposing counsel.

When all was said and done, the Supreme Court, by a 7–1 vote, struck down as unconstitutional the Virginia law prohibiting prescription advertising and extended the protections of the First Amendment to advertising that simply urges a commercial transaction at a certain price.[11] Blackmun dismissed the *Chrestensen* precedent, saying the case had no "continuing validity." Blackmun viewed the *Virginia Pharmacy* case as a straightforward extension of *Bigelow*. "I have no difficulty," he wrote in a memo to himself before the argument, "in concluding that the principles enumerated in *Bigelow* are applicable here and that this statute must fall."[12] Nevertheless, his opinion stressed the unique facts of this case, emphasizing that Virginia regulated and licensed pharmacists and that 95 percent of the drugs to be advertised were manufactured by pharmaceutical companies, not compounded by pharmacists. Again, the Court emphasized the *customers'* First Amendment right to know prices, claiming that this was the right at stake, not the sellers' advantages in promoting their products. Along the way, Blackmun's opinion observed the wide disparities in prescription drug prices in Virginia localities, endorsed the benefits of advertising to a free market economy, and re-affirmed the government's ability to limit misleading information and prohibit advertising of illegal products or enterprises.

Both Burger and Powell were concerned that the *Virginia Pharmacy* decision might potentially open a constitutional right of lawyers and doctors to advertise. Powell suggested a paragraph distinguishing these professionals on the ground that they do not dispense standardized products, but instead render professional services of almost infinite variety and nature. Powell was satisfied when Blackmun agreed to add this observation as footnote 25 in his opinion; Burger wrote a separate concurrence to emphasize the point.

William Rehnquist was the sole dissenter—and the only justice who foresaw the far-reaching implications of extending First Amendment protections to commercial advertising. Rehnquist, who found the First Amendment less seductive than did his colleagues, deplored the Court's willingness to override the Virginia legislature's judgment, even though he agreed that the Court's criticisms of the Virginia law were sound as a "matter of desirable public policy." [13] Responding to the footnote in Blackmun's opinion and Burger's concurrence insisting that the Court's decision had no implications for advertising by lawyers and doctors, Rehnquist presciently predicted that "surely the difference between pharmacists' advertising and lawyers' and doctors' advertising can be only one of degree and not of kind." [14] "Under the Court's opinion," Rehnquist said, "the way will be open not only for dissemination of price information but for active promotion of prescription drugs, liquor, cigarettes and other products the use of which has previously been thought desirable to discourage." [15]

Upon reading a draft of Rehnquist's dissent, Powell wrote, "strong dissent with some persuasive arguments, but I will stay with the Court's opinion." [16] So did everyone else.

A year later, the issue of lawyer advertising came to the Court. Two young Arizona lawyers who had opened an office to provide moderately priced legal services to middle-class clients had placed an advertisement in the *Arizona Republic* promising "very reasonable fees" and giving some specific examples of their prices.[17] The state bar then disciplined them by a one-week suspension for violating its prohibition on lawyer advertising. The Arizona Supreme Court upheld the suspension, relying on Blackmun's *Virginia Pharmacy* footnote. Blackmun himself, however, refused to be bound by the footnote and—after he tried to limit the decision's implications by conceding the state's ability to regulate lawyer advertising and insisting that the decision applied only to "truthful advertisement concerning the availability and terms of routine legal services"—he mustered four additional votes to reverse the Arizona decision.[18] This time Burger, Powell, and Stewart joined Rehnquist in dissenting. But the die had been cast; commercial speech now enjoyed firm First Amendment protection.

Three years passed before the Court confronted a state advertising ban grounded in sound public policy. The case involved an electric company's challenge to a rule of the New York public utility commission banning advertising to promote electricity consumption—a prohibition that was without doubt desirable. Dramatic changes in the energy sector had prompted the public utility commission to institute the ban. During the 1970s, our nation experienced a major transformation of energy supplies; a series of events—including an Arab oil embargo, the Iranian revolution, shortages of natural gas, and a moratorium on nuclear power plant construction—had led to a quadrupling of the price of oil.[19] President Carter had made energy conservation an urgent national priority. To aid consumers in the conservation effort, the New York Public Service Commission prohibited utility advertisements that promoted electricity use. But in 1980, by an 8–1 vote in *Central Hudson Gas and Electric Co. v. Public Service Commission of New York*, the Court ruled that the prohibition violated the First Amendment.[20]

The *Central Hudson* decision removed any doubt that the Burger Court had created an important new constitutional constraint on federal and state laws limiting corporate commercial speech, creating a controversial, but enduring, constitutional right that corporations could invoke to strike down both sensible and senseless laws and regulations. As law professor Bruce Ledewitz said, "Through advertising's information and conditioning, corporations became persons, while people become consumers."[21] Only William Rehnquist saw it coming.

Lewis Powell's Four-Step

By insisting in the *Virginia Pharmacy* case that untrue or misleading advertising is not constitutionally protected, the Court made clear that First Amendment protections for commercial speech are less robust than for political speech.[22] The Court then turned to spelling out the limits of its commercial speech doctrine. Having strongly disagreed with Blackmun's decision on lawyer advertising, Chief Justice Burger assigned the *Central Hudson* opinion to Lewis Powell. Powell took the opportunity to detail how courts should apply the new constitutional protection for commercial speech. This produced the usual back-and-forth with his clerks and more than usual dialogue with his colleagues. Just eight days before the opinion was published, Powell's law clerk described a "crossfire" of criticism from Powell's colleagues on both his left and right.[23]

In *Central Hudson*, Powell insisted that the legal protection for commercial speech turns on its value to the audience, not the speaker: "The First Amendment's concern for commercial speech is based on the informational function of advertising."[24] He then proceeded to set forth a four-step test for lawful government constraints that he claimed had been "developed" in earlier cases: First, the commercial speech must be about a legal product, truthful, and not misleading. Second, if so, the government cannot prohibit the speech unless the governmental interest is "substantial" (which, for example, the state's interest in energy conservation was in *Central Hudson*). Third, if the government interest is substantial, the regulation of speech must directly advance the governmental interest (which the ban on promoting energy consumption did). Finally, the governmental constraint must not be more extensive than necessary to serve the government's purpose. Here, the Court concluded, was where the New York Public Service Commission foundered.

Blackmun and Stevens concurred in the result in *Central Hudson*, but insisted that prior decisions failed to support Powell's four-part test. They urged giving commercial speech constitutional protections equivalent to political speech—a view that seems to command a majority of today's Supreme Court.

William Rehnquist was once again the lone dissenter. Even accepting the conclusion of *Virginia Pharmacy* that commercial speech is entitled to some First Amendment protection, Rehnquist objected to extending such protection to a state-created and regulated monopoly, such as this electric company. Rehnquist pointed out that the New York utility commission could have constitutionally promoted energy conservation by increasing electricity prices, an action that consumers certainly would have regarded as "more extensive" than the ban on promotional advertising. He also—correctly as it would turn out—described the "no more extensive than necessary" fourth prong of Powell's test as an invitation to courts to substitute their own judgment "for that of the State in deciding how a proper ban on promotional advertising should be drafted." Rehnquist insisted that the discretion given to courts under *Central Hudson*—indeed the constitutional protection accorded to commercial speech under *Virginia Pharmacy*—had "unlocked a Pandora's Box" of issues whose resolution "on a judicial battlefield will be a very difficult one." Invoking the Founders, Rehnquist said: "Nor do I think those who won our independence, while declining to 'exalt order at the cost of liberty' would have viewed a merchant's unfettered freedom to advertise in hawking his wares as a 'liberty' not subject to extensive regulation in light of the government's substantial interest in attaining order in the economic sphere." The Court, Rehnquist said, ignored that "in a democracy, the economic is subordinate to the political, a lesson that our ancestors learned long ago, and that our descendants will undoubtedly have to relearn many years hence."[25]

Unleashing the *Lochner* Monster

One of the first things every law student learns about constitutional law is the Supreme Court's repudiation in the late 1930s and early 1940s of the decisions of the "*Lochner* era"—a three-decade period, dating from the end of the nineteenth century, when the Court struck down both federal and state laws that regulated private economic contracts. The *Lochner* case itself was a 1905 decision in which the Court, by a 5–4 vote, invalidated a New York law providing that bakers could not work more than ten hours a day or sixty hours a week.[26] The majority opinion by Justice Rufus Peckham described the New York maximum hours law as "unreasonable and entirely arbitrary" and "counter to that liberty of person and of free contract provided for in the Federal Constitution."[27]

After more than thirty years of striking down many laws on this ground, including early New Deal statutes, the Supreme Court abandoned *Lochner* in 1937—the year that Franklin Roosevelt attempted to pack the Court by expanding the number of justices. That year the Court upheld a state of Washington minimum wage statute for women, the federal National Labor Relations Act and the Social Security Act.[28] By 1938, two of Franklin Roosevelt's eight appointments, including Hugo Black, had joined the Court.[29] Within a few years, the Court had ratified the broad power of Congress to regulate commerce and had sustained much New Deal legislation.

By the late 1970s, when the Burger Court invented the commercial speech doctrine, *Lochner* and its progeny had been repudiated for decades. The justices understood this well and were loath to explicitly resurrect *Lochner*. This is why it was crucial to the Court that the parties agreed that *Virginia Pharmacy* was a case moored in the Free Speech Clause rather than in due process (which is where the *Lochner* era cases had found their constitutional grounding).

During the justices' conference in *Virginia Pharmacy*, Justice Stewart observed that the case raised issues of economic due process, which he was not inclined to resuscitate. Ultimately, however, he was convinced by the consumers' First Amendment claims and joined Harry Blackmun's majority opinion. Even so, Stewart wrote separately to emphasize that the Court's decision did not bar state or federal legislation regulating false or deceptive advertising.[30]

Only William Rehnquist recognized that the Court was—perhaps inadvertently—treading back into *Lochnerian* waters. In *Virginia Pharmacy*, he deplored the era of economic due process and pointed to the cases overruling *Lochner*. To emphasize his point, Justice Rehnquist said, "While there is much to be said for the Court's observation as a matter of desirable public policy, there is certainly nothing in the United States Constitution which requires the Virginia Legislature to hew to the teachings of Adam Smith in its legislative decisions regulating the pharmacy profession."[31] Rehnquist also quoted an earlier observation of Justice Black that the idea that "due process authorizes courts to hold laws unconstitutional when they believe the legislature has acted unwisely—has long since been discarded."[32]

Dissenting in *Central Hudson*, Rehnquist became even more explicit.

The Court today, he said, "returns to the bygone era of *Lochner v. New York*."[33] "By labeling economic regulation of business conduct as a restraint on 'free speech' [the Court has] gone far to resurrect the discredited doctrine of cases such as *Lochner*."[34] The New York Public Service Commission's ban on advertising promoting electricity use, Rehnquist said, is "akin to an economic regulation to which virtually complete deference should be accorded by this Court."[35]

Despite Rehnquist's objections, which have been widely echoed and amplified in the scholarly literature, the Burger Court's grant of constitutional protection to commercial speech has endured and even been expanded. The four-part test set forth by Justice Powell in *Central Hudson* has also demonstrated remarkable staying power, perhaps because of the discretion it provides courts in deciding commercial speech cases.

The complaint that granting constitutional protection to commercial speech involves a return to the archaic and discredited judicial control over economic affairs of the *Lochner* era is only one of the criticisms of the Burger Court's creation of constitutional protection for commercial speech. The other is that commercial advertising has nothing to do with the fundamental values and concerns of the First Amendment—that business advertising is far afield from the free-flowing political discourse that sits at the core of the First Amendment.[36] Nor does promotion of commercial transactions fit into the category of speech vital to individual freedom and self-fulfillment, which includes, for example, books, movies, and art.[37]

Instead, as the Court emphasized in *Virginia Pharmacy*, support for constitutional protection of commercial speech resides in economic values, in the view that unconstrained truthful commercial advertising promotes a free market economy and improves consumers' well-being.[38] By limiting the ability of federal and state governments to regulate such advertising, the Court deployed its primacy over constitutional interpretation to validate an unregulated free enterprise system of the sort that Lewis Powell had applauded in his 1971 Chamber of Commerce memorandum.[39]

The scope and nature of valid economic regulations had long been recognized as the bailiwick of state and federal legislators, not the courts. Nevertheless, First Amendment protection for commercial speech constrains state and federal legislators today. Indeed, the Court under the leadership of Chief Justice John Roberts now seems determined to use the First Amendment to serve a deregulatory agenda.

In the pharmaceutical industry, detailers bring to doctors drug samples and medical studies extolling the virtues of their high-priced, high-profit prescription drugs. Knowing a particular physician's prescription practices enhances the ability of a detailer to effectively promote purchases of expensive pharmaceuticals. Information identifying the specific drugs a doctor has prescribed is routinely provided to pharmacies when they fill prescriptions.

In 2007, Vermont enacted a "prescription confidentiality law" that required a prescribing physician to consent to the sale by pharmacies, health insurers, or others of prescriber-identifying information for the purpose of "marketing or promoting a prescription drug." The law also prohibited pharmaceutical manufacturers or marketers from using such prescriber-specific information for "marketing or promoting a prescription drug" without the prescribing physician's consent. The use of such information for health care research, however, was permitted.

The Vermont legislature banned using prescriber-identifying data for marketing after it found that detailing "caused doctors to make decisions based on 'incomplete and biased information' " and that detailing "increases the cost of health care and health insurance, encourages hasty and excessive reliance on brand-name drugs . . . as compared with older and less expensive generic alternatives, and fosters disruptive and repeated marketing visits tantamount to harassment." [40] Similar laws were enacted for similar reasons by Maine and New Hampshire.

Three data-mining companies and an association of pharmaceutical manufacturers who produce brand-name drugs sued to invalidate the law as an infringement of their First Amendment commercial speech rights. On June 24, 2011, the Supreme Court, by a 6–3 vote, struck down the Vermont law as a violation of the right of free speech under the First Amendment. In doing so, the Court majority awarded constitutional protection to the ability of pharmaceutical companies and data-mining companies to target individual physicians in their marketing campaigns.

Unlike the Burger Court, which had grounded its First Amendment protection for commercial speech in the rights and benefits of the recipients of such information, the Roberts Court, in an opinion by Anthony

Kennedy, emphasized the rights of the pharmaceutical companies and data miners. That is exactly what the amicus brief of the U.S. Chamber of Commerce urged the Court to do.[41] The statute here, Justice Kennedy said, "disfavors marketing, that is speech with a particular content" and "disfavors specific speakers, namely pharmaceutical manufacturers."[42] The state's remedy, the Court said, is to combat the pharmaceutical manufacturers' efforts by its own speech.

Justice Breyer (joined by Justices Ginsburg and Kagan) responded with a lengthy dissent. The ban on detailing, he said, "is inextricably related to a lawful government effort to regulate a commercial enterprise. . . . Some ordinary regulatory programs can affect speech, particularly commercial speech, in myriad ways," Breyer said. "To apply a 'heightened' First Amendment standard of review when ever such a program burdens speech would transfer from legislatures to judges the primary power to weigh ends and to choose means, threatening to distort or undermine legitimate legislative objectives."[43] Breyer then quoted from Rehnquist's dissent in *Central Hudson* warning that strong First Amendment rights for commercial speech would "return us to the bygone era of *Lochner v. New York.*"[44] "Until today," Breyer said, "this Court has *never* found that the *First Amendment* prohibits the government from restricting the use of information gathered pursuant to a regulatory mandate." Pointing out that the Court had judged state law by a standard even "stricter than *Central Hudson*," Breyer observed that "given the sheer quantity of regulatory initiatives that touch upon commercial messages, the Court's vision of its reviewing task threatens to return us to a happily bygone era when judges scrutinized legislation for its interference with economic liberty. . . . Today's majority," he said, "risks repeating the mistakes of the past in a manner not anticipated by our precedents."[45] The *Lochner* monster, which William Rehnquist had seen unleashed nearly three decades earlier, had been resurrected.[46]

Corporations Are People Too

Writing in the *Harvard Law Review* in 1980, Archibald Cox described the Burger Court's extension of constitutional protection for commercial speech as "the most venturesome rulings of the Burger Court dealing with freedom of expression."[47] But the debilitating mischief set in motion by the Burger Court's granting of First Amendment protection to commercial speech of businesses is minor compared to the forces unleashed by its crucial decisions concerning campaign finance and corporate political speech—rulings welcomed by some as vindicating the important political speech rights of the First Amendment and bemoaned by others as doing far more to expand "the political power of money" than to advance First Amendment goals.[48]

The first, and by far the more famous, Burger Court decision arose out of Richard Nixon's Watergate scandal. It involved the Federal Election Campaign Act Amendments of 1974 (FECA), one of the first acts of Congress signed into law by Gerald Ford after Nixon resigned. This far-reaching legislation was spurred by improprieties of Nixon's reelection campaign and related concerns about potential corruption and the role money was playing in politics. A number of corporate contributions to Nixon had received great publicity, including, for example, a $2 million pledge to Nixon from milk producers simultaneous with the Nixon administration's increase in milk price supports, unlawful large contributions to the Republican Party from American Airlines (laundered through a Lebanese agent and a Swiss bank) followed immediately by the airline's applications for new profitable routes, and the settlement of an antitrust suit against International Telephone & Telegraph Corporation soon after an ITT subsidiary agreed to fund a large share of the costs of the Republican National Convention.[49] Secret cash from millionaires along with piles of illegal corporate contributions used by Nixon's reelection campaign officials to fund the Watergate break-in and other shady activities added to the stench.[50]

Congress's fundamental goal in enacting the contribution and expenditure limits of FECA, along with disclosure provisions and public financing of presidential campaigns, was to promote political equality by limiting the influence of the wealthy in political campaigns.[51] But, in striving for greater equality, the law's limitations raised serious constitutional questions involving First Amendment protections for political speech.

The 1974 law imposed criminal penalties for (1) a candidate exceeding spending limitations in contests for nomination or election; (2) individuals exceeding limits on amounts they contribute to a particular campaign or overall annual contribution limits; and (3) individuals not formally connected with a candidate's campaign organization exceeding limits for expenditures on behalf of or against a candidate. FECA also introduced a mechanism for public financing of presidential conventions and campaigns, which favored major party candidates over those of minor parties.[52]

At the behest of New York's senator James L. Buckley, who opposed the law and intended to challenge its constitutionality, FECA contained special rules providing for expedited judicial review of a constitutional challenge: a lawsuit would be filed with the federal district court in Washington, D.C., which would certify questions to be decided by the federal Court of Appeals for the D.C. Circuit, sitting en banc, and then appealed to the Supreme Court.

Soon after the law was signed by a reluctant President Ford, it was challenged by Senator Buckley, together with Minnesota senator Eugene McCarthy, Stewart Mott (a wealthy liberal contributor to Senators George McGovern and McCarthy), and a rather strange amalgam of groups, which included the American Civil Liberties Union, the Libertarian Party, and the Mississippi Republican Party. Describing the challengers to the law's validity, Senator Buckley said, "What we had in common was a concern that the restrictions imposed by the new law would squeeze independent voices out of the political process by making it even more difficult than it already was to raise effective challenges to the political status quo."[53]

After hearing argument on twenty-eight constitutional questions that had been certified by the D.C. district court, an eight-judge en banc panel of the federal appellate court for the D.C. Circuit (the court where Warren Burger had originally served) on August 15, 1975, issued a lengthy opinion upholding all of the major provisions of FECA.[54] The appellate court majority emphasized the "compelling government interests" in avoiding corruption and securing political equality. Money, it concluded, was not the same as speech.

This court determined that the First Amendment objections to FECA's limits on contributions to candidates and on expenditures supporting a political candidacy had to give way to the importance of reducing the influence of money in our nation's political process. "The corrosive influence of money blights our democratic processes," the court said.[55] "By reducing in good measure disparity due to wealth, the Act tends to equalize both the relative ability of all voters to affect electoral outcomes, and the opportunity of all interested citizens to become candidates for elective federal office."[56] The court viewed greater equality in our political process as essential. The contribution and expenditure limits, along with other provisions of the act, the court concluded, "should not be rejected because they might have some incidental, not clearly defined, effect on First Amendment freedoms."[57]

The decision was appealed to the Supreme Court, which heard a full day of oral arguments on November 10, 1975. The Court—cognizant of the need to decide the case well before the 1976 elections—announced its decision and published opinions totaling nearly three hundred pages on January 30, 1976. The nearly 150-page majority opinion in *Buckley v. Valeo* was per curiam and was cobbled together from partial drafts by a five-justice "drafting team,"[58] composed of Burger, Brennan, Stewart, Powell, and Rehnquist. Separate opinions concurring and dissenting in parts of the per curiam opinion were filed by Burger, White, Marshall, Blackmun, and Rehnquist. (John Paul Stevens, who didn't take his seat on the Court until December 19, 1975, did not participate in the case.)

The Court's decision established the constitutionally permissible ground rules that still govern our nation's financing and regulation of political campaigns. Richard Hasen, professor at the University of California Irvine School of Law and an expert on campaign finance regulation, calls *Buckley v. Valeo* the "Rosetta Stone of American campaign finance jurisprudence."[59] In fashioning that stone, the Burger Court paid far less heed to the goal of political equality than had either the Congress or the Court of Appeals for the D.C. Circuit.

The conflict within the Supreme Court over FECA's constitutionality had been foreshadowed in disputes within the Ford administration over how vigorously to defend the law.[60] Robert Bork, Ford's solicitor general, wanted to file a brief claiming that much of the law was unconstitutional. Attorney General Edward Levi wanted to be more neutral. Members of the newly formed Federal Elections Commission, who were defending the law, urged the Justice Department to remain silent. Ford himself ultimately refereed the dispute, and the Justice Department filed a brief skeptical of the act's constitutionality, especially in its limitations on individual expenditures on behalf of political candidates.

Given the length and complexity of the various opinions, we can only summarize the Court's most important conclusions here. The Court upheld the voluntary public financing of presidential campaigns that was one centerpiece of the 1974 legislation. But public financing was never extended to House and Senate races. Then in 2008, after Barack Obama amassed prodigious sums for his campaign, he rejected public funding. In 2012, for the first time, both major candidates for president rejected public funding. Since then, public financing has fallen into desuetude.

The Court reached conflicting conclusions concerning the constitutionality of the act's limitations on campaign contributions versus "independent" expenditures on behalf of a candidate. Allowing unlimited independent expenditures in support of a political candidate, the Court concluded, was essential to maintain core First Amendment values. The Court said that "in the absence of prearrangement or coordination with the candidate or his agent," such expenditures do not partake of the potential corruption or appearance of corruption attendant to large political contributions. Contrariwise, the Court upheld the act's limits on contributions. It regarded restricting the ability to contribute large sums to campaigns as a less intrusive imposition on an individual's ability to speak in support of a candidate, and it viewed such contributions as raising the specter of potential corruption.

For the Court's majority, actual or apparent corruption were the only governmental interests sufficient to justify these kinds of encroachment on the First Amendment. The Court brushed aside as "ancillary" the "governmental interest in equalizing the relative ability of individuals and groups to influence the outcome of elections."[61] "The concept that government may restrict the speech of some elements of our society in order to enhance the relative voice of others," the Court said, "is wholly foreign to the First Amendment. . . . The First Amendment's protection against governmental abridgment of free expression cannot properly be made to depend on a person's financial ability to engage in public discussion."[62]

Only Byron White and Thurgood Marshall disagreed with striking down the limits on individual expenditures. White viewed the limits on expenditures as an essential complement to the contribution limits, and he foresaw that "widespread evasion" would result from the Court's decision. He also predicted, quite correctly, that the Court's decision would return political candidates to the "treadmill" of "the endless job of raising increasingly large sums of money."[63]

Unsurprisingly, Marshall was most concerned about "the interest in promoting the reality and appearance of equal access to the political arena" and ensuring that candidacy for public office "not become, or appear to become, the exclusive province of the wealthy."[64] Marshall would not be at all surprised that the U.S. Senate today is a "millionaires' club."

Burger wrote separately to say that he would strike down both the contribution and expenditure limits as "two sides of the same First Amendment coin."[65] He also considered the public financing provisions to be unconstitutional and regarded the act's provisions requiring disclosure of contributions as overly broad and unduly chilling of political activity.[66]

The 1974 campaign finance law and its subsequent revisions have failed entirely in their goal of limiting lawmakers' quest for money, which is now a principal activity of our representatives and senators (and many other elected officials). Nor did campaign finance legislation or the Supreme Court decisions remove the potential for corruption or the appearance of corruption from our political process. The Court's greatest success was in shunting to the sidelines the quest for greater equality in our nation's politics between those with and without money. In the generation since *Buckley v. Valeo*, the Supreme Court has come close to striking down as unconstitutional all limits on campaign contributions, but, so far, it has not done so.[67]

The Burger Court's next move was to enhance the influence of corporations in our nation's elections and political discourse. Money may not be speech, but—in politics, as with advertising—it greatly affects what the American people hear.

Corporate Political Speech

Early in the 1970s, business interests suffered significant legislative failures, especially on environmental, health, and safety issues. In the first half of that decade, when labor unions, newly emergent consumer advocacy organizations, and environmentalists secured important victories, the public believed that ongoing economic growth was inevitable. This meant that members of Congress felt little need to kowtow to business interests. Large segments of the prosperous, well-educated middle class had become disdainful of business interests, and the titans of the national news media tended to side with the goals of public interest entities, such as Common Cause and Ralph Nader's numerous consumer organizations. The result was an outburst of congressional regulation of business operations and activities. Despite some ups and downs, environmental organizations have demonstrated staying power, but by the 1980s both organized labor and the consumer movement were losing sway.

The worm began to turn once "stagflation"—a destructive and unprecedented combination of unemployment and inflation—infected the economy in the mid-1970s. At first, business interests were unable to gain political traction, especially in the wake of the post-Watergate revelations of illegal corporate contributions to Nixon's 1972 reelection campaign. Ironically, however, the 1974 campaign finance legislation expanded opportunities for corporations to influence political campaigns. That legislation explicitly permitted corporations and labor unions to establish funds—so-called political action committees (PACs)—to aggregate contributions for political purposes and to use corporate and union resources to administer the PACs and to solicit contributions from employees, shareholders, and union members.[68]

The Court in *Buckley* concluded that the way in which members were appointed to the Federal Election Commission was unconstitutional, but nevertheless it expressly validated the decisions that the FEC had announced prior to the date of the Court's opinion.[69] One of these FEC opinions, which Lewis Powell kept in his *Buckley* files, had blessed the Sun Oil PAC and allowed the Sun Oil corporation to control its PAC, subject to disclosure of its political expenditures.[70] After that, corporations using multiple PACs to funnel campaign contributions to political candidates, especially powerful incumbents, became commonplace. Powell wanted to add text and footnotes to the *Buckley* opinion, pointing out that the legislation would validate the "special interest" power of unions and corporations. Powell also wanted to note that in the 1974 campaign unions donated $4.3 million to congressional campaigns while business groups gave $1.6 million. Potter Stewart, the author of the opinion's section on the limits on contributions, rejected Powell's requests, and suggested that

Powell should instead write separately to make these points. Powell declined that invitation. (Until the mid-1970s, union PAC contributions generally equaled or exceeded those from business, but never since then.)

In his 1971 memorandum to the Chamber of Commerce, Powell lamented that "in terms of political influence with respect to the course of legislation and government action, the American business executive is truly the 'forgotten man.'" And, as we have described, he strongly urged that the Chamber "consider assuming a broader and more vigorous role in the political arena."[71] Business interests soon took Powell's advice. By the end of 1974, the year the campaign finance limits were enacted, only eighty-nine companies had created PACs, but by July 1980 that number had grown to 1,204. In the 1976 elections, corporate and business trade association PACs contributed $10 million to candidates for Congress—outspending labor unions for the first time; by 1980, business contributions had nearly doubled to $19.2 million.

By the mid-1970s, business groups had started forming ad hoc coalitions to support or oppose particular legislation, coalitions that dissolved once the fate of the legislation was resolved. Business interests also changed Washington's political landscape in the 1970s by funding new, vibrant, conservative think tanks, most notably the Heritage Foundation. These think tanks and their allies routinely produce and disseminate analyses and position papers that arm members of Congress and their staffs with intellectual ammunition on behalf of pro-business positions, and over time they have come to play an increasingly important role in the legislative process. One senator (South Carolina's Jim DeMint) even thought he would be more powerful heading Heritage than staying in the Senate.

In 1977, a case came to the Court that gave Lewis Powell an opportunity to enhance businesses' opportunities to expand their political influence. The case, *First National Bank of Boston v. Bellotti*, involved a challenge to the constitutionality of a Massachusetts criminal law that prohibited expenditures by business corporations for the purpose of influencing any referendum other than "one materially affecting any of the property, business or assets of the corporation."[72] The First National Bank of Boston and other business corporations wanted to spend corporate money to oppose a Massachusetts referendum that would have permitted the state legislature to enact a graduated personal income tax.

The Massachusetts Supreme Judicial Court upheld the restrictions of the statute, but, by a 5–4 vote, the Burger Court reversed and, in an opinion by Powell, struck down the Massachusetts law as violating the corporation's First Amendment rights.

Sharp divisions over this case emerged slowly within the Court, and they came as something of a surprise. At the November 11, 1977, conference, two days after the case had been argued, the justices voted 8–1 to reverse the Massachusetts court and strike down the statute. Only White disagreed. He held the view, expressed 160 years earlier by Chief Justice John Marshall, that: "A corporation is an artificial being, invisible, intangible, and existing only in contemplation of law. Being the mere creature of law, it possesses only those properties which the charter of creation confers upon it." [73] At oral argument, the Massachusetts attorney general had put the point sharply but less eloquently: corporations, he said, are creatures of the state and, as such, the state can regulate them however it sees fit.

After the conference, Burger assigned the opinion to Brennan. But, on December 1, Brennan informed his colleagues that he "would presently write to sustain [the statute's] constitutionality." "I doubt," he said, "I can write an opinion that will command majority support." [74] Powell, who harbored no doubt that the Massachusetts statute should be struck down as a violation of the corporation's First Amendment rights, penned "Wow!" in the margin of his copy of Brennan's memo. [75] On December 6, Powell sent a memo to his colleagues, citing the *Virginia Pharmacy* decision and insisting that it was "too late to hold that persons who elect to do business in the corporate form . . . may not express opinions through the corporation on issues of general public interest. . . . Circumscribing speech on the basis of its source in the absence of a compelling interest that could not be attained otherwise," he said, "would be a most serious infringement of First Amendment rights." [76] This signaled vigorous conflict among the justices over the merits of the case. Powell, not William Brennan, would ultimately secure a majority.

After much back-and-forth, the Court announced its decision in *First National Bank of Boston v. Bellotti* on April 26, 1978. Powell's opinion began by emphasizing the rights of the recipients of information rather than the rights of the corporate speaker. "The proper question," he said, "is not whether corporations 'have' First Amendment rights, and, if so, whether they are coextensive with those of natural persons. . . . Instead," he continued, "the question must be whether [the Massachusetts statute] abridges expression that the First Amendment was meant to protect. . . . The speech proposed by appellants," he said, "is at the heart of the First Amendment's protections. . . . The people in our democracy," Powell wrote, "are entrusted with the responsibility for judging and evaluating the relative merits of conflicting arguments."[77] Quoting *Buckley*'s contempt for claims of political equality, he added, "We noted only recently that the concept that government may restrict the speech of some elements of our society in order to enhance the relative voice of others is wholly foreign to the First Amendment."[78]

Chief Justice Burger wrote a separate concurring opinion claiming that allowing business corporations to engage in the political process was essential to combat the power of "media conglomerates," who enjoy the First Amendment protections of freedom of the press. Media conglomerates, he said, "pose a much more realistic threat to valid interests" than other business corporations in terms of "unfair advantage in the political process" and "corporate domination of the political process."[79] Freedom of the press, he said, applies to all corporations and confers no special status on the media.

Justice White, joined by Brennan and Marshall, dissented at length, restating the question as "whether a state may prevent corporate management from using the corporate treasury to propagate views having no connection with the corporate business."[80] He answered with a resounding "yes." While expressing "now little doubt that corporate communications come within the scope of the First Amendment," White emphasized that the Court's decision "casts considerable doubt upon the constitutionality of legislation passed by some 31 states restricting corporate activity." He pointedly rejected Powell's assertion that corporate political speech is at the "core" of First Amendment values. Nor did White regard the public's "right to hear" as impinged by the state's curtailment of corporate political speech or activities. Addressing the political equality issue and disagreeing sharply with Powell, White described the state's concern here as one of "preventing institutions which have been permitted to amass wealth as a result of special advantages extended by the state for certain economic purposes from using that wealth to acquire an unfair advantage in the political process." "The state, he said, "need not permit its own creation to consume it." [81]

Justice Rehnquist—unsurprisingly, given his refusal to accept any constitutional status for commercial speech—also dissented. He emphasized that the Court's decision conflicted not only with the views of the Massachusetts legislature and the state's highest court, but also with Congress and thirty other states, which "have considered the matter and have concluded that restrictions on the political activity of business corporations are both politically desirable and constitutionally permissible." [82] Quoting Chief Justice John Marshall, Rehnquist distinguished the First Amendment rights of business corporations from those of "natural persons." Rehnquist concluded: "the interest of the public in receiving the information offered by the speaker seeking protection" is "in no way diminished" by the "limited rights of political expression" granted to business corporations by the Commonwealth of Massachusetts. [83]

Corporations now had a constitutional right to engage in political speech, and under *Buckley* limitations on expenditures on behalf of political candidates were constitutionally prohibited. It would require no great leap for the Supreme Court to conclude—as it would a generation later in the notorious *Citizens United* case—that corporate expenditures on behalf of political candidates enjoy similar constitutional protection. [84] All the Court had to do was to reject a footnote in Powell's *Bellotti* opinion suggesting that corporate expenditures on behalf of a candidate might not enjoy the same constitutional protection as those supporting or opposing a referendum. [85] *Bellotti*'s significance was matched only by its obscurity. The vast swath of the public that expressed surprise at the *Citizens United* decision—how can corporations have First Amendment rights?—were obviously unfamiliar with the fact that the Burger Court had decided that question thirty-two years earlier.

Citizens United

Presidents commonly criticize decisions of the Supreme Court, but, until January 27, 2011, no president had done so in front of a national television audience watching his State of the Union address. Barack Obama that night, standing at a podium high above six Supreme Court Justices seated below him, sharply criticized the Court's decision in *Citizens United v. Federal Election Commission*, which, as mentioned, struck down a federal statute limiting independent expenditures by corporations and unions supporting a political candidate. The Court's decision, the president said, would "open the floodgates for special interests—including foreign companies—to spend without limit on our elections." "I don't think American elections," Obama said, "should be bankrolled by America's most powerful interests." The president also asserted that the Court had "overruled a century of law" in holding that the First Amendment prohibited legislative restrictions on independent corporate spending on behalf of political candidates. To that, Justice Samuel Alito, who had been in the Court's majority in *Citizens United*, shook his head in disagreement and mouthed the words "not true." Alito was right. What the Court had done was take a logical step along the path the Burger Court had paved in its *Buckley* and *Bellotti* decisions.

During the interval between these Burger Court decisions and the 2010 decision of the Roberts Court in *Citizens United*, the Court had on several occasions considered congressional limitations on corporate and union political expenditures and activity. We shall not describe those here, but merely observe that a number of the Court's 5–4 decisions in this area were decided by the votes (and vacillations) of Sandra Day O'Connor, who stepped down in 2006. She was replaced by Samuel Alito, who views any limitations on campaign contributions and expenditures as unconstitutional.[86]

In *Citizens United*, the Supreme Court, by a 5–4 vote, struck down limits on such spending enacted by Congress in 2002, and, in the process, overruled two recent decisions that had upheld limits on corporate and union spending in support of political candidates.[87] The *Citizens United* majority claimed that the Court continued to accept *Buckley*'s anticorruption rationale as the basis for these kinds of limits (although some of the justices would clearly like to strike those down as well). Thus, the Supreme Court has never yet overruled *Buckley*, notwithstanding a generation of harsh criticisms from both the left and right of that decision's distinction allowing limits on campaign contributions while outlawing limits on expenditures in support of particular candidates.

The political equality rationale for the limitations on both contributions and expenditures, embraced by the Congress in 1974 and validated by the federal Court of Appeals for the D.C. Circuit in its *Buckley* decision, has never been able to muster a Supreme Court majority. In his oral argument on September 9, 2009, in *Citizens United*, Seth Waxman, a former solicitor general, arguing to uphold the limitations on corporate expenditures, described corporations as "great aggregations of wealth," quoting from an opinion of the Court by Justices O'Connor and Stevens in a 2003 decision upholding restrictions on corporate campaign contributions.[88] Antonin Scalia intervened. "Great aggregations of wealth," the justice said. "The amicus brief by the Chamber of Commerce," Scalia continued, "points out that 96 percent of its members employ less than 100 people. These are not aggregations of great wealth."[89]

If *Buckley's* anticorruption rationale lives on, as the Court insists, it is barely alive. In 2012, the Court summarily reversed, by a 5–4 vote, a decision of the Montana Supreme Court that would have retained limits on corporate spending because of that state's long history of corporate corruption of state officials.[90]

The Burger Court's invention of First Amendment protection for commercial speech and its grant (by one vote) of political speech rights to corporations now rest on constitutional *terra firma*. Even Justice Stevens's ninety-page dissent in *Citizens United* confirmed that "we have long since held that corporations are covered by the First Amendment." During the period 2005–2011, the United States Chamber of Commerce alone spent more than $385 million in political expenditures, including lobbying. In total, eight business associations spent more than $1.5 billion during the same six-year period.[91] (The limited disclosure requirements do not permit any reliable estimates of the amount of political spending by individual business corporations.) Between 2006 and 2011, the Chamber filed eighty-three amicus briefs in the Supreme Court; it got the result it wanted in two thirds of the cases.[92] Lewis Powell would be proud.

The Burger Court created constitutional rules that allow corporations virtually unfettered leeway to convince the public to support both their commercial interests and their political preferences. During the Court's consideration of the *Buckley* case, Powell was concerned that the 1974 campaign finance law might enhance the voice of unions over corporations: he was worried that shoe leather would become more important than leather wallets. Today—when private sector unions have dwindled to represent only a small percentage of American workers and when unions' political activities pale in comparison to those of businesses— Powell's fears of the political and economic power of unions seem farfetched. As business interests were becoming more adept at influencing legislation and judicial decisions, unions were continuing a long decline from which they have yet to recover. Except for legislation directly affecting their ability to organize, unions have become both less active and less effective in the legislative process. The Burger Court cannot be held responsible for the decline of unions in America, but, as we show in the next chapter, the Court gave unions a push downhill.

CHAPTER 11

Battling Workplace Inequality

O f all the Burger Court decisions that struck false notes about where the Court and the country were heading, few in retrospect sound from as uncommon a songbook as the 1979 decision in *United Steelworkers v. Weber*.[1] The Court, in its first case dealing with affirmative action in employment, upheld a voluntary agreement between Kaiser Aluminum and Chemical Corporation and the United Steelworkers of America (USWA) concerning a company training program for unskilled workers to obtain promotions. The agreement provided that admission to the program would generally be based on seniority but that half the new trainees would be black.

In the first year of the plan, Kaiser admitted seven blacks and six whites to the program. After being denied admission to the program, despite his seniority over several black employees, Brian Weber, a white employee at the company's plant in Gramercy, Louisiana, challenged the program as violating Title VII of the Civil Rights Act of 1964.[2] Title VII prohibits employers and unions from discriminating in employment or in admission to "any program established to provide apprenticeship or other training" based on "race, color, religion, sex, or national origin." Prior to 1974, when Kaiser and the union entered into their agreement, only five of the 273 skilled workers at the Gramercy plant were African American, even though the area's workforce was almost 40 percent African American. Writing for a 5–2 majority, Justice Brennan said that Title VII does not forbid "voluntary race-conscious affirmative action efforts" to "eliminate manifest racial imbalances in traditionally segregated job categories."[3] Brennan—emphasizing that the "plan does not unnecessarily trammel the interests of the white employees"—concluded that the "adoption of the Kaiser-USWA plan for the Gramercy plant falls within the area of discretion left by Title VII to the private sector voluntarily to adopt affirmative action plans designed to eliminate conspicuous racial imbalance in traditionally segregated job categories."[4] Justice Rehnquist (joined by Burger) wrote a strong dissent characterizing the majority's reading of Title VII as Orwellian and a "tour de force reminiscent not of jurists . . . but of escape artists such as Houdini." After an extensive review of its legislative history, Rehnquist insisted that Title VII clearly prohibits the affirmative action program. Title VII, he wrote, "prohibits a covered employer from considering race when making an employment decision, whether the race be black or white."[5] Rehnquist concluded: "There is perhaps no device more destructive to the notion of equality than the *numerus clausus*—the quota. Whether described as 'benign discrimination' or 'affirmative action' the racial quota is nonetheless a creator of castes, a two-edged sword that must demean one in order to prefer another."[6]

Benjamin Hooks, executive director of the NAACP, described *Weber* as "probably the most important civil rights decision in recent history."[7] James Nailor, a black electrician hired into the Kaiser training program, said: "The decision means my children will have a chance to do better than I will. That's the American Dream."[8] But the decision hardly heralded a new era in employment race relations. The year after the program began, Kaiser terminated it, so the Court was evaluating a program that no longer existed. Steel plants were closing across America, facing international competition from which they have yet to recover. Outsourcing work became the norm for Kaiser and many other U.S. companies. Between 1974 and 1988 African American electricians grew from 5.3 to 8.4 percent of the total, but there were 40 percent fewer electrician jobs. In 1974, there were nearly forty thousand black workers in the steel industry; by 1988 there were less than ten thousand.[9] As Judith Stein wrote, "The Supreme Court sustained the USWA-Kaiser plan, but the recession of 1975–76 did not."[10]

Even the 5–2 vote for the Court's decision in *Weber* sends misleading signals. Lewis Powell, who had written the *Bakke* case the year before, did not participate, having missed the oral argument because of surgery.

He followed *Weber*, however, and his files imply that he would have voted with the dissenters. He described Rehnquist's dissent as "powerful," and when Justice Brennan informed the conference that Rehnquist's dissent required no changes to his own draft, Powell expressed surprise, adding: "There may be an answer to [Rehnquist], but apparently no one will try to advance it." [11] After *Weber* was announced, Powell sent Burger a copy of a critical editorial in *The Virginian Pilot*, written by his former clerk J. Harvie Wilkinson, which Powell described as "quite perceptive." [12] John Paul Stevens, who also did not participate in *Weber*, wrote a concurring opinion eight years later in *Johnson v. Transportation Agency*, a case challenging an affirmative action plan voluntarily adopted by the Transportation Agency of Santa Clara County, California, indicating that he, too, would have sided with the dissenters in *Weber*.[13] In that same case, Byron White, who had voted with the majority in *Weber*, voted to strike down the plan, calling it "a perversion of Title VII." [14] And Harry Blackmun wrote separately in *Weber* to "share some of the misgivings" expressed in Rehnquist's dissent.[15]

The harmony *Weber* projects between an employer and its union, litigating hand-in-hand to improve the economic position of African Americans, is also delusive. Convergence of interests between unions and employers was rare. Unions responded to their majority, which typically meant white workers, and—given the growing disparity between union and nonunion wages—employers endeavored to thwart union efforts to organize their workforce and to shed unions where they existed.[16] Employers generally emerged victorious.

The lower courts in *Weber* had not made any finding of prior racial discrimination by either Kaiser or the steelworkers union. But it was not in the company's nor the union's interest to establish past discrimination. Despite a long history of racial segregation in the craft unions and among Louisiana employers, silence allowed both the company and the union to avoid any responsibility for racial discrimination.[17] *Weber*'s ongoing significance lies in the wedge the controversy exposes between white and minority workers. Rather than engaging in a joint project to enhance their economic well-being, they had become caught up in a contest over the legal and social meaning of discrimination and in a competition for scarce, well-paid industrial jobs.

On August 5, 1981, President Ronald Reagan fired more than eleven thousand air traffic controllers who had walked off the job two days earlier in an illegal strike. Reagan not only broke the strike; he destroyed the air controllers' union. By portraying the union as caring only for its narrow self-interest, Reagan incited widespread hostility to unions, especially unions of public employees. It was the first time since a nationwide 1894 railroad strike that the federal government had broken a union. Unsurprisingly, Reagan's appointees to the National Labor Relations Board (NLRB) were notoriously hostile to unions.

Alan Greenspan (who Reagan appointed in 1987 to chair the Federal Reserve) described Reagan's destruction of the workers' union, the Professional Air Traffic Controllers Organization (PATCO) as "perhaps the most important" of Reagan's domestic accomplishments.[18] The historian Joseph McCartin, who has written a book about the episode, calls it "one of the most significant events in 20th Century U.S. labor history"— a catalyst that helped make "the years 1979–1983 the most vulnerable moment for American workers since the Great Depression."[19] Reagan's action apparently emboldened large numbers of private and other public employers to fire striking workers, an action that had long been legally permissible.

Reagan's decision to fire the air traffic controllers, however, was just one reason for unions' decline.[20] Demographic changes were also important: the fastest growing segment of the labor force was female employees in the South, often performing traditionally nonunion work in a traditionally antiunion region. Selfish and corrupt union leaders also abetted unions' decline.[21] The economic shocks and challenges of the 1970s and the deep recession of the early 1980s threatened middle-class workers' livelihood.[22] Rampaging inflation was eroding workers' purchasing power, as was competition from products from Japan and Europe, newly resurgent after the devastation of World War II. Many economists were emphasizing a new era of limits: the bestselling economics book of the times was *The Zero-Sum Society*.[23] Workers could no longer count on economic growth to produce good jobs or growing wages. As country songwriter Dwight Yoakam sang: "All those years of payin' union dues . . . sure didn't seem to count for much when we got our layoff news."[24]

Congress has long been bedeviled about how to ameliorate the difficulties individual employees have in attempting to bargain successfully with their employers over wages and working conditions.[25] Over time, it has vacillated between specific legislation, such as limits on maximum hours or requirements of minimum wages, and relying on collective bargaining by union representatives to redress individual employees' weaknesses in negotiations with their employers. Robert F. Wagner, the New York senator who led the effort for the 1935 National Labor Relations Act (often called the Wagner Act), viewed collective bargaining as a better alternative than government regulation of labor contracts.[26] Extensive government regulation of labor contracts, he feared, risks creating a "despotic state."[27]

In 1947, following an especially strike-torn year, Congress—overriding a veto by President Harry Truman—enacted the antiunion Taft-Hartley Act curtailing unions' ability to strike. That law expanded protections for employers' efforts to stop unionization and opened the door to vigorous antiunion campaigns.[28] It also affirmed states' rights to enact "right to work" laws that allow workers to refuse to pay union dues even when the union is obligated to bargain on their behalf. Three decades later, in 1978, the Senate failed by one vote to break a filibuster blocking pro-union legislation that would have increased the prospects of collective bargaining by limiting employers' ability to engage in antiunion activities and increasing sanctions for doing so.[29] That was the last hurrah for union rights in Congress.

The gaps in the ability of collective bargaining to support individual workers left a vacuum that Congress and state legislatures attempted to fill with more legal protections for individual workers.[30] In the 1960s, Congress enacted nondiscrimination legislation directed at both employers and unions, most notably the Equal Pay Act of 1963, which bars lower pay for women performing the same jobs as men, and Title VII of the 1964 Civil Rights Act. In the Equal Employment Act of 1972, Congress extended Title VII to public employees. During the 1970s, Congress added other laws protecting workers, such as the Occupational Safety and Health Act of 1970 (OSHA) and the Employee Retirement Income Security Act of 1974 (ERISA). State legislatures and courts also added legal protections for wrongful terminations of employment.[31] Once all workers enjoyed protections such as these, potential gains from collective bargaining were diminished.

Now fewer than 7 percent of private workers are unionized, and half of the nation's 14.5 million union members are government employees.[32] Some economists often advance limited union representation as one important explanation for the wage stagnation since the 1970s of middle-class workers.[33]

When Warren Burger took his Supreme Court seat, union representation was already declining, dropping another 10 percentage points while Burger was chief justice.[34] In contrast to Lewis Powell's commitment to enhancing the power of American business, the Burger Court contained no effective union advocate. The Court's only two reliable liberals, William Brennan and Thurgood Marshall, were quite conflicted when it came to labor unions. Brennan's father, a stationary fireman in the boiler room of the P. Ballantine & Sons New Jersey brewery, was a local leader and national vice president of the International Brotherhood of Stationary Firemen and president of the Essex County Trades Council.[35] Before becoming a judge, Brennan himself had been an effective labor lawyer— but he represented employers resisting unions, not unions or employees.[36] A 1939 profile described Brennan as having "pitted his legal skill against counsel for a great many labor unions."[37] In 1946, after representing Western Electric Company, when it was facing a strike that had turned violent, Brennan showed some empathy for unions, saying that except in industries "of vital public importance," "strikes are not too great a penalty for industrial freedom."[38] But a few months later, speaking to the Newark Rotary Club and endorsing the antiunion Taft-Hartley legislation, Brennan described organized labor as "a powerful giant . . . inclined to play bully and . . . dictate its own terms without regard to the common good."[39] William Brennan, the liberal lion, was hardly the unions' ally.

The Court's other reliable liberal, Thurgood Marshall, was ambivalent toward unions. As a young civil rights lawyer, he had urged blacks to join labor unions, but he also complained of the rampant racial discrimination prevalent in many unions.[40] Marshall had personally litigated, for example, an employment discrimination case against the boilermakers union in Rhode Island.[41] When forced to choose between unions and blacks or other minorities complaining of union discrimination, Thurgood Marshall usually sided with the minorities.

Potter Stewart, an Ohio Republican, had long been associated with Ohio's notoriously antiunion senator Robert A. Taft, having supported Taft for president in the late 1940s.[42] Richard Nixon's four appointees— Burger, Blackmun, Powell, and Rehnquist—were quite conservative in labor cases. Speaking for the four Nixon appointees and William Douglas in a 1974 decision limiting application of the Wagner Act for a group of middle-management employees, Powell said: "It seems wrong, and it is wrong, to subject people . . . who have demonstrated their initiative, their ambition, and their ability to get ahead, to the leveling process of seniority, uniformity, and standardization . . . fundamental principles of unionization."[43] Harry T. Edwards (a University of Michigan labor law professor who in 1980 was appointed by Jimmy Carter to replace David Bazelon on the Federal Court of Appeals for the D.C. Circuit) complained that the Nixon appointees voted together in three-fourths of the labor and employment discrimination cases that were not unanimous. The Burger Court, he said, reduced "labor's arsenal of economic weaponry."[44] Former head of the NLRB and Stanford law professor William Gould agrees: the Burger Court, he said, demonstrated a "declining sympathy for organized labor."[45]

Favoring Businesses over Unions

While the loss of union membership, influence, and power was attributable to a complex interplay of economic, political, and societal forces, the Court was not unaffected by these forces. Employees and unions won about half the time in the Burger Court, but this provides a poor signal of the Court's impact.[46] In the most important labor cases, unions lost. And once Reagan was elected president, Supreme Court deference to decisions of his antiunion NLRB tended to produce antiunion results.[47] The Burger Court's labor law decisions facilitated union decline.

One of the Burger Court's greatest blows against unions came in 1974. Until 1970, the NLRB had frequently recognized union representation when the union presented the board with cards signed by a majority of employees. In the last major labor decision of the Warren Court in June 1969, the Court unanimously rejected employers' claims that authorization cards were inherently unreliable and ordered employers who had engaged in intimidating antiunion campaigns to bargain with unions that had obtained signed cards from a majority of employees authorizing the union as their bargaining agent.[48] Five years later, the Burger Court, in an opinion by Justice Douglas for a 5–4 majority, concluded that employers may refuse to accept authorization cards signed by a majority of employers, forcing unions to win a secret-ballot election before an employer is required to bargain with it.[49] Unions have long attempted to get Congress to overturn this decision. Barack Obama supported such "card-check" legislation as a senator, and he urged its enactment after becoming president. In 2009, the Democratic majority in the House of Representatives passed a card-check bill, but it died in the Senate.[50]

The Burger Court also expanded employers' ability to enjoin strikes. Reversing a Warren Court precedent, the Court in 1976 decided that striking warehouse workers have no First Amendment right to peacefully picket their company's store located in a shopping center mall.[51] Consumer boycotts—a long-standing technique used by unions in their disputes with employers—did not fare any better than picketing. In 1980, the Court rejected the Warren Court's conclusion that First Amendment protections for speech demand considerable leeway for consumer boycotts by unions, and, for the first time, banned picketing of customers by striking workers.[52] Powell's plurality opinion brushed aside the lower court's suggestion that halting the picketing might violate the First Amendment, observing that "such picketing spreads labor discord by coercing a neutral party to join the fray."[53] This disdain contrasts sharply with the support Powell and his colleagues accorded commercial and political speech by business corporations.

The Burger Court frequently upheld employers' prerogatives in their confrontations with unions. The Court made clear that when all or part of a business is sold or merged into a new company, the new business may generally shed an existing collective bargaining agreement by refusing to hire the previous workforce even if the new enterprise engages in the same business operations as its predecessor.[54] In combination with other Burger Court decisions, this gave corporations disincentives to hire a substantial number of the predecessor's employees except when it is unavoidable because of the employees' unique knowledge or skills.[55] Employers also became more adept at forcing employees to strike and then permanently replacing the strikers with nonunion workers.[56]

When an employer goes into bankruptcy, the Burger Court unanimously determined that the bankruptcy court has the power to void a collective bargaining agreement.[57] So employers in financial difficulty often rely on bankruptcy judges to break or modify union contracts.

Sometimes employers will threaten a bankruptcy petition in an effort to persuade unions to modify existing collective bargaining agreements and reduce wages and benefits. Airline companies shedding unions have been the most notorious beneficiaries of this regime.[58]

Finally, lest any doubt remains regarding the Burger Court's tilt toward business over labor, consider the Court's decision in *First National Maintenance Corp. v. NLRB*,[59] decided in 1981, the year that Ronald Reagan broke the air traffic controllers' union. The employer was a small New York firm, First National Maintenance (FNM), that provided cleaning and maintenance services at a variety of locations in the New York area. The controversy concerned the status of maintenance workers at a Brooklyn nursing home, who had voted to be represented by a union, District 1199, which represented hospital and health care workers nationally. Once the union was certified, FNM closed its Brooklyn nursing home operation without notifying the union or bargaining with it. The thirty-five workers there no longer had jobs nor any right to transfer to a job in any of the company's other locations.[60] The NLRB determined that FNM had violated the Wagner Act by failing to bargain with the union over its decision to abandon this location. The Court of Appeals for the Second Circuit agreed.

Then, someone at the Chamber of Commerce decided—because FNM was losing money at the Brooklyn nursing home and there was nothing in the record reflecting FNM's animus toward the union—that this was an ideal case to take to the Supreme Court. The attorney hired by the Chamber—Marvin Frankel, a former federal judge, Columbia law professor, and well-known lawyer—drafted FNM's petition for certiorari and its Supreme Court briefs, in addition to the *amicus* brief he filed on behalf of the Chamber of Commerce.[61] As the Chamber predicted, the Supreme Court treated this case as one involving a management decision reflecting no antiunion sentiment, even though FNM's lawyer had advised his client that District 1199 was a "difficult" and "militant" union that the company should strongly resist.[62] At conference, the justices voted 7–2 (with only Brennan and Marshall dissenting) in favor of FNM. Burger assigned the majority opinion to Blackmun. Blackmun's *FNM* opinion incorporates a 1964 concurrence of Potter Stewart, which had insisted that some "managerial decisions, which lie at the heart of entrepreneurial control" are completely free of any legal obligation to bargain with workers or their union and endorses management's needs for "speed, flexibility, and secrecy in meeting business opportunities."[63] *First National Maintenance* leaves employers free unilaterally to close plants, move business locations, and automate business processes without any legal requirement to bargain with their union or their employees.[64] The Court made a clear choice: when a company decides to relocate or downsize, the costs of such decisions often fall on workers whose jobs are lost or replaced.[65]

Race Divides America's Workers

Conflicts between unions and employers were only one chapter in the story of workplace controversies in the Burger era. As *Weber* illustrates, the Burger Court played a key role in controversies over nondiscrimination and affirmative action in employment (and in government contracting), disputes that drove a wedge between white and minority workers, helped destroy the Democrats' working-class coalition, and transformed American politics.[66]

Although some unions, such as the United Packinghouse Workers and the United Auto Workers, were integrated, many more unions had long been segregated. Racial conflicts were common.[67] George Meany, the longtime head of the AFL-CIO, refused in 1959, for example, to support an effort by black workers and their leaders to bar segregated unions or segregated local branches. Instead, Meany simply defended "the democratic rights of Negro members to maintain the unions they want."[68] That year, a Washington, D.C., electricians union barred African Americans from working on construction of the AFL-CIO's national headquarters.[69]

In October 1961, the U.S. Commission on Civil Rights concluded in a lengthy report on employment discrimination that "most international unions have failed to exhibit any profound concern over civil rights problems." The report continued: "within the labor movement itself, civil rights goals are celebrated at the higher levels, but fundamental internal barriers tend to preserve discrimination at the workingman's level." "Race prejudice," the commission said, is "sometimes a convenient vehicle to deter Negro workers from becoming competitors for jobs. . . . Even those unions which admit Negroes to membership . . . may discriminate against them with respect to job opportunities. . . . Existing federal law," the commission concluded, "has little impact on the discriminatory practices of labor organizations."[70] A year later, Roy Wilkins, head of the NAACP, said that despite "much talk and few deeds on civil rights," a "Negro worker needs the patience of Job, the hide of an elephant, plus a crowbar to get into Mr. Meany's own union—the plumbers."[71]

Few remember it today, but when Martin Luther King gave his famous "I Have a Dream" speech late in the afternoon of August 28, 1963, before a crowd of 200,000 gathered on the Washington Mall, his audience had marched on Washington for "Jobs and Freedom." King was the last speaker of the day; the first was A. Philip Randolph, a seventy-four-year-old black labor activist, who had spent decades trying to break down racial barriers in America's unions.[72] Just over a year later, Lyndon Johnson signed the Civil Rights Act of 1964, with Title VII barring employment discrimination by private employers or unions based on race, color, religion, sex, or national origin.[73] King had spoken before of a "duality of interests of labor and Negroes." "The labor-hater," he said, "is virtually always a twin-headed creature spewing anti-Negro epithets from one mouth and anti-labor propaganda from the other mouth."[74] When he was assassinated at the age of thirty-nine on April 4, 1968, King had traveled to Memphis in support of thirteen thousand black sanitation workers striking because of dangerous working conditions and discriminatory pay. King's efforts to link the civil rights and labor movements went for naught in the decade after his assassination.

Seniority Trumps Equal Employment Opportunity

As with segregated schools, the Burger Court was forced to decide what remedies are appropriate to redress generations of employment discrimination. In a "zero-sum society" with limited economic growth, those remedies might pose risks to the livelihood of white workers who enjoyed seniority over more recently hired African Americans. Union majoritarianism frequently clashed with the individual rights of minority workers. Claims of discrimination by black workers often threatened the pay, and sometimes the jobs, of white workers. Title VII of the 1964 Civil Rights

Act contains a proviso protecting seniority by allowing employers "to apply different standards of compensation, or different terms, conditions or privileges of employment pursuant to a bona fide seniority . . . system, provided that such differences are not the result of an intention to discriminate because of race, color, religion, sex, or national origin."[75]

Divisions among workers based on race, ethnicity, and gender— contesting among themselves and with their employers for slices of the economic pie—burst to the surface while Warren Burger was chief justice. As the historian Daniel T. Rodgers has put it: "Defense of the privileges of whiteness ran as a constant thread through labor movement history."[76] Like Brian Weber, white workers were determined to defend the advantages that their seniority accorded them, even when such seniority thwarted the goal of Title VII to end workplace discrimination. Unlike Brian Weber, they usually prevailed.

The seniority exception was added to the Civil Rights Act in the Senate at the behest of the AFL-CIO, which conditioned its support of Title VII on the protection of seniority arrangements.[77] Overriding seniority as a remedy for racial discrimination, AFL-CIO counsel Thomas Harris argued, "would be unjust to the white workers who have been working there 15 or 20 years."[78] The AFL-CIO believed that the seniority provision would protect the racial status quo of seniority systems for a generation.[79]

For the first decade or so following Title VII's enactment, lower courts interpreted the seniority exception narrowly, reasoning that Congress had not intended to "freeze an entire generation of African American employees out of jobs or promotions based on the ongoing effects of past discriminatory patterns of seniority systems."[80] And, in 1976, in its first case involving the seniority exception, the Burger Court, in an opinion by William Brennan, signaled that existing seniority systems were not inviolate by granting retroactive seniority to black truck drivers who had been discriminated against by both their employer and their union.[81] Justice Powell, however, in a memorandum to his colleagues described his views and Brennan's as "irreconcilable."[82] Both Powell (joined by Rehnquist) and Burger wrote separately to emphasize their concerns that the seniority granted to the black truck drivers should not adversely affect "wholly innocent employees."[83] Those employees' interests, they said, should be weighed heavily in fashioning an appropriate remedy for the black victims of discrimination.[84] These worries echo the anxieties these justices expressed for white students in cases involving public school integration.

The next year, Powell and Burger secured a majority of the Court to preserve seniority despite its racially discriminatory effects. The case, *Teamsters v. United States*, again involved African American truck drivers.[85] The lower courts found that the employer, a nationwide freight trucking firm, had engaged "in a pattern and practice of employment discrimination against Negroes and Spanish-surnamed Americans" and that the teamsters union had violated Title VII "by agreeing with the employer to create and maintain a seniority system that perpetuated the effects of past racial and ethnic discrimination."[86] In what some commentators described as a "bombshell," the Court, by a 7–2 majority (with only Brennan and Marshall dissenting), overturned a decade of lower court precedent and upheld the seniority system.[87] Along with a companion case involving female flight attendants (issued the same day with the same majority), the *Teamsters* decision made clear that a seniority system that is facially applicable to all racial and ethnic groups but has the effect of perpetuating racially discriminatory employment opportunities does not violate Title VII so long as the seniority system itself "was negotiated and [is] maintained free from any [discriminatory] purpose."[88] Proving a discriminatory purpose is, of course, manifestly difficult.

After *Teamsters*, the Burger Court made clear that, absent proof of a discriminatory purpose in establishing and continuing the system, it would protect seniority systems despite their impact in limiting employment opportunities of African Americans and other minorities.[89] In a 5–4 decision (with Stevens, Blackmun, Marshall, and Brennan in dissent), the Court decided in 1982 that a seniority system that adversely affected black employees was immune from challenge even if it was adopted after Title VII had taken effect by an employer who had a prior history of "overt race discrimination."[90] That same year, a case brought by black employees of an Alabama manufacturer of railroad freight cars, claiming that a seniority system was adopted by its employer and its unions for the purpose of maintaining racial discrimination, reached the Court.[91] At trial, the Alabama district court determined that despite "ample discrimination by the company in its employment practices and some discriminatory practices by the union," the seniority system was "in no way related to the discriminatory practices."[92] The Fifth Circuit Court of Appeals reversed, finding that the seniority system was invalid because "the differences in the terms, conditions, and standards of employment for black workers and white workers resulted from an intent to discriminate because of race."[93] In an opinion by Justice White for a 7–2 majority, the Court reversed the Fifth Circuit, concluding that a finding of discriminatory intent is purely a factual matter for the trial court to determine, one that cannot be satisfied by "something less than actual motive."[94] Thurgood Marshall dissented (joined by Brennan), insisting that the appellate court had found "overwhelming evidence of discriminatory intent."

Another question remained: would the Burger Court uphold a seniority system that clearly had an adverse racially discriminatory impact on black workers when it conflicted with a court-ordered consent decree entered into by an employer to settle charges of racial discrimination?[95] In a 6–3 decision (with Brennan, Marshall, and Blackmun dissenting), the Burger Court—siding with a firefighters union and relying on its *Teamsters* decision—concluded that the seniority system prevailed. Even though a disproportionate number of black firemen would be laid off and the goals of the consent decree disrupted, the Court said that the black firemen had failed to show that the city or the union had a motive to discriminate in establishing the seniority system. After this decision, Ronald Reagan's Justice Department, with Reagan's approval, sent letters to over fifty state and city governments informing them that they must modify consent decrees to eliminate timetables and affirmative action goals.[96]

Then, in May 1986, just months before Burger stepped down to lead the nation's bicentennial celebration of the Constitution, the Court confronted a challenge to provisions of a collective bargaining agreement between a teachers union and the public school board of Jackson, Michigan, which provided that if layoffs became necessary, white teachers with greater seniority would be laid off before minority teachers with less seniority in order to maintain the same percentage of minority teachers that existed before the layoffs.[97] Lewis Powell, in an the opinion for a sharply divided Court, insisted that such a provision, explicitly based on race, could survive "strict scrutiny" only if the minority teachers could prove prior racial discrimination by the school board.[98] As he had in the contexts of school desegregation and higher education, Powell "expressed concern over the burden that a preferential-layoffs scheme imposes on innocent parties."[99] Hiring goals, Powell said, "do not impose the same kind of injury that layoffs impose. Denial of a future employment opportunity is not as intrusive as loss of an existing job."[100] Emphasizing the "adverse financial as well as psychological effects" of the layoffs and the "serious disruption" of the lives of the senior white employees,[101] Powell failed to comment concerning the similar consequences that the Court's decision imposed on the more recently hired minority teachers. As Marshall said in dissent, Powell's "analysis overlooks the important fact that [the collective bargaining agreement] does not cause the loss of jobs, someone will lose a job under any layoff plan and, whoever it is, that person will not deserve it."[102] Nevertheless, the collective judgment of Jackson's school board and its union about who would bear these costs was, according to a 5–4 majority, unconstitutional.

As our nation struggled for a new labor market free from racial discrimination, a majority of the Burger Court came down on the side of white workers protected by seniority. Absent proof of an "actual" discriminatory purpose, seniority systems—no matter when established or how long they might perpetuate employment disadvantages for black employees—became invulnerable to challenge under Title VII.

The Burger Court's solicitude for seniority has had lasting impact. In 2009 the Supreme Court relied on *Teamsters* in determining that an employer does not violate Title VII's prohibition against sex discrimination when it credits women, who took pregnancy leave before the enactment of the Pregnancy Discrimination Act of 1978, with less seniority than other employees who took medical or disability leaves for the same period of time, but for different reasons.[103] Unsurprisingly, Ruth Bader Ginsburg dissented, insisting that the Pregnancy Discrimination amendments to Title VII were meant to protect women "against repetition or continuation of pregnancy-based disadvantageous treatment."[104] As many as fifteen thousand women may receive smaller pension benefits because of this decision.[105]

Before the Burger Court entered the fray, all that the lower courts had generally required to modify a seniority system was that its racially discriminatory effects were foreseeable. Employers and unions were treated as having intended the consequences of their actions. The Burger Court, however, claimed that proof of an employer's or union's "actual motive" to racially discriminate was a congressional mandate. Before long—with no statutory hook—the Burger Court would also limit constitutional race discrimination claims to circumstances where an actual discriminatory purpose could be proved.

Employment Discrimination and Affirmative Action

The boundary between eliminating employment discrimination and affirmative action has been blurry from the beginning. Ironically, given the split it ultimately provoked between white and black union members, the phrase "affirmative action" appeared first in the Wagner Act, which provided that an employer who is found to be discriminating against union members or organizers must stop and take "affirmative action" to put the victims where they would have been absent such discrimination.[106] In the civil rights context, the phrase originated as a legal matter in John Kennedy's Executive Order 10925, issued on March 6, 1961, establishing the President's Committee on Equal Employment Opportunity (chaired then by Vice President Lyndon Johnson) to review federal government employment and government contractors and their unions to ensure that they did not discriminate based on race, creed, color, or national origin. The executive order told the commission to recommend "affirmative steps" to "realize more fully the national policy of nondiscrimination," and told government contractors to "take affirmative action to ensure that applicants are employed" on a nondiscriminatory basis.[107] Title VII of the Civil Rights Act, enacted a year later, explicitly permits courts to order "affirmative action" where employers or unions have intentionally engaged in racial discrimination.[108] A year after that, on September 24, 1965, President Johnson issued his own executive order repeating the requirement that federal contractors take "affirmative action" to ensure that applicants are employed and treated without discrimination based on race.[109] (In 1967, Johnson added women to the list.)

When Richard Nixon followed Johnson to the presidency, he took steps toward implementing Johnson's vision by requiring specific racial hiring goals and timetables in government construction contracts in Philadelphia.[110] George Meany described this "Philadelphia Plan" as part of Nixon's war against unions, of "trying to make a whipping boy out of the Building Trades."[111] Some analysts view Nixon's affirmative action program as reflecting his sincere desire to increase black employment opportunities.[112] Others regard this as a typically Nixonian ploy to enrage white working-class Democrats. Historian and journalist Rick Perlstein says that Nixon's affirmative action plan "drove a wedge through the Democratic coalition at its most vulnerable joint: between "blacks and hardhats"—while making Nixon look noble.[113] Whatever Nixon's motive, division followed. Affirmative action in university admissions was controversial and received most of the publicity, but, during the bad economic times of the 1970s, white resentment became targeted at affirmative action in employment and in government programs that favored hiring minorities and contracting with minority-owned businesses.

The manner in which Title VII's discrimination prohibition was enforced added fuel to the fire. Title VII created the Equal Employment Opportunity Commission (EEOC) and assigned it the task of investigating discrimination complaints and attempting to cajole employers and unions into compliance with the law's nondiscrimination mandate. If this conciliation effort failed, however (until amendments to Title VII in 1972), the EEOC had no independent enforcement power but had to refer cases to the Justice Department, which would decide whether to take legal action. By the late 1960s, the EEOC was receiving and investigating fifteen thousand complaints annually; it typically managed to settle only about five hundred of these, often taking up to two years to complete an investigation.[114] John David Skrentny has described how the bureaucratic necessity of identifying which employers to investigate induced the EEOC to require all large employers to detail the racial composition of their workforce.[115] Such reporting not only exposed companies with few minority employees; it also identified comparable companies with many more. Enforcement based on numbers soon became the norm. In an early influential study of EEOC's enforcement efforts, Columbia University law professor (and later university president) Michael Sovern pointed out that an employer with "about the 'right' proportion of Negroes" would be "virtually invulnerable to a charge of discrimination."[116] Employment discrimination enforcement based on a company employing the "right proportion" of minorities inevitably produced charges that Title VII was requiring racial quotas.

The Burger Court first directly confronted Title VII enforcement in a lawsuit by thirteen African American janitors and workers at other menial jobs against a Duke Power Company electricity generation plant in rural North Carolina.[117] The facility employed ninety-five employees, including fourteen blacks. Workers at the plant were divided into five divisions. All the black employees worked in the "labor" division, where the highest pay was less than the lowest pay in the other four divisions, even though many of the whites had not finished high school.[118] Duke Power explicitly engaged in racial discrimination in its hiring and promotion practices prior to the enactment of Title VII.[119] On the day Title VII went into effect, the company instituted a new policy requiring employees in all divisions other than the labor division to achieve a certain score (approximately the national median for high school graduates) on two aptitude and intelligence tests, in addition to graduating high school.[120] The trial court concluded that these requirements did not violate Title VII, and the Fourth Circuit Court of Appeals agreed, because there had been no proof that Duke Power had a discriminatory purpose in adopting the diploma and test requirements.[121]

After the Supreme Court heard oral argument, there were clearly six votes to reverse the lower courts and uphold the black plaintiffs' claims of discrimination. (Brennan did not participate in the case, which was decided before Powell and Rehnquist joined the Court.) Only Burger and Black were unsure how to rule. Black said he was "inclined to affirm," regarding Duke Power as "doing its best to comply" with a "new act."[122] Having initially expressed his unease with upholding the company's policies and then learning of a possible 6–2 split, Burger joined the majority and chose to write the opinion himself.[123] In what ultimately turned out to be a unanimous decision finding a Title VII violation, Burger said "Good intent or absence of discriminatory intent does not redeem employment procedures or testing mechanisms that operate as 'built-in headwinds' for minority groups and are unrelated to measuring job capability."[124] Recognizing that the black plaintiffs had received an inferior segregated education, the Court demanded that the diploma and test requirements "bear a demonstrable relationship to successful performance of the jobs for which [they are] used." "The touchstone," Burger said, "is business necessity."[125]

The Court's 1971 decision in *Griggs v. Duke Power Company* was widely heralded as affirming the EEOC's emphasis on hiring and promotion results. The Court had accepted the argument advanced by both the NAACP and Erwin Griswold, Nixon's solicitor general, that Title VII "may no more be frustrated by apparently neutral employment practices, not justified by business necessity, which have racially exclusionary effects than by overtly discriminatory practices." [126] After *Griggs*, an ostensibly neutral standard for employment or promotion could violate Title VII if it would have a foreseeable racially disparate impact not justified by business necessity.

As had the Burger Court's early segregated-school decisions, *Griggs* induced great optimism for Title VII enforcement among civil rights advocates, optimism bolstered by numerous lower court decisions applying the disparate impact standard to strike down employment practices by both public and private employers. [127] As with school desegregation, however, it did not take very long for the Burger Court to alter direction. The turning point came in a 1976 decision, *Washington v. Davis*, where the Court rejected the use of racially disparate impact to evaluate the lawfulness of an employment examination that the District of Columbia used in hiring police. [128]

African American applicants who had been rejected for employment as police officers sued the District of Columbia in 1970, two years before Congress made Title VII applicable to local governments. Consequently, the plaintiffs brought their case directly under the Constitution's equal protection guarantee. In the beginning, that distinction seemed without a difference: lawyers assumed that the disparate-impact standard the Supreme Court had applied to Title VII in *Griggs* also governed discrimination cases brought directly under the Constitution. The Court had never ruled to the contrary. Indeed, the justices had never considered the issue.

So *Washington v. Davis* proceeded on its path to the Supreme Court, where it arrived in the spring of 1975, just like a Title VII case. The District of Columbia required applicants for the police force to pass a written test of verbal aptitude, which black applicants failed at a rate four times that of whites. The question was whether the District could show, as *Griggs* had demanded of Duke Power Company, that the requirement was job-related—that success on the test, which consisted of eighty multiple-choice questions, actually correlated with success as a police officer. The U.S. Court of Appeals for the District of Columbia Circuit held that the department failed to carry this burden and ruled for the black plaintiffs. But by a vote of 7–2, the Supreme Court reversed.

Washington v. Davis would prove to be one of the Burger Court's foundational constitutional rulings. In an opinion by Byron White, the court held that the Constitution's guarantee of equal protection was violated only by official action undertaken with the intent to discriminate. Evidence of disparate impact was not sufficient to prove a constitutional violation. Although decided in the context of public employment, the discriminatory intent requirement of *Washington v. Davis* has had major ramifications for any claim that a law or policy neutral on its face nonetheless discriminates on the basis of race, sex, or other protected category. Often in such cases, plaintiffs can amass statistical evidence, but a smoking gun—proof of discriminatory intent—remains elusive. *Washington v. Davis* has thus migrated far beyond employment, cutting off claims of unconstitutional discrimination in the context of the death penalty,[129] the disenfranchisement of prisoners and former prisoners, and numerous others.[130]

What is remarkable about the case is how no one, not even the justices, anticipated the crucially important question the court would end up deciding. A fascinating and unexplored episode of the Burger years, the story of *Washington v. Davis*, a landmark, illustrates the almost random way that law evolves.

When the District of Columbia's appeal reached the Supreme Court, a law clerk named Kenneth W. Starr drew the assignment of writing the "pool memo" for the justices, summarizing the issues for their consideration in deciding whether to grant review. Later to gain fame as the independent counsel investigating President Bill Clinton in the Whitewater affair, Starr (who also served as a federal appeals court judge, U.S. solicitor general, dean of Pepperdine University Law School, and president of Baylor University) was clerking for Burger. Nothing in his memo indicated that the case was anything special or that it involved anything other than an application of *Griggs*. This was hardly surprising, because neither the parties nor the lower court had suggested that the constitutional claim required a different standard from that of Title VII.

"The majority's result is arguably consistent with some of *Griggs'* sweeping language prohibiting any employment practice which *cannot be shown* to be related to job performance if an adverse racial impact results," Starr wrote in his memo, dated August 22, 1975. Without making a specific recommendation on whether the court should take the case, Starr observed that the employer here seemed to be on firmer ground than Duke Power was in *Griggs*: "Everyone seems to admit that verbal skills are job-related in nature." [131]

Even after the Court took the case, the justices regarded it as just one among many, and not a very interesting one at that. (The court heard argument in 172 cases during the 1975 term, well over twice the number it hears today.) "Is this case really very important?" Harry Blackmun asked himself in notes he made while preparing for argument. In any event, he said, "the test is demonstrably job related. . . . A policeman must obviously possess a substantial degree of verbal skill." [132] Nowhere in Blackmun's six pages of notes to himself is there any hint that the disparate-impact standard might itself be in question. The solicitor general had asked the Court for extra argument time. Blackmun wrote to his colleagues opposing the request. "I regard the case as not that important and the issue as not that difficult," he said. "I could find other uses for the time." [133]

But another view began to emerge as the justices prepared for argument. Lewis Powell's clerk, Christina B. Whitman, urged him to consider whether the case might not present a deeper question than appeared on the surface. "This Court must decide (either explicitly or implicitly) whether ordinary equal protection analysis or Title VII law is to be applied in this case," she wrote. She reviewed an emerging jurisprudence in which the Court had suggested that mere discriminatory impact was insufficient in constitutional cases without some evidence of discriminatory purpose. She continued: "Both parties—and the courts below—assumed that the inquiries set forth in *Griggs* are appropriate. The issue is not briefed at all. But I am unconvinced. It is not surprising that the applicability of Title VII standards has been assumed. The lower courts have generally made no distinction between Title VII standards and those appropriate under the Equal Protection Clause."

Whitman, who went on to a long career as a law professor at the University of Michigan, offered a suggestion for how to proceed: "If it is decided eventually that equal protection analysis is appropriate, the case should be [sent back to the trial court] so that the complaint can be amended. I realize that all this sounds like a drastic move this late in the game, but it is better to do this than to constitutionalize *Griggs* and Title VII *sub silentio*." In the margin is Powell's handwritten annotation: "Yes."[134]

The court heard the case on March 1, 1976. At the justices' conference two days later, the vote was 7–2 to reverse the appeals court and rule for the District of Columbia.[135] Burger evinced no particular interest in what standard to apply. The court of appeals had simply "misread *Griggs*," he said. "The test doesn't have to be the best possible." Blackmun expressed a similar view. It was "not a bad test," he said. Stevens said he would reverse under either Title VII or Equal Protection. "The difference in standards may not be very different in a case of this kind," he said. "The total picture here is not one of discrimination."

But four other justices drove the conversation deeper as they explained their reasons for voting to reverse. It would be a difficult case under Title VII, Stewart said. "But this is not a Title VII case." He said the plaintiffs had to prove discriminatory intent and "such a showing is not made here." He concluded: "That is the end of this case." White, Powell, and Rehnquist agreed with Stewart. "The test was neutral and the Constitution requires no more," White said.

Only Brennan spoke at length urging a different outcome. There is "no difference between Equal Protection and Title VII standards," he said, "but in any event, the D.C. Circuit was entitled to rely on Title VII standards." *Griggs*, he said, "required the city to show by professionally competent witnesses that the test is job-related." Marshall agreed.

Despite the emergence of a consensus, the case still presented a problem: the Court was about to answer a question that no one had asked of it. The parties had not briefed the question—a fact that had led Powell's law clerk to recommend a remand. But the Court's appetite was whetted. White's opinion for the Court dealt with the problem succinctly. The court of appeals had applied the wrong standard, White wrote. "Although the petition for certiorari did not present this ground for reversal, our Rule 40(1)(d)(2) provides that we 'may notice a plain error not presented'; and this is an appropriate occasion to invoke the Rule."[136]

White then moved directly to the merits:

> As the Court of Appeals understood Title VII, employees or applicants proceeding under it need not concern themselves with the employer's

possibly discriminatory purpose but instead may focus solely on the racially differential impact of the challenged hiring or promotion practices. This is not the constitutional rule. We have never held that the standard for adjudicating claims of invidious racial discrimination is identical to the standards applicable under Title VII, and we decline to do so today.[137]

While acknowledging that "there are some indications to the contrary in our cases,"[138] and that the many lower court decisions applying disparate impact "impressively demonstrate that there is another side to the issue,"[139] White went on:

> A rule that a statute designed to serve neutral ends is nevertheless invalid, absent compelling justification, if in practice it benefits or burdens one race more than another would be far-reaching and would raise serious questions about, and perhaps invalidate, a whole range of tax, welfare, public service, regulatory, and licensing statutes that may be more burdensome to the poor and to the average black than to the more affluent white.[140]

Yet, despite the sweeping nature of these statements, there is ambiguity in White's opinion. It appears to leave the door at least ajar to invoking discriminatory effect in order to show discriminatory purpose. "This is not to say that the necessary discriminatory racial purpose must be express or appear on the face of the statute," White wrote, "or that a law's disproportionate impact is irrelevant in cases involving Constitution-based claims of racial discrimination."[141] "Invidious discrimination," he said, "may often be inferred from the totality of the relevant facts.[142]

John Paul Stevens, in a concurring opinion, did not read the court as foreclosing evidence of effects. "The line between discriminatory purpose and discriminatory impact is not nearly as bright, and perhaps not quite as critical, as the reader of the Court's opinion might assume," Stevens wrote.[143] He suggested that for future cases, context would matter. "Frequently," he said, "the most probative evidence of intent will be objective evidence of what actually happened rather than evidence describing the subjective state of mind of the actor."[144] The foreseeability of a discriminatory impact might suffice to show discriminatory intent, "for normally the actor is presumed to have intended the natural consequences of his deeds." [145]

But the Burger Court quashed that possibility three years later in resolving an equal protection sex discrimination challenge to an especially generous preference in all of its civil service hiring by the state of Massachusetts for veterans who scored passing marks on civil service examinations. [146] This was an unfortunate case to bring to the Supreme Court. Preferences for veterans in state and federal civil service hiring have a long history in America. [147] As the Court observed, veterans' hiring preferences had long "been justified as a measure designed to reward veterans for the sacrifice of military service, to ease the transition from military to civilian life, to encourage patriotic service, and to attract loyal and well-disciplined people to civil service occupations." [148] So it is hardly surprising that the Court rebuffed the sex discrimination claim of Helen Feeney. Feeney, having worked effectively for the state for twelve years, had been passed over for promotions many times by veterans who had scored considerably lower on civil service exams. She was understandably frustrated. Her battle with Massachusetts, however, was of no avail to her, and it substantially set back the prospects for successful discrimination claims by other disadvantaged women and minorities. [149] By a 7–2 vote, with only Brennan and Marshall dissenting, the Court—in a decision that Eleanor Smeal, president of the National Organization for Women, described as "devastating"—upheld the state's preference for veterans, while recognizing that the law predictably "benefits an overwhelmingly male class." [150] (Few women had served in the military by then. Over one quarter of Massachusetts's population were veterans; only 1.8 percent of these were women.) [151]

Justice Stewart's opinion for the Court emphasized that the Massachusetts law involved a facially neutral classification. "When the basic classification is rationally based," Stewart said, "uneven effects upon particular groups within a class are ordinarily of no constitutional concern. The calculus of effects, the manner in which a particular law reverberates in a society, is a legislative and not a judicial responsibility." [152] The existence of an inevitable and foreseeable discriminatory impact was of little relevance. "Discriminatory purpose," Stewart continued, "implies more than . . . intent as awareness of consequences. It implies that the decisionmaker . . . selected or reaffirmed a particular course of action at least in part 'because of,' not merely 'in spite of,' its adverse effects upon an identifiable group." [153]

Reva Siegel, a Yale constitutional law professor, describes the Burger Court's decisions in *Davis* and *Feeney* as having "changed the structure of Equal Protection doctrine . . . first by sharply differentiating review of race-based and facially neutral statutes, and, then, by sharply differentiating proof of purpose and proof of impact." [154] After 1979, minorities and women advancing constitutional challenges to laws that would inevitably harm them had to prove they were enacted or maintained because of an actual purpose to discriminate. [155] Laws or policies that explicitly advantage minorities, in contrast, after *Bakke*, are subject to "strict scrutiny" and struck down unless they further a "compelling" state interest and do so by "the least restrictive means."

In 1984, Clarence Thomas—who headed Ronald Reagan's EEOC, and in 1991 would take Thurgood Marshall's place on the Supreme Court—attacked the use of disparate impact under Title VII. [156] Once on the Supreme Court, Thomas's antipathy to both disparate impact as a basis for evaluating claims of discrimination and to affirmative action in any form became legendary. [157] In 1988, Reagan's Justice Department made clear its intention to limit affirmative action and to require proof of an actual intent to discriminate to bring any racial discrimination claim. [158] In 1989, it achieved Supreme Court success after William Rehnquist had become chief justice. [159] Congress, however, two years later, reaffirmed the role of disparate-impact testing for discrimination under Title VII. [160] The ongoing validity of that legislation is under threat in the Supreme Court. [161]

After Warren Burger stepped down, the Supreme Court, led first by William Rehnquist, then by Rehnquist's former law clerk John Roberts (who had served in Reagan's Justice Department), continued an effort to halt, if not dismantle, affirmative action programs and to limit discrimination claims by minorities and women. A 2009 Roberts Court decision resolving a complaint by a white firefighter who had been passed over for promotion by the city of New Haven, Connecticut, exposes how far the ground has shifted. The case was brought by Frank Ricci, who in 2003 took a written civil service exam used by the city in assessing promotions to lieutenant or captain in its fire department. [162] Of the 118 firefighters who took the exam, forty-one whites, nine blacks, and six Hispanics passed, but under city rules none of the blacks qualified for promotion. The collective bargaining agreement between the firefighters union and the city required that the written exam count for 60 percent of the total score with the oral portion counting for 40 percent, a ratio that blacks had long complained about. After the city announced that no blacks and only one Hispanic would be promoted, a group of minority firefighters threatened to sue, claiming that the city's promotion process had a racially discriminatory disparate impact on them.[163] The city responded by announcing that it would void the test results and retest all the applicants. Ricci, a dyslexic fireman who had worked diligently to score highly on the test, sued the city, claiming that its decision to throw out the original test results unlawfully discriminated against him based on his race.

In a 5–4 decision, with opinions spanning nearly one hundred pages, the Supreme Court agreed. Anthony Kennedy, writing for the majority, described the city's decision to substitute a new test as intentional discrimination based on race. The city, he said, had rejected the test results—which the Court found to be "job-related and consistent with business necessity"—"solely because the higher scoring candidates were white."[164] In a concurring opinion, Antonin Scalia complained that the Court had ducked, for the time being at least, a decision that the 1991 law codifying the disparate impact test of *Griggs* was unconstitutional.

Ruth Bader Ginsburg authored a passionate dissent, emphasizing the "long shadow" of the legacy of racial discrimination by cities in hiring firefighters and by firefighter unions, including in New Haven.[165] She questioned in detail the evidence of job relatedness or business necessity of the written test and complained of the 60/40 weighting of the written portion required by the city's agreement with the union—pointing out that in Bridgeport, a city of similar size just down the highway that gave primacy to the oral portion of its exam, minority firefighters held one third of lieutenant and captain positions. Disparate treatment and disparate impact, she said, are "twin pillars of Title VII," and they "advance the same objectives: ending workplace discrimination and promoting genuine equal opportunity."[166] But Ginsburg's view garnered only four votes.

Toward the end of his opinion for the Court, Justice Kennedy claimed that the *Ricci* decision "clarifies how Title VII applies to resolve competing expectations under the disparate-treatment and disparate-impact provisions." [167] The disparate-impact pillar now stands on shaky ground—ground that the Burger Court weakened when it began to require a finding of discriminatory purpose. The Court's decisions in *Davis* and *Feeney* laid the groundwork, allowing the even more conservative courts that followed to ignore the foreseeable (and sometimes inevitable) adverse consequences of laws and policies on the employment opportunities of blacks, other minorities, and women. Coupled with the requirement, first announced in *Bakke*, that courts must view with heightened scrutiny policies or legislation that explicitly advantage blacks or other minorities, the Burger Court set the table for the ongoing legal attacks on affirmative action.

Is "Diversity" a Lifeline?

The Burger Court decided hundreds of cases concerning employees' complaints of disadvantages in their workplace. In the most important conflicts between businesses and unions, business interests prevailed. When African American workers tried to advance employment opportunities at the potential expense of white workers with greater seniority, the Court ensured that seniority practices established by employers or through collective bargaining with unions remained inviolate. Finally, as in the context of school desegregation, after appearing ready to advance vigorously the interests of blacks and minorities in achieving equal opportunity, the Burger Court retreated, circumscribing the ability of minority and women workers to redress grievances and limiting both public and private employers' ability to engage in affirmative actions on behalf of blacks or other minorities.

In taking these steps, the Court conformed the legal landscape to better match the economic, social, and political changes that were taking hold. Our nation moved to the right during Warren Burger's time on the Court. The energy of the civil rights revolution dissipated, replaced by white working-class anxieties about economic security and cultural decline. Jim Crow had been dismantled; widespread working-class perceptions of unfair advantages for blacks and other minorities in hiring and promotions had come to the fore. This anxiety replaced the earlier emphasis on redressing the country's long history of racial subjugation and discrimination. These were forces that the Burger Court chose not to resist.

Largely through initiatives by corporate human resources departments, Lewis Powell's reliance in *Bakke* on "diversity" as a constitutionally appropriate basis for allowing colleges and universities to admit more blacks and minorities disseminated into the employment context. Businesses became convinced that a racially and ethnically diverse workforce is a business asset in an increasingly global marketplace.[168] Companies' efforts to achieve diversity among their employees became a crucial source of employment opportunity for African Americans, women, Hispanics, and Asians. Despite those efforts, however, disadvantages remain. *The New York Times* has reported that the commitment of private sector employers to affirmative action has often been ineffective and may be diminishing.[169] Even so, minority workers now appropriately rely more for economic opportunities on the volition of employers than on the Supreme Court; this speaks volumes about how far the law has moved since the Burger Court in 1971 in *Griggs* upheld the challenge by Duke Power's black workers.

―――――――――― PART FIVE ――――――――――

The Presidency

The Founders, having witnessed and rejected the tyranny of kings, split governmental power into many pieces, first in the states and subsequently for the national government. The separation of powers—with its "checks and balances"—is a fundamental feature of the government of the United States. The first three (of seven) Articles of our Constitution describe the composition, method of selection, and responsibilities of the three branches, providing that (1) "all legislative power herein granted shall be vested in a Congress of the United States"; (2) "the executive power shall be vested in a President of the United States"; and (3) "the judicial power of the United States shall be vested in one Supreme Court and in such inferior courts as the Congress may . . . establish."

No one expected the relationships among the three to be perfectly harmonious. Before he became president, Woodrow Wilson, speaking of the separate branches, said:

> Government is not a machine, but a living thing. . . . It is accountable to Darwin, not to Newton. It is modified by its environment, necessitated by its tasks, shaped to its functions by the sheer pressure of life. . . . There can be no successful government without leadership or

without the intimate, almost instinctive, coordination of the organs of life and action.[1]

Disputes between the Congress and the president are common, but rarely have they reached the fever pitch of the Nixon presidency. Nixon's has been described as an "Imperial Presidency," and not just because he outfitted the White House police in European palace style uniforms with starred epaulets, gold piping, draped braids, and tall black plastic hats festooned with a large White House crest.[2] (In 1980, the outfits, which only Nixon had used, became uniforms of the Southern Utah State marching band.) Soon after his inauguration, Nixon began impounding funds that Congress had appropriated in laws that he had signed, because he disagreed with the congressional purposes and policies.[3] This was a direct challenge to Congress's power of the purse and its primacy in domestic affairs. The Burger Court rejected the president's assertions of such broad power in a dispute between the executive branch and the state of New York.[4]

In foreign affairs and national security, where the president has always enjoyed more constitutional sway than in domestic affairs, Nixon regarded the president as completely unconstrained, not only in his role as commander in chief over decisions about where and how to deploy force, but also in the ability to engage in domestic wiretaps and other surveillance without any judicial permission or oversight. In a May 1977 interview—nearly three years after Nixon had resigned the presidency—the English journalist David Frost asked the former president about his approving "the systematic use of wiretapping, burglaries, or so-called black bag jobs, mail openings and infiltrations against anti-war groups and others." Nixon famously responded: "Well, when the president does it, that means it's not illegal."[5] Elections and congressional appropriations, he said, provide adequate checks on potential presidential abuse. Nixon elaborated: "If the President, for example, approves something because of the national security, or . . . because of a threat to internal peace and order of significant magnitude, then the President's decision in that instance is one that enables those who carry it out, to carry it out without violating the law. Otherwise they're in an impossible position."[6]

During Warren Burger's time as chief justice, the Court confronted what was potentially the greatest constitutional crisis since the Civil War. Richard Nixon's involvement in the Watergate affair led to the first resignation of a president in the nation's history. Disputes between Congress and the president led Congress to enact legislation to enhance its own power vis-à-vis the president—most notably the War Powers Resolution of 1973 and the Budget and Impoundment Control Act of 1974.[7] The conflicts concerning presidential power that arose out of Nixon's presidency required the Court to resolve crucial disputes with the press and among the branches of government.

Nowhere does the Constitution say that the judiciary shall serve as the final arbiter of disputes among the three branches or as the referee of disputes between Congress and the president. The Constitution does not even say that the Supreme Court shall have the ultimate say over the Constitution's meaning or the power to invalidate on constitutional grounds laws passed by Congress and signed by the president. But the Court has for two centuries exercised that power, after it was established by Chief Justice John Marshall in 1803.[8] Today, no one challenges these functions—powers that, as Yale constitutional law professor Alexander Bickel said, were "summoned up out of the constitutional vapors."[9] The reach of the power the Supreme Court exercises over the other branches of government is unimaginable in most other democracies.

Richard Nixon may have created the Burger Court, but he did not control it. The Court forced the president from office through a unanimous opinion ordering him to yield tapes of the White House–orchestrated cover-up of the crimes that came to be known as Watergate—tapes that Nixon himself, remarkably, had created, tapes that demonstrated his guilt beyond any doubt. That is, of course, the fundamental irony at the heart of Richard Nixon's relationship to Warren Burger's Supreme Court.

But another irony cuts in the opposite direction. While helping to push this grievously lawless president out the White House door, the Burger Court also strengthened the presidency. In the Nixon tapes case itself, the Court for the first time recognized the concept of presidential executive privilege (while finding that the needs of the criminal justice system overcame the privilege in Nixon's case). And in a subsequent decision rejecting a Pentagon whistle-blower's suit against Nixon for dismissing him, the Court established every president's absolute immunity from liability for actions taken in the course of his official duties.

This complex and fascinating tale of the Supreme Court's confrontation with the essence and excesses of the presidential power of Richard M. Nixon—a legacy with enduring significance—is the subject of the next two chapters.

CHAPTER 12

Power and Its Abuse

Richard Nixon detested the unruly young protesters against the Vietnam War. His hatred of the press was also legendary; his principal speechwriter, William Safire (who became a *New York Times* columnist after Nixon's resignation), said, "I must have heard Richard Nixon say 'the press is the enemy' a dozen times."[1] But most of all Nixon loathed "leakers," government employees who made unauthorized disclosures to the press, disclosures that often produced news reports adverse to his administration. Nixon's national security adviser, Henry Kissinger, shared Nixon's abhorrence of leakers. Their determination to stop such leaks became evident just months after Nixon's inauguration when they began wiretapping the phones of national security officials and a few reporters. When these wiretaps were first initiated, they were not clearly illegal, but, as this chapter will describe, the Supreme Court determined that such wiretaps without a court-authorized warrant were unlawful.

Wiretaps, however, did not long satisfy Nixon. Beginning in 1971, he created a new unit within the White House, the so-called plumbers, who conducted a number of nefarious activities on the president's behalf, culminating in the break-in of the Democratic headquarters in the Watergate office building. The event that triggered this escalation was *The New York Times*'s publication in June 1971 of the *Pentagon Papers* and the Burger Court's refusal—in its first test of Nixon's presidential power—to halt that publication.

Publication of the *Pentagon Papers*

The *Pentagon Papers*, formally titled "History of U.S. Decisionmaking on Vietnam Policy," is a seven-thousand-page, forty-seven-volume, sixty-pound review of the history of the United States' involvement and military escalations in Vietnam.[2] In January 1969, only fifteen copies of the history, which was classified "Top Secret" and marked "sensitive," existed. This document was prepared at the request of Defense Secretary Robert McNamara, beginning in June 1967. It was finished on January 15, 1969, five days before Nixon's inauguration. McNamara assigned responsibility for the project to two of his Defense Department aides, Leslie Gelb and Morton Halperin. In the summer of 1967, Halperin and Gelb fatefully asked Daniel Ellsberg to work on the history. Ellsberg had previously served as a defense contractor with the RAND Corporation, joined the Defense Department in 1964, and done a civilian tour in Vietnam. Gelb did not trust Ellsberg and denied him access to the full set of papers, but Halperin persuaded Gelb to allow Ellsberg, who had all the necessary security clearances, full access. After Nixon's inauguration, Ellsberg, along with Halperin, worked briefly for Kissinger, but Ellsberg, who had become a vocal antiwar critic, left Kissinger's staff in March 1969, less than two months after Nixon's inauguration.

On Sunday, June 13, 1971—two columns to the right of a photo of Richard Nixon proudly walking his older daughter, Tricia, down the aisle at her White House wedding the previous day—*The New York Times* published an article, based on the *Pentagon Papers*, summarizing the history of United States involvement in Vietnam during the previous three decades and revealing deliberate deceptions of the public by its presidents and their cabinet officers.[3] Excerpts from the *Pentagon Papers* were included on six inside pages. Rick Perlstein describes the *Times* article as "a polite way of saying Americans had been lied to for twenty-five years."[4] The next day, the *Times* published another article and another six pages of excerpts from the Defense Department's history, and it promised more to come.

President Nixon's initial instinct was to take political advantage of the disclosures since they revealed duplicity by his Democratic predecessors, John Kennedy and Lyndon Johnson. Nixon wanted everyone to call them the Kennedy-Johnson Papers.[5] At a press conference that Monday,

Nixon's secretary of state, William Rogers, took this tack by saying that he hoped when Nixon left office there would be a study of how Richard Nixon got the United States out of Vietnam.[6]

But Nixon's calm was short-lived. Spurred on by the insistence of Kissinger and his deputy Alexander Haig that the leak was damaging to U.S. interests, Nixon on Monday evening ordered his attorney general, John Mitchell, to file a lawsuit to halt the *Times's* publication. Mitchell then sent a telegram to Arthur Ochs Sulzberger, the *New York Times* publisher, claiming that publication of this classified material violated the Espionage Act, alleging that further publication "will cause irreparable injury to the defense interests of the United States," and requesting that the *Times* cease publication and return the documents to the government.[7] Assistant Attorney General Robert Mardian was put in charge of preparing for litigation, and another assistant attorney general, William Rehnquist, was tasked with evaluating the government's prospects of successfully restraining further publication.[8] The *New York Times* hired Alexander Bickel and Floyd Abrams, a young First Amendment lawyer, to represent it in court.

Initially, Gelb, Halperin, and Ellsberg were each suspected of providing the *Times* with the *Pentagon Papers*, but within a few days the Nixon administration settled on Ellsberg—who had been trying for months to get a senator or congressman to release the *Papers*—as the most likely source. Daniel Ellsberg, with assistance from Anthony Russo, a friend who shared Ellsberg's antiwar views, had indeed provided the *Times* with a copy of the papers.

The Nixon administration soon learned that trying to halt publication of the *Pentagon Papers* was like pushing on a balloon. On Tuesday, June 15, 1971, the government secured a temporary order from a New York federal district court judge prohibiting the *Times* from further publication of the *Papers*. The *Times* complied and did not publish its third installment on Wednesday. On Monday, June 14, however, *The Washington Post* had obtained about two hundred pages of the *Pentagon Papers*—material that the *Times* published on Tuesday. On Wednesday, the *Post* acquired several thousand additional pages from someone (probably Ellsberg) in Boston.[9] After much agonizing by the *Post's* owner, editorial staff, and lawyers about the propriety of publishing this material in light of the court order against the *Times*, the *Post* on Thursday ran a "first of series" story with a four-column front-page headline: "Documents Reveal U.S. Effort in '54 to Delay Viet Election." [10]

The next day, Assistant Attorney General William Rehnquist called the *Post*'s executive editor, Ben Bradlee, and read to him a message from the attorney general identical to the telegram that Mitchell had sent to the *Times* earlier that week. [11] The Justice Department then went to the federal district court for the District of Columbia seeking to restrain publication by the *Post*. In the *Post* case, the court denied the government's request. The government appealed. Fearful that the Justice Department might ask Chief Justice Burger for an immediate order restraining publication, the *Post* sent two reporters to Burger's home in Arlington, Virginia, to watch for government lawyers. Near midnight, the *Post* reporters, who had been unable to reach Burger by telephone, knocked on his door to tell him what they were doing there. The chief justice answered the door in his bathrobe, carrying a long pistol which he held in his right hand, muzzle down, throughout the few minute conversation with the reporters, whom he told to wait down the street. The reporters wanted the *Post* to publish the story of Burger's attire and weapon, but Bradlee was fearful of the cartoons that might result and antagonize the chief justice just as the paper was about to appear before him, so he killed the story. [12]

By the weekend, other newspapers had obtained portions of the papers. All told, articles based on excerpts from the *Pentagon Papers* were published by seventeen different newspapers.

The activity in the courts was hectic. Within two weeks, federal appellate courts in New York and D.C. had issued conflicting orders in the *Times* and *Post* cases. On June 24, the Supreme Court granted certiorari in *The New York Times* case and by a 5–4 vote restrained both the *Times* and the *Post* from publishing any more from the *Papers* until the Court decided the case. [13] The Court gave the parties less than twenty-four hours to brief the case, and, on June 26, heard oral argument. Four days later, on June 30, 1971—seventeen days after the *Times*'s initial article—the Court announced its decision. [14]

After oral argument, the justices quickly realized that crafting a majority opinion with the normal give-and-take among them would substantially delay both the decision and their summer break. [15] They agreed instead to issue a very brief per curiam opinion setting forth the result and stating simply that the government had not met the "heavy burden" necessary to justify a "prior restraint" of publication. Each of the justices then wrote separately, with their nine opinions reflecting their divergent views of the case. The vote was 6–3 with Burger, Harlan, and Blackmun voting to uphold the injunction prohibiting publication and to return the case to the lower courts for a more careful evaluation of the government's claim that publishing the *Pentagon Papers* would seriously impair national security. The three dissenters agreed that the Court had treated the case with too much haste. At the conference following the argument, Burger said that he could not vote on the merits because of the way the Court had been rushed. Harlan agreed, saying that "the judicial process has been made a travesty." [16] As Harlan put it in his dissenting opinion, the Court "has been almost irresponsibly feverish in dealing with these cases." [17] In contrast, the six-justice majority concluded that restraining publication of the papers was unwarranted: the government had failed to prove that publication of this history would sufficiently impair national security to justify restraining their publication. But they agreed on little else.

Justice Black, writing his last opinion before retiring, reiterated his long-standing view—with which only Douglas agreed—that the First Amendment was an absolute bar against enjoining publication, regardless of the potential damage to national security. The majority's view that publication may sometimes be enjoined, Black said, "would make a shambles of the First Amendment." [18] Black was angry that Alexander Bickel had not argued the case solely on First Amendment grounds and had put so much emphasis on the limitations of presidential power. Bickel's concession that there might be a time when national security could outweigh the First Amendment rights of the press galled Black, prompting him to say to his law clerks, "Too bad the *New York Times* couldn't find someone who believes in the First Amendment." [19] But Bickel needed five votes, not just two.

In his own concurrence (joined by Black), Justice Douglas added that the "dominant purpose of the First Amendment was to prohibit the widespread practice of governmental suppression of embarrassing information." [20]

At conference, Justice Brennan said that he did not agree with Black and Douglas, [21] and he left some room in his opinion for enjoining publication, in "a single, extremely narrow class of cases," such as identifying troop movements when the nation is at war. [22] But the government, he said, "comes here with a heavy burden."[23] The government's claim, Brennan said, is that "publication of the material sought to be enjoined 'could' or 'might' or 'may' prejudice the national interest in various ways. But the First Amendment tolerates absolutely no prior judicial restraints of the press predicated upon surmise or conjecture that untoward consequences may result."[24]

The three other justices in the majority agreed that the government faced a "heavy burden" to overcome in obtaining an injunction against publication. To Justices Stewart, White, and Marshall, however, the central question was the nature of the checks and balances on what Stewart (in an opinion joined by White) described as the "enormous power" of the president "in the two related areas of national defense and international relations."[25] Stewart observed that the president's power in these two areas has been "largely unchecked by the Legislative and Judicial branches," and that our Constitution grants the president "vastly greater constitutional independence" in these arenas than "a prime minister of a country with a parliamentary form of government." He added, "the only effective restraint upon executive policy and power in the areas of national defense and international affairs may lie in an enlightened citizenry."[26] Stewart said that if publication "would result in the sentencing to death of one hundred young men," he would enjoin that sort of publication.[27] But neither Stewart nor White was convinced that publication would "surely result in direct, immediate, and irreparable damage to our Nation or its people." Absent that, they were unwilling to prohibit publication. Offering a bit of advice to the executive branch—advice that has been ignored—Stewart said that wisdom requires "avoiding secrecy for its own sake." "When everything is classified," he said, "then nothing is classified."[28]

Justice White (in an opinion joined by Stewart) rejected the government's claim that "the President is entitled to an injunction whenever he can convince a court that the information to be revealed threatens 'grave and irreparable' injury to the public interest." White emphasized the criminal penalties Congress had provided for disclosure of classified material under the Espionage Act and observed that, given "the hazards of criminal sanctions, a responsible press may choose never to publish the more sensitive materials." At the justices' conference, White had described the *Times* as "criminally liable."[29]

White also underscored how infrequently prior restraint cases will arise. "Normally," he said, "publication will occur and the damage be done before the Government has either opportunity or grounds for suppression.[30] During the conference after oral argument—contrary to Solicitor General Erwin Griswold's statement at argument that no additional injunctions would be needed—law clerks informed the justices that the government had obtained a restraining order against the *St. Louis Post-Dispatch*.[31]

Justice Marshall's concurring opinion, like White's and Stewart's, treated the case as raising separation of powers issues. Picking up on an argument advanced by Professor Bickel, Marshall said that Congress had provided no authority for courts to enjoin publication of material that might damage national security, but instead had provided in the Espionage Act only a criminal penalty for doing so. In such circumstances, Marshall said, the courts and the executive branch cannot "make law" to enjoin publication of potentially damaging classified material.[32] Marshall never mentioned the First Amendment in his opinion, reflecting his agreement with Justice Harlan's comment at conference that the key question here was "the scope of judicial review over the Executive."[33]

Chief Justice Burger conceded that the potential harms to the national interest were uncertain, but he nevertheless would have left the injunctions in place during further proceedings in the lower courts to delve into the merits of the government's claims. Justices Harlan and Blackmun also preferred more extensive hearings below, but, based on the potential for harm to the nation and their views of the proper deference to the executive branch in matters concerning national security, they would have upheld the government's position and prohibited publication.

In this conflict between the newspapers' right to publish and national security, the newspapers won. But only on the question whether a "prior restraint" should halt publication. Despite the nine different opinions—and the impending retirement of Hugo Black, followed a few years later by William Douglas, who were the only advocates of the absolute primacy of the First Amendment—the *Pentagon Papers* case continues to warn against judicially enforced prior restraints on press publication of classified materials, even when publication might harm the national security.[34] But the ability to publish does not provide the press with immunity against criminal prosecution. Five justices made clear that they saw no bar to criminal prosecution of *The New York Times* and *The Washington Post* under the Espionage Act. As John Jeffries has emphasized, such a prosecution would ratify Justice Blackmun's claim in dissent that "what is needed here is a weighing, upon properly developed standards, of the broad right of the press to print and of the very narrow right of the Government to prevent."[35] This sentiment was also expressed by Erwin Griswold during oral argument when he admitted seeing "no alternative" to the Court serving as a "censorship board."[36] Justice White was right, however, when he observed that opportunities for prior restraint are rare, so the necessary standards for weighing these competing interests have not developed. With the exception of cases where authors have explicitly contracted not to reveal government secrets, Blackmun's balancing hardly ever occurs.[37]

The July 1, 1971, edition of *The New York Times* rolls off the press as the newspaper resumes publication of the *Pentagon Papers* following the Supreme Court's decision.

At oral argument, Justice White asked Griswold whether the government would criminally prosecute the newspapers if it failed to obtain injunctions prohibiting publication. Griswold responded that, although it would "technically be a crime" to publish, he found it "exceedingly difficult to think that any jury would convict or that an appellate court would affirm a conviction of a criminal offense for the publication of materials which this Court has said could be published."[38] Griswold was prescient: following the *Pentagon Papers* decision, the government has largely abandoned efforts either to enjoin publication or to impose criminal sanctions on publishers of leaked classified information. Although the government vigorously pursued a criminal prosecution of Daniel Ellsberg for leaking the *Pentagon Papers*, it never brought any criminal charges against the newspapers that published the material.

A key legacy of the *Pentagon Papers* case, therefore, is what Columbia law professor David Pozen, in a comprehensive 2013 *Harvard Law Review* article on national security leaks, calls the "source/distributor divide." The way the law is now applied, Pozen says, affords "so little protection for the leaker and yet so much protection for the journalist who knowingly publishes the fruits of the leaker's illicit conduct and thereby enables the very harm—revelation of sensitive information to the public and to foreign adversaries—that the leak laws were designed to combat."[39] This dichotomy was not necessitated by or even contemplated in the Court's opinions in the *Pentagon Papers* case, but in subsequent decades, such disparate treatment has become an important legacy of this decision.

In fact, prosecutions for leakers are themselves quite rare. The Obama administration—in what Attorney General Eric Holder described as a logical legal response to an increasing number of serious leaks—brought twice as many prosecutions for leaking classified information as all of its predecessors combined: eight between 2009 and 2013.[40]

Although the *Pentagon Papers* decision makes clear that such a prosecution is constitutionally permissible, the government has never prosecuted the media for possessing or publishing classified information. Prosecutors have, however, on occasion sought information identifying reporters' sources of classified information.[41] Two notorious instances involved *New York Times* reporters: Judith Miller, who in connection with the 2005 prosecution of Vice President Dick Cheney's aide I. Lewis "Scooter" Libby spent eighty-five days in jail for refusing to identify the source of a leak of the identity of a CIA agent,[42] and James Risen, who faced possible criminal prosecution in 2013 for refusing to testify against Jeffrey Sterling, a former CIA official charged with leaking classified information about a CIA program designed to interfere with Iran's effort to produce nuclear weapons.[43] The Justice Department has issued guidelines limiting the occasions in which the government will make such requests from reporters, but no court has yet upheld a privilege for reporters allowing them to withhold information about their sources in a criminal trial.[44] As the Court of Appeals said in Risen's case: "There is no First Amendment testimonial privilege, absolute or qualified, that protects a reporter from being compelled to testify by the prosecution or defense in criminal proceedings about criminal conduct that the reporter personally witnessed or participated in."[45] Risen asked the Supreme Court to review his case, but it refused. Then, Risen again refused to testify and the Justice Department backed down.[46] Sterling, however, was convicted, demonstrating the truth of the source-distributor divide.

Two days before the Supreme Court announced its *Pentagon Papers* decision, Daniel Ellsberg was indicted for violating the Espionage Act and a federal criminal law prohibiting the theft of government property. His first trial was dismissed before verdict after the prosecutors revealed that the government had wiretapped a conversation between the defendant and his lawyers. A second trial commenced in January 1973, but in April, the government prosecutors admitted to the judge that Howard Hunt and G. Gordon Liddy, two key operatives of the White House's plumbers unit, had broken into the offices of Ellsberg's psychiatrist in an effort to obtain information helpful to the prosecution. Four days later, the *Washington Star-News* revealed that the judge in the case had met with Nixon and domestic policy adviser John Ehrlichman to discuss potentially being appointed FBI director. A few days after that, the government disclosed that wiretaps of Ellsberg dated from 1969 or 1970. The judge then dismissed all the charges against Ellsberg on the ground of government misconduct.[47]

The government's case against Ellsberg did not founder because the threats to national security from publication of the *Pentagon Papers* were imaginary, but it might have. Many years later, Erwin Griswold—who had argued to halt publication in both the D.C. appellate court and the Supreme Court and submitted to the Court a secret brief containing eleven alleged national security threats—admitted: "I have never seen any trace of a threat to the national security from the publication. Indeed, I have never seen it even suggested that there was such an actual threat."[48] It is "apparent," he added, that "the principal concern of the classifiers is not with national security but rather with governmental embarrassment of one sort or another."[49]

The lies that were revealed by publication of the *Pentagon Papers*, along with Nixon's expansive views of executive power, prompted Congress in 1973 to enact the War Powers Resolution in an effort to limit the circumstances under which the president could initiate military hostilities without congressional approval. That law has not been completely successful.

The political consequences of the *Pentagon Papers* episode surpassed its legal fallout. The leak and publication of the *Pentagon Papers* in 1971 prompted Nixon to set up the plumbers unit within the White House, and, with Nixon's blessing, that group initiated illegal activities (including the Ellsburg break-in) that ultimately led to the Watergate break-in and Nixon's resignation.[50] The publication of the *Pentagon Papers* also ended the American people's willingness to believe what the government told them about Vietnam and took an enduring toll on the public's belief in and respect for government.[51] The history of government officials' lies concerning Vietnam, followed closely by Watergate, inculcated a distrust of government that played an important role in generating the anti-government sentiment that moved our nation's politics to the right.

For the Burger Court, the *Pentagon Papers* case was the opening act in a drama concerning the president's authority in the national security realm. The next important decision occurred in what started out as an ordinary criminal case involving "national security" wiretaps.

Restraining Warrantless Domestic Wiretaps

If he were a fictional character, Lawrence "Pun" Plamondon would seem a caricature of a radical 1960s hippie.[52] He was born in a mental hospital in Traverse City, Michigan, the son of an alcoholic father and syphilitic mother, both of Native American descent. A high school dropout, he spent a hyperactive childhood in Catholic schools and reform schools. In the late 1960s, he lived in Detroit, partaking amply of sex, drugs, and rock 'n' roll, but after the 1967 Detroit riots, he became a political radical who helped found the White Panther Party as a counterpart to the Black Panther Party, a group of militant black radicals. In 1968, he and another White Panther exploded a dynamite bomb at a clandestine CIA office near the University of Michigan's Ann Arbor campus. Hiding from the law abroad and in the United States, Plamondon soon made the FBI's Ten Most Wanted Fugitives list. In 1970, he was arrested in Michigan when he and some friends were stopped by the Michigan State Police for throwing empty beer cans out of a van, and he was recognized by the police officer. Plamondon later described this incident as exhibiting a "lack of revolutionary discipline."[53]

At Plamondon's trial for bombing the CIA, his defense lawyers learned from an affidavit by John Mitchell that some of Plamondon's conversations had been overheard in government wiretaps authorized by the attorney general but not approved by any court. The wiretaps, Mitchell said, "were being employed to gather intelligence information deemed necessary to protect the nation from attempts of domestic organizations to attack and subvert the existing structure of the Government."[54] Mitchell's affidavit said that it "would prejudice the national interest to disclose the particular facts concerning these surveillances other than to the court *in camera*."[55] The government claimed that "the surveillance was lawful, though conducted without judicial approval, as a reasonable exercise of the president's power (exercised through the Attorney General) to protect the national security."[56]

The Supreme Court disagreed by an 8–0 vote (with Rehnquist not participating because of his former Justice Department boss John Mitchell's involvement). The Court concluded that presidential claims concerning national security do not create an exception to the Fourth Amendment's requirement that domestic electronic surveillance must be approved by a court, a requirement that had been confirmed by the Warren Court in 1967 for ordinary law enforcement wiretaps.[57] The majority opinion by Justice Powell (joined by Douglas, Brennan, Marshall, Stewart, and Blackmun) begins by describing the issue as "an important one for the people of our country and their Government. . . . It involves the delicate question," Powell said, "of the President's power, acting through the Attorney General, to authorize electronic surveillance in internal security matters without prior judicial approval."[58] But, he insisted, the question before the Court is a "narrow one," limited to whether the special circumstances applicable to "domestic security surveillance" necessitate an exception to the Fourth Amendment's requirement that the government obtain prior judicial approval in a warrant authorizing the surveillance.[59] Despite "the pragmatic force" of the government's position, the majority concluded that "an appropriate prior warrant procedure" was required. Powell's opinion explicitly refused to address surveillance of "activities of foreign powers or their agents."[60]

Justice White wrote a separate concurring opinion stating that he viewed statutory limitations on wiretapping under the Omnibus Crime Control and Safe Streets Act of 1968 as prohibiting the warrantless wiretapping here. Unlike the majority, he saw no need to reach the constitutional issue as to whether this wiretap was barred by the Fourth Amendment's prohibition on unreasonable searches and seizures.

Warren Burger was clearly unhappy with Powell's opinion and refused to join it. He also refused to join White's concurrence. Rather than say what he thought, Burger simply asked Powell to note that the chief justice concurred in the result. At the justices' conference, Burger had said "I am not ready to vote," but he indicated that he was inclined to agree with White that the statute required the government to obtain a warrant in this case. Justice Douglas then complained about Burger's practice of refusing to take a position at conference but nevertheless controlling opinion assignments. "He usually passes," Douglas said, "hoping to be in the majority and able to assign."[61] Burger did, in fact, try to assign the majority opinion to White, but Douglas refused to go along, saying (correctly) that White would not command a majority. Douglas insisted that Powell write for the majority, an astute strategic move intended to ensure that Powell, who had expressed support for the government's ability to engage in such wiretaps when he was president of the American Bar Association, stayed with the majority.[62] After Burger acquiesced in the assignment to Powell, he shared no further views of the case with his colleagues.

The Supreme Court's 1972 decision in the *Keith* case (formally styled *United States v. U.S. District Court*, but known as *Keith*, the name of the federal district judge) required the government to reveal to Plamondon and his attorneys the conversations that the government had unconstitutionally intercepted. But the government refused and instead dropped its case against Plamondon and his co-defendant.

The prosecution had repeatedly insisted that Plamondon was not the target of the wiretaps, nor had they been intended to collect information about him.[63] One of the defense lawyers speculated that the wiretap was of a conversation among Huey Newton at the Black Panthers' headquarters and Plamondon and Eldridge Cleaver while Plamondon and Cleaver were fugitives together in Algeria.[64] This seems right. Justice Powell examined the wiretaps *in camera* and described them in a file memo as six conversations over a five-month period containing "rather fragmentary exchanges between Plamondon, who is a member of the White Panther Party, with several members of the Black Panther Party." These conversations, according to Powell, related to "possible cooperation between the two organizations on relatively minor matters." Powell concluded that the conversations had no relationship to Plamondon's crime, reflected no foreign involvement, and contained no evidence of planned violence.[65] Nevertheless, the Justice Department preferred abandoning its case against Plamondon rather than establishing the precedent of releasing such wiretaps to defendants and their counsel. The government feared that this case might become the first step in a flood of required releases of extensive wiretaps of domestic political groups. By the early 1970s, domestic FBI wiretaps with no judicial warrant had become commonplace in the United States.

Warrantless wiretaps had been used against organized crime and in domestic security cases at least since 1946 when President Truman's attorney general (and future Supreme Court Justice), Tom Clark, advised Truman that they were necessary "in cases vitally affecting the domestic security."[66] With the exception of a sharp curtailment under Attorney General Ramsey Clark toward the end of the Johnson administration, warrantless wiretaps had been used ever since. In 1956, the FBI established COINTELPRO (Counter Intelligence Program) to break the back of the decaying Communist Party USA.[67] In 1963 COINTELPRO began infiltrating and surveilling many more domestic groups, including the Ku Klux Klan in 1964, black militants (especially the Black Panther Party) in 1967, and the New Left, including civil rights and antiwar organizations, in 1968.

Ironically, the FBI's COINTELPRO activities came to light due to a burglary of an FBI field office in Media, Pennsylvania, by a group calling itself the Citizens' Commission to Investigate the FBI. The burglary occurred on March 8, 1971, when the occupants of the apartment building containing the FBI office were distracted by the heavyweight championship fight between Muhammad Ali and Joe Frazier. A 2014 book, *The Burglary*, reveals the "Citizens' Commission" to have been eight ordinary antiwar citizens, led by a Haverford College physics professor and including a day-care director, a cab driver, a lock picker, and a professor of religion and his graduate-student wife.[68] The burglars provided some of the stolen FBI documents to journalists and members of Congress. A leftist journal called *WIN* published eighty-two pages from the files, revealing the existence of COINTELPRO and broad FBI surveillance of antiwar groups. Two years later, in response to a Freedom of Information Act lawsuit, the Justice Department provided NBC correspondent Carl Stern and CBS correspondent Fred Graham many more documents revealing widespread FBI abuses—abuses that were subsequently confirmed in a 1974 Justice Department report from Attorney General Edward Levi to President Ford. L. Patrick Gray, who served as acting FBI director after J. Edgar Hoover's death in 1972; Mark Felt, who was associate FBI director (and later revealed to be Bob Woodward and Carl Bernstein's "Deep Throat" Watergate source); and Edward Miller, Felt's deputy, were all indicted for illegal break-ins of homes of relatives of members of the radical Weather Underground.

These revelations of FBI misconduct prompted well-publicized congressional hearings, which found that warrantless wiretaps had been commonly used against U.S. citizens who posed no real threat to U.S. security.[69] A Senate staff report concluded that the FBI had been waging a "secret war against those citizens it considers threats to the established order."[70]

In 1976, the Senate established an intelligence oversight committee, followed the next year by a similar House committee. Congress also limited the term of the FBI director to ten years. (J. Edgar Hoover had served in that position from 1924 until his death in 1972.) On March 10, 1976, Attorney General Levi curtailed the ability of the FBI to investigate domestic groups unless it has evidence that the group is preparing to commit an act of violence. The FBI's emphasis then shifted to solving such crimes after they were committed.

In 1978, Congress enacted the Foreign Intelligence Surveillance Act (FISA) as "a response to the revelations that warrantless electronic surveillance in the name of national security had been seriously abused."[71] FISA provides for the use within the United States of "electronic surveillance," a significant purpose of which is to acquire "foreign intelligence information," which the legislation describes rather broadly.[72] FISA generally requires that warrants for such surveillance be obtained from the

FISA Court. The FISA Court is composed of judges appointed by the chief justice, meets secretly in a secure Washington, D.C., facility, and uses expedited procedures to allow prompt action under standards for warrants that are considerably more lenient than in ordinary criminal cases.[73] These procedures closely follow those suggested by Justice Powell in his *Keith* opinion for surveillance concerning domestic security. By empowering the chief justice to appoint members of the FISA Court, Congress actually enhanced the Court's power.[74] In 2013, the FISA regime came under pressure following disclosures by Edward Snowden that revealed the breadth of surveillance and intelligence gathering by the National Security Agency.

Interestingly, FISA does not apply to purely domestic security surveillance where no foreign power or persons are involved. In such cases, *Keith* continues to govern, and a warrant must be obtained in the normal manner from a federal judge or magistrate.

Following the terrorist attacks of September 11, 2001, both George W. Bush and Barack Obama claimed that congressional enactments of Patriot Act laws expanded their powers to act unilaterally regarding domestic surveillance in an effort to prevent or halt terrorist acts. But, as New York University Law School dean Trevor Morrison has observed, Justice Powell's opinion in *Keith* "is still the Supreme Court's most important statement on the general topic of electronic surveillance."[75] Both the Supreme Court in *Keith* and Congress in FISA made clear that—even where the national security is potentially at stake—electronic surveillance is too powerful and too intrusive to be left solely to the discretion of the president and his subordinates.

But the *Keith* case did not address the question as to whether the National Security Agency has the unilateral authority to find out whom Americans are calling (without listening to the calls) in the absence of a warrant. That issue is heading toward the Supreme Court as we write. The key precedent is a decision of the Burger Court in a more routine criminal case.[76]

In 1979, in *Smith v. Maryland*, the Court in a 5–3 decision upheld police installation without any warrant of a "pen register" at a telephone switching office to identify and record the numbers dialed from the telephone of a man accused of a robbery and harassing phone calls to the victim.[77] In a short opinion upholding the police, Justice Blackmun emphasized that the telephone company automatically obtains such information. "It is too much to believe," he said, "that telephone subscribers, under the circumstances, harbor any general expectation that the numbers they dial will remain secret."[78] Since the person who makes the calls has no "legitimate expectation of privacy," the Court concluded that the police action to discover the numbers called was not a "search" entitled to the protections of the Fourth Amendment. Justices Stewart, Brennan, and Marshall dissented.

Chief Justice Burger, who joined Blackmun's majority opinion, agreed in a memorandum to Blackmun that the caller's "urge for privacy" did not mean that he had "a constitutionally protected right." "Congress," Burger said, "could require a warrant but the Constitution does not." He closed with a P.S.: "I'm going to use a public phone for my calls to my bookie."[79]

In 2012, the Supreme Court unanimously required a warrant for police placing a GPS tracking device on an automobile to monitor a suspect's travels for several weeks.[80] Justice Scalia, writing for the majority, relied on the traditionally salient fact that the police had physically trespassed onto the suspect's property when they attached the GPS device. A majority of the justices, however, would have decided the case on less formalistic grounds. Justice Sonia Sotomayor (appointed to the Court in 2009 by President Obama) wrote separately, suggesting that it may be time to rethink *Smith v. Maryland.* The Burger Court's approach in that case, she said, "is ill suited to the digital age, in which people reveal a great deal about themselves to third parties in the course of carrying out mundane tasks."[81]

In 2014, the Court unanimously rejected as unconstitutional a warrantless search of smartphones incident to the arrest of a person stopped for a traffic violation and of a man who witnesses said was selling drugs.[82] "Cell phones," Chief Justice Roberts said, "differ in both a quantitative and qualitative sense from other objects that might be carried on an arrestee's person." They often contain "the sum of an individual's private life." So a warrant is required to search a cell phone. "Privacy," Roberts said, "comes at a cost."[83] He distinguished *Smith v. Maryland*, saying that the Court found no search had occurred there.

The key question is whether the Burger Court's decision in *Smith v. Maryland* will survive challenges to the National Security Agency's warrantless collection and evaluation of bulk telephone data throughout America.

A decade after the Burger Court concluded that the domestic wiretaps ordered by top officials of the Nixon administration without obtaining a court order were unlawful, the Court faced the question whether a victim of illegal wiretaps could obtain damages from the perpetrators. It did so, however, in an illusory case, a case that seems to be about something else altogether.

Liability for Illegal Acts

When the Court finally addressed the question of the liability of government officials, including the president, for illegal acts, Richard Nixon was a party. In Nixonian fashion, the contest was deceptive: it appeared to concern the firing of Ernest Fitzgerald, a Defense Department whistle-blower who, to Nixon's dismay, told Congress about massive cost overruns on a defense transport plane. Fitzgerald sued Nixon and some of his aides, including Bryce Harlow and Alexander Butterfield, for damages, claiming that his firing was illegal.[84] By the time the dispute reached the Supreme Court, however, Fitzgerald and Nixon had entered into a "contingent settlement" under which Nixon paid Fitzgerald $142,000 and agreed to pay an additional $28,000 if the Court failed to find the former president immune from liability. The settlement made the lawsuit a charade, but a majority of the Court wanted to use Fitzgerald's claim to resolve a highly contentious dispute that had split the Court 4–4 the previous term.[85]

The protagonist then was Morton Halperin—the Defense Department aide who had co-authored the *Pentagon Papers* and a former member of Henry Kissinger's national security staff who Nixon believed was leaking adverse information to the press.[86] In spring 1969, Nixon and Kissinger had Attorney General John Mitchell order the FBI to place a wiretap on Halperin's home phone, a tap that lasted twenty-one months, from May 1969 until February 1971. After installing the Halperin wiretap, the White House arranged for wiretaps of other Kissinger assistants and several members of the press.

When Halperin learned of the wiretap in 1973, he, along with his wife and children, sued Nixon, Kissinger, Mitchell, and seven other Nixon Administration officials for damages. The federal district court dismissed the suit against all the defendants except Nixon; White House Chief of Staff and Nixon's closest aide, H. R. "Bob" Haldeman; Kissinger; and Mitchell because there was insufficient evidence of the others' responsibility. The judge then concluded that the remaining defendants had acted in "good faith," which he said barred any liability for damages. The court of appeals disagreed and reversed.[87] The Supreme Court's brief opinion in *Halperin v. Kissinger*, issued on June 22, 1981, announced: "The judgment with respect to petitioners Kissinger, Nixon, and Mitchell is affirmed by an equally divided Court."[88] Only eight justices participated in the *Halperin* case: William Rehnquist had recused himself because his former Justice Department boss, John Mitchell, was a defendant. Rehnquist, however was willing to participate in *Nixon v. Fitzgerald* and its companion case, *Harlow v. Fitzgerald*, which together raised similar legal issues concerning the immunity of the president and his aides.

In the months before the Court issued its three-sentence evasion in *Halperin*, hundreds of pages of analysis, principally by Lewis Powell and Byron White, had been circulated among the justices. Powell was determined to provide absolute immunity from liability for the president and quite broad, but qualified, immunity for his aides. He thought he had four more votes: Burger, Stewart, Stevens, and Marshall. By March, White had written several drafts of a proposed dissenting opinion. In a memo to Powell, circulated to the other justices on March 19, White wrote: "The more I get into this case, the more I think that the majority is on a most mistaken course that will disserve the law and the country. . . . Denying remedies across the board for Presidential violations of known constitutional and statutory duties seems to me gross overkill."[89] Marshall had originally said at conference that he agreed with Powell, but ultimately he changed his mind and urged that the justices wait for another case with a full court to decide these issues.[90]

Powell remained unbowed, writing and rewriting a proposed opinion in an effort to secure a fifth vote, but at the end of May he finally gave up. On June 2, Powell accepted a 4–4 outcome in *Halperin* and looked to the *Fitzgerald* dispute to vindicate his position the next term. White wrote only that he would not dissent. The Court's cryptic opinion masked how bitterly the justices had divided over Halperin's right to recover damages for the illegal twenty-one-month wiretap of his home phone. Halperin's case would take another decade to resolve.

The Court then turned to Fitzgerald's quite different complaint. The legal issues concerning immunity of the president and his aides were essentially the same.

The justices attend their former colleague Potter Stewart's funeral at Arlington National Cemetery, December 11, 1985. Stewart died at seventy, four years after retiring. Left to right: Warren E. Burger, William J. Brennan, Jr., Byron R. White, Harry A. Blackmun, Lewis F. Powell, Jr., William H. Rehnquist, John Paul Stevens, and Stewart's successor, Sandra Day O'Connor. Thurgood Marshall is not in this photograph.

The outcome of Fitzgerald's lawsuit seemed to depend solely on William Rehnquist, but on June 18, 1981, Potter Stewart, age sixty-six, announced his resignation from the Court after twenty-three years of service. Ronald Reagan then appointed Sandra Day O'Connor to succeed Stewart. The argument in *Nixon v. Fitzgerald* on November 30, 1981 was among the first she heard.

At the December 2 conference, Rehnquist and O'Connor agreed that the president had absolute immunity against damages resulting from acts while in office. Burger, Stevens, and Powell also continued to favor absolute immunity. However, as Powell began to write an opinion granting absolute immunity to the president—now for a firm five-vote majority—serious doubts about Fitzgerald's case emerged. Six Justices, Brennan, Blackmun, Marshall, Rehnquist, O'Connor, and even Powell himself, were all troubled: some because of the settlement agreement, others because they thought Fitzgerald's lawsuit had no firm legal basis.[91]

But Burger, with strong support from Rehnquist and O'Connor, insisted that the Court had taken Fitzgerald's case to resolve the question of the president's immunity from civil liability.[92] The Chief Justice strongly urged Powell and Stevens, who had supported absolute immunity for the president in *Halperin*, to ratify that view here. In a December 17, 1981, letter to Burger, Powell agreed, and he tailored his opinion to overcome the specific obstacles in the *Fitzgerald* litigation. So, by a 5–4 vote, the Court concluded that a president is "entitled to absolute immunity from damages for liability predicated on his official acts."[93]

Unsurprisingly, Byron White wrote a strong dissent based on his *Halperin* drafts, joined by Brennan, Marshall, and Blackmun. Characterizing the majority's approach as "completely unacceptable," White wrote, "I do not agree that, if the office of the President is to operate effectively, the holder of the office must be permitted, without fear of liability and regardless of the function he is performing, deliberately to inflict injury on others by conduct that he knows violates the law."[94] Making clear that he was not simply raising "a hypothetical example," White referred back to the *Halperin* case, noting the irony that this decision was issued on the "tenth anniversary of the Watergate affair."[95]

Within the Court's chambers, no one who had witnessed the Court's struggle in *Halperin* found the *Fitzgerald* decision surprising, but outside the Court Nixon's escape from any liability for his wrongdoing while in office was major news. Roger Mudd, anchoring the *NBC Nightly News*, described Nixon as again succeeding in "bitterly dividing a branch of the government" and said that the Court's decision placed Nixon "above the law." NBC's Court reporter Carl Stern said that "about half a dozen other lawsuits pending against Mr. Nixon will probably now have to be dropped."[96] Morton Halperin's was one of those.

On the same day it announced its *Nixon v. Fitzgerald* decision, the

Court also issued an opinion in the companion case, *Harlow v. Fitzgerald*, addressing Fitzgerald's suit for civil damages against Nixon's aides Bryce Harlow and Alexander Butterfield.[97] This time the vote was 8–1 in favor of "qualified immunity," with Powell again writing for the majority, joined by all his colleagues except Burger, who was the sole holdout for absolute immunity for the president's aides.[98]

Powell's opinion in *Harlow* has proved to be even more important than the one he authored in *Nixon v. Fitzgerald*. After *Fitzgerald*—with notable exceptions for the president, judges, and prosecutors—absolute immunity has become a rarity. The scope, meaning, and application of the qualified immunity doctrine as transformed by the Burger Court in *Harlow*, however, remains an especially contentious legal doctrine—one that frequently is in conflict with the legal rights the Court has granted to victims of violations of constitutional rights.

In 1971 (before Powell and Rehnquist had joined the Court), in *Bivens v. Six Unknown Named Agents of Federal Bureau of Narcotics*,[99] the Court, over strong dissents by Burger, Blackmun, and Hugo Black, greatly expanded the potential for lawsuits against government officials by deciding that a person who is injured by a federal violation of his constitutional rights—in this case a warrantless search illegal under the Fourth Amendment—may sue to recover damages even if Congress has not authorized such a lawsuit by legislation. The Court in *Bivens*, however, did not address whether the federal narcotics agents might enjoy immunity from personal liability for the damages because that issue had not been decided by the Court of Appeals.

The immunity question came to the Court three years later in a suit for damages on behalf of three students who had been demonstrating against Nixon's bombing of Cambodia in connection with the Vietnam War at Kent State University on May 4, 1970, and were killed by members of the Ohio National Guard. (The Ohio National Guard soldiers fired sixty-seven shots into the crowd of students, killing four, paralyzing one, and wounding eight others.) In an opinion by Chief Justice Burger, a unanimous Supreme Court concluded that the qualified immunity of state officials and guardsmen turned on the scope of each defendant's responsibilities and discretion, the "circumstances as they reasonably appeared at the time," and the defendants' "good faith."[100] Ultimately, the case was settled by a payment of $675,000 by the state of Ohio to the plaintiffs.[101]

In *Harlow*, the Court expanded the ability of government officials to claim that they are immune from liability by eliminating the requirement that the official must have acted "in good faith," and shielded government officials from liability as long as their conduct "does not violate clearly established statutory or constitutional rights of which a reasonable person would have known." [102] What that meant became clear three years later, when the Court addressed the scope of qualified immunity in another warrantless wiretapping case—once again involving John Mitchell.[103] In 1970, Attorney General Mitchell had ordered a wiretap on the phone of a Haverford College physics professor, a member of a group that the FBI believed was planning to bomb heating tunnels serving federal office buildings and to kidnap Henry Kissinger (the same Haverford physics professor who was involved in the burglary of the FBI in Media, Pennsylvania). After being arrested on unrelated charges, a person whose innocent conversations had been overheard in the wiretap of the professor sued Mitchell for damages for violating his Fourth Amendment rights. The wiretap clearly required a warrant under the standards the Court had established for domestic surveillance in its *Keith* decision, but, because the wiretap had been put in place before the *Keith* decision, the Court decided that the qualified immunity standard it announced in *Harlow* protected Mitchell from liability for any damages.

The Burger Court never retreated from its decision in *Bivens* that a citizen whose constitutional rights have been violated has a right to sue the responsible government officials for damages; it just made it extremely difficult for a victim to find anyone who would actually be required to pay.[104] Morton Halperin's efforts to obtain a dollop of justice for the nearly two-year wiretap of his family's phone demonstrate the dilemma. In 1989, sixteen years after he first filed his lawsuit and after two decisions by the Court of Appeals and three others by district court judges—after John Mitchell (who almost certainly would have enjoyed qualified immunity anyway) had died and Richard Nixon had achieved absolute immunity and been dropped from the suit—a district court judge determined that, for the period of the wiretap from February 1969 through May 1970, the remaining two defendants, Henry Kissinger and Bob Haldeman, had met the good faith and reasonableness requirements for qualified immunity announced by the Burger Court in *Harlow v. Fitzgerald*.[105] The appellate court had previously concluded that a trial would be necessary to develop sufficient facts to assess Kissinger's and Haldeman's immunity claims for the period of the wiretap for the year after May 1970.[106] Then in 1991, the lower court dismissed Halperin's lawsuit on qualified immunity grounds for that period as well.[107] While that decision was on appeal, Halperin in 1992 dropped his twenty-year dispute in exchange for a $1 payment and a public apology from Kissinger.[108]

CHAPTER 13

Richard Nixon in
Warren Burger's Court

Shortly after midnight on June 17, 1972, five men—paid out of a secret cash stash of Nixon's campaign organization, the Committee to Re-Elect the President (known to many as CREEP)—broke into the Democratic National Committee headquarters in the Watergate office building. The Watergate break-in soon produced the indictment of the burglars plus two former White House staffers. Then, in October 1972, the FBI revealed that the burglary was only one instance of widespread political spying by Nixon and his reelection committee. On January 30, 1973, shortly after Nixon had won an overwhelming vote for reelection and had been sworn in for his second term, the burglars pled guilty, and former Nixon aides G. Gordon Liddy and James McCord were convicted of conspiracy, burglary, and illegal wiretapping in connection with the Watergate break-in. A week after that, by a unanimous vote, the Senate created a special Watergate investigation committee.[1] That committee, headed by North Carolina Democrat Sam Ervin, held televised hearings that riveted the nation during the spring and summer of 1973. Ninety percent of American adults either listened to or watched the hearings.[2] The committee's vice chairman, Tennessee Republican Howard Baker, repeatedly asked the question everyone wanted answered: "What did the president know, and when did he know it?"

Nixon's Tapes

On June 25, John Dean, former counsel in Nixon's White House, told the committee that there was a "cancer" in the White House and claimed that he had frequently discussed a cover-up with the president. Three weeks later, on July 16, Alexander Butterfield, who had been Nixon's appointments secretary, stunned the nation by revealing to the Watergate Committee that since 1970 the president had secretly recorded all Oval Office conversations and telephone calls.

In the late 1940s, Richard Nixon, serving as a congressman on a House committee investigating supposed communists in President Truman's administration, viewed Truman's refusal to provide information to Congress as a "cover-up" by the executive branch.[3] Truman's position, Nixon said, "cannot stand from a constitutional standpoint or on the basis of the merits."[4] Now sitting in the White House, Nixon had changed his tune.

Archibald Cox, who had been appointed by Attorney General Elliot Richardson as special prosecutor for Watergate-related crimes, and the Senate Watergate Committee immediately demanded the tapes. A week later, on July 23, 1973, Nixon claimed that the tapes were shielded from release by "executive privilege," and he refused to turn them over to either the committee or Cox. Nixon told Senator Ervin that he had "personally listened to a number of them" and that they "would not finally settle the issues before your committee." He added (in uncharacteristic understatement) that "there are inseparably interspersed in them a great many very frank and very private comments." The tapes, Nixon insisted, would remain under his "sole personal control."

Ervin responded, "I love my country. I venerate the office of President and I have best wishes for the success of the incumbent president." But, he added, "I am certain that the doctrine of separation of powers does not impose on any president the duty or the power to undertake to separate a congressional committee from access to the truth concerning alleged criminal activities." Ervin's committee immediately voted to subpoena the tapes. Special prosecutor Cox moved to subpoena them too.[5] When Cox refused to accept summaries of the tapes (to be verified by Mississippi senator John Stennis), Nixon ordered his attorney general, Richardson, to fire Cox. On October 20, 1973, in what was instantly labeled the "Saturday Night Massacre," Richardson refused and resigned in protest, as did his deputy, William Ruckelshaus. The Justice Department's third in command, Solicitor General Robert Bork, complied with Nixon's demand, dismissed Cox, and said that the office of the special prosecutor had been abolished as an independent entity. That evening NBC News reported, "The country tonight is in the midst of what may be the most serious constitutional crisis in history."[6]

On November 1, in response to massive public and congressional pressure, Bork appointed Leon Jaworski, a Texas lawyer, to replace Cox. To Nixon's dismay, Jaworski retained virtually all of Cox's legal staff, refused to curb the criminal investigations of the White House, and persisted in seeking the tapes. A constitutional struggle had commenced. No one doubted that it would ultimately be resolved by the Supreme Court.

The following year, on the evening of July 24, 1974, Peter Rodino, the New Jersey Democrat who headed the House Judiciary Committee, convened his committee to consider Articles of Impeachment against Nixon.[7] As he banged his gavel to begin the somber proceedings, an anxious nation waited, glued to its TV sets. But the impeachment articles the committee would adopt were not the worst news that Nixon heard that day. Ensconced in his San Clemente retreat, Nixon had learned that in the Supreme Court courtroom that morning—less than a block away from the House Judiciary Committee room but well outside the reach of television cameras—Chief Justice Warren Burger had solemnly announced the Court's unanimous 8–0 decision in *United States v. Nixon*, requiring the president to turn over to District Court Judge John J. Sirica tapes of conversations of the president and his aides discussing what to do in response to the Watergate burglary.[8] The Court's decision soon proved to be the fatal blow for Nixon's presidency.

Alexander Haig, the president's chief of staff, learned of the Court's action at about 8:25 a.m. Pacific time, five minutes after Burger had finished announcing the decision. When Haig informed Nixon, who was sitting in his California study gazing at the ocean, the president exploded. He cursed his three appointees, Warren Burger, Harry Blackmun, and Lewis Powell, who had all voted against him. (Nixon's fourth appointee, William Rehnquist, who had served as an assistant attorney general in Nixon's Justice Department, did not participate in the case.) Nixon apparently had believed a report published in *The New York Times* the previous weekend claiming that Burger and Blackmun were preparing a dissent, so he had been confident of their votes, and he had also expected Powell not to "desert" him.[9]

An hour or so later, James St. Clair, the Boston attorney who had argued the case for the president, came to Nixon's study and spent several hours going over the opinion with him. Nixon's press secretary had announced months earlier that the president would abide by a "definitive decision" of the Supreme Court, which everyone had interpreted as leaving him some wriggle room if the Court split. Confronted with a unanimous Court, Nixon now pressed St. Clair to find some "air" in the Court's decision. St. Clair became increasingly exasperated at Nixon's desperation to avoid complying. At one point, he told the president that legal ethics might compel him to withdraw from further representation if Nixon defied the court order.

What Nixon knew, but St. Clair did not, was that obeying the Supreme Court would end his presidency. Three taped conversations between Nixon and his closest aide, Bob Haldeman, in the morning and afternoon of June 23, 1972, six days after the burglary, supplied the "smoking gun" his opponents had been looking for. The June 23 tape unmistakably refuted all of Nixon's denials of obstructing justice and revealed that he had ordered a cover-up by attempting to use the CIA to deflect the FBI's investigation of the burglary in order to conceal his closest associates' complicity in the crime. As the journalist J. Anthony Lukas has written, the tape was "a weapon so redolent of powder, so smeared with prints that no defendant could hope for acquittal."[10] Conservative columnist George Will called it a "smoking howitzer."[11]

The night before the Supreme Court's announcement, Nixon had asked his White House counsel, Fred Buzhardt, to listen to this tape. Upon learning of the Court's decision, Buzhardt told Haig and St. Clair that the tape was devastating and directly contradicted information the White House had provided the House Judiciary Committee. "In my opinion," Buzhardt later said, "the tape was conclusive evidence. It was no longer a question of the president leaving office, but how he was leaving."[12]

At 4:00 p.m. California time, James St. Clair read to the media a statement from Nixon: "While I am, of course, disappointed in the result, I respect and accept the Court's decision, and I have instructed Mr. St. Clair to take whatever measures are necessary to comply with the decision in all respects." Speaking for himself, St. Clair added that reviewing the tapes and complying with the Court's order would be "time-consuming." With no sense of irony, he added: "As we all know, the President has always been a firm believer in the rule of law and he intends his decision to comply with the Court's ruling as an action in furtherance of that belief." [13]

Richard Nixon boards a helicopter to leave the White House following his resignation on August 9, 1974.

The House Judiciary Committee voted three Articles of Impeachment on July 31 and August 1. On August 5, the White House released transcripts of the tapes. On the evening of August 8, Richard Nixon told the nation that resignation was "abhorrent to every instinct in my body," but it had become "evident . . . that I no longer have a strong enough base in

Congress to justify continuing the effort." [14] At noon, on August 9, 1974, two weeks and two days after the Court announced its decision, Richard Nixon left office, becoming the only U.S. president to resign.

The Supreme Court knew, of course, that the stakes of *United States v. Nixon* were unusually high, but the justices did not know what the president had said on the tapes, so they were not certain that Nixon's fate resided with them.[15] The justices might conceivably have ducked this fray if the contest over the tapes had been a dispute solely between Congress and the president. The Court has sometimes stepped aside from such controversies, labeling them "political questions" and leaving them to the political branches to resolve.[16] The Burger Court, for example, refused to review challenges to decisions of the Democratic National Committee concerning which delegates would represent California and Illinois at the 1972 Democratic convention.[17] And nearly two decades after the *Nixon* decision, in a case coincidentally styled *Nixon v. United States*,[18] the Court unanimously determined that it had no power to review the Senate's procedures in the impeachment case of Walter Nixon, a federal judge who had been convicted of making false statements to a grand jury.

In *United States v. Nixon*, however, the contest over the tapes did not involve a request by a congressional committee but instead rose out of the March 1, 1974, criminal indictment of seven of Richard Nixon's closest aides—including John Mitchell, Nixon's former attorney general and director of the Committee to Re-Elect the President, Nixon's chief of staff Bob Haldeman, and his domestic policy adviser John Ehrlichman. All seven defendants had been charged with a variety of Watergate-related offenses, including conspiracy to obstruct justice; the grand jury's indictment had also named Nixon himself as "an unindicted co-conspirator." On April 18, the district court judge, John Sirica, granted a request by Jaworski and issued a subpoena duces tecum (a requirement to bring specified materials to court) to President Nixon for tapes and documents relating to several specific meetings between the president and his aides. Among the tapes requested was the smoking-gun tape of June 23, 1972. St. Clair, representing the president, moved to quash the subpoena, claiming that the requested documents and tapes were shielded from judicial inspection by the constitutional separation of powers and executive privilege. Judge Sirica denied this claim, but he delayed his order while it was appealed.

Given the extraordinary nature of the case, the Supreme Court granted certiorari and scheduled three hours of oral argument for Monday, July 8, skipping the Court of Appeals altogether. Such expedited review and the attendant postponement of the Court's usual summer break were rarities. Justices White and Blackmun opposed skipping the appellate court, and Burger was also reluctant, but the Court ultimately voted 6–2 to do so.[19]

The justices often have at least tentatively decided how a case should come out before they hear oral argument, and the *Nixon* tapes case was no exception. Lewis Powell, for example, had recorded his "tentative" thoughts about the Watergate tapes cases many months before the case even reached the Court.[20] In a memo dictated in his Virginia residence on September 13, 1973, a month before the Saturday Night Massacre, he observed that "few problems of great national consequence have been handled quite so badly by all concerned as what is called 'Watergate.' " Powell scorned the "political and media attack" against the "president himself," the "insatiable zest for sensationalism" of the media, and all the "pious protestations to the contrary." To Powell, the stakes were unmistakable: "Many who hope to destroy if not impeach the President (as they destroyed Johnson) have long since convicted him of personal responsibility of all the crimes committed. They now want the tapes to confirm the 'hanging.' " Powell said that he would deny the Ervin Committee access to the tapes, but he viewed the criminal investigation as "far more difficult." Like everyone else, Lewis Powell regarded the cover-up as "more shocking than the initial crimes." The case, Powell said, "might look quite different if the circumstances were less intertwined with merciless political hostilities, sensational journalism, publicity seeking senatorial proceedings before television, and the titillating possibility that the Head of State is himself guilty of high crimes and misdemeanors."

As he continued to dictate, Powell got his emotions under control, and his lawyerly training and judicial temperament took hold. As he so often did, Powell resisted what he viewed as the "absolutist positions" of both sides. He had little regard for Nixon's claim that a decision about whether and what to provide the court was a matter to be left entirely in the president's discretion. Acknowledging the "possibility that any President conceivably could be involved in criminal conduct or the deliberate concealment of such conduct by his aides or associates," Powell rejected the notion that the president could "be the sole judge as to what, if anything, to disclose to an investigating grand jury." But he also renounced the special prosecutor's claim that the prosecutor and grand jury had an unbridled right to obtain any and all of a president's private communications, even if national security was at stake. Powell characteristically sought a middle ground that would command a majority of the Court. He concluded his memo by describing himself as "essentially open minded and indeed deeply troubled as I see no clear, satisfactory resolution of this unfortunate confrontation between the Executive and Judicial Branches of government." [21]

At the July 9, 1974, oral argument, the Court got little help from the lawyers for either side. Despite its unusual length and dramatic buildup, the argument added nothing. James St. Clair tried to warn the Court away from any decision that would influence the politics of impeachment or its proceedings. And he repeatedly insisted that the president had sole discretion over releasing any of the tapes. At one point, Justice White asked him, "Would you automatically say every conversation about Watergate is in the course of the performance of the duties of the President of the United States?" St. Clair insisted that the answer was yes. And in responses to both Powell and Marshall, he held firm to his claim that the president's privilege and discretion were absolute—even for conversations involving a criminal conspiracy. [22] The justices would have none of that. Since by then there was overwhelming evidence of a criminal conspiracy within the White House—whether or not involving the president himself—this position was untenable. Nor did St. Clair's refusal to confirm that the president would be bound by the Court's decision sit well with the justices.

Leon Jaworski fared only a bit better. He was so eager to portray Nixon as a crook that he overplayed the fact that the grand jury had named Nixon an unindicted co-conspirator. Justices Douglas, Brennan, and Stewart all made clear that they thought that fact irrelevant, but Jaworski still would not let it go. Finally Justice White intervened. "I thought," he said, "we had put that issue aside. I just don't understand what the relevance of that is to this case." After Jaworski continued to press the point, White once again insisted that "it is irrelevant" and added: "I am just wondering, Mr. Jaworski, why you aren't content." [23]

By the time the Court convened for its conference the next day, the justices and their clerks had spent months researching, discussing, and reflecting on the case. Powell's notes to himself in preparation for the conference put into words everyone's disquiet: "We decide and write not just as to Nixon and Watergate, but for the long term. The principles involved relate to the basic structure of our Government."[24] At the conference, the justices unanimously voted to uphold Judge Sirica's subpoena. They also agreed to duck the question whether the grand jury had overstepped by naming a sitting president a co-conspirator; all of the justices regarded that question as irrelevant to the central issue of the district court judge's right to hear the tapes.

Chief Justice Burger, who, like Powell, viewed the press and the Ervin Committee as character assassins, assigned the opinion to himself, quashing an extensive effort by Brennan to have the justices produce one jointly authored opinion signed by all.[25] Unsurprisingly—especially because this was the sole case then occupying the attention of the other justices and their clerks—Burger's effort to craft an opinion that satisfied his colleagues did not go smoothly.[26] Two weeks later, however, after much back-and-forth and many important revisions to Burger's drafts, all joined his opinion for the Court. Nixon lost, but the presidency prevailed.[27] As did the Supreme Court.

The Court conclusively rejected the president's claim that it lacked the power to resolve the issue. Instead, the decision emphatically reaffirmed the Court's responsibility, duty, and power to say "what the law is," including delineating the powers and privileges of each branch of the federal government.

Then, for the first time in the nation's history, the Court explicitly confirmed a "presumptive privilege for Presidential communications . . . fundamental to the operation of Government, and inextricably rooted in the separation of powers under the Constitution."[28] But, Burger's opinion continued, "This presumptive privilege must be considered in light of our historic commitment to the rule of law. . . . The allowance of the privilege to withhold evidence that is demonstrably relevant in a criminal trial would cut deeply into the guarantee of due process of law and gravely impair the basic function of the Court."[29] The president's "generalized assertion of privilege," therefore, "must yield to the demonstrated, specific need for evidence in a criminal trial."[30]

Burger concluded by describing the duties of the district court judge upon receipt of the materials to "treat the subpoenaed material as presumptively privileged" and to "require the Special Prosecutor to demonstrate that the Presidential material was 'essential to the justice of the [pending criminal] case.' "[31] The district court judge "has a very heavy responsibility to see to it that Presidential conversations, which are either not relevant or not admissible, are accorded that high degree of respect due the President of the United States."[32]

In response to his colleagues' tenacious and repeated requests, Burger made many changes to the opinion. He reluctantly accepted Blackmun's rewrite of the statement of facts, White's detailed revisions of the section concluding that the district court's subpoena complied with the standards of the applicable rule of criminal procedure, and Stewart's overhaul of the executive privilege section.[33] But Burger was firmly committed to the part of the opinion describing the duties of the district court judge in this delicate balancing endeavor. There Burger relied heavily on what he regarded as the precedent set by Chief Justice John Marshall in the 1807 treason trial of Aaron Burr.[34]

The *Burr* trial was the only previous time in American history that a judge in a criminal prosecution had issued a subpoena to a sitting president demanding him to produce the contents of private conversations and communications. Aaron Burr was a Revolutionary War hero who in 1800 had tied Thomas Jefferson for the presidency in the electoral college but ultimately lost in the House of Representatives and became vice president when Alexander Hamilton threw his support to Jefferson. Burr subsequently killed Hamilton in a duel, supposedly in response to insults Hamilton had made during Burr's campaign for governor of New York. During Jefferson's second term, after having left the vice presidency, Burr became involved in a campaign to attack Mexico, and he was accused of conspiring with the British to free the western territories from the United States. Jefferson publicly pronounced Burr guilty of treason in January 1807 in a special message to Congress, but the ultimate determination of Burr's guilt was left to a trial in federal court in Richmond, Virginia, with Chief Justice John Marshall presiding. During the course of these proceedings—which ultimately acquitted Burr, thanks largely to a very sympathetic instruction to the jury by Chief Justice Marshall—Marshall subpoenaed letters and other documents involving communications between President Jefferson and General James Wilkinson, who was serving both as governor of the Louisiana Territory and commander of the U.S.

army.[35] Jefferson turned the subpoenaed documents over to his counsel with instructions to provide them to the court as he saw fit.

After that, things get a bit murky. Some scholars view Jefferson's role in the case as a precedent for the president's sole discretion over whether to provide private communications to a court for a criminal trial.[36] Others view the *Burr* case as authority for the limits of presidential discretion.[37] The latter was Warren Burger's position. At the initial conference in the *Nixon* case, when the Court was deciding whether to grant expedited review, Burger said, with respect to Nixon's executive privilege claim, "It is the Burr situation."[38] Lewis Powell, in contrast, felt that President Jefferson and Chief Justice Marshall had avoided any "final confrontation," so he regarded the *Burr* case's precedential value as "limited."[39]

Warren Burger had a special affinity for the *Burr* saga. While a night student at St. Paul College of Law (now William Mitchell College of Law), Burger and a few friends regularly convened what they called the "smokers" club to reargue famous trials. Burger argued three: an abuse of power trial of Warren Hastings in the British House of Commons, the Senate's impeachment trial of President Andrew Johnson, and the treason trial of Aaron Burr.[40] Two decades later, in the spring of 1953, when he was serving as an assistant attorney general in the Eisenhower administration, Burger, who was a talented artist, painted in oil a still life of "some familiar objects" in his office: a desk with a small, largely depleted candle in a small holder and two books.[41] One of those books was the volume of case reports containing *United States v. Aaron Burr*. When he sat at his desk in the Supreme Court working on his *Nixon* opinion, that painting hung on the wall above him.

Years later, reflecting on the *Nixon* decision, Burger said it was "painful" because "I knew it was likely to produce terminal results for a president. But I couldn't have come out any differently." He added: "Chief Justice John Marshall had written it all in the *Aaron Burr* case. . . . The details of how Marshall handled that case made it almost an exact duplicate." The only distinction Burger drew was that in *Burr* the defendant wanted the material, while in *Nixon*, it was the prosecution.[42] His colleagues did not begin to fathom the parallels that Burger saw between the *Nixon* and *Burr* cases, nor the depth of his feelings that he was, more than a century and a half later, ratifying Chief Justice Marshall's wise resolution of Burr's challenge to Jefferson's discretion and authority and validating Marshall's insistence on the supremacy of the Supreme Court in such matters. Had his colleagues understood this, they might have wasted less energy trying to wrestle the *Nixon* opinion away from him.

Familiar Objects, an oil painting in color by Warren Burger that depicts the official volume containing Chief Justice John Marshall's opinion in the Aaron Burr case.

Burger, however, misjudged the importance of the distinction he drew between the *Burr* and *Nixon* litigation. Burger's *Nixon* opinion insisted that the constitutional right to due process and a fair criminal trial demanded that the president produce the evidence. But in *Nixon*, the prosecutor wanted the tapes to secure convictions, while in *Burr*, the defendant wanted the president's evidence to prove his innocence.

Had Jefferson refused to produce the material in *Burr*, John Marshall's only remedy would have been to dismiss the treason charges and free Burr—a result Jefferson did not want. In *Nixon*, the Burger Court allowed the prosecution to secure evidence adverse to the defendants by overriding a constitutional privilege in order to make it possible to prove their guilt. But common legal privileges of confidentiality, such as the attorney-client privilege, the husband-wife privilege, and the physician-patient privilege, routinely deny prosecutors access to relevant and often damaging evidence of guilt. Burger's *Nixon* opinion offers no hint about its implications for these privileges, and state and federal courts have subsequently evinced some confusion about the *Nixon* decision's meaning in these far more ordinary circumstances.

Legal scholars have found much to fault in Burger's *Nixon* opinion.[43] First—for which the Court surely can be forgiven under the circumstances—is its rush to take the case before the Court of Appeals had spoken and its willingness to resolve what was, formally at least, a dispute between two members of the executive branch (Nixon and Jaworski). More significant is the Court's audacity in insisting that the desires of a prosecutor in a criminal trial trump the president's right to confidential communications, a right that the Court found to be grounded in Article II of the Constitution.

Whatever its legal shortcomings, the Court certainly got the politics right. Nixon was a criminal; by then everyone knew so, and his being forced to resign was well deserved. The nation exhaled a huge collective sigh of relief when he left office. When Gerald Ford was sworn in on August 9, 1974, as our thirty-eighth president, he captured a grateful nation's sentiment, saying, "our long national nightmare is over."[44] The Supreme Court had spared the nation the agony of an impeachment trial.

Banishing the President, but Strengthening the Presidency

Without a doubt, Richard Nixon fared rather badly in what he had rightly viewed as Nixon's Court. The Supreme Court forced him to release his tapes, which drove him from office. Then it awarded government archivists complete control over the tapes' disposition, resulting over time in virtually unfettered public access.[45] Nixon's journeys through the Supreme Court made for an unparalleled, even unimaginable saga. But the drama of his repudiation by his handpicked justices obscures the fact that while driving one president from office, the Burger Court actually strengthened the presidency.[46] It ratified a constitutional basis for claims of executive privilege, a privilege that Nixon's successors have frequently invoked. It spared Nixon—and future presidents—from risk of civil damages for wrongful acts committed while in office. Those who lived through the cataclysmic events of summer in 1974 might well have imagined that they were watching the institution of the presidency crumble. But such an outcome was neither the Court's intent nor its effect. A stronger presidency, insulated in important ways from liability and accountability, is one more lasting legacy of the Burger Court.

Conclusion

A Lasting Legacy

In August 1986, a weary Lewis Powell, fresh from the trauma of *Bowers v. Hardwick* and facing the start of a new Supreme Court term under a new chief justice, addressed a group of lawyers at the American Bar Association's annual meeting in New York. The topic of his untitled speech was the Burger Court.

"There has been no conservative counterrevolution by the Burger Court," Powell told the lawyers. He went on to explain: "None of the landmark decisions of the Warren Court was overruled, and some were extended."[1]

The "no counterrevolution" verdict was thus joined by a key member of the Burger Court even before Burger left office.[2] (Burger's retirement became effective on September 26, when William Rehnquist took the oath as his successor.) Powell's remarks remain of more than passing interest as we look back on the Burger Court after the passage of three decades. His assessment was at once both highly selective and internally contradictory—a mixed message that draws us down a path to a conclusion quite different from his own.

"We have not diminished the constitutional protections afforded to those suspected of committing crime," Powell declared,[3] a statement that overlooked the Court's new exceptions to the exclusionary rule, deprecated the hollowing-out of the *Miranda* protections against compelled self-incrimination, and ignored altogether the hurdles the Court had created for showing ineffective assistance of counsel. It also failed to account for the weakening and explicit overturning of Warren Court precedents that had empowered federal judges, through habeas corpus, to supervise the quality of criminal justice delivered by the state courts and to repair those courts' errors.[4]

Powell's lengthy inventory of cases dealing with desegregation and racial equality in the wake of *Brown*—"the great legacy of Earl Warren's Court," he observed—omitted any mention of *Milliken v. Bradley*,[5] the Detroit schools case that prevented integration remedies from crossing the district line. Nor, on the subject of equal protection, did he mention his own majority opinion in *San Antonio Independent School District v. Rodriguez*,[6] which left resource-poor school districts without a constitutional claim for more equal funding.

Equally puzzling, on another subject, is Powell's assertion that "no prior Court has been more zealous to assure separation of church and state, and at the same time to protect the rights guaranteed by the Free Exercise Clause."[7] The description is not only oversimplified but logically inconsistent. As we have seen, the Establishment and Free Exercise Clauses are in tension with one another. When does government solicitude for religious exercise cross the line into establishment? When does policing of the Establishment Clause's prohibition go too far and stifle free exercise? No Court can answer those questions consistently or elevate both clauses equally—certainly not the Burger Court, from which the Establishment Clause emerged weakened, ripe for further weakening in the years to come.

By a handwritten note on the title page, Powell instructed his secretary, Sally Smith, to file the speech with the *Bowers v. Hardwick* case material[8]—a puzzling choice, but one perhaps explained by the paragraph devoted to that decision. Unlike the rest of the fifteen-page text, dry and composed as if at arm's length, the *Bowers* paragraph reads as if Powell invested some emotion in it. The tone is defensive. With sodomy laws "now moribund and rarely enforced," the paragraph says, "the case may not be as significant as press reports suggest." And in any event, "we had no occasion to consider possible defenses, such as one based on the Eighth Amendment, to an actual prosecution."[9]

Powell concluded his remarks with this coda:

> It has been fashionable for critics to say that the Burger Court "lacked a sense of direction," appeared to "drift," or lacked a coherent "pol-

icy." To lawyers, and certainly to Article III judges, these observations should make little sense. The great strength of the Supreme Court is that we have no "policy" or purpose other than "faithfully and impartially" to discharge our duties "agreeably to the Constitution and laws of the United States." [Quoting the federal judicial oath.] This is our sworn duty.[10]

No policy or purpose? In the preceding chapters, we have seen abundant examples of both. Powell's denial that the Court advanced any policy views is especially jarring given the force with which he had promoted his own preferred policies concerning public schools and business speech rights, not to mention his singular insistence on the constitutional right of colleges and universities to promote diversity in their admissions policies.

The contrast between the Burger Court's "policies and purposes" and those of the Warren Court is stark. For Earl Warren and his Court, the Constitution was an engine of social change. It was the quest for greater equality—in the schools, in the voting booth and the legislatures, in the courtroom—that drove constitutional interpretation. No such lodestar drew the Burger Court. Equality took a backseat to other values: to the prerogatives of states and localities within the federal system, to the preservation of elite institutions, to the efficiency of the criminal justice system, to the interests of business, and above all, to rolling back the rights revolution the Warren Court had unleashed. Certainly both Courts shared a deep concern for racial equality—but the Burger Court's concern was to make sure that white applicants to schools and jobs were not being asked to pay too heavy a price for the nation's racial past.

When Powell spoke, Ronald Reagan was in the midst of his second term, on his way to becoming the first president since Eisenhower to serve two full terms. Eighteen months before Powell's speech in New York to a few hundred lawyers, Reagan—fresh off an unprecedented victory in the electoral college where he had carried all but one state (his opponent's home state of Minnesota)—delivered the first State of the Union address of his second term to a packed House Chamber of the Capitol and millions of Americans watching at home. There Reagan proclaimed a "Second American Revolution," detailing the policies and values that the country would soon come to know as the "Reagan Revolution."[11]

Reagan cited individual rights and responsibilities, greater freedom, lower taxes, a stronger military, and deregulation of businesses as core components of his revolution. He emphasized the importance of faith, even calling for the restoration of school prayer, and made clear how little he thought of the social transformation of the 1960s and 1970s. "As the family goes, so goes our civilization," he said. Echoing Nixon, Reagan emphasized law and order, saying that an "explosion of violence" in the previous two decades had posed "the greatest threat to our sense of national well-being." Following the lead of Burger's Court, he called for the admission of "all reliable evidence that police officers acquire in good faith," for tightening habeas corpus, and for permitting the death penalty "where necessary." Drawing a breathtakingly explicit link between race and crime, Reagan added: "There can be no economic revival in ghettos when the most violent among us are allowed to roam free."

With the glaring exception of abortion, which Reagan insisted "must be stopped," the overlap between the Reagan Revolution and the decisions of the Burger Court is undisputable: limiting the rights of criminal defendants, freeing businesses from burdensome regulations, elevating individualism over equality. In Reagan's first State of the Union address, he had called for a "New Federalism," a devolution of power to the states, which he claimed would make government "more accountable to the people," reflecting a similar devolution of constitutional responsibility that we have seen the Burger Court promote in criminal law, obscenity, abortion funding, and school finance, for example.[12]

In his memorandum for the Chamber of Commerce, Lewis Powell himself had targeted the courts, especially the Supreme Court, for advocacy by conservative forces.[13] Business interests responded first, but the U.S. Chamber of Commerce was not the only institution to accept his invitation. Imitating the litigation strategies of the American Civil Liberties Union (ACLU) and the NAACP Legal Defense Fund that had enjoyed success during the Warren Court era, public interest law firms with a contrary agenda emerged and matured during Burger's tenure.[14] Since 1973, when the first conservative public interest law firm was founded, the conservative legal movement has enjoyed enormous influence over the agenda of courts and the development of American law. The Federalist Society, a self-described group of conservatives and libertarians, held its first conference at Yale Law School in April 1982 and is now one of the most influential legal organizations in the United States. Supreme Court justices Antonin Scalia, Clarence Thomas, and Samuel Alito were members, and Chief Justice John Roberts served on its leadership council. Numerous federal district and appellate court judges have also been members. The Society's membership now numbers in the tens of thousands and chapters can be found at more than 140 law schools. Conservative donors and their foundations, including those of the Koch, Scaife, and Olin families, have provided generous funding to the Federalist Society and the conservative public interest law firms.

Speaking of the Supreme Court, Richard Nixon's speechwriter and advisor Patrick Buchanan in 1972 told the president that he had "recaptured the institution from the Left."[15] Indeed he had. And the Burger Court was just the opening act.

————

Suppose Richard Nixon had filled only three Supreme Court vacancies by 1972 and not four, or that Hubert Humphrey had defeated Nixon for the presidency in the close election of 1968. A switch of one vote could have carried desegregation remedies across school district lines and given impoverished school systems a constitutional claim on a greater share of the state's wealth.[16] However alluring it might be as literature, however, such an alternative history would necessarily oversimplify the complex social and political landscape the Burger Court navigated and on which its actual decisions fell. How might the country have responded to a flood of cross-district busing orders in both North and South? Would wealth equalization in the nation's school districts have meant leveling up or bringing wealthy suburban districts down? What would that scenario have meant for private schools or homeschooling? And with what political impact?

The purpose of thought experiments like these is not to answer such questions but to raise them. The Burger Court took shape during a time of dramatic political, social, and economic change. The Burger justices didn't stand apart from the turmoil of the times, but neither could they have known where the paths they chose would ultimately lead. In many respects, they simply ratified the changes that were taking place: the movement for women's rights was, up to a point, irresistible. The movement for gay rights proved a step too far—but the *Bowers* decision can be seen now as having prompted a reaction that made the movement's eventual success not only possible but inevitable.

Chief Justice Burger, flanked by Judge Antonin Scalia (left) and Justice William H. Rehnquist, speaking to the White House press corps on June 17, 1986, immediately following President Reagan's announcement of Burger's retirement, Rehnquist's proposed elevation, and Scalia's nomination to take Rehnquist's seat as an associate justice.

By the time Warren Burger stepped down to head the Constitution's bicentennial celebration, the country was very different from what it had been when he arrived at the Supreme Court at the dawn of the Nixon administration. It was more conservative politically and socially. Ronald Reagan's two elections as president had enjoyed strong support from social conservatives and the Religious Right as well as from libertarians who wanted to shrink the federal government and from business interests eager for deregulation. We don't mean here to depict the Burger Court as serving the Reagan Revolution—that would be inaccurate. But Warren Burger's Court played a crucial role in establishing the conservative legal foundation for the even more conservative Courts that followed. Once again, Supreme Court justices are seeking to harness the Constitution as an instrument of social change—but in a direction opposite from the Warren Court's of a half century ago.

Americans' appetite, observed by Tocqueville long ago, for turning to the courts to resolve their most profound disputes has invested the Supreme Court, as the highest court of all, with enormous power over American life. The Burger Court essentially forced a president from office. The Rehnquist Court, a quarter century later, essentially installed one. Yet the Supreme Court is also constrained by the very nature of an institution expected to follow a path marked out by precedent. Precedent, of course, can be discarded, either incrementally or abruptly, by any five justices acting in concert, but not without a price in terms of the Court's legitimacy. It is a contradiction that lies at the Supreme Court's heart: tethered to the past, defined by the present, the Supreme Court inevitably shapes the future. So it was with the Burger Court and its lasting legacy.

The justices assembled in their conference room, joined by President Reagan, for Sandra Day O'Connor's investiture, September 25, 1981. This was the last Burger "natural court," remaining intact until Burger's retirement five years later. Left to right: Harry A. Blackmun, Thurgood Marshall, William J. Brennan, Jr., Warren E. Burger, the president, O'Connor, Byron R. White, Lewis F. Powell, Jr., William H. Rehnquist, and John Paul Stevens.

Appendix

The Members of the Burger Court

Warren Burger served with twelve justices—two for only fifteen months (Hugo L. Black and John Marshall Harlan, Jr., both of whom retired in September 1971) and three for the entirety of his seventeen-year tenure (William J. Brennan, Jr., Byron R. White, and Thurgood Marshall.) Here, we provide capsule biographies of the Burger Court justices.[1]

Burger himself was born on September 17, 1907 in St. Paul, Minnesota, the fourth of seven children. Unable to afford college, Burger held a full-time job selling life insurance while taking night classes, first at the University of Minnesota, from which he did not receive a degree, and then at the St. Paul College of Law (later renamed William Mitchell College of Law and merged in 2015 with Hamline University School of Law.) He received his law degree with honors in 1931 and practiced law for the next twenty-one years as a member of one of St. Paul's leading law firms.

Burger was active in Republican politics in Minnesota, attending the 1952 Republican National Convention as floor manager for the state's favorite son, Harold Stassen. He was a key player in persuading his delegation to give its votes to Dwight Eisenhower, helping Eisenhower defeat Robert Taft for the presidential nomination. Burger was rewarded with an invitation to join the Eisenhower administration as assistant attorney general in charge of the Justice Department's Civil Division. He remained in Washington, D.C., for the rest of his life, spending thirteen years on the United States Court of Appeals for the District of Columbia Circuit (1956–1969) before taking his seat on the Supreme Court on

June 23, 1969. He retired on September 26, 1986, and died on June 25, 1995, at age eighty-seven.

The justices who served on the Burger Court are listed here in order of their Supreme Court appointments.

HUGO L. BLACK

Black was serving in the United States Senate from Alabama at the time of his appointment by President Franklin D. Roosevelt on August 12, 1937. He was born on February 27, 1886, in Harlan, Alabama, the last of eight children, and grew up in the small Alabama town of Ashland. He did not attend college, graduating in 1906 from the University of Alabama Law School. Moving to Birmingham, he served as a police court judge and later as a prosecutor. In a highly successful private practice, he specialized in personal injury cases and for two years (1923–1925) was a member of the local Ku Klux Klan chapter. In 1926, he was elected to the Senate, where he sponsored progressive labor legislation and provided strong support for the New Deal.

Black was the first of FDR's nine Supreme Court appointees. He served thirty-four years, retiring on September 17, 1971, after suffering a stroke. He died eight days later at age eighty-five.

WILLIAM O. DOUGLAS

Douglas, born on October 16, 1898, in Maine, Minnesota, the son of a Presbyterian minister, was the fourth of Franklin Roosevelt's nine justices. At the time of his appointment on March 20, 1939, he was the forty-year-old chairman of the Securities and Exchange Commission. He was a graduate of Whitman College in Walla Walla, Washington and Columbia Law School. After graduating second in his class, he practiced law briefly before beginning an academic career at Columbia and subsequently Yale Law School, where he taught for five years. His specialty was corporate law, expertise that he deployed as a securities regulator.

As a Supreme Court justice, Douglas retained a connection to politics, and came close in 1940 and again in 1944 to being named FDR's running mate. In 1970, his liberal jurisprudence and flamboyant personal life (four marriages) inspired a Republican-led impeachment effort, which failed. In late 1974, Douglas suffered a serious stroke from which he never recovered. He returned to work at the Court after a months-long absence, but retired on November 12, 1975. He died on January 19, 1980, at the age of eighty-one. His thirty-six-year tenure is the longest in Supreme Court history.

JOHN MARSHALL HARLAN II

Grandson of a Supreme Court justice of the same name, Harlan was serving on the United States Court of Appeals for the Second Circuit, in New York, at the time of his appointment to the Supreme Court by President Eisenhower. He took his seat on March 28, 1955.

Harlan was born in Chicago on May 20, 1899, and was a Rhodes Scholar at Oxford after graduating from Princeton in 1920. He read law at Oxford and received his law degree from New York Law School in 1924. As a partner in a Wall Street law firm, he became a well-known trial lawyer and leader of the New York City bar. He was a conservative voice on the Supreme Court during his sixteen-year tenure, dissenting from many of the Warren Court's landmark decisions. Suffering from cancer, he retired on September 23, 1971, and died on December 29 that year at the age of seventy-two.

WILLIAM J. BRENNAN, JR.

Brennan was born in Newark, New Jersey on April 25, 1906, the second of eight children of Irish immigrants. His father, William Sr., was active in labor union politics, and Brennan specialized in labor law (representing employers, not unions) after graduating from the University of Pennsylvania's Wharton School and from Harvard Law School in 1931. He gave up law practice in 1949 to take a seat on a state trial court. From there, he received promotions to the state court of appeals and in 1952 to the New Jersey Supreme Court. On the eve of the 1956 presidential election, Eisenhower named him to the vacant "Catholic seat" on the U.S. Supreme Court. Brennan took his seat under a recess appointment on October 16, 1956. The Senate confirmed him on March 19, 1957.

During his thirty-three-year tenure, Brennan was a close ally of Chief Justice Warren and was the leader of the liberal wing of the Court during the Burger years. He retired on July 20, 1990, following a stroke and died on July 24, 1997 at the age of ninety-one.

POTTER STEWART

Stewart, the last of Eisenhower's five Supreme Court appointees, was born on January 23, 1915, in Jackson, Michigan. He grew up in Cincinnati in a prominent Republican family; his father, James Garfield Stewart, served as mayor from 1938 to 1947, when he was named to the Ohio Supreme Court. Stewart was a Phi Beta Kappa graduate of Yale College and graduated in 1941 from Yale Law School. His early law practice in New York was interrupted by service in the Navy during World War II. Returning to Cleveland, he built a successful law practice and took part in Republican politics as an ally of the conservative Taft wing of the party. At the unusually young age of thirty-nine, he was named to the United States Court of Appeals for the Sixth Circuit.

Four years later, on October 14, 1958, Eisenhower named him to the Supreme Court as a recess appointment. He was confirmed by the Senate on May 5, 1959, and retired on July 3, 1981. He died on December 7, 1985, at the age of seventy.

BYRON R. WHITE

White was born in Fort Collins, Colorado, on June 8, 1917, and won national fame as an All-American football player for the University of Colorado. He graduated from the university in 1938 as valedictorian and a member of Phi Beta Kappa, having lettered in basketball and baseball as well as football. He delayed his Rhodes Scholarship to Oxford until the spring of 1939 so he could play for the Pittsburgh Steelers during the 1938 football season. He entered Yale Law School in the fall of 1939, cutting short his Rhodes Scholarship due to the outbreak of World War II. After finishing his first year with the highest class rank, he took a leave to play football for the Detroit Lions. He joined the Navy after Pearl Harbor and, as an intelligence officer, investigated the sinking of John F. Kennedy's PT-109.

After his military service, White returned to Yale Law School, graduating in 1946. He then clerked on the Supreme Court for Chief Justice Fred Vinson. In Washington, he reencountered Kennedy, who had just been elected to Congress. White returned to Colorado to practice law and became deeply involved in Kennedy's presidential campaign. After the 1960 election, Attorney General Robert Kennedy selected White as deputy attorney general. In that capacity, he traveled to the South to oversee civil rights enforcement. President Kennedy named him to the Supreme Court on April 3, 1962. He retired after thirty-one years on June 28, 1993, and died on April 15, 2002, at the age of eighty-four.

THURGOOD MARSHALL

When President Lyndon Johnson named Thurgood Marshall to the Court on June 13, 1967, every Supreme Court justice in history had been a white man. A famous civil rights lawyer and leader who supervised the litigation that led to *Brown v. Board of Education*, Marshall took his seat on October 2, 1967, after a contentious confirmation hearing during which southern senators tried to humiliate him with questions about the minutiae of constitutional history. At the time, Marshall was serving as U.S. solicitor general, in charge of the federal government's Supreme Court cases. He had previously spent four years as a judge on the United States Court of Appeals for the Second Circuit, to which President Kennedy appointed him in 1961.

Marshall was born in Baltimore on July 2, 1908. His mother was a teacher and his father, a former dining car waiter, was a steward at an all-white club. Marshall attended a segregated public high school in Baltimore; an all-black college, Lincoln University in Chester, Pennsylvania; and Howard University Law School, from which he graduated in 1933. He was inspired by the law school's dean, Charles Hamilton Houston, to devote his legal career to improving the circumstances of African Americans. From 1939 until becoming a federal judge, Marshall headed the NAACP Legal Defense and Educational Fund. The organization challenged segregation in higher education and in housing before turning to the public schools.

Marshall served on the Supreme Court for twenty-four years, retiring on October 1, 1991. He died on January 24, 1993, at the age of eighty-four.

HARRY A. BLACKMUN

Blackmun was President Nixon's third choice for the vacancy caused by Abe Fortas's forced resignation nearly a year earlier. The Senate had rejected two earlier choices, Clement Haynsworth and G. Harrold Carswell, before Nixon named Blackmun—who forever after referred to himself as "Old Number Three"—on April 15, 1970. The Senate confirmed the nomination unanimously on May 12, 1970.

Blackmun and Burger grew up together in St. Paul, Minnesota, and were lifelong friends when they joined the Court in successive years. But they grew apart as their judicial outlooks diverged during their joint tenure. Blackmun was born in Nashville, Illinois on November 12, 1908. Like Burger, he came from a family beset by financial insecurity. He was able to attend Harvard on a scholarship from the Harvard Club of Minnesota. He graduated in 1929 summa cum laude and a member of Phi Beta Kappa. In 1932, he graduated from Harvard Law School and returned to St. Paul to clerk for Judge John B. Sanborn, Jr., of the United States Court of Appeals for the Eighth Circuit. He practiced law for sixteen years with a major Minneapolis law firm and then became resident general counsel for the Mayo Clinic in Rochester, Minnesota, a client of his law firm. In 1959, President Eisenhower named him to the appeals court seat from which Judge Sanborn had retired.

Early in his twenty-four-year Supreme Court tenure, Blackmun received Burger's assignment to write for the 7–2 majority in *Roe v. Wade*, the decision that was to define the rest of his life as well as his legacy. He retired on August 3, 1994, and died on March 4, 1999, at age ninety.

LEWIS F. POWELL, JR.

Powell had earlier rejected President Nixon's offer of a Supreme Court nomination. But in 1971, he allowed himself to be persuaded to accept, and on October 22, Nixon named him to succeed Hugo Black. Powell took his seat on January 7, 1972, at the age of sixty-four. At the time of his nomination, he was conducting a major corporate law practice in Richmond, Virginia, where he had been active in civic life for many years. From 1951 to 1961—the years including and following *Brown v. Board of Education*—Powell was chairman of the Richmond school board. Although the school board's efforts at integration were exceedingly modest, at best, the Richmond schools did stay open despite the wave of "massive resistance" that closed schools throughout the South during those years. Powell also served as a member of the Virginia Board of Education and spent a one-year term as president of the American Bar Association, 1964–1965.

Powell was born on September 19, 1907, in Suffolk, Virginia. He graduated in 1929 from Washington and Lee University, where he was elected student body president and was a member of Phi Beta Kappa. He was first in his class at the university's law school, graduating in two years in 1931. The next year, he earned a master's degree from Harvard Law School. Powell's legal career was interrupted by service during World War II as an Army Air Force intelligence officer. He was highly decorated and rose in thirty-three months from lieutenant to colonel.

Powell retired on June 26, 1987, and died on August 25, 1998, at age ninety.

WILLIAM H. REHNQUIST

President Nixon announced Rehnquist's appointment, to succeed Justice Harlan, simultaneously with Powell's appointment on October 22, 1971. But while Powell's confirmation vote, on December 6, 1971, was 89–1, Rehnquist was confirmed four days later after a contentious hearing by a vote of 68–26. While Powell had no obvious political ties, Rehnquist had entered Republican politics in his adopted state of Arizona in the 1950s and was closely affiliated with the party's most conservative wing. He played a strategic role in Barry Goldwater's 1964 presidential campaign and joined the Nixon administration in 1969 as assistant attorney general in charge of the Office of Legal Counsel.

Rehnquist was born in Shorewood, Wisconsin, on October 1, 1924. He attended Kenyon College in Gambier, Ohio, for a semester before joining the Army in the spring of 1943. He spent much of his military service as a weather observer in North Africa, and upon returning to civilian life in 1946 decided to head for a warmer climate than that of the upper Midwest. He enrolled in Stanford, graduating in 1948. He then attended Harvard's graduate school for one year, earning a master's degree in political science, before returning to Stanford for an accelerated law school program. He graduated first in his class in 1952 and clerked on the Supreme Court for Justice Robert H. Jackson. Following his clerkship, he moved to Phoenix, where he practiced law for sixteen years before moving back to Washington.

Rehnquist served as an associate justice for fifteen years, until his elevation to chief justice upon Burger's retirement. He died in office at the age of eighty on September 3, 2005, after a nearly year-long struggle with an aggressive form of thyroid cancer.

JOHN PAUL STEVENS

Stevens was President Gerald Ford's only Supreme Court nominee, named on November 28, 1975, to succeed William Douglas. Ford said years later that the nomination of John Paul Stevens was the presidential achievement of which he was most proud. Stevens was born in Chicago on April 20, 1920, into a family that had once owned the Stevens Hotel, now the Chicago Hilton, a Chicago landmark that was the biggest hotel in the world when it opened in 1927. He graduated Phi Beta Kappa from the University of Chicago in 1941. He joined the Navy the day before the attack on Pearl Harbor and served as a code breaker until the end of the war. He then returned to Chicago and entered Northwestern University Law School, graduating first in his class in 1947. He clerked on the Supreme Court for Justice Wiley B. Rutledge.

Turning down an offer to teach at Yale Law School, Stevens returned to Chicago to practice law. He specialized in antitrust law, and gained local fame by conducting an investigation of corruption on the Illinois Supreme Court. In 1970, he was named to the United States Court of Appeals for the Seventh Circuit, where he served until his Supreme Court confirmation. During his thirty-four and a half years on the Supreme Court, his voting pattern grew more liberal as the Court itself grew more conservative. He left the Court at the age of ninety on June 29, 2010, to begin an active off-the-bench life of writing and speaking.

SANDRA DAY O'CONNOR

Being the first woman on the Supreme Court ("F.W.O.T.S.C." as she sometimes called herself) was not Sandra O'Connor's only distinction. She was the only member of the Burger Court to have served in elective office. Active in Republican politics in Arizona, she was appointed in 1969 to fill a vacant seat in the State Senate. She won two subsequent elections, and in 1973 became the Senate's majority leader, the first woman in the country to hold so high an office in a state legislature. O'Connor was also distinctive for her upbringing on a remote cattle ranch near Arizona's Mexican border. She was born Sandra Day in El Paso, Texas, on March 26, 1930, and had to return to El Paso for high school, living there with her grandparents, because there was no high school near the ranch. She graduated from Stanford in 1950 and from its law school in 1953. At Stanford, she met two men who would play a prominent role in her life: William Rehnquist, with whom she would serve on the Supreme Court for twenty-four years, and John O'Connor, whom she married.

Unable as a woman to find a law firm job—one Los Angeles firm offered to hire her as a secretary—she took a job as a deputy county attorney in San Mateo, California, before joining her husband in Germany while he performed his military service as an Army lawyer. The couple settled in Phoenix in 1957. O'Connor practiced law and gave birth to three sons. She entered state government in 1965 as a lawyer in the Arizona attorney general's office. In 1974, following four years in the attorney general's office and five years in the legislature, she won an elected judgeship on the state trial court. In 1979, the state's Democratic governor, Bruce Babbitt, appointed her to Arizona's middle-level appeals court. She was serving there when President Reagan, acting to fulfill a campaign promise to name a woman to the Supreme Court, nominated her on August 19, 1981, to succeed Potter Stewart.

On July 1, 2005, O'Connor announced that she would retire from the Court in order to care for her husband, who was suffering from Alzheimer's disease. President Bush initially named John G. Roberts, Jr., to fill her seat, but moved the Roberts nomination to that of chief justice following Rehnquist's death in September. O'Connor delayed her retirement until January 31, 2006, when Samuel A. Alito, Jr., was sworn in to take her place.

THE BURGER "NATURAL COURTS"

Political scientists use the term "natural court" to refer to any period during which a court's membership is unchanged. There were five "natural" Burger courts:

1. From June 23, 1969, to June 9, 1970: Burger, Black, Douglas, Harlan, Brennan, Stewart, White, Marshall. (One seat was vacant during this time.)
2. From June 9, 1970, to January 7, 1972: Burger, Black, Douglas, Harlan, Brennan, Stewart, White, Marshall, Blackmun.
3. From January 7, 1972, to December 19, 1975: Burger, Douglas, Brennan, Stewart, White, Marshall, Blackmun, Powell, Rehnquist.
4. From December 19, 1975, to September 25, 1981: Burger, Brennan, Stewart, White, Marshall, Blackmun, Powell, Rehnquist, Stevens.
5. From September 25, 1981, to September 26, 1986: Burger, Brennan, White, Marshall, Blackmun, Powell, Rehnquist, Stevens, O'Connor.

Acknowledgments

W e have had much generous support in writing this book. The idea emerged out of a seminar for Yale law and history students that Michael Graetz taught for several years with the historian Daniel Kevles, a course designed to counter the widespread idea that the 1970s—a transformative period when our nation's politics and society changed dramatically—were years when nothing important happened. This mistaken view was echoed by the accepted wisdom that during the Burger years what didn't happen was much more important than what did. The readings and discussions in those classes served as a catalyst for this book. More recently, numerous students have provided important insights and research in courses and seminars on the Burger Court that Michael Graetz and Linda Greenhouse taught at Columbia and Yale law schools. Participants at the Columbia Law School faculty workshop also contributed valuable comments and criticisms on partial drafts of our manuscript. Our colleagues Mark Barenberg, Kent Greenawalt, Daniel Richman, and Reva Siegel offered especially valuable help. Tom Franklin and Adam Haslett also offered important and timely criticism and comments. Columbia Law School students Alexander Nourse Gross, Megan Larkin, Linda Moon, Bruce Wilson, and Sasha Zheng generously assisted us with the form and substance of our endnotes. Our deans at Columbia and Yale, Gillian Lester, David Schizer, and Robert Post, offered us unstinting support and encouragement. Michael Graetz is also grateful for support from the Phillipe P. Dauman Faculty Research Fund.

We thank our agent, Wendy Strothman, for helping us shape this project and guide it to print. Our editor at Simon & Schuster, Bob Bender, and his colleague Johanna Li made enormous contributions to bringing the finished product to fruition. Special thanks are also due to Steve Petteway, the Supreme Court's curator, for giving us access to the Court's amazing photo archive, from which we selected some of the memorable images in the book. No one was more crucial to this book's production or more deserving of our thanks than Marianne Carroll, who typed, retyped, and typed again this manuscript in its many iterations with great care, skill, and remarkable goodwill.

Finally, we want to thank our families—Brett, Lucas, Dylan, Jake, Sydney, Casey on the Graetz side, and Gene and Hannah on the Greenhouse side—whose support, encouragement, patience, and good humor make everything possible. Without you, there is nothing.

Notes

INTRODUCTION: A COUNTERREVOLUTION RECLAIMED

1 "Bicentennial Observance of the U.S. Constitution," CQ Electronic Library, http://www.cqpress.com/incontext/constitution/docs/bicentennial_observance html.

2 "Remarks of Thurgood Marshall at the Annual Seminar of the San Francisco Patent and Trademark Law Association in Maui, Hawaii, May 6, 1987," http:// thurgoodmarshall.com/speeches/constitutional_speech.htm.

3 *Baker v. Carr,* 369 U.S. 186 (1962) (reapportionment); *Brown v. Board of Education,* 347 U.S. 483 (1954) (desegregation); *Gideon v. Wainwright,* 372 U.S. 335 (1963) (right to counsel). Warren's assessment can be found in Fred P. Graham, "Warren Era Ending Today After 16 Years of Reform," *New York Times,* June 23, 1969, A1.

4 Gallup Poll: "63% in Gallup Poll Think Courts Are Too Lenient on Criminals," *New York Times,* March 3, 1968, 40.

5 Louis Harris poll: "81% in a Poll See Law Breakdown," *New York Times,* September 10, 1968, 31.

6 Republican Party Platform of 1968, http://www.presidency.ucsb.edu/ws /?pid=25841.

7 Robert B. Semple, Jr., "Warren E. Burger Named Chief Justice by Nixon; Now on Appeals Bench," *New York Times,* May 22, 1969, A1.

8 See, for example, Warren E. Burger, "Who Will Watch the Watchman?: The Fourth Annual Edwin A. Mooers Lecture, April 17, 1964," *American University Law Review* 14 (1964–65): 1.

9 Harry A. Blackmun Papers (Box 50, Folder 1), Manuscript Division, Library of Congress.

10 Id.

11 Semple, "Warren E. Burger Named Chief Justice by Nixon."

12 Vincent Blasi, ed., *The Burger Court: The Counter-Revolution That Wasn't* (New Haven: Yale University Press, 1983).

13 Bernard Schwartz, *The Ascent of Pragmatism: The Burger Court in Action* (New York: Addison-Wesley, 1990), 413.

14 Benjamin N. Cardozo, *The Nature of the Judicial Process* (New Haven: Yale University Press, 1921), 168.

15 531 U.S. 98 (2000).

INTRODUCTION TO PART I: CRIME

1 Ramsey Clark, *Crime in America: Observations on its Nature, Causes, Prevention, and Control* (New York: Simon & Schuster, 1970).

2 James Q. Wilson, *Thinking About Crime* (New York: Basic Books, 1975).

3 William J. Stuntz, *The Collapse of American Criminal Justice* (Cambridge: Belknap Press, 2011), 294–95.

4 Id., 255, 287–88, 379n15.

5 The facts are collected in Eduardo Porter, "In the U.S., Punishment Comes Before the Crimes," *New York Times*, April 29, 2014. The FBI report for 2013 reflects a continuing downturn in violent crime. The estimate of 1.16 million violent crimes is the lowest since 1.09 million in 1978, despite population growth in the interval. A number of factors are offered for the decline, including an aging population, more effective policing, increased use of security cameras, and the extraordinary number of prisoners in the United States. See, e.g., Ian Simpson, "Violent U.S. Crime Drops Again, Reaches 1970s Level: FBI," Reuters, November 10, 2014; and Federal Bureau of Investigation, "Crime Statistics for 2013 Released," November 10, 2014, http://www.fbi.gov/news/stories/2014/november/crime-statistics-for-2013-released.

6 Christian Henrichson and Ruth Delaney, "The Price of Prisons: What Incarceration Costs Taxpayers" (New York: Vera Institute of Justice, 2012), 9, http://www.vera.org/sites/default/files/resources/downloads/price-of-prisons-updated-version-021914.pdf; The Reset Foundation, Poverty to Prison Cycle, http://theresetfoundation.org/the-issue.

7 For descriptions of this political transformation see Jonathan Simon, *Governing Through Crime: How the War on Crime Transformed American Democracy and Created a Culture of Fear* (New York: Oxford University Press, 2007), and Michael W. Flamm, *Law and Order: Street Crime, Civil Unrest, and the Crisis of Liberalism in the 1960s* (New York: Columbia University Press, 2007).

8 Stuntz, *The Collapse of American Criminal Justice*, 234.

9 Porter, "In the U.S., Punishment Comes Before the Crime."

10 *Gideon v. Wainwright*, 372 U.S. 335 (1963); *Miranda v. Arizona*, 384 U.S. 436 (1966); *Mapp v. Ohio*, 367 U.S. 643 (1961).

11 Simon, *Governing Through Crime*, 114–16.

12 Stephan Lesher, *George Wallace: American Populist* (New York: Addison-Wesley, 1994), 294.

13 Richard Nixon, "Radio Address About the State of the Union on Law Enforcement and Drug Abuse Prevention, March 10, 1973," in *Public Papers of the Presidents of the United States: Richard Nixon, 1973* (Washington, D.C.: Government Printing Office, 1991), 182.

14 Warren E. Burger, Ripon College Commencement Lecture on Crime and Punishment, Ripon, Wisconsin (May 21, 1967); Warren E. Burger, "Who Will Watch the Watchman?," *American University Law Review* 14 (1964): 1.

CHAPTER I: THE FALL AND RISE OF THE DEATH PENALTY

1 Lee Epstein and Joseph Fiske Kobylka, *The Supreme Court and Legal Change: Abortion and the Death Penalty* (Chapel Hill: University of North Carolina Press, 1992), 34–35; Carol S. Steiker, "*Furman v. Georgia*: Not an End but a Beginning," in *Death Penalty Stories*, eds. John H. Blume and Jordan M. Steiker (New York: Foundation Press, 2009), 95.

2 Brief for Petitioner, *Furman v. Georgia* 408 U.S. 238 (1972) (No. 69-5003), 11, quoted in Epstein and Kobylka, *The Supreme Court and Legal Change*, 35.

3 See 408 U.S. at 316 and 417.

4 James Liebman, "Slow Dancing with Death: The Supreme Court and Capital Punishment, 1963–2006," *Columbia Law Review* 107 (2007): 1; *Graham v. Florida*, 130 S. Ct. 2011, 2021 (2010); *Kennedy v. Louisiana*, 554 U.S. 407, 419, 422 (2008).

5 The history is told in Epstein and Kobylka, *The Supreme Court and Legal Change*, 34–82.

6 *Boykin v. Alabama*, 395 U.S. 238 (1969).

7 An Arkansas jury had sentenced William Maxwell, a twenty-one-year-old black man, to death for raping Stella Spoon, a thirty-five-year-old white woman. In appealing Maxwell's sentence, the NAACP Legal Defense Fund had amassed extensive data supporting racial bias in death sentences where the perpetrator was black and the victim white. In its initial conference, the Court voted 6–3 for Maxwell on both issues, but Justice Douglas, who had been assigned the opinion, wrote a draft opinion so broad that he lost his majority. Del Dickson, *The Supreme Court in Conference, 1940–1985: The Private Discussions Behind Nearly 300 Supreme Court Decisions* (New York: Oxford University Press, 2001), 610–12; see also Epstein and Kobylka, *The Supreme Court and Legal Change*, 63–65 (asserting that the initial vote for Maxwell was 8–1). The Court then scheduled the case to be reargued the next year. By then Earl Warren and Abe Fortas had been replaced by Warren Burger and Harry Blackmun; this changed two votes in death penalty cases. Blackmun, however, did not participate because he had written the Court of Appeals opinion affirming Maxwell's death sentence. The Supreme Court deadlocked 4–4 on whether bifurcated trials were necessary. Unable to sort out the muddle, the Court dodged and, by a 7–1 vote, sent the case back to the lower court on the ground that several jurors had been excluded

after voicing moral or religious objections to the death penalty, contrary to the 1968 Supreme Court decision in *Witherspoon v. Illinois*, 391 U.S. 510 (1968). *Maxwell v. Bishop*, 308 U.S. 262 (1970). Dickson, *The Supreme Court in Conference*, 614.

8 *McGautha v. California*, 402 U.S. 183 (1971).

9 402 U.S. at 204, 207 (Harlan, J., majority) (emphasis added).

10 410 U.S. at 210. Justice Black wrote a separate concurrence (agreeing with virtually all of Harlan's opinion) to emphasize his view that it is inappropriate for justices to interpret the Constitution based on modern sensibilities. Justices Douglas, Brennan, and Marshall dissented.

11 *People v. Anderson*, 493 P. 2d. 880 (Cal. 1972).

12 Chief Justice Burger asked William Brennan and Byron White to review the nearly two hundred certiorari petitions in death penalty cases that had been submitted to the Court and identify appropriate cases for the Court to take. Dickson, *The Supreme Court in Conference*, 616n372; Epstein and Kobylka, *The Supreme Court and Legal Change*, 70. Woodward and Armstrong say that it was Justice Stewart who insisted on further review. *The Brethren: Inside the Supreme Court* (New York: Simon & Schuster, 1979), 206.

13 *Furman v. Georgia*, 408 U.S. 238, 239 (1971) (per curiam), quoted in Epstein and Kobylka, *The Supreme Court and Legal Change*, 70.

14 *Furman v. Georgia*, 408 U.S. at 242 (Douglas, J.); Dickson, *The Supreme Court in Conference*, 617.

15 Dickson, *The Supreme Court in Conference*, at 616–18.

16 Id. at 619.

17 408 U.S. at 239–40.

18 Woodward and Armstrong, *The Brethren*, 209.

19 408 U.S. at 307 (Stewart, J.).

20 Id. at 308.

21 Id. at 310.

22 Id.

23 408 U.S. at 310–12 (White, J.).

24 408 U.S. at 405, 414 (Blackmun, J., dissenting).

25 Id. at 417–18 (Powell, J., dissenting).

26 Id. at 375–408 (Burger, C.J., dissenting).

27 Marie Gottschalk, *The Prisons and the Gallows: The Politics of Mass Incarceration in America* (Cambridge: Cambridge University Press, 2006), 221.

28 Woodward and Armstrong, *The Brethren* at 207.

29 William J. Stuntz, *The Collapse of American Criminal Justice* (Cambridge: Belknap Press, 2011), 216.

30 Hugo Adam Bedau, *The Death Penalty in America: Current Controversies* (New York: Oxford University Press, 1997).

31 Epstein and Kobylka, *The Supreme Court and Legal Change*, 87.

32 James B. Ginty, Memorandum to the Conference, January 8, 1976 (Lewis F. Powell, Jr.'s *Gregg* file, Folder 1, p. 4, Attachment D).

33 *Trop v. Dulles*, 356 U.S. 86, 100–101n10 (1958). In 1910 the Supreme Court had concluded that fifteen years of imprisonment in chains with hard labor was disproportionate cruel and unusual punishment for a Philippine resident who had falsified an official government document. Writing for the majority, Justice Joseph McKenna said: "time works changes [and] brings into existence new conditions and purposes." *Weems v. United States*, 217 U.S. 349 (1910) (McKenna, J., majority).

34 408 U.S. at 382 (Burger, C.J., dissenting).

35 Id. at 383.

36 *Gregg v. Georgia*, 428 U.S. 153 (1976).

37 *Fowler v. North Carolina*, 428 U.S. 904 (1976).

38 Memorandum from Chris Whitman to Lewis F. Powell, Jr., January 16, 1976 (Lewis F. Powell, Jr.'s, *Gregg* file, Folder 3, p. 5).

39 Woodward and Armstrong, *The Brethren*, 431.

40 *Jurek v. Texas*, 428 U.S. 262, 265–66 (1976).

41 Epstein and Kobylka, *Supreme Court and Legal Change*, 97–99; Bedau, *The Death Penalty in America*, 135.

42 All descriptions of the conference are based on Lewis F. Powell, Jr.'s, Conference Notes, April 2, 1976 (Lewis F. Powell, Jr.'s, *Gregg* file, Folder 5). See also Dickson, *The Supreme Court in Conference*, 620–21.

43 Id.; Woodward and Armstrong, *The Brethren*, 435–36.

44 Contrary to Burger's wishes, they refused to issue a separate opinion—which would have produced a majority—saying only that the Constitution permits the death penalty in some circumstances. Memorandum from Potter Stewart to Warren Burger, May 7, 1976 (Lewis F. Powell, Jr.'s, *Gregg* file, Folder 6).

45 When the Court initially issued its decisions in the five death penalty cases, the opinions of the three justices were described as opinions of Justice Stewart in which Justices Powell and Stevens concurred. By the beginning of October, Lewis Powell had taken umbrage with this characterization. He wrote to Henry Putzel, the Court's Reporter of Decisions, saying that the way in which the cases were recorded had occasioned a "great deal of confusion in the media and at the bar." Powell requested that the official reports be changed to describe the plurality opinion as "by Stewart, Powell, and Stevens." Memorandum from Lewis F. Powell, Jr. to Henry Putzel, Jr., October 1, 1976 (Lewis F. Powell, Jr.'s *Gregg* file, Folder 12). A surprising amount of correspondence then ensued about the precise formulation of such a change. For some reason, Chief Justice Burger insisted on "consideration of the entire Court." Letter from Warren Burger to Lewis F. Powell, Jr., October 4, 1970 (Lewis F. Powell, Jr.'s, *Gregg* file, Folder 12). By November 4, all the justices had approved Powell's request, and the official reports now describe the opinion as by all three justices. In a note to Powell, indicating that

he did not object to the change, William Rehnquist said, "I think Henry Putzel could far more profitably have devoted his time to changing other parts of your opinion." Letter from William Rehnquist to Lewis F. Powell, Jr., October 21, 1976. Id.

46 428 U.S. at 199 (Plurality opinion).

47 Id. at 189 (Plurality opinion).

48 See Norman Mailer, *The Executioner's Song* (Boston: Little, Brown and Company, 1979).

49 For greater detail, see, e.g., James Liebman and Lawrence C. Marshall, "Less Is Better: Justice Stevens and the Narrowed Death Penalty," *Fordham Law Review* 74 (2006): 1607; Liebman, "Slow Dancing with Death," 1; and Epstein and Kobylka, *The Supreme Court and Legal Change.*

50 See, e.g., *Ford v. Wainwright*, 477 U.S. 399 (1986); *Penry v. Lynaugh*, 492 U.S. 302 (1989); and *Atkins v. Virginia*, 536 U.S. 304 (2002).

51 *Thompson v. Oklahoma*, 487 U.S. 815 (1988) (holding that defendant who committed first degree murder at the age of fifteen could not be sentenced to death); *Stanford v. Kentucky*, 492 U.S. 361 (1989) (upholding death penalty for juveniles under the age of sixteen); *Roper v. Simmons*, 543 U.S. 551 (2005) (holding that the death penalty cannot be applied to defendants under the age of eighteen).

52 *Coker v. Georgia*, 433 U.S. 584 (1977); see also *Eberheart v. Georgia*, 433 U.S. 917 (1977). See, generally, Epstein and Kobylka, *The Supreme Court and Legal Change*, 118–20; and Liebman, "Slow Dancing with Death," 37–38.

53 After *Furman* there had been three states that had death sentences for such rapes, but the Court had struck down the mandatory death penalty statutes of North Carolina and Louisiana the previous year. Three other states, Florida, Mississippi, and Tennessee, imposed death sentences for sexual assault of a child, but one of the three, Tennessee, was also mandatory and therefore invalid.

54 See, e.g., Marvin E. Wolfgang, "Racial Discrimination in the Death Sentence for Rape," in *Executions in America*, ed. William J. Bowers (Lanham: Lexington, 1974); and Marc Riedel, "Rape, Race, and the Death Penalty in Georgia," *American Journal of Orthopsychiatry* 45 (1975): 663.

55 *Coker v. Georgia*, 433 U.S. at 596.

56 "*Coker v. Georgia*," The Oyez Project at IIT Chicago-Kent College of Law, http://www.oyez.org/cases/1970-1979/1976/1976_75_5444.

57 "The Law: Arguing About Death for Rape," *Time*, April 11, 1977.

58 Lewis F. Powell, Jr., Conference Notes, *Coker* file, folder 2.

59 Convictions for rape increased beginning in the 1980s. In 2008, in a contentious 5–4 decision, the Court extended *Coker* to strike down the death penalty (then applicable in five states) for the rape of a child when the crime does not result, and was not intended to result, in the child's death. *Kennedy v. Louisiana*, 554 U.S. 407 (2008).

60 *Lockett v. Ohio*, 438 U.S. 586 (1978). In *Woodson v. North Carolina*, 428 U.S. 280 (1976), one of the five death penalty cases decided along with *Gregg v. Georgia*, Woodson, along with three others, had participated in an armed robbery of a convenience store during which a customer and cashier were shot and killed. There was dispute at Woodson's trial over who had fired the deadly shots, but no one claimed that Woodson, who had stayed outside the store as a lookout, did. Nevertheless, he was convicted by a North Carolina jury of first-degree murder, which resulted in a mandatory sentence of death. The Court did not have to deal with the question of whether the death penalty was unconstitutional disproportionate punishment for such a crime because it struck down North Carolina's statute on the ground that its mandatory imposition of death sentences was unconstitutional. See also *Enmund v. Florida*, 458 U.S. 782 (1982) (striking down death penalty for participation in robbery and killings where defendant was, at most, sitting in a car outside the farmhouse where these crimes occurred).

61 *Lockett v. Ohio*, 438 U.S. at 589–92.

62 438 U.S. at 605 (Burger, C.J., majority). See also Liebman, "Slow Dancing with Death," 38–40.

63 438 U.S. at 639 (Rehnquist, J., dissenting).

64 Liebman, "Slow Dancing with Death," 40.

65 Id., 57, citing *Barefoot v. Estelle*, 463 U.S. 880 (1983); *Zant v. Stephens*, 462 U.S. 862 (1983); and *Barclay v. Florida*, 463 U.S. 939 (1983).

66 E.g., *Simmons v. South Carolina*, 512 U.S. 154, 171 (1994) (plurality opinion) (the state may not treat future dangerousness of defendant as an aggravating factor if in the alternative to the death penalty the defendant would be held in jail for life without parole); *Espinosa v. Florida*, 505 U.S. 1079, 1080–81 (1992) (per curiam); and *Sochor v. Florida*, 504 U.S. 527, 540–41 (1992) (the state's "coldness" aggravating factor was unconstitutional).

67 Linda Greenhouse. "Supreme Court: A New Angrier Mood on Death Penalty Appeals," *New York Times*, November 11, 1983.

68 *Coleman v. Balkcom*, 451 U.S. 949, 957–58 (1981) (Rehnquist, J., dissenting from denial of certiorari).

69 Justice O'Connor never voiced similar complaints publicly, but her opinions imply that she agreed.

70 *Maggio v. Williams*, 464 U.S. 46 (Brennan, J.), 58 (Blackmun, J.) (1983).

71 See Liebman, "Slow Dancing with Death," 51–60.

72 In 1984, for example, it rejected a claim that death sentences must be imposed by a jury. *Spaziano v. Florida*, 488 U.S. 447 (1984).

73 "Death Cases Straining Justices," *New York Times*, May 13, 1986.

74 This history is from Kate Pickett, "A Brief History of Lethal Injection," *Time*, November 10, 2009.

75 *Heckler v. Chaney*, 470 U.S. 821 (1985). In recent years, lethal injections, which have long been thought to be the most humane method of execution, experi-

enced some serious malfunctions. In 2014, for example, in Ohio, Oklahoma, and Arizona, executions by lethal injections were botched. The Arizona execution of Joseph Rudolph Wood III took nearly two hours before he died, with Wood struggling to breathe much of the time. Mark Berman, "Arizona Execution Lasts Nearly Two Hours: Lawyer Says Joseph Wood Was 'Gasping and Struggling to Breathe,' " *Washington Post*, July 23, 2014. Wood's execution prompted Alex Kozinski, a federal appellate judge, to urge a return to firing squads. "I personally think we should go to the guillotine, but shooting is probably the right way to go," Kozinski said. Maura Dolan, "Executions Should Be by Firing Squad, Federal Appeals Court Judge Says," *Los Angeles Times*, July 23, 2014. Saying that firing squads would be "messy but effective," Kozinski added, "If we as a society cannot stomach the splatter from an execution carried out by a firing squad, then we shouldn't be carrying out executions at all." Id.

76 Epstein and Kobylka, *The Supreme Court and Legal Change*, 122, quoting David A. Kaplan, "Death Row Inmate Prevails—Finally," *National Law Journal*, January 11, 1998; "Disorder in the Court: The Death Penalty and the Constitution," *Michigan Law Review*, 85 (1987): 1817–18.

77 *McKleskey v. Kemp*, 481 U.S. 279, 283–85 (1987).

78 See Brennan's dissent at id., 326, for the statistics.

79 Summarized further at Epstein and Kobylka, *The Supreme Court and Legal Change*, 123.

80 *McKleskey v. Kemp*, 753 F.2d 877, 898 (1985).

81 Brief for Petitioner, *McCleskey v. Kemp*, 481 U.S. 279 (1987) (No. 84-6811), quoted in Epstein and Kobylka, *The Supreme Court and Legal Change*, 125.

82 481 U.S. at 306, 311, 312 (Powell, J., majority).

83 Id. at 313.

84 Stuntz, *The Collapse of American Criminal Justice*, 120, 291. Proving that a prosecutor or judge or jury deliberately discriminated against a black murderer of a white victim is usually a hopeless endeavor—even when it is clear that the system discriminates extensively. So *McCleskey* allows the state to punish by death crimes when the victim is white more frequently than the same crime when the victim is black. Nearly a decade after deciding *McCleskey*, the Supreme Court eliminated the potential for successful claims of discrimination against black defendants. *United States v. Armstrong*, 517 U.S. 456 (1996).

85 481 U.S. at 315–19 (Powell, J., majority).

86 On the morning of October 15, 1986, just before the oral argument, White handed Powell a twelve-page memorandum expressing similar views. Unsurprisingly, Rehnquist and Scalia agreed. As did O'Connor, who in a handwritten note to Powell, after he circulated the first draft of his opinion in November, congratulated him on his "splendid opinion." "No one could have done better," she said.

87 481 U.S. at 336 (Brennan, J., dissenting).

88 Id. at 345 (Blackmun, J., dissenting).

89 George Will, "The Death Penalty by One Vote," *Washington Post*, April 30, 1987, in Lewis F. Powell, Jr.'s, *McCleskey* file, Folder 2, p. 12.

90 Peter Applebome, "Georgia Inmate Is Executed After 'Chaotic' Legal Move," *New York Times*, September 26, 1991; "Warren McCleskey Is Dead," *New York Times*, September 29, 1991.

91 Applebome, "Georgia Inmate Is Executed After 'Chaotic' Legal Move."

92 Liebman, "Slow Dancing with Death," 84.

93 John C. Jeffries, Jr., *Justice Lewis F. Powell, Jr.* (New York: Fordham University Press, 2001), 451.

94 Stephen B. Bright, "The Politics of Crime and the Death Penalty: Not 'Soft on Crime' but Hard on the Bill of Rights," *St. Louis University Law Journal* 39 (1995): 484.

95 The case is *Ford v. Wainwright*, 477 U.S. 399 (1986).

96 William Fletcher, "Madison Lecture: Our Broken Death Penalty," *NYU Law Review* 89 (2014): 820–21.

97 *Walton v. Arizona*, 497 U.S. 639, 669 (1990).

98 James Liebman, "Opting for Real Death Penalty Reform," *Ohio State Law Journal* 63 (2002): 318.

99 Between 1976 and 2013, Texas executed nearly six times as many people (493) as the second closest state, Virginia (110). After that came Florida (74), Missouri (68), Alabama (56), and Georgia (53). New Mexico, Colorado, and Wyoming have each executed one person. California and Pennsylvania have executed the lowest percentage of their death row inmates: 13 of 731 in California, 3 of 198 in Pennsylvania. These numbers are from Fletcher, "Our Broken Death Penalty," at 809.

100 Id. at 811.

101 We thank Robert Ferguson for emphasizing this point. Life without parole, for example, was Texas' response to the Supreme Court's 2005 decision (in *Roper*) banning the death penalty for juveniles.

102 Carol S. Steiker and Jordan M. Steiker, "Entrenchment and/or Destabilization? Reflections on (Another) Two Decades of Constitutional Regulation of Capital Punishment," *Law and Inequality* 30 (2012): 212.

103 Death Penalty Information Center, "The Death Penalty in 2014: Year-End Report," http://www.deathpenaltyinfo.org/yearend2014#pressrelease.

104 Jeffries, *Justice Lewis F. Powell, Jr.*, 451–2.

105 481 U.S. at 345 (Blackmun, J., dissenting).

106 *Callins v. Collins*, 510 U.S. 1141, 1145 (1994) (Blackmun, J., dissenting).

107 Id.

108 *Payne v. Tennessee*, 501 U.S. 808 (1991), overruling *Booth v. Maryland*, 482 U.S. 496 (1987) (which had struck down a statute that permitted juries to consider victim impact evidence as an aggravating factor in death penalty

sentencing hearings). Victim impact statements are now allowed in capital cases.

109 *Atkins v. Virginia*, 536 U.S. 304 (2002).

110 *Baze v. Rees*, 553 U.S. 35, 86 (2008); see also John Paul Stevens, *Five Chiefs: A Supreme Court Memoir* (New York: Little Brown and Company, 2011), 218.

111 *Furman*, 408 U.S. 238, 369 (Marshall, J., concurring); Fletcher, "Our Broken Death Penalty," 828.

112 When the Supreme Court upheld Oklahoma's use of lethal injections in 2015, Justice Stephen Breyer dissented to "reopen the question" whether the death penalty is an unconstitutional punishment. In his dissent, he detailed how *Gregg*'s effort to eliminate arbitrariness in the penalty's imposition had failed. *Glossip v. Gross*, 135 S. Ct. 2726, 2755 (2015) (Breyer, J., dissenting). Justice Scalia responded dismissively: "Welcome to Groundhog Day." Id. at 2746 (Scalia, J., concurring).

113 *Jones v. Chapell*, No. W09-02158-CJC, July 16, 2014 (Central District of California), reversed, *Jones v. Davis*, No. 14–56373 (9th Cir. 2015); Maura Dolan, "Federal Judge Rules California Death Penalty Is Unconstitutional," *Los Angeles Times*, July 16, 2014.

CHAPTER 2: TAMING THE TRILOGY

1 384 U.S. 436 (1966).

2 372 U.S. 335 (1963). See also *Massiah v. United States*, 377 U.S. 201 (1964).

3 367 U.S. 643 (1961).

4 The description is from Yale Kamisar, "On the Fortieth Anniversary of the *Miranda* Case: Why We Needed It, How We Got It—and What Happened to It," *Ohio State Journal of Criminal Law* 5 (2007): 178.

5 See, e.g., Yale Kamisar, "What Is an 'Involuntary' Confession? Some Comments on *Inbau* and *Reid*'s Criminal Interrogation and Confessions," *Rutgers Law Review* 17 (1963): 728.

6 Kamisar, "On the Fortieth Anniversary of the *Miranda* Case," 168.

7 *Miranda v. Arizona*, 384 U.S. 436, 483–84 (1966).

8 Id. at 536 (White, J., dissenting). Justice Tom C. Clark also dissented. He retired in 1967; unlike the other dissenters, he was never a member of the Burger Court.

9 Id. at 526 (White, J., dissenting).

10 Id. at 542.

11 Kamisar, "On the Fortieth Anniversary of the *Miranda* Case," 197; Yale Kamisar, "*Miranda*'s Reprieve," *ABA Journal* 92 (2006): 50.

12 Id.

13 For a comprehensive discussion of this legislation and its litigation history, see Michael Edmund O'Neill, "Undoing *Miranda*," *BYU Law Review* 2000 (2000): 185.

14 *Dickerson v. United States*, 530 U.S. 428, 443; (2000) (Rehnquist, C.J., majority).

15 Charles D. Weisselberg, "Mourning *Miranda*," *California Law Review* 96 (2008): 1523–24.

16 Kamisar, "On the Fortieth Anniversary of the *Miranda* Case," 203.

17 *Harris v. New York*, 401 U.S. 222 (1971). The Court soon extended this impeachment ability to instances when the defendant had requested but had been refused legal counsel by the police. *Oregon v. Hass*, 420 U.S. 714 (1975).

18 384 U.S. at 478.

19 *Oregon v. Mathiason*, 429 U.S. 492 (1977); *California v. Beheler*, 463 U.S. 1121 (1983). The Burger Court also concluded that no *Miranda* warnings are required when an IRS agent questions the target of a tax fraud investigation at the suspect's home. *Beckwith v. United States*, 425 U.S. 341 (1976). Nor are the warnings required for a person called before a grand jury. *United States v. Mandujano*, 425 U.S. 564 (1976); *United States v. Wong*, 431 U.S. 174 (1977).

20 *New York v. Quarles*, 467 U.S. 649 (1984). In an opinion by Justice Rehnquist, joined by Burger, White, Blackmun, and Powell, the Court concluded that "the need for answers to questions in a situation posing a threat to public safety outweighs the need for the prophylactic rule protecting the Fifth Amendment's privilege against self-incrimination." 465 U.S. at 657 (Rehnquist, J., majority). Justice O'Connor, no fan of *Miranda*, in a separate opinion said that the Court had failed to provide "sufficient justification for departing from [*Miranda*] or for blurring its now clear strictures." Id. at 660 (O'Connor, J., concurring in part, dissenting in part). She predicted that the "end result will be a finespun new doctrine on public safety exigencies incident to custodial interrogation, complete with hair-splitting distinctions." Id. at 663–64. The dissent by Marshall, joined by Brennan and Stevens, pointed out that hair-splitting had already occurred. Marshall disputed the majority's assertion that the public was at risk during Quarles's interrogation: the police officer had testified that "the situation was under control," the New York court had described the perpetrator "as reduced to a condition of physical powerlessness," and it had found no evidence that Kraft's question was prompted by any concern for public safety. Id. at 675–76 (Marshall, J., dissenting). On the other hand, there was a loaded gun hidden in a supermarket.

21 The Burger Court allowed to be used at trial testimony of a witness whose identity had been learned by police only through questioning the defendant without giving *Miranda* warnings. *Michigan v. Tucker*, 417 U.S. 433 (1974). The Court allowed a second confession after *Miranda* warnings had been given when a first confession had previously been improperly obtained. *Oregon v. Elstad*, 470 U.S. 298 (1985). The lower courts interpreted these decisions to permit any evidence obtained when *Miranda* warnings are not given, other than the defendant's confession, to be admissible at his trial—an outcome the Supreme Court ratified in

2004. Kamisar, "On the Fortieth Anniversary of the *Miranda* Case," 163–203; Weisselberg, "Mourning *Miranda*," 1519–1601; Richard A. Leo and Welsh S. White, "Adapting to *Miranda*: Modern Interrogators' Strategies for Dealing with the Obstacles Posed by *Miranda*," *Minnesota Law Review* 84 (1999): 397–472.

22 See, e.g., Weisselberg, "Mourning *Miranda*," 1551–58; and Leo and White, "Adapting to *Miranda*," 431–450.

23 *North Carolina v. Butler*, 441 U.S. 369 (1979).

24 441 U.S. at 378 (Brennan dissenting, joined by Marshall and Stevens).

25 *Connecticut v. Barrett*, 479 U.S. 523 (1987).

26 *Moran v. Burbine*, 475 U.S. 412 (1986).

27 George C. Thomas III, "Separated at Birth but Siblings Nonetheless: *Miranda* and the Due Process Notice Cases," *Michigan Law Review* 99 (2001): 1082.

28 William J. Stuntz, "Waiving Rights in Criminal Procedure," *Virginia Law Review* 75 (1989): 762, 808.

29 Leo and White, "Adapting to *Miranda*," 397; Richard A. Leo, "The Impact of *Miranda* Revisited," *Journal of Criminal Law and Criminology* 86 (1996): 621; Barry C. Feld, "Police Interrogation of Juveniles: An Empirical Study of Policy and Practice," *Journal of Criminal Law and Criminology* 97 (2006): 219; David Simon, *Homicide: A Year on the Killing Streets* (New York: Houghton Mifflin, 1991) at 595; Yale Kamisar, "Killing *Miranda* in Baltimore: Reflections on David Simon's *Homicide*," *Jurist* 2 (1999).

30 Kamisar, "On the Fortieth Anniversary of the *Miranda* Case," 178.

31 Id. at 177n65.

32 John F. Decker, *Revolution to the Right: Criminal Procedure Jurisprudence During the Burger-Rehnquist Court* (Portland: Taylor & Francis, 1992); Lewis R. Katz, "In Search of a Fourth Amendment for the Twenty-first Century," *Indiana Law Journal* 65 (1990): 575; Silas J. Wasserstrom, "The Incredible Shrinking Fourth Amendment," *American Criminal Law Review* 21 (1984): 271; Michael Campbell, Note, "Defining a Fourth Amendment Search: A Critique of the Supreme Court's Post-*Katz* Jurisprudence," *Washington Law Review* 61 (1986): 200.

33 *Schnecloth v. Bustamonte*, 412 U.S. 218 (1973). The Court also upheld warrantless searches by flying over and photographing fenced backyards and industrial complexes (*California v. Ciraolo*, 476 U.S. 207 [1986]; *Dow Chemical Co. v. United States*, 476 U.S. 227 [1986]); by obtaining an individual's records from his bank (*United States v. Miller*, 425 U.S. 435 [1976]); and by setting up a pen register to record telephone numbers called from one's home (*Smith v. Maryland*, 442 U.S. 735 [1979]).

34 See Carol S. Steiker, "Counter-Revolution in Constitutional Criminal Procedure? Two Audiences, Two Answers," *Michigan Law Review* 94 (1996): 2497.

35 469 U.S. 325 (1985).

36 Id. at 328.

37 Id. at 340, 346–47 (White, J., majority).

38 Id. at 351, 353 (Blackmun, J., concurring). Powell also wrote a concurring opinion, joined by Justice O'Connor, saying that the Court's decision turned "on the special characteristics of the elementary and secondary school" setting. Id. at 348 (Powell, J., concurring).

39 Steiker, "Counter-Revolution in Constitutional Criminal Procedure?," 2498–2500; *O'Connor v. Ortega*, 480 U.S. 709 (1987); *Griffin v. Wisconsin*, 483 U.S. 868 (1987); *New York v. Burger*, 482 U.S. 691 (1987); *Skinner v. Railway Labor Executives' Association*, 489 U.S. 602 (1989); *National Treasury Employees Union v. Von Raab*, 489 U.S. 656 (1989); *Vernonia School District v. Acton*, 515 U.S. 646 (1995); in the order listed.

40 *Weeks v. United States*, 232 U.S. 383 (1914). Some scholars date the exclusionary rule from *Boyd v. United States*, 116 U.S. 616 (1886).

41 *Katz v. United States*, 389 U.S. 347, 357 (1967) (Stewart, J.).

42 Potter Stewart, "The Road to *Mapp v. Ohio* and Beyond: The Origins, Development and Future of the Exclusionary Rule in Search-and-Seizure Cases," *Columbia Law Review* 83 (1983): 1392–93.

43 The Burger Court also restricted individuals' standing to bring such claims. See, e.g., *Rakas v. Illinois*, 439 U.S. 128 (1978) (denying standing to protest an illegal search to an automobile passenger); and *United States v. Salvucci*, 448 U.S. 83 (1980) (overruling *Jones v. United States*, 362 U.S. 257 [1960]). See also Steiker, "Counter-Revolution in Constitutional Criminal Procedure," 2505–11.

44 *United States v. Leon*, 487 U.S. 897 (1984).

45 487 U.S. at 918–25 (White, J., majority).

46 *Nix v. Williams*, 467 U.S. 431 (1984) (ratifying an "inevitable discovery exception" to the exclusionary rule).

47 *United States v. Havens*, 446 U.S. 620 (1980).

48 *United States v. Janis*, 428 U.S. 433 (1976) (civil tax); *Immigration and Naturalization Service v. Lopez-Mendoza*, 468 U.S. 1032 (1984) (deportation).

49 Decker, *Revolution to the Right*, 18.

50 *Herring v. United States*, 555 U.S. 135, 144 (2009). Three justices (Alito, Scalia, and Thomas) are ready to throw out the exclusionary rule altogether. In a 2006 opinion for the Court, Scalia minimized the benefits of the exclusionary rule by emphasizing the increased professionalism of the police, including internal review procedures and civilian review boards (*Hudson v. Michigan*, 547 U.S. 586, 598–99 [2006]), thereby ratifying Burger's call for the latter as a substitute for the exclusionary rule in his law review article more than four decades earlier.

51 Steiker, "Counter-Revolution in Constitutional Criminal Procedure?," 2521.

52 *Gideon v. Wainwright*, 372 U.S. 335 (1963).

53 Id. at 344 (Black, J., majority).

54 Anthony Lewis, *Gideon's Trumpet: How One Man, a Poor Prisoner, Took His Case to the Supreme Court—and Changed the Law of the United States* (New

York: Random House, 1964). See also Stephen Holden, "Foot Soldiers in the Battle for a Fair Shake," *New York Times*, June 27, 2013. The challenges public defenders face were documented in an award-winning 2013 HBO film, *Gideon's Army*, which focused on two Georgia public defenders, who typically represent more than one hundred defendants at a time.

55 Burger seemed to agree. In 1975, writing for a 6–3 majority, Justice Stewart concluded that the Constitution permits a criminal defendant to waive his right to counsel and defend himself, despite the fact that a lawyer may be necessary "to assure the defendant a fair trial." *Faretta v. California*, 422 U.S. 806 (1975). Burger, in a dissenting opinion joined by Rehnquist and Blackmun, said that the goal of ensuring justice is "ill-served and the integrity of and public confidence in the system are undermined when an easy conviction is obtained due to the defendant's ill-advised decision to waive counsel." In a separate dissent, Harry Blackmun put this objection more sharply: "If there is any truth to the old proverb that 'one who is his own lawyer has a fool for a client,' the Court by its opinion today now bestows a *Constitutional* right on one to make a fool of himself." 422 U.S. at 839 (Burger, C.J., dissenting), and 853 (Blackmun, J., dissenting) (1975).

56 In addition to police interrogation, the Warren Court had extended the right to counsel to lineups, guilty-plea hearings, sentencing hearings, direct appeals of convictions, and juvenile delinquency proceedings. *United States v. Wade*, 388 U.S. 218 (1967) (lineups); *White v. Maryland*, 373 U.S. 59 (1963) (guilty-plea proceedings); *Mempa v. Rhay*, 389 U.S. 128 (1967) (sentencing hearings); *Douglas v. California*, 372 U.S. 353 (1963) (direct appeals); and *In re Gault*, 387 U.S. 1 (1967) (juvenile delinquency proceedings). In 1972 the Burger Court unanimously extended the right to misdemeanor charges that could result in imprisonment. *Argersinger v. Hamlin*, 407 U.S. 25 (1972). Despite the Court's unanimity, fissures among the justices appeared in four separate opinions. That same year the Court, in a 5–4 decision, concluded that no counsel is required for a lineup before the defendant has been formally charged. *Kirby v. Illinois*, 406 U.S. 682 (1972). Then the Court determined that no right to counsel exists for a probation-revocation hearing (*Gagnon v. Scarpelli*, 411 U.S. 778 [1973]); for a prosecutor's presentation of a photo display to a witness after indictment but before trial (*United States v. Ash*, 413 U.S. 300 [1973]); for an indigent defendant's discretionary appeals of his conviction (*Ross v. Moffitt*, 417 U.S. 600 [1974]); or for prison disciplinary proceedings (*Wolff v. McDonnell*, 418 U.S. 539 [1974]). See also *Fuller v. Oregon*, 417 U.S. 40 (1974) (permitting states to recoup the costs of counsel from previously indigent defendants). In 1975, the Court denied any right to counsel in a pretrial judicial hearing of probable cause for arrest and detention. *Gerstein v. Pugh*, 420 U.S. 103 (1975). Subsequently, the Court decided that counsel was not required to be appointed for a "putative" defendant called before a grand jury, *United States v. Mandu-*

jano, 425 U.S. 564 (1976); for military court-martials, *Middendorf v. Henry*, 425 U.S. 25 (1976); or for cases where a fine and probation are imposed, but not imprisonment, *Scott v. Illinois*, 440 U.S. 367 (1979).

57 The Supreme Court has frequently said so—at least since 1932. *Powell v. Alabama*, 287 U.S. 45, 53 (1932).

58 *McMann v. Richardson*, 397 U.S. 759, 771 and n. 14 (1970) (White, J., majority).

59 *Strickland v. Washington*, 466 U.S. 668, 685 (1984).

60 466 U.S. at 686 (O'Connor, J., majority).

61 Id. at 672.

62 Id. at 708, 710 (Marshall, J., dissenting).

63 Stephen Bright, "Counsel for the Poor: The Death Sentence Not for the Worst Crime but for the Worst Lawyer," *Yale Law Journal* 103 (1994): 1843n53.

64 American Bar Association Guidelines for the Appointment and Performance of Counsel in Death Penalty Cases, 1989, 30–38, http://www.americanbar .org/content/dam/aba/migrated/2011_build/death_penalty_representation /1989guidelines.authcheckdam.pdf. In a careful empirical study of 2,249 Philadelphia cases involving indigent murder defendants, RAND Corporation researchers estimated that replacing private court-appointed attorneys with public defenders would have resulted in 270 fewer convictions and a total decrease of 6,400 years in the total time served. James Anderson and Paul Heaton, "How Much Difference Does the Lawyer Make?" *Yale Law Journal* 122 (2012): 154, 212.

65 Anthony Lewis, *Gideon's Trumpet* at 205.

66 *Padilla v. Kentucky*, 130 S. Ct. 1473 (2010).

67 In *Missouri v. Frye*, 132 S.Ct. 1399 (2012), the defendant's attorney failed to tell his client about a prosecutor's offer of ninety days imprisonment if he pled guilty. After the offer had expired, Frye did plead guilty and was sentenced to three years in prison. The Court held that the attorney's failure constituted ineffective assistance under *Washington*. In the second case, *Lafler v. Cooper*, 132 S.Ct. 1376 (2012), the Court required a state court to consider resentencing a defendant who had turned down a plea offer based on erroneous advice from counsel and was subsequently convicted in a "full and fair trial before a jury." Both cases were decided by 5–4 majorities, with vigorous dissents by Justice Scalia. Whether these decisions signal more robust judicial oversight of claims of ineffective assistance of counsel remains to be seen. See, e.g., Carol S. Steiker, "Gideon's Problematic Promises," *Daedalus* 143 (2014): 51.

CHAPTER 3: CLOSING THE FEDERAL COURTHOUSE DOORS

1 *Shelton v. United States*, 242 F. 2d. 101, en banc 246 F. 2d. 571 (1957).

2 Bureau of Justice Statistics, Sourcebook of Criminal Statistics, Table 5-24-2010, http://www.bjs.gov/content/pub/ascii/fdluc06.txt.

3 William J. Stuntz, "The Pathological Politics of Criminal Law," *Michigan Law Review* 100 (2001): 509.

4 *Boykin v. Alabama*, 395 U.S. 238, 242 (1969).

5 Id. at 242–43 (Douglas, J., majority).

6 As Chapters 1 and 2 have explained, under Burger Court precedents, the silence of Mr. Boykin's attorney would have waived his rights unless Boykin could prove that he was likely innocent, but Boykin's sentence would have nevertheless been reversed after the Court determined that a death sentence was an unconstitutional punishment for robbery.

7 *Santobello v. New York*, 404 U.S. 257, 261 (1971). See also *Brady v. United States*, 397 U.S. 742 (1970); and *Parker v. North Carolina*, 397 U.S. 790 (1970).

8 *Brady v. United States*, 397 U.S. 742, 750, 757–58 (White, J., majority). The defendant, represented by competent counsel, had entered a guilty plea to a kidnapping, which carried a maximum sentence of death. He was sentenced to fifty years imprisonment, later reduced to thirty. Justice White concluded by observing: "we have no reason to doubt that [the defendant's] solemn admission of guilt was truthful." Id. at 758.

9 See H. Mitchell Caldwell, "Coercive Plea Bargaining: The Unrecognized Scourge of the Justice System," *Catholic University Law Review* 61 (2011): 83n147, 85n158, and 86n163 et seq.

10 434 U.S. 357 (1978). See also William J. Stuntz, "*Bordenkircher v. Hayes*: The Rise of Plea Bargaining and the Decline of the Rule of Law," in *Criminal Procedure Stories*, ed. Carol S. Steiker (New York: Foundation Press 2006), 377–8.

11 434 U.S. at 358.

12 *Hayes v. Cowan*, 547 F.2d 42, 44 (6th Cir. 1976).

13 We thank Boris Bittker for the tango image.

14 434 U.S. at 363–65 (Stewart, J., majority).

15 Lewis F. Powell, Jr., Initial Memorandum, September 14, 1977 (Lewis F. Powell, Jr.'s, *Bordenkircher* file, Folder 1, p. 9), plus handwritten notes on Clark's memorandum.

16 Memorandum from Nancy Bregstein to Lewis F. Powell, Jr., November 7, 1977 (Lewis F. Powell, Jr.'s, *Bordenkircher* file, Folder 1, p. 10).

17 434 U.S. at 369–70 (Powell, J., dissenting).

18 434 U.S. at 368 (Blackmun, J., dissenting).

19 *Imbler v. Pachtman*, 424 U.S. 409 (1976). The Warren Court had provided such immunity for judges. *Pierson v. Ray*, 386 U.S. 547 (1967). For more on immunity of government officials, see Chapter 12.

20 Stuntz, "*Bordenkircher v. Hayes*," 30n73 (citing U.S. Department of Justice, Bureau of Justice Statistics, *Prosecutors in State Courts in 1990* [1998], 1–2).

21 Id., at 376 sources at notes 75–77.

22 Id.

23 Stephanos Bibas, "Incompetent Plea Bargaining and Extrajudicial Reforms," *Harvard Law Review* 126 (2012): 150–74.

24 445 U.S. 263, 264–66 (1980).

25 Id. at 272 (Rehnquist, J., majority).

26 Id. at 284.

27 Id. at 295 (Powell, J., dissenting).

28 In January 1982, in *Hutto v. Davis*, the Court, in a brief per curiam opinion, applied *Rummel* to uphold a forty-year Virginia sentence of a man convicted of possessing less than nine ounces of marijuana with the intent to distribute and of distributing marijuana. *Hutto v. Davis*, 454 U.S. 370 (1982). Powell "reluctantly" concurred, conceding that the crime here was more severe than Rummel's, and Davis's sentence was less. Id. at 375. Brennan dissented, joined by Marshall and Stevens, insisting that the majority's refusal to consider whether the sentence was grossly disproportionate to the crime was an "abdication of our responsibility to enforce the Eighth Amendment." Id. at 383.

29 *Solem v. Helm*, 463 U.S. 277 (1983).

30 One of the "consistent themes" of the constitutional era in the United States, Powell said, was that "Americans had all the rights of English subjects." 463 U.S. at 286.

31 Id. at 304 (Burger, C.J., dissenting).

32 Id.

33 Id. at 314–15.

34 Letter from Harry A. Blackmun to Lewis F. Powell, Jr., June 6, 1983. Lewis F. Powell, Jr., *Helm* file, folder 3.

35 *Hamelin v. Michigan*, 501 U.S. 957 (1991); Kelly A. Patch, "*Hamelin v. Michigan*: Is Proportionate Sentencing Merely Legislative Grace?," *Wisconsin Law Review* 1992 (1992): 1718. Kennedy's opinion rejected the relevance of the comparative prongs of Powell's opinion in *Helm*.

36 There is evidence that the nation's taste for mass incarceration may be abating. California, for example, has recently reformed the three-strikes law that the Rehnquist Court had upheld in *Ewing v. California*, 538 U.S. 11 (2003).

37 E.g., Stephanos Bibas, "Prosecutorial Regulation Versus Prosecutorial Accountability," *University of Pennsylvania Law Review* 157 (2009): 966; and William J. Stuntz, "The Pathological Politics of Criminal Law," 100 *Michigan Law Review* 100 (2001): 506–7.

38 Stuntz, "*Bordenkircher v. Hayes*," 378–79 (emphasis in original).

39 There is much literature on this issue. We have relied upon Joseph C. Hoffman and William J. Stuntz, *Habeas After the Revolution* (Chicago: University of Chicago Press, 1994); John C. Jeffries, Jr., and William J. Stuntz, "Ineffective Assistance and Procedural Default in Federal Habeas Corpus," *University of Chicago Law Review* 57 (1990): 691–92; Louis Michael Seidman, "Factual Guilt and the Burger Court: An Examination of Continuity and Change in

Criminal Procedure," *Columbia Law Review* 80 (1980): 436–503; Robert M. Cover and T.Alexander Aleinkoff, "Dialectical Federalism: Habeas Corpus and the Court," *Yale Law Journal* 86: 1035 (1977); Neil McFeeley, "Habeas Corpus and Due Process: From Warren to Burger," *Baylor Law Review* 28 (1976): 553; Henry J. Friendly, "Is Innocence Irrelevant? Collateral Attack on Criminal Judgments," *University of Chicago Law Review* 38 (1970): 142; Jordan M. Steiker, "Innocence and Federal Habeas," *UCLA Law Review* 41 (1993): 303; Todd E. Pettys, "Killing Roger Coleman: Habeas, Finality, and the Innocence Gap," *William & Mary Law Review* 48 (2007): 2313; and Yale Rosenberg, "The Federal Habeas Corpus Custody Decisions: Liberal Oasis or Conservative Prop?," *American Journal of Criminal Law* 23 (1995): 99.

40 U.S. Const. art. I, § 9, cl. 2.

41 Act of February 5, 1867, Ch. 28, *Statutes at Large of the United States* XIV (1868), at 385.

42 *Fay v. Noia*, 372 U.S. 391, 400 (1963). Blackstone called the writ "the most celebrated writ in the English law." *Commentaries on the Laws of England: A Facsimile of the First Edition of 1765–1769* (Chicago: University of Chicago Press, 1979), 3:129.

43 Robert M. Cover, *Justice Accused: Antislavery and the Judicial Process* (New Haven: Yale University Press, 1975); Burt Neuborne, "The Myth of Parity," *Harvard Law Review* 90 (1977): 1111–14.

44 *Fay v. Noia*, 372 U.S. 391 (1963); *Townsend v. Sain*, 372 U.S. 293 (1963); *Sanders v. United States*, 373 U.S. 1 (1963).

45 *Fay v. Noia*, 372 U.S. 391 (1963); *Townsend v. Sain*, 372 U.S. 293 (1963).

46 *United States ex rel Noia v. Fay*, 183 F. Supp. 222 (S.D.N.Y. 1960) *reversed* 300 F.2d 345 (2d Cir. 1962). The language quoted is from the contemporaneous habeas jurisdictional statute, 28 U.S.C. § 2254.

47 372 U.S. 391 (1963) (Brennan, J., majority).

48 Id. at 399.

49 Id. at 426–27.

50 Id. at 438.

51 372 U.S. 293 (1963), overruled in part by *Keeney v. Tamayo-Reyes*, 504 U.S. 1 (1992).

52 Id. at 312 (Warren, C.J., majority).

53 Id.

54 *Sanders v. United States*, 373 U.S. 1 (1963). In 1969, during Earl Warren's last term, the Court expanded habeas to prisoners whose Fourth Amendment rights (under *Mapp*) to exclude illegally seized evidence had been violated. *Kaufman v. United States*, 394 U.S. 17 (1969).

55 Annual Report of the Director of the Administrative Office of the United States Courts (1964).

56 Friendly, "Is Innocence Irrelevant?," 143.

57 Id.

58 *LaVallee v. Della Rose*, 410 U.S. 690 (1973).

59 Stewart, another *Townsend* dissenter, surprisingly dissented in *LaVallee*, perhaps out of respect for a recent Court precedent. He, along with Douglas and Brennan, joined Marshall's strong dissent. Marshall complained that the majority had undermined the "inquiry contemplated by *Townsend*" and a recently amended habeas statute. 410 U.S. at 697. But, he said, given the "majority's firmly held views," there was "no reason to set the case for oral argument." Id. at 695 (Marshall, J., dissenting).

60 *Estelle v. Williams*, 425 U.S. 501 (1976); *Francis v. Henderson*, 425 U.S. 536 (1976).

61 *Francis v. Henderson*, 425 U.S. at 542–43.

62 The quote is from *Johnson v. Zerbst*, 304 U.S. 458, 464 (1938), quoted in Justice Brennan's dissent in *Williams*, 425 U.S. 516, 525. Brennan was joined by Marshall in *Williams*, who did not participate in *Francis*. Stewart did not participate in either case.

63 *Stone v. Powell*, 428 U.S. 465 (1976).

64 In *Stone v. Powell*, the attorneys of the two defendants had both objected to the constitutional violations. Nevertheless, the Burger Court denied habeas relief because the constitutional claims had been denied by the state courts.

65 428 U.S. at 469–70 (Powell, J., majority).

66 Memorandum, May 7, 1975 (Lewis F. Powell, Jr.'s, *Stone* file, Folder 1, p. 17).

67 The quote is from *Fay v. Noia*, 372 U.S. at 422.

68 Robert M. Cover and T. Alexander Aleinikoff, "Dialectical Federalism: Habeas Corpus and the Court," *Yale Law Journal* 86 (1977): 1035–1102; Burt Neuborne, "The Myth of Parity," *Harvard Law Review* 90 (1977): 1105–31.

69 *Schneckloth v. Bustamonte*, 412 U.S. 218, 253, 259 (1973) (Powell, J., concurring).

70 Letter of William Rehnquist, Assistant Attorney General, to Senate Judiciary Committee, September 1, 1971.

71 *Congressional Record*, December 3, 1971, 44644 (Statement of Edmund S. Muskie [D. ME]).

72 *Stone v. Powell*, 428 U.S. at 491 n31 (Powell, J., majority).

73 E.g., Friendly, "Is Innocence Irrelevant?," 142.

74 428 U.S. at 494 n. 36 (Powell, J., majority).

75 A year after *Stone v. Powell*, the Court further restricted criminal defendants' opportunities for habeas corpus. In a 7–2 opinion by William Rehnquist, with only Brennan and Marshall dissenting, the Court explicitly rejected the Warren Court's decision in *Fay v. Noia* that federal habeas relief was available so long as the defendant did not "deliberately bypass" state court procedural requirements. Describing the state court criminal trial as the "main event," Rehnquist said that a criminal defendant will have no recourse to federal habeas corpus

unless he can show both "cause" for failing to raise his constitutional claims in state court in accordance with its procedures and "prejudice" from failing to do so. *Wainwright v. Sykes*, 433 U.S. 72, 87–90 (1977). Rehnquist insisted that the Court was merely limiting *Noia*. Id. at 87–88. But one did not need a fortune-teller to know that *Noia* was left standing on very shaky ground, if still standing at all. Henceforth, a criminal defendant would suffer the consequences of his counsel's shortcomings whenever the attorney failed to raise objections concerning violations of the defendant's constitutional rights at the time and in the manner required under a state's procedural rules. The Court in *Sykes* also insisted that the defendant must show "actual prejudice" from a constitutional violation. Rehnquist left little doubt that the prejudice requirement demanded a strong likelihood that the defendant was innocent—a showing that the defendant "will be the victim of a miscarriage of justice." Id. at 91.

76 Sandra Day O'Connor, "Trends in the Relationship Between Federal and State Courts from the Perspective of a State Court Judge," *William & Mary Law Review* 22 (1981): 802.

77 Id. at 805.

78 *Rose v. Lundy*, 455 U.S. 509 (1982).

79 Id. at 512–13.

80 Id. at 518–19 (O'Connor, J., plurality).

81 Id. at 520.

82 Memorandum from Rehnquist to O'Connor, November 25, 1981, Lewis F. Powell, Jr., Papers, *Rose v. Lundy* file, p. 80. During the remainder of Chief Justice Burger's tenure, state prisoners seeking habeas corpus review continued to fare poorly. See, e.g., *Summer v. Mata*, 455 U.S. 591 (1982); and *Murray v. Carrier*, 477 U.S. 478 (1986). But also see *Vasquez v. Hillary*, 474 U.S. 254 (1986), where the petitioner prevailed.

83 *Coleman v. Thompson*, 501 U.S. 722 (1991).

84 Id. at 726 (O'Connor, J., majority).

85 Roger Keith Coleman was executed by the state of Virginia less than a year later, on May 21, 1992, despite widespread doubts about his guilt. Three days before that, *Time* magazine had pictured Coleman on its cover with the headline: "This Man Might Be Innocent: This Man Is Due to Die." *Time*, May 18, 1992. (Fourteen years later, in 2006, a DNA analysis confirmed Coleman's guilt.) Todd E. Pettys, "Killing Roger Coleman: Habeas, Finality and the Innocence Gap," 48 *William and Mary Law Review* (2007): 2313, 2319.

86 Antiterrorism and Effective Death Penalty Act of 1996, Pub. L. No. 104–132, 110 Stat. 1214 (1996) (codified as amended in varied sections of 28 U.S.C.).

87 Mark Tushnet and Larry Yackle, "Symbolic Statutes and Real Laws: The Pathologies of the Antiterrorism and Effective Death Penalty Act and the Prison Litigation Reform Act," *Duke Law Journal* 47 (1997): 5.

88 *Miranda v. Arizona*, 384 U.S. at 457 (Warren, C.J., majority).

89 See, e.g., "The Challenges of Mass Incarceration in America: Does Locking Up More People Reduce Crime?" *Daedalus* 139 (July 2010): 5–144.

90 E.g., Michelle Alexander, *The New Jim Crow: Mass Incarceration in the Age of Colorblindness* (New York: New Press, 2013); William J. Stuntz, *The Collapse of American Criminal Justice* (Cambridge: Belknap Press, 2011); Michael J. Klarman, "The Racial Origins of Modern Criminal Procedure," *Michigan Law Review* 99 (2000): 48–97; and William J. Stuntz, "Unequal Justice," *Harvard Law Review* 121 (2008): 1969–2040.

91 Vesla Weaver, "Frontlash: Race and the Development of Punitive Crime Policy," *Studies in American Political Development* 21 (2007): 230.

INTRODUCTION TO PART II: RACE

1 The legal historian Lawrence Friedman, for example, has said, "no decision, perhaps, in all of American history has been quite so momentous." Lawrence M. Friedman, *American Law in the 20th Century* (New Haven: Yale University Press, 2002), 288–94.

2 *Mayor of Baltimore v. Dawson*, 350 U.S. 877 (1955).

3 *Holmes v. Atlanta*, 350 U.S. 879 (1955).

4 *Loving v. Virginia*, 388 U.S. 1, 7, 8 (1967).

5 The phrase is from Gunnar Myrdal's *An American Dilemma: The Negro Problem and Modern Democracy*, 20th Anniversary ed. (New York: Harper & Row, 1962).

CHAPTER 4: STILL SEPARATE, STILL UNEQUAL

1 J. Harvie Wilkinson III, *From Brown to Bakke: The Supreme Court and School Integration, 1954–1978* (New York: Oxford University Press, 1979), 6.

2 Michael J. Klarman, *From Jim Crow to Civil Rights: The Supreme Court and the Struggle for Racial Equality* (New York: Oxford University Press, 2004), 293–300.

3 *Brown v. Board of Education*, 347 U.S. 483, 495 (1954); Klarman, *From Jim Crow to Civil Rights*, 302 (citing Douglas's papers); see also Richard Kluger, *Simple Justice: The History of Brown v. Board of Education and Black America's Struggle for Equality* (New York: Knopf, 1976).

4 E.g., Kluger, *Simple Justice*; Klarman, *From Jim Crow to Civil Rights*; and Wilkinson, *From Brown to Bakke*. Justices Frankfurter and Jackson, who viewed segregation as morally wrong but not necessarily illegal, agreed that unanimity was essential and joined the majority. After much coaxing, Stanley Reed of Kentucky, who thought the decision wrong but cared deeply about the role of the Court, was the last to sign on. Klarman, From *Jim Crow to Civil Rights*, 304–6.

5 Kluger, *Simple Justice* at 605. This memorandum, which Rehnquist insisted reflected Justice Jackson's views, not his own, caused controversy in Rehnquist's 1971 Senate confirmation debate.

6   Klarman, *Jim Crow* at 295, 302.

7   Mark V. Tushnet, *Making Civil Rights Law: Thurgood Marshall and the Supreme Court, 1936–1961* (New York: Oxford University Press, 1994), 217–18; Klarman, *Jim Crow*, 313.

8   *Brown v. Board of Education of Topeka*, 349 U.S. 294, 300–301 (1955).

9   Klarman, *Jim Crow*, 315.

10 Philip Elman, "The Solicitor General's Office, Justice Frankfurter, and Civil Rights Litigation, 1946–1960: An Oral History," *Harvard Law Review* 100 (1987): 842n2; also quoted in Klarman, From *Jim Crow to Civil Rights*, 315.

11 Numan V. Bartley, "Looking Back at Little Rock" and Tony Freyer, "Politics and Law in the Little Rock Crisis, 1954–57," both in *An Epitaph for Little Rock: A Fiftieth Anniversary Retrospective on the Central High Crisis*, ed. John A. Kirk (Fayetteville: University of Arkansas Press, 2008); Ronnie Dugger, "They *Like* Faubus," *The New Republic*, October 14, 1957; Numan V. Bartley, *The Rise of Massive Resistance: Race and Politics in the South during the 1950's* (Baton Rouge: Louisiana State University Press, 1969), 251–69; and Virgil T. Blossom, *It Has Happened Here* (New York: Harper, 1959). Fifty years later, one of the nine, Minnijean Brown-Trickey, described the day:

> We lived in the segregated society of Little Rock, Arkansas, Jim Crow South. The rules were you have to know your place. You drink out of the colored water fountains. . . . Central High was named the most beautiful high school in America when it was built. . . . It's got a gym. It's got a track. . . . a great contrast to where I was going to school. So why not? . . . [O]n September 3rd, nine kids showed up to enter Central High School. We were rejected by the Arkansas National Guard and the mob that was screaming hatred.

"Fifty Years Since Little Rock Nine, New HBO Documentary Tells the Story of a Defining Civil Rights Struggle," DemocracyNow.org, September 20, 2007, http://www.democracynow.org/2007/9/20/fifty_years_since_little_rock_nine. Little Rock's school superintendent, Virgil Blossom, chose Central High to be integrated and spared Hall, a new high school located in the upper-crust side of town. Little Rock's white working class resented being forced to integrate while the city's more affluent residents were protected—a situation frequently repeated throughout the nation. Bartley, *The Rise of Massive Resistance*, 254.

12 In a private comment to Earl Warren at a White House dinner, just weeks before the Court announced its *Brown* decision, Eisenhower said, "These are not bad people. All they are concerned about is to see that their sweet little girls are not required to sit in school alongside some big black bucks." William Lee Miller, *Two Americans: Truman, Eisenhower, and a Dangerous World* (New York: Knopf,

2012), 344; Arthur Montoya, *America's Original Sin: Absolution and Penance* (Bloomington: Xlibris, 2011), 135. Steven Ambrose has substituted "big overgrown Negroes" in his *Eisenhower: Soldier and President* (New York: Simon & Schuster, 1990), 367. For a more positive view of Eisenhower's attitude, see Jean Edward Smith, *Eisenhower in War and Peace* (New York: Random House, 2012), 705–30. Eisenhower never publicly endorsed the *Brown* decision. Ambrose, *Eisenhower*, 341–42, 367–68.

13 As Minnijean Brown-Trickey describes it, "we were surrounded by 101st Airborne guards, who had fixed bayonets and helmets, and walked into history." But her time at Central High was difficult: "seventy-five to a hundred people who were just constantly violating our bodies and minds, twenty nice kids, and 1,900 plus silent witnesses . . . people who stood by, watched and said nothing." "Fifty Years Since Little Rock Nine"; Harry S. Ashmore, *The Easy Chair: The Untold Story Behind Little Rock* (Atlanta: Southern Regional Council, 1958), 16.

14 *Cooper v. Aaron*, 358 U.S. 1 (1958).

15 Id. at 16.

16 Bernard Schwartz, *Swann's Way: The School Busing Case and the Supreme Court* (New York: Oxford University Press, 1986), 56.

17 *Griffin v. School Board of Prince Edward County*, 377 U.S. 218, 233, 234 (Black, J., majority) (1964); *Bradley v. School Board, City of Richmond Va.*, 382 U.S. 103, 105 (1965) (a per curiam opinion addressing Richmond's refusal to desegregate public school teachers: "Delays in desegregating school systems are no longer tolerable"). After reopening its schools, Virginia's next gambit was a "pupil placement plan," under which a state board accepted applications and placed students in schools; race determined where students were placed.

18 *Green v. County School Board of New Kent County*, 391 U.S. 430, 438, 442 (Brennan, J., majority) (1968). For the internal machinations, see Schwartz, *Swann's Way*, 60–61 and Bruce Ackerman, *We the People, Volume 3: The Civil Rights Revolution* (Cambridge: Belknap Press, 2014), 238–39.

19 391 U.S. at 436. The Court rejected the country's "freedom of choice" plan as insufficient "to effectuate a transition to a unitary system." Id. at 437.

20 In 1964, Congress passed the Elementary and Secondary Education Act, greatly increasing federal funding of K–12 education. The next year, the Departments of Justice and Health, Education, and Welfare (HEW) started negotiating with recalcitrant southern school districts to gradually desegregate their schools or lose their federal funds. According to HEW, the number of blacks attending southern white schools more than tripled from 2 percent in 1964 to 7.5 percent in 1965, doubled again to about 14 percent by 1967, and reached 23 percent by 1968. Ackerman, *We the People, Volume 3*, 232–35, 379. Civil rights groups had a lower estimate for 1965 of 5 percent. U.S. Commission on Civil Rights, *Survey of School Desegregation in the Southern and Border States*, 1965–1966 (Washington D.C., 1966).

21 The final Warren Court school desegregation case was handed down in spring 1969. *United States v. Montgomery County Board of Education*, 395 U.S. 225 (1969). The Court unanimously approved an Alabama district court order requiring the Montgomery County school board to achieve, on a specific timetable, a goal "so that in each school the ratio of white to Negro faculty members is substantially the same as it is throughout the system." 289 F. Supp. 647, 654 (M.D. Ala. 1968). The school board had challenged the order as an illegal quota, and the federal appellate court had essentially agreed. 400 F.2d. 1, 8 (5th Cir. 1968). As with *Brown* itself, the Montgomery County case marked the beginning, not the end, of a saga. The question of how to respond to specific numerical racial goals would divide the Court for the next half century.

22 Two important exceptions are Schwartz, *Swann's Way*, Chapter 4; and Ackerman, *We the People, Volume 3*, Chapter 11. See Schwartz, *Swann's Way*, 62 ("most important" case of Burger's first term).

23 *Alexander v. Holmes County Board of Education*, 396 U.S. 19 (1969).

24 Bernard Schwartz, a New York University legal historian, describes Burger's draft opinion as "more like the rambling first draft by a new law clerk than the finished product of an experienced judge." Schwartz, *Swann's Way*, 80. The final, more carefully crafted per curiam opinion was rewritten principally by Justice Brennan. Id., Chapter 4.

25 Id., at 87.

26 Ackerman, *We the People, Volume 3*, 229–56. By the end of March 1970, the Justice Department was preparing lawsuits to force desegregation of two hundred school districts in Arkansas, Florida, Mississippi, North Carolina, and South Carolina. Peter Milius, "Justice Department to Make Final Overture to Holdout School Districts in South," *Washington Post*, March 30, 1970.

27 Richard Nixon, "Statement About Desegregation of Elementary and Secondary Schools, March 24, 1970," in *Public Papers of the Presidents of the United States: Richard Nixon, 1970* (Washington, D.C.: Government Printing Office, 1971), 304.

28 Schwartz, *Swann's Way*, 88.

29 Id. at 8.

30 *Swann v. Charlotte–Mecklenburg County Board of Education*, 402 U.S. 1, 9n4 (1971) (Burger, C.J., majority).

31 Id. at 30.

32 John C. Jeffries, Jr., *Justice Lewis F. Powell, Jr.* (New York: Fordham University Press, 2001), 284.

33 Id. at 285–86.

34 Id. at 287.

35 Schwartz, *Swann's Way*, 207–21.

36 402 U.S. at 25 (Burger, C.J., majority).

37 Id. at 26.

38 Id. at 30–31.

39 Schwartz, *Swann's Way*, 216.

40 Id. at 149.

41 Id. See also Richard R. W. Brooks and Carol M. Rose, *Saving the Neighborhood: Racially Restrictive Covenants, Law, and Social Norms* (Cambridge: Harvard University Press, 2013); Joyce A Baugh, *The Detroit School Busing Case:* Milliken v. Bradley *and the Controversy over Desegregation* (Lawrence: University Press of Kansas, 2011).

42 402 U.S. at 23 (Burger, C.J., majority).

43 *Newsweek*, May 3, 1971, 26, quoted in Schwartz, *Swann's Way*, 186.

44 *Winston–Salem/Forsyth County Board of Education v. Scott*, 404 U.S. 1221, 1228 (1971), quoted in Schwartz, *Swann's Way*, 189. See *Swann*, 402 U.S. at 25.

45 404 U.S. at 1229–30.

46 Schwartz, *Swann's Way*, 193. Charlotte's first black mayor was Harvey Gantt, the first black person admitted to a public university in South Carolina; see Chapter 5.

47 Before Denver, the Burger Court had to resolve one more dispute from Virginia. *Wright v. Council of City of Emporia*, 407 U.S. 451 (1972). In a 5–4 decision—with all five Warren Court veterans in the majority and all four Nixon appointees in dissent—the Court upheld the district court's comprehensive desegregation order requiring the city of Emporia to allow its students to attend schools in Greenville County, which surrounds the city. Chief Justice Burger's dissent, joined by Blackmun, Powell, and Rehnquist, presaged future majorities. The dissenters emphasized that the Emporia and Greenville systems would each be desegregated and would "completely eliminate all traces of *state-imposed* desegregation." Id. at 473 (emphasis added). The dissent rejected any notion of seeking "any particular degree of racial balance;" and—echoing Justice Powell's brief in *Swann*—applauded local control over schools. The dissent also claimed that there was no basis for concluding "that Emporia's decision to operate a separate school system was the manifestation of a discriminatory purpose." Id. at 482. The city of Emporia lost its case. But the die was cast.

48 Richard Nixon, "Statement About Desegregation of Elementary and Secondary Schools, March 24, 1970," in *Public Papers of the Presidents of the United States: Richard Nixon, 1970* (Washington, D.C.: Government Printing Office, 1971), 315; also Schwartz, *Swann's Way*, 92; and Ackerman, *We the People, Volume 3*, 259–63.

49 Joyce A. Baugh, *The Detroit School Busing Case*: Milliken v. Bradley *and the Controversy over Desegregation* (Lawrence: University Press of Kansas, 2011), 126.

50 *Keyes v. School District No. 1*, 413 U.S. 189 (1973). Much of our discussion of *Keyes* is based on a thorough review of Justice Powell's papers on the case. It largely agrees with John Jeffries's biography based on the same papers. See also, e.g., Phoebe A. Haddon, "Has the Roberts Court Plurality's Colorblind Rhetoric Finally Broken *Brown*'s Promise?," *Denver University Law Review* 90 (2013): 1251.

51 Justice White did not participate in the case because his old law firm had once represented the Denver school district. Bob Woodward and Scott Armstrong, *The Brethren: Inside the Supreme Court* (New York: Simon & Schuster, 1979), 314–16. For more detail on the *Keyes* case, see Rachel F. Moran, "Untoward Consequences: The Ironic Legacy of *Keyes v. School District No. 1,*" *Denver University Law Review* 90 (2013): 1209. Rehnquist's dissent explicitly rejected extending *Brown* to situations like Denver's where segregation was neither established nor required by law. And he objected to the majority's suggestion that a city-wide remedy was appropriate to remedy the school board's discrimination that had been found to be deliberate in only one area of the city.

52 Jeffries, *Justice Lewis F. Powell, Jr.*, 285; and see, e.g., Memorandum from Lewis F. Powell, Jr., to J. Harvie Wilkinson III, February 18, 1973 (Lewis F. Powell, Jr.'s, *Keyes* file, Folder 1, p. 88).

53 413 U.S. 189, 238 (Powell, J., dissenting).

54 Memorandum from Lewis F. Powell, Jr., to Larry Hammond, March 1, 1973 (Lewis F. Powell, Jr.'s, *Keyes* file, Folder 1, p. 91).

55 Lewis F. Powell, Jr., Memorandum, December 28, 1972 (Lewis F. Powell, Jr.'s, *Keyes* file, Folder 1, p. 62). Only the urging of one of his clerks kept Powell from quoting Burger's *Winston-Salem* opinion to restrict *Swann*. Memorandum from William C. Kelly to Lewis F. Powell, Jr., March 15, 1973 (Lewis F. Powell, Jr.'s, *Keyes* file, Folder 1, p. 99).

56 413 U.S. at 245–51, 253. Memorandum from Lewis F. Powell, Jr., to J. Harvie Wilkinson, III, March 22, 1973 (Lewis F. Powell, Jr.'s, *Keyes* file, Folder 1, p. 127); and Jeffries, *Justice Lewis F. Powell, Jr.*, 285–98.

57 *San Antonio Independent School District v. Rodriguez*, 411 U.S. (1973).

58 *Keyes*, 413 U.S. at 241 (Powell, J., dissenting).

59 Memorandum from Lewis F. Powell, Jr., to J. Harvie Wilkinson, III, January 6, 1973. *Keyes* file, Folder 1, 374–79.

60 Memorandum from Lewis F. Powell, Jr., to J. Harvie Wilkinson, III, March 22, 1973 (Lewis F. Powell, Jr.'s, *Keyes* file, Folder 1, p. 129).

61 Memorandum from Larry Hammond to Lewis F. Powell, Jr., October 2, 1972 (Lewis F. Powell, Jr.'s, *Rodriguez* file, Folder 2).

62 411 U.S. 1, 12–13.

63 Id.

64 *Serrano v. Priest*, 487 P.2d 1241 (Cal. 1971).

65 411 U.S. 1, 71 (Marshall, J., dissenting).

66 Memorandum from Lewis F. Powell, Jr., to Larry Hammond, October 12, 1972 (Lewis F. Powell, Jr.'s, *Rodriguez* file, Folder 3, p. 24).

67 Powell quoted with approval Burger's dissent in the *Emporia* case asserting that "local control is not only vital to continued public support of the schools, but it is of overriding importance from an educational standpoint as well." 411 U.S. at 49–50 (Powell, J., majority).

68 Id. at 55.

69 Jeffries, *Justice Lewis F. Powell, Jr.*, 308–18 for this and the discussion of the case.

70 *Bradley v. School Board of the City of Richmond*, 338 F. Supp. 67 (E.D. Va. 1972); also Jeffries, *Justice Lewis F. Powell, Jr.*, 31;1 and James E. Ryan, *Five Miles Away, A World Apart: One City, Two Schools, and the Story of Educational Opportunity in Modern America* (Oxford: Oxford University Press, 2011).

71 462 F.2d 1058 (4th Cir. 1972).

72 *Richmond School Board v. State Board of Education of Virginia*, 412 U.S. 92 (1973).

73 Woodward and Armstrong, *The Brethren*, 323.

74 412 U.S. at 93 (1973) (per curiam).

75 For an excellent detailed analysis of the Detroit school case, see Baugh, *The Detroit School Busing Case*; Judge Roth's trial is described in Chapter 5.

76 See Reynolds Farley, Sheldon Danziger, and Harry J. Holzer, *Detroit Divided* (New York: Russell Sage, 2008).

77 Id.

78 Baugh, *The Detroit School Busing Case*, 107–8, 111, 116, and 123.

79 Id. at 132–37.

80 *Milliken v. Bradley*, 418 U.S. 717 (1974).

81 Lewis F. Powell, Jr., Written Notes on Warren Burger's Draft Opinions (Lewis F. Powell, Jr.'s, *Milliken* file, Folders 7–9).

82 For a comprehensive discussion, see Ackerman, *We the People, Volume 3*. See also Baugh, *The Detroit School Busing Case*.

83 See Ronald P. Formisano, *Boston Against Busing: Race, Class, and Ethnicity in the 1960s and 1970s* (Chapel Hill: University of North Carolina Press, 1991).

84 418 U.S. at 753 (Stewart, J., concurring).

85 418 U.S. 761 (Douglas, J., dissenting).

86 418 U.S. at 782, 783, 814 (Marshall, J., dissenting).

87 Dennis J. Hutchinson, *The Man Who Once Was Whizzer White: A Portrait of Justice Byron R. White* (New York: Free Press, 1998).

88 *Bradley v. Milliken*, 338 F. Supp. 582, 592 (1971).

89 418 U.S. at 766, 778 (White, J., dissenting).

90 Michael Klarman blurb on Baugh, *The Detroit School Busing Case*.

91 Baugh, *The Detroit School Busing Case*, 200–202.

92 *Keyes v. Congress of Hispanic Educators*, 902 F. Supp. 1274 (D. Colo. 1995).

93 Gary Orfield, *Schools More Separate: Consequences of a Decade of Resegregation* (Civil Rights Project, Harvard University Press, 2001).

94 Charles T. Clotfelter, "Are Whites Still Fleeing? Racial Patterns and Enrollment Shifts in Urban Public Schools, 1987–1996," *Journal of Policy Analysis and Management* 20 (2001): 199–221.

95 E.g., Niraj Chokshi, "The Most Segregated Schools May Not Be in the States You'd Expect," *Washington Post*, May 1, 2014.

96 Rachel F. Moran, "Untoward Consequences: The Ironic Legacy of *Keyes v. School District No. 1*," *Denver Law Review*, 90 (2013), 1209–1222.

97 *Parents Involved in Community Schools v. Seattle School District No. 1*, 551 U.S. 701 (2007). In June 2007, in a decision announced on the last day before the Court's summer recess, the justices, by a 5–4 vote, struck down voluntary efforts of the school boards in Seattle and Louisville that had sought to create and maintain integrated schools by using the student's race as a factor in school assignments. For detailed discussion see Marcia Coyle, *The Roberts Court: The Struggle for the Constitution* (New York: Simon & Schuster, 2014): 28–47; J. Harvie Wilkinson III, "The Seattle and Louisville School Cases: There is No Other Way," *Harvard Law Review* 121 (2007): 158–83. The plurality opinion by Chief Justice Roberts (joined by Scalia, Thomas, and Alito) said that such programs were designed to achieve "racial balance," which the Chief Justice said was a goal forbidden under the Constitution. In dissent, Justice Stevens observed that "no Member of the Court I joined in 1975 would have agreed with today's decision." Stevens described Roberts' claim that his opinion was "more faithful to the heritage of *Brown*" as "a cruel irony" that "rewrites the history of one of this Court's most important decisions." 551 U.S. at 799, 803 (2007). Justice Breyer, in a seventy-seven-page dissent (joined by Stevens, Souter, and Ginsburg) described this decision as a "radical" wrong turn "that the Court and the nation will come to regret." Breyer quoted extensively (and ironically) from *Swann, Rodriguez*, and *Milliken* to emphasize the Roberts Court's willingness to trample local autonomy and control over schools in circumstances where local school boards had *voluntarily* undertaken measures to integrate their communities' schools. Announcing his dissent to a packed courtroom, Breyer added: "It is not often in the law that so few have so quickly changed so much." Linda Greenhouse, "Justices Reject Diversity Plans in Two Districts," *New York Times*, June 28, 2007, A1. (This sentence does not appear in his written dissent.) Justice Kennedy joined in the result urged by Roberts and his colleagues, but rejected their claim that the Constitution requires local school boards and other political actors always to be "colorblind."

98 Janet L. Yellen, "Perspectives on Inequality and Opportunity," from the Survey of Consumer Finance, Boston, Massachusetts, October 17, 2014, 2, 11–13, http://www.federalreserve.gov/newsevents/speech/yellen20141017a.htm.

99 *Brown v. Board of Education*, 347 U.S. at 495.

CHAPTER 5: SEEKING A HIGHER EDUCATION

1 *DeFunis v. Odegaard*, 416 U.S. 312, 320–21 (1974) (Douglas, J., dissenting).

2 *DeFunis v. Odegaard*, 82 Wash. 2d 11, 507 P. 2d 1169 (1973).

3 82 Wash. 2d at 35.

4 Id.

5 Memorandum from John C. Jeffries, Jr., to Lewis F. Powell, Jr., February 12, 1974 (Lewis F. Powell, Jr.'s, *DeFunis* file, Folder 1, p. 30).

6 416 U.S. 312 (1974).

7 416 U.S. at 314, 340, 343 (Douglas, J. dissenting).

8 *Grutter v. Bollinger*, 539 U.S. 306, 350 (2003) (Thomas, J., dissenting).

9 Anthony Lewis, "President Asks Mississippi to Comply with U.S. Laws," *New York Times*, October 1, 1962, 1.

10 Claude Sitton, "Negro at Mississippi U as Barnett Yields; 3 Dead in Campus Riot, 6 Marshals Shot; Guardsmen Move In; Kennedy Makes Plea," *New York Times*, October 1, 1962, 1.

11 Meredith describes his quest for admission and his years at Ole Miss in his book *Three Years in Mississippi* (Bloomington: Indiana University Press, 1966).

12 Id. at 232.

13 George Wallace, Inauguration Speech, Montgomery, Alabama, January 14, 1963, http://www.npr.org/2013/01/14/169080969/segregation-forever-a-fiery-pledge-forgiven-but-not-forgotten.

14 *Lucy v. Adams*, 350 U.S. 1, 1–2 (1955) (per curiam). Descriptions of Autherine Lucy and the events at the University of Alabama in 1956 and 1957 are based on E. Culpepper Clark, *The Schoolhouse Door: Segregation's Last Stand at the University of Alabama* (New York: Oxford, 1993).

15 Quoted in Jerome Karabel, *The Chosen: The Hidden History of Admission and Exclusion at Harvard, Yale, and Princeton* (New York: Houghton Mifflin Harcourt, 2005), 378.

16 Clark, in *The Schoolhouse Door*, says Thursday, February 2; *Encyclopedia of Alabama* says Friday, February 3: "Autherine Lucy," *Encyclopedia of Alabama*, http://www.encyclopediaofalabama.org/face/Article.jsp?id=h-2489.

17 Clark, *The Schoolhouse Door*, 79.

18 Id. at 80.

19 Id. at 102. Marshall was assisted in Lucy's case by Constance Baker Motley, who also represented the African Americans who later sought admission to the public universities in Mississippi, Georgia, South Carolina, and Alabama. Constance Baker Motley, *Equal Justice Under Law: An Autobiography* (New York: Farrar Strauss and Giroux, 1998).

20 Clark, *The Schoolhouse Door*, 169.

21 On June 5, 1963, after Wallace reiterated publicly that he will be present to bar the entrance of the students, the court issued a temporary injunction preventing him from obstructing the order. *United States v. Wallace*, 218 F. Supp. 290, 291 (N.D. Ala. 1963).

22 Clark, *The Schoolhouse Door*, 198. None of the city, state, or university leaders wanted a repeat of Mississippi's violence. Neither did George Wallace. Appearing on *Meet the Press* on June 2, in his first national television appearance, Wallace insisted that there would be no violence in Alabama. "I am not hoping

to have myself arrested," he said. "This is a dramatic way to express to the American people the omnipotent march of centralized government to destroy the rights and freedom and liberty of the people of this country." Id. at 199, 225–33.

23 Id. at 231.

24 Id. at 154.

25 "Report to the American People on Civil Rights, 11 June 1963," John F. Kennedy Presidential Library and Museum, http://www.jfklibrary.org/Asset -Viewer/LH8F_0Mzv0e6Ro1yEm74Ng.aspx.

26 Despite overwhelming evidence, all-male, all-white Mississippi juries twice refused to convict his killer, Byron De La Beckwith. He was not brought to justice until thirty years later, when in 1994 a jury of eight blacks and four whites finally convicted him of the murder. He died in prison in 2001 at the age of eighty. David Stout, "Byron De La Beckwith Dies; Killer of Medgar Evers was 80," *New York Times*, January 23, 2001.

27 See John David Skrentny, *The Ironies of Affirmative Action: Politics, Culture, and Justice in America* (Chicago: University of Chicago Press, 1996), 72.

28 Howard Ball, *The Bakke Case: Race, Education, and Affirmative Actions* (Lawrence: University Press of Kansas, 2000), 3.

29 Karabel, *The Chosen*, 379.

30 Id. at 395.

31 Id. at 405. John David Skrentny, *The Minority Rights Revolution* (Cambridge: Harvard University Press, 2002), 166, says that Harvard admitted 109 blacks in 1969, double the previous year's number. In April 1969, the Harvard faculty voted to add a Department of Afro-American Studies. Karabel, *The Chosen*, 403.

32 Id. at 402.

33 Skrentny, *Ironies of Affirmative Action*, at 167.

34 Karabel, *The Chosen*, 392.

35 Skrentny, *Ironies of Affirmative Action*, at 168–69.

36 Id. at 169.

37 Id. at 169n.24.

38 Wilkinson, *From Brown to Bakke*, 289.

39 Id. at 169n25.

40 Ball, *The Bakke Case*, 49.

41 Karabel, *The Chosen*, 404.

42 Id. at 409.

43 Id.

44 E.g., Nathan Glazer, *Affirmative Discrimination* (Cambridge: Harvard University Press, 1975); Lino Graglia, *Disaster by Decree: The Supreme Court Decisions on Race and the Schools* (Ithaca: Cornell University Press, 1977).

45 Glazer, *Affirmative Discrimination*; John Hart Ely, "The Constitutionality of Reverse Racial Discrimination," *University of Chicago Law Review* 41 (1974):

723–41 (arguing for its constitutionality). Columbia's Louis Henkin called it "benign discrimination." Louis Henkin, *"DeFunis:* An Introduction," *Columbia Law Review* 75 (1975): 483–94. Conservative columnist James J. Kilpatrick liked "benevolent cruelty." Kilpatrick, "The *DeFunis* Syndrome," *Nation's Business,* June 1974, 13, cited in Wilkinson, *From* Brown *to* Bakke, 255.

46 Ball, *The* Bakke *Case,* 54.

47 The quote and description of Bakke are from id. at 46–48, 49.

48 UCD's admissions policies are detailed in id. at 49–52.

49 Id. at 55–56.

50 Id. at 52.

51 Id.

52 Id. at 49.

53 Id. at 56–58.

54 Id. at 56, 61.

55 Id. at 77.

56 E.g., Lincoln Caplan, *The Tenth Justice: The Solicitor General and the Rule of Law* (New York: Knopf, 1987).

57 For a detailed discussion, see Asher Smith, "The Interests of the United States: Affirmative Action and the Strange Position of the Office of the Solicitor General Within the Executive Branch" (Unpublished manuscript, Yale Law School, 2013).

58 Ball, *The* Bakke *Case,* 76.

59 Brief for the United States as Amicus Curiae, *Regents of the University of California v. Bakke,* 438 U.S. 265 (1978) (No. 76–811).

60 Jeffries, *Justice Lewis F. Powell, Jr.,* 469.

61 Linda Greenhouse, *Becoming Justice Blackmun: Harry Blackmun's Supreme Court Journey* (New York: Times Books, 2006), 128–33.

62 Ball, *The* Bakke *Case,* 123.

63 Jeffries, *Justice Lewis F. Powell, Jr.,* 494–95.

64 *Regents of the University of California v. Bakke,* 438 U.S. 265, 279 (1978) (Powell, J.).

65 Id. at 316.

66 Id. at 317–18.

67 Id. at 316.

68 Id. at 324 (Brennan, J.).

69 Id. at 395, 402 (Marshall, J.).

70 Id. at 407 (Blackmun, J.). Blackmun's line concerning the need to take account of race in order to "get beyond" racism became the most often quoted of the entire set of opinions. It was, however, not original with the justice, but rather was borrowed, without attribution, from an article that McGeorge Bundy published in *The Atlantic Monthly* in November 1977, following the *Bakke* oral argument. One of Blackmun's law clerks had brought the article to the justice's attention.

McGeorge Bundy, "The Issue Before the Court: Who Gets Ahead in America," *Atlantic Monthly*, November 1977, 41–54. See Linda Greenhouse, *"A Tale of Two Justices," Green Bag* 11 2d. (2007): 40.

71 For a compilation, see Ball, *The* Bakke *Case*, 140–41.

72 Id. at 142.

73 Anthony Lewis, "A Solomonic Decision," *New York Times*, June 29, 1978, quoted in Jeffries, *Justice Lewis F. Powell, Jr.*, 495; and Ball, *The* Bakke *Case*, 141.

74 Lewis, "A Solomonic Decision" and quoted in Ball, *The* Bakke *Case*, 141.

75 Ball, *The* Bakke *Case*, at ix.

76 Id. at 124.

77 The history of black admissions at the University of Michigan is from Barbara A. Perry, *The Michigan Affirmative Action Cases* (Lawrence: University Press of Kansas, 2007), 52–53.

78 Id. at 52–55.

79 One was by Jennifer Gratz, an excellent student and her high school's homecoming queen, the ambitious daughter of a police sergeant and a secretary, whose dream to attend the University of Michigan as an undergraduate had been thwarted when her application was rejected. The other was by Barbara Grutter, a forty-three-year-old mother of two, who applied to the University of Michigan Law School in 1997 and, despite high grades and test scores, was rejected. This litigation has been described effectively in Barbara A. Perry's *The Michigan Affirmative Action Cases*.

80 "Justice Powell's opinion in *Bakke*," Rehnquist said, "emphasized the importance of considering each particular applicant as an individual, assessing all of the qualities that individual possesses, and in turn, evaluating that individual's ability to contribute to the unique setting of higher education." *Gratz v. Bollinger*, 539 U.S. 244, 271 (2003). The university's granting of bonus points to "every single" minority applicant had "the effect of making 'the factor of race . . . decisive' for virtually every minimally qualified underrepresented minority applicant." Id. at 272 (quoting *Bakke*, 438 U.S. at 317 [Powell, J.]) (Rehnquist, C.J., majority).

81 *Grutter v. Bollinger*, 539 U.S. 306, 323 (2003) (O'Connor, J., majority).

82 Id. at 325.

83 Id. at 334–37.

84 Id. at 339–42.

85 *Fisher v University of Texas*, 133 S. Ct. 2411 (2013); cert. granted again June 29, 2015. Abigail Fisher, a white applicant rejected by the University of Texas, had already graduated from Louisiana State University before her case reached the Supreme Court the first time in 2012—making her case even more moot than Marco DeFunis's had been—but the Supreme Court's appetite for reaching the affirmative action challenge was so great that it took her case twice. Justice Kagan did not participate.

86 See Joan Biskupic, "Special Report: Behind U.S. Race Cases, a Little-Known Recruiter," Reuters.com, December 4, 2012, available at http://www.reuters .com/article/2012/12/04/us-usa-court-casemaker-idUSBRE8B30V22012 1204.

87 *Shelby County v. Holder*, 133 S. Ct. 2612 (2013).

88 *Students for Fair Admissions, Inc. v. Harvard*, No. 14-14176, filed in the Boston federal district court and *Students for Fair Admissions, Inc. v. University of North Carolina*, No. 114-954, filed in the federal district court in Winston-Salem, North Carolina.

89 *Schuette v. Coalition to Defend Affirmative Action*, 134 S.Ct. 1623, 1638 (2014). None of the Court's five separate opinions garnered a majority. Justice Kennedy's opinion (joined by Chief Justice Roberts and Justice Alito) described the Court's decision as a narrow one, insisting that "this case is not about how the debate over racial preferences should be resolved. It is about who may resolve it." "There is no authority in the Constitution of the United States or in this Court's precedents," Kennedy wrote, "for the judiciary to set aside Michigan laws that commit this policy determination to the voters." Id. at 1638.

90 Adam Liptak, "Court Backs Michigan on Affirmative Action," *New York Times*, April 22, 2014.

91 In 1946, when Heman Marion Sweatt applied to the University of Texas' law school, the state's constitution barred his admission because he was black. When he challenged his rejection, the Texas court ordered the university to provide him a separate black law school, which it did—but without any permanent staff, building, library, or accreditation. Sweatt, represented by Thurgood Marshall, took his case to the Supreme Court, and in 1950 the Court unanimously ordered the all-white University of Texas Law School to admit him. *Sweatt v. Painter*, 339 U.S. 629 (1950). Cross burnings, vandalism, and other forms of racial harassment, along with his physical challenges, however, proved too much for Sweatt, and he soon left. Discrimination against blacks and Mexican Americans continued at the university into the 1970s, and in 1978 the Department of Education found the University of Texas in violation of the nondiscrimination requirements of Title VI of the Civil Rights Act. Fearful of losing federal funding, the university then embarked on a program to admit more minority students.

92 "President Lyndon B. Johnson's Commencement Address at Howard University: 'To Fulfill These Rights,' June 4, 1965," Lyndon B. Johnson Presidential Library, accessed January 3, 2015, http://www.lbjlib.utexas.edu/johnson /archives.hom/speeches.hom/650604.asp.

93 William G. Bowen, Martin A. Kurzweil, and Eugene M. Tobin, *Equity and Excellence in American Higher Education* (Charlottesville: University of Virginia Press, 2006), 142.

94 Id. at 141.

95 Alan Krueger, Jesse Rothstein, and Sarah Turner, "Race, Income and College in 25 Years: Evaluating Justice O'Connor's Conjecture" (working paper, Center for Studies in Higher Education, University of California Berkeley, 2006); eventually published in *American Law and Economics Review* 8, no. 2 (2006): 282–311. This quotation appears in the working paper but was toned down in the published version. The language in the final version was not nearly as succinct and forthright. See the published version at: http://0-aler.oxfordjournals.org.pegasus.law.columbia.edu/content /8/2/282.full.

96 Lee Bollinger, "The Real Mismatch: The Supreme Court Should Not Force Schools to Trade Affirmative Action for Socioeconomic Diversity," *Slate.com*, May 30, 2013.

97 Richard Pérez-Peña, "Colleges Show Uneven Effort to Enroll Poor," *New York Times*, May 31, 2013, A1.

CHAPTER 6: PRIVACY AT A PRICE

1 410 U.S. 113 (1973).

2 *Doe v. Bolton*, 410 U.S. 179 (1973).

3 Linda Greenhouse and Reva B. Siegel, *Before Roe v. Wade: Voices That Shaped the Abortion Debate Before the Supreme Court's Ruling*, 2nd ed. (New Haven: Yale Law School, 2012), 265, http://documents.law.yale.edu/before-roe.

4 See, for example, David J. Garrow's monumental *Liberty and Sexuality: The Right to Privacy and the Making of Roe v. Wade* (Berkeley: University of California Press, 1994); and N. E. H. Hull and Peter Charles Hoffer, Roe v. Wade: *The Abortion Rights Controversy in American History*, 2nd ed. (Lawrence: University Press of Kansas, 2010).

5 *Hall v. Lefkowitz*, 305 F. Supp. 1030 (1969).

6 351 F. Supp. 224 (1972).

7 381 U.S. 479 (1965).

8 405 U.S. 438 (1972).

9 For women's experience of illegal abortion, see Leslie J. Reagan, *When Abortion Was a Crime: Women, Medicine, and Law in the United States, 1867–1973* (Berkeley: University of California Press, 1998). For a less academic but powerful anecdotal account, see Ellen Messer and Kathryn E. May, *Back Rooms: Voices from the Illegal Abortion Era* (Amherst: Prometheus, 1994).

10 Mary Steichen Calderone, "Illegal Abortion as a Public Health Problem," *American Journal of Public Health* 50 (July 1960): 948.

11 The original pre-*Roe* name was the National Association for Repeal of Abortion Laws.

12 Greenhouse and Siegel, *Before Roe*, 38–40.

13 Reva B. Siegel, "Sex Equality Arguments for Reproductive Rights: Their Critical Basis and Evolving Constitutional Expression," *Emory Law Journal* 56

(2007): 826–28; Twiss Butler, "Abortion Law: 'Unique Problem for Women' or Sex Discrimination?," *Yale Journal of Law and Feminism* 4 (1991): 133.

14 Brief of California Committee to Legalize Abortion et al. as Amicus Curiae, *Roe v. Wade*, 410 U.S. 113 (1973) (Nos. 70–18, 70–14), 5. Justice Blackmun, for one, was distinctly unimpressed by the slavery argument, making the notation "NG," for "no good," at that point in his copy of the brief. Linda Greenhouse, "How the Supreme Court Talks About Abortion: The Implications of a Shifting Discourse," *Suffolk University Law. Review* 42 (2008): 46n39.

15 In 1992, the controlling opinion in *Planned Parenthood v. Casey* observed that women's control over their reproductive lives was necessary for "the ability of women to participate equally in the economic and social life of the nation." 505 U.S. 833, 835. In 1967, a group of ministers and rabbis had formed the Clergy Consultation Service on Abortion, based at Rev. Howard Moody's Judson Memorial Church in New York City. It later expanded into a nationwide network of thousands of clergy members and volunteers who referred women to safe abortion providers. See Suzanne Staggenborg, *The Pro-Choice Movement: Organization and Activism in the Abortion Conflict* (New York: Oxford University Press, 1994), 23–24.

16 For liberal clergy statements, see Greenhouse and Siegel, *Before Roe v. Wade*, 29–31, 69–71.

17 314 F. Supp. 1217 (1970).

18 For a fascinating content analysis of leading newspapers during these years, see Vincent Vecera, "The Supreme Court and the Social Conception of Abortion," *Law and Society Review* 48 (2014): 345.

19 George Gallup, "Abortion Seen up to Woman, Doctor," *Washington Post*, August 25, 1972.

20 Amici curiae brief of the Planned Parenthood Federation of America, Inc., and the American Association of Planned Parenthood Physicians, *Roe v. Wade*, 410 U.S. 113 (1973) (Nos. 70-18, 70-14), 11. See Arthur Selwyn Miller and Jerome A. Barron, "The Supreme Court, the Adversary System, and the Flow of Information to the Justices: A Preliminary Inquiry," *Virginia Law Review* 61 (1975): 1217n70. The newspaper clipping is in Harry A. Blackmun Papers (Box 152, Folder 2).

21 Robert N. Karrer, "The Formation of Michigan's Anti-Abortion Movement, 1967–1974," *Michigan Historical Review* 22 (1996): 67.

22 Michael J. Perry, "Abortion, the Public Morals, and the Police Power: The Ethical Function of Substantive Due Process," *UCLA Law Review* 23 (1975): 733n204.

23 Harry A. Blackmun Papers, Memorandum to the Conference, May 18, 1972 (Box 151, Folder 6).

24 Id. First Draft Opinion in *Roe v. Wade*, p. 16 (labeled "1st DRAFT").

25 388 U.S. 1 (1967).

26 Harry A. Blackmun Papers, Memorandum on *Doe v. Bolton* (Box 152, Folder 8, pp. 9–11) (labeled "1st DRAFT").

27 Harry A. Blackmun Papers, Memorandum to the Conference, May 31, 1972 (Box 151, Folder 3).

28 410 U.S. 113, 129.

29 Id. at 148–49.

30 Harry A. Blackmun Papers, handwritten notes in preparation for conference of October 13, 1972. (Box 151, Folder 8).

31 Id.

32 Harry A. Blackmun Papers, Memorandum to the Conference, November 21, 1972 (Box 151, Folder 6, p. 47).

33 Id., cover page, p. 48.

34 Harry A. Blackmun Papers, Letter from Lewis F. Powell, Jr., to Harry A. Blackmun, November 29, 1972 (Box 151, Folder 4).

35 Id., Letter from Harry A. Blackmun to Lewis F. Powell, Jr., December 4, 1972 (Box 151, Folder 3).

36 Id., Thurgood Marshall to Harry A. Blackmun, December 12, 1973 (Box 151, Folder 4).

37 Id., Memorandum to the Conference re Abortion Cases, December 21, 1973 (Box 151, Folder 6, p. 50).

38 Memorandum from Larry A. Hammond to Lewis F. Powell, Jr., November 27, 1972 (Lewis F. Powell, Jr.'s, *Roe* file, Box 5).

39 Harry A. Blackmun Papers, Hand-down Draft Opinion (Box 151, Folder 3) (marked "confidential—not for distribution, 1-22-73").

40 For a modern account of the post-*Roe* political story, see Linda Greenhouse and Reva B. Siegel, "Before (and After) *Roe v. Wade:* New Questions About Backlash," *Yale Law Journal* 120 (2011): 2028.

41 Linda Greenhouse, "Justice John Paul Stevens as Abortion-Rights Strategist," *UC Davis Law Review* 43 (2010): 749.

42 For the role the abortion issue played in the 1980 election, see Donald Grier Stephenson, Jr., *Campaigns and the Court: The U.S. Supreme Court in Presidential Elections* (New York: Columbia University Press, 1999), 190. Stephenson, however, mistakenly views the *Roe* decision as at odds with "both parties, their presidential candidate, [and] public opinion." Id. at 197. See also id. at 199–217 (discussing the political effects of *Roe*, in the elections of 1980 and 1984 and on the Democratic and Republican parties' positions).

43 See Greenhouse and Siegel, *Before* Roe v. Wade, 71–73.

44 410 U.S. at 177 (Rehnquist, J., dissenting).

45 428 U.S. 52 (1976).

46 See, e.g., *Bellotti v. Baird I*, 428 U.S. 132 (1976); *Bellotti v. Baird II*, 443 U.S. 622 (1979); and *Hodgson v. Minnesota*, 497 U.S. 417 (1990).

47 505 U.S. 933 (1992).

48 462 U.S. 416 (1983).

49 For a lively account of O'Connor's confirmation hearing, see Joan Biskupic, *Sandra Day O'Connor: How the First Woman on the Supreme Court Became Its Most Influential Justice* (New York: HarperCollins, 2005), 92–98.

50 *Akron v. Akron Center for Reproductive Health*, 462 U.S. 416 (1983), O'Connor, J., dissenting at 452–74. In a subsequent abortion case, *Webster v. Reproductive Health Services, Inc.*, 492 U.S. 490 (1989), the medical community mobilized to refute Justice O'Connor's assumption that the date of viability would ever approach the date of conception. A brief filed by the American Medical Association and other major professional organizations explained that even though some 10 percent of babies born between twenty-four and twenty-eight weeks of gestation—near the start of the third trimester—were now surviving, up from 2 percent a decade earlier, an "anatomic threshold" existed that would make it impossible for the foreseeable future for newborns younger than that to survive. The brief explained in detail that the fetal lungs were not sufficiently mature before twenty-three or twenty-four weeks to enable even mechanically assisted respiration to sustain life outside the womb. The amicus brief did not directly address Justice O'Connor, but it was clearly aimed at her assertion in her *Akron* dissent. Evidently persuaded, she never again raised the issue as a basis for objecting to *Roe*. See Linda Greenhouse, "The Counter-Factual Court," *University of Louisville Law Review* 47 (2008): 1.

51 432 U.S. 438 (1977).

52 432 U.S. 519 (1977).

53 432 U.S. 464 (1977).

54 *Roe v. Norton*, 408 F. Supp. 660, 663n3 (D. Conn. 1975).

55 Lewis F. Powell, Jr., Notes for Conference (Lewis F. Powell, Jr.'s, *Maher* file, Folder 2, p. 4).

56 411 U.S. 1 (1973). See Chapter 5 for a lengthier description.

57 432 U.S. at 472–76 (Powell, J.).

58 432 U.S. at 483 (Brennan, J., dissenting).

59 432 U.S. 460, 463 (Blackmun, J., dissenting).

60 Lewis F. Powell, Jr., Notes on Draft Opinion (Lewis F. Powell, Jr.'s, *Maher* file, Folder 7).

61 *McRae v. Califano*, 491 F. Supp. 630 (1980).

62 448 U.S. 297 (1980).

63 Lewis F. Powell, Jr., Conference Notes (Lewis F. Powell, Jr.'s, *Harris* file, Folder 1).

64 Harry A. Blackmun Papers, Conference Notes (Box 316, Folder 8).

65 Lewis F. Powell, Jr., Conference Notes (Lewis F. Powell, Jr.'s, *Harris* file, Folder 1).

66 Potter Stewart Papers, Letter from Powell (Box 146, Folder 1244).

67 448 U.S. at 316.

68 Potter Stewart Papers (Box 146, Folder 1242).

CHAPTER 7: THE ROCKY ROAD TO SEX EQUALITY

1 Ruth Bader Ginsburg, "Sex Equality and the Constitution," *Tulane Law Review* 52 (1978): 457.

2 This was often referred to as the equal treatment versus special treatment debate. See, e.g., Wendy W. Williams, "Equality's Riddle: Pregnancy and the Equal Treatment/Special Treatment Debate," *NYU Review of Law and Social Change* 13 (1984–1985): 325.

3 See Neil S. Siegel and Reva B. Siegel, "Equality Arguments for Abortion Rights," *UCLA Law Review Discourse* 60 (2013): 162. "*Roe v. Wade* grounds constitutional protections for women's decision whether to end a pregnancy in the Due Process Clauses. But in the four decades since *Roe*, the U.S. Supreme Court has come to recognize the abortion right as an equality right as well as a liberty right." The authors cite, primarily, *Planned Parenthood v. Casey*, 505 U.S. 833 (1992) and Justice Ginsburg's dissenting opinion for four justices in *Gonzales v. Carhart*, 550 U.S. 124, 172 (2007), referring to "a woman's autonomy to determine her life's course, and thus to enjoy equal citizenship stature."

4 414 U.S. 632 (1974).

5 Harry A. Blackmun Papers (Box 175, Folder 1). His handwritten note actually says "N sex related," the capital N being Blackmun's own consistent shorthand for "not."

6 Lewis F. Powell, Jr., Notes on Memorandum Dated January 8, 1973 (Lewis F. Powell, Jr.'s, *LaFleur* file, Folder 1, p. 1) (italics in original).

7 Ruth Bader Ginsburg, "Sex Equality and the Constitution," 457n1.

8 404 U.S. 71 (1971).

9 Harry A. Blackmun Papers, Notes for Conference (Box 135, Folder 10).

10 See Cary Franklin, "The Anti-Stereotyping Principle in Constitutional Sex Discrimination Law," *NYU Law Review* 85 (2010): 83.

11 *Reed v. Reed*, Brief for Appellant. For the characterization of Ginsburg's "grandmother brief," see Serena Mayeri, *Reasoning From Race* (Cambridge: Harvard University Press, 2011), 61.

12 Harry A. Blackmun Papers, Notes for Conference (Box 135, Folder 10).

13 *Reed v. Reed*, 404 U.S. at 76–77.

14 The quotation Burger used in his majority opinion in *Reed* (404 U.S. at 76) is from *Royster Guano Co. v. Virginia*, 253 U.S. 412, 415 (1920). Ginsburg had cited this obscure tax case in brief. See Fred Strebeigh, *Equal: Women Reshape American Law* (New York: W.W. Norton, 2009), 40.

15 Gerald Gunther, "The Supreme Court, 1971 Term—Foreword: In Search of Evolving Doctrine on a Changing Court: A Model for a Newer Equal Protection," *Harvard Law Review* 86 (1972): 1.

16 411 U.S. 677 (1973).

17 Lewis F. Powell, Jr., Conference Notes, January 19, 1973 (Lewis F. Powell, Jr.'s, *Frontiero* files).

18 William J. Brennan, Jr., Memorandum to Conference, February 14, 1973 (Lewis F. Powell, Jr.'s, *Frontiero* files).

19 Brennan's third draft, *Frontiero v. Richardson*, at 9 (Lewis F. Powell, Jr.'s, *Frontiero* files). The illegitimacy case cited is *Weber v. Aetna Casualty & Surety Company*, 406 U.S. 164 (1972).

20 Letter from Lewis F. Powell, Jr., to William J. Brennan, Jr., March 2, 1973. (Lewis F. Powell, Jr.'s, *Frontiero* files.)

21 Memorandum from Lewis F. Powell, Jr., to William C. Kelly, Jr., March 8, 1973 (Lewis F. Powell, Jr.'s, *Frontiero* file, Folder 1, p. 54).

22 "*Frontiero v. Richardson* File," Wahlbeck, Paul J., James F. Spriggs II, and Forrest Maltzman. 2011. The Burger Court Opinion-writing Database. http://supreme courtopinions.wustl.edu/files/opinion_pdfs/1972;sh71-1694.pdf.

23 *Frontiero v. Richardson*, 411 U.S. 677, 692 (1973), Powell, J., concurring in the judgment. For a lively account of the *Frontiero* case, see Serena Mayeri, "When the Trouble Started: The Story of *Frontiero v. Richardson*," in Elizabeth M. Schneider and Stephanie M. Wildman, eds., *Women and the Law Stories* (New York: Foundation Press, 2011), 57–92. For an account of the case in a broader context, see Serena Mayeri, *Reasoning from Race: Feminism, Law, and the Civil Rights Revolution* (Cambridge: Harvard University Press, 2011), 70–75.

24 See Chapter 6 for an extensive discussion of this point.

25 This history is recounted by Jane J. Mansbridge, *Why We Lost the ERA*, 2nd ed. (Chicago: University of Chicago Press, 1986).

26 See Donald T. Critchlow, *Phyllis Schlafly and Grassroots Conservatism: A Woman's Crusade* (Princeton: Princeton University Press, 2005).

27 In addition to *Frontiero*, the cases Ginsburg argued were: *Kahn v. Shevin*, 416 U.S. 351 (1974) (her only loss, in which the court rejected a challenge to the $500 property tax exemption that Florida law granted to widows but not to widowers); *Edwards v. Healy*, 421 U.S. 772 (1975), a challenge to Louisiana's system of exempting women from jury duty unless they affirmatively volunteered, dismissed after argument as moot when the state revised the applicable provision of its constitution; *Weinberger v. Wiesenfeld*, 420 U.S. 636 (1975), striking down a provision of the Social Security law that provided survivors' benefits to widows with minor children but not to widowers; *Califano v. Goldfarb*, 430 U.S. 199 (1977), striking down a Social Security provision granting survivors' benefits to widows regardless of their economic dependence on their late husbands while requiring a widower to have received half his support from his late wife in order to qualify; and *Duren v. Missouri*, 439 U.S. 357 (1979), striking down a state's jury system that automatically granted women's requests for exemption from jury service.

28 Jessica Weisberg, "Reigning Supreme," *Elle*, October 2014, 359.

29 Potter Stewart Papers (Box 91, Folder 793). Around this time, Stewart visited Harvard Law School and in informal remarks to the students offered, perhaps

unwittingly, a window into his thinking. He observed that "the female of the species has the best of both worlds. She can attack laws that unreasonably discriminate against her while preserving those that favor her." *Harvard Law School* 15 (March 23, 1973), quoted in Ginsburg, "Sex Equality and the Constitution," 466n68.

30 *Cohen v. Chesterfield County School Board*, 326 F. Supp. 1159 (1971). The justices granted *certiorari* to both cases on April 20, 1973, consolidating them for argument and deciding both by a single opinion on January 21, 1974.

31 *LaFleur v. Cleveland Board of Education*, 465 F. 2d 1184 (6th Cir. 1972).

32 Handwritten Annotation on Jack B. Owens's Memorandum to Lewis F. Powell, Jr., September 24, 1973 (Lewis F. Powell, Jr.'s, *LaFleur* file, Folder 1, p. 63) (italics in original).

33 Lewis F. Powell, Jr., Notes for Conference, October 17, 1973 (Lewis F. Powell, Jr.'s, *LaFleur* file, Folder 1, p. 72).

34 Lewis F. Powell, Jr., Conference Notes (Lewis F, Powell, Jr.'s, *LaFleur* file, Folder 1).

35 Brief for the United States, *Cleveland Board of Education v. LaFleur*, 414 U.S. 632 (1973) (No. 72-777); *Cohen v. Chesterfield County School Board* (No. 72-1129), 8–9.

36 Motion and brief of American Civil Liberties Union et al., *Cleveland Board of Education v. LaFleur*, 414 U.S. 632 (1973) (No. 72-777); *Cohen v. Chesterfield County School Board* (No. 72-1129), 6–9.

37 414 U.S. 632, 644 (Stewart, J., majority).

38 412 U.S. 441, 446 (1974).

39 414 U.S. 632, 646–7.

40 Id. at 653 (Powell, J., concurring in the result).

41 Id. at 654n2.

42 417 U.S. 484 (1974).

43 *Aiello v. Hansen*, 359 F. Supp. 792, 798–9, 801 (N.D. Cal. 1973).

44 Harry A. Blackmun, Memorandum (Box 188, Folder 12) (headed: "No. 73-640—Geduldig v. Aiello").

45 Lewis F. Powell, Jr., Notes from Conference, March 29, 1974 (Lewis F. Powell, Jr.'s, *Geduldig* file, Folder 1, p. 16).

46 *Geduldig v. Aiello*, 417 U.S. 484, 494 (1974).

47 Id. at 501 (Brennan, J., dissenting).

48 Id. at 497n20.

49 429 U.S. 125 (1976).

50 Brief for the United States, *General Electric Company v. Gilbert*, 429 U.S. 125 (1976) (No. 74-1589), 8.

51 429 U.S. 125, 136 (Rehnquist, J., majority).

52 Id. at 125, 161 (Stevens, J., dissenting).

53 Lesley Oelsner, "Supreme Court Rules Employers May Refuse Pregnancy Sick Pay," *New York Times*, December 8, 1976, 1.

54 Ginsburg, "Sex Equality and the Constitution," 462.

55 S. Rep. No. 331, 95th Cong., 1st Sess. 4 (1977).

56 429 U.S. 190 (1976); Lewis F. Powell, Jr., Written Note on Memorandum, July 9, 1976 (Lewis F. Powell, Jr.'s, *Craig* file, Folder 1, p. 1).

57 Brief of American Civil Liberties Union for Appellants as Amicus Curiae, *Craig v. Boren*, 429 U.S. 190 (1976) (No. 75-628), 10, 22.

58 Lewis F. Powell, Jr.'s, *Craig v. Boren*, file, Notes from Conference, October 8, 1976.

59 See Seth Stern and Stephen Wermiel, *Justice Brennan: Liberal Champion* (New York: Houghton Mifflin Harcourt, 2010), 406–8.

60 *Craig v. Boren*, 429 U.S. 190, 197 (1976).

61 Potter Stewart Papers (Box 121, Folder 1035).

62 Potter Stewart agreed with the judgment but did not endorse Brennan's choice of the standard of review, writing separately to say that the statute should be invalidated for making a distinction that amounted to "total irrationality."

63 *Craig v. Boren*, 429 U.S. 190, 211 (Powell, J., concurring).

64 Id. at 211–12 (Stevens, J., concurring).

65 518 U.S. 515 (1996). (Justice Clarence Thomas did not participate.)

66 See especially Reva B. Siegel, "Constitutional Culture, Social Movement Conflict and Constitutional Change: The Case of the *de facto* ERA," *California Law Review* 94 (2006): 1323.

67 *Goldberg v. Rostker*, 509 F. Supp 586 (E.D. Pa. 1980).

68 *Rostker v. Goldberg*, 453 U.S. 57 (1981).

69 Brief of Women's Equity Action League Educational and Legal Defense Fund et al. as Amicus Curiae, *Rostker v. Goldberg*, 453 U.S. 57 (1981) (No. 80–251), 2–3.

70 Brief of Stacey Acker et al. as Amicus Curiae, *Rostker v. Goldberg*, 453 U.S. 57 (1981) (No. 82–251), 20–21.

71 Linda Greenhouse, "Justices, 6–3, Rule Draft Registration May Exclude Women," *New York Times*, June 26, 1981, A1. The justices in the majority were Burger, Stewart, Blackmun, Powell Stevens, and Rehnquist, who wrote the opinion for the court.

72 453 U.S. at 78–79.

73 Phyllis Schlafly, "Panetta's Cowardly Decision," *Human Events*, January 30, 2013. http://www.humanevents.com/2013/01/29/schlaflypanetta-cowardly-decision/.

CHAPTER 8: EXPRESSION AND REPRESSION

1 "Beyond the (Garbage) Pale," *New York Times*, April 1, 1969, 46.

2 Henry Raymont, " 'Che!' Tests the Limits of Sex Onstage," *New York Times*, March 24, 1969, 56.

3 Id.

4 Lesley Oelsner, "8 in 'Che!' Are Found Guilty of Obscenity," *New York Times*, February 26, 1970, 31.

5 354 U.S. 476, 489 (1957). It was in this decision that the Warren Court declared obscenity to lack all First Amendment protection. Brennan, writing for the Court, declared that "implicit in the history of the First Amendment is the rejection of obscenity as utterly without redeeming social importance. . . . We hold that obscenity is not within the area of constitutionally protected speech or press." 354 U.S. at 484–85.

6 378 U.S. 184, 197 (1964) (Stewart, J., concurring).

7 Justice Brennan's dissenting opinion in *Paris Adult Theatre 1 v. Slaton*, 413 U.S. 49 (1973), provides a list (413 U.S. at 82n8). The one-case-at-a-time approach was derived from the Warren Court's decision in *Redrup v. New York*, 386 U.S. 767 (1967).

8 E.g., "Justices Decide Obscene Matter in Home Is Legal," *New York Times*, April 8, 1969, A1.

9 394 U.S. 557 (1969).

10 Leigh Ann Wheeler, *How Sex Became a Civil Liberty* (New York: Oxford University Press, 2013), 169–71.

11 Richard Nixon, "Statement About the Report of the Commission on Obscenity and Pornography," in *Public Papers of the President of the United States: Richard Nixon, 1970* (Washington, D.C.: Government Printing Office, 1971), 940.

12 Kevin J. McMahon, *Nixon's Court: His Challenge to Judicial Liberalism and Its Political Consequences* (Chicago: University of Chicago Press, 2011), 181.

13 Id. at 180, quoting William Safire, *Before the Fall: An Inside View of the Pre-Watergate White House* (New York: Doubleday, 1975), 557.

14 413 U.S. 15 (1973).

15 Letter from Warren Burger to William J. Brennan, Jr., June 14, 1972. Potter Stewart Papers, Yale University, Box 272, folder 3256.

16 413 U.S. 49, 62 (1973).

17 Potter Stewart Papers (Box 272, Folder 3256).

18 413 U.S. at 24.

19 Potter Stewart Papers (Box 272, Folder 3256).

20 Id. (William J. Brennan, Jr., Memorandum to the Conference, June 13, 1972, p. 1–3.)

21 Id. at 15–16.

22 Potter Stewart Papers (Box 272, Folder 3256).

23 Potter Stewart Papers (Box 272, Folder 3259). The internal Court struggle is described by Seth Stern and Stephen Wermiel in *Justice Brennan: Liberal Champion* (New York: Houghton Mifflin Harcourt, 2010), 366–68.

24 McMahon, *Nixon's Court*, 182.

25 413 U.S. at 25, 30.

26 Ravi Somaiya, "As Old Pornographic Magazines Ebb, Newer Entries to Genre Tilt Artistic," *New York Times*, January 19, 2015, B3.

27 Charles V. Bagli, "Times Square's Crushing Success Raises Questions About Its Future," *New York Times*, January 27, 2015, A16.

28 381 U.S. 479 (1965).

29 405 U.S. 438 (1972).

30 *Baker v. Nelson*, 191 N.W. 2d 185 (1971).

31 388 U.S. 1 (1967).

32 Congress, responding to the justices' long-standing request, repealed nearly all the Supreme Court's mandatory appellate jurisdiction in 1988, leaving the Court with complete discretion whether to accept cases in the formerly mandatory categories, which now arrive as ordinary petitions for certiorari.

33 409 U.S. 810 (1972).

34 Harry A. Blackmun Papers (Box 785, Folder 7). See also Linda Greenhouse, "Wedding Bells," *New York Times*, March 20, 2013, accessed February 15, 2015, http://opinionator.blogs.nytimes.com/2013/03/20/wedding-bells/

35 *Obergefell v. Hodges*, 135 S. Ct. 2584 (2015); *Baker v. Nelson* described, 135 S. Ct. at 2598; *Baker v. Nelson* overruled, 135 S. Ct. at 2605.

36 *Doe v. Commonwealth's Attorney for the City of Richmond*, 403 F. Supp. 1199 (1975), *affirmed*, 425 U.S. 901 (1976).

37 "A Summary of Supreme Court Actions," *New York Times*, October 11, 1972, 20.

38 Lesley Oelsner, "Justices Decline to Remove Curb on Homosexuals," *New York Times*, March 30, 1976, A1.

39 Among many sources for the history of the period from the gay rights perspective are: Dudley Clendinen and Adam Nagourney, *Out for Good: The Struggle to Build a Gay Rights Movement in America* (New York: Simon & Schuster, 1999); George Chauncey, *Why Marriage: The History Shaping Today's Debate over Gay Equality* (New York: Basic Books, 2004); Fred Fejes, *Gay Rights and Moral Panic: The Origins of America's Debate over Homosexuality* (New York: Palgrave Macmillan, 2008); William N. Eskridge, Jr., *Dishonorable Passions: Sodomy Laws in America, 1861–2003* (New York: Penguin, 2008); and David A. J. Richards, *The Sodomy Cases: Bowers v. Hardwick and Lawrence v. Texas* (Lawrence: University Press of Kansas 2009).

40 Israel Shenker, "Political Scientists Vary on Constitutional Theme," *New York Times*, April 10, 1976, 21.

41 Steven O. Ludd, "The Aftermath of *Doe v. Commonwealth's Attorney*: In Search of the Right to Be Let Alone," *University of Dayton Law Review* 10 (1985): 705.

42 David A. J. Richards, "Sexual Autonomy and the Constitutional Right to Privacy: A Case Study in Human Rights and the Unwritten Constitution," *Hastings Law Journal* 30 (1979): 958.

43 *People v. Onofre*, 51 N.Y. 2d 476 (1980); *cert. denied, New York v. Onofre*, 451 U.S. 987 (1981).

44 *People v. Uplinger,* 58 N.Y. 2d 936 (1983).

45 *New York v. Uplinger,* 467 U.S. 245 (1984).

46 Id. at 252 (White, J., dissenting).

47 *National Gay Task Force v. Board of Education of the City of Oklahoma City,* 729 F. 2d 1270 (10th Cir. 1984).

48 *Board of Education of the City of Oklahoma City v. National Gay Task Force,* 470 U.S. 903 (1985).

49 According to Eskridge, *Dishonorable Passions,* 226–28, citing William Brennan's and Harry Blackmun's files, the division was between Brennan, Marshall, Blackmun, and Stevens, who voted to affirm the lower court's overturning of the state law, and Burger, White, Rehnquist, and O'Connor, who voted to reverse. Burger, assuming that Powell would be a fifth vote to reverse, wanted to set the case for reargument before a full court, but none of the other justices supported that course of action.

50 Among other sources, the background of the case is recounted at length by Eskridge, *Dishonorable Passions,* 229–64.

51 *Hardwick v. Bowers,* 760 F. 2d 1202 (1985).

52 478 U.S. 186 (1986).

53 Preliminary Memorandum (Lewis F. Powell, Jr.'s, *Bowers* file, Folder 1, p. 2).

54 The cases were *Dronenburg v. Zech,* 741 F. 2d 1388 (D.C. Cir. 1984); and *Baker v. Wade,* 769 F. 2d 289 (5th Cir. 1985). White's draft opinion is in Lewis F. Powell, Jr.'s, *Bowers* file, Folder 1, p. 18.

55 The incident is recounted in Dennis J. Hutchinson, *The Man Who Once Was Whizzer White* (New York: Free Press, 1998), 451–52; and John C. Jeffries, Jr., *Justice Lewis F. Powell, Jr.: A Biography* (New York: Fordham University Press, 1994), 514.

56 Brief for Petitioner, *Bowers v. Hardwick,* 478 U.S. 186 (No. 85-140), 20.

57 Id. at 37.

58 Brief for Petitioner, *Bowers v. Hardwick,* 478 U.S. 186 (No. 85-140), 6.

59 Id. at 4.

60 Id. at 27.

61 "Memo to Mike," March 31, 1986 (Lewis F. Powell, Jr.'s, *Bower* files, Folder 1, p. 36).

62 Harry A. Blackmun Papers (Box 451, Folder 9).

63 370 U.S. 660 (1962).

64 Letter from Warren Burger to Lewis F. Powell, Jr. April 3, 1986, Lewis F. Powell Jr.'s *Bowers v. Hardwick* file.

65 Jeffries, *Justice Lewis F. Powell, Jr.,* 521.

66 478 U.S. 186, 190–91 (1986).

67 Id. at 194.

68 Id. at 197 (Burger, J., concurring).

69 Id. at 198 (Powell, J., concurring).

70 Harry A. Blackmun Papers (Box 451, Folder 7).

71 *Minersville School District v. Gobitis*, 310 U.S. 586 (1940).

72 319 U.S. 624 (1943).

73 For background on the flag salute cases, see Douglas E. Abrams, "Reason and Passion: Justice Jackson and the Second Flag Salute Case," Parts I and II, *Precedent* (Summer 2011): 22; and (Fall 2011): 16.

74 478 U.S. at 214 (Blackmun, J., dissenting).

75 *Obergefell v. Hodges*, 135 S. Ct. 2584 (2015).

76 Al Kamen, "Powell Changed Vote in Sodomy Case," *Washington Post*, July 13, 1986, A1.

77 Linda Greenhouse, "Washington Talk: When Second Thoughts in a Case Come Too Late," *New York Times*, November 5, 1990.

78 *Lawrence v. Texas*, 539 U.S. 558, 577 (2003).

79 *Obergefell v. Hodges*, 135, S. Ct. 2584 (2015).

80 *Lawrence v. Texas*, 539 U.S. at 578. Kennedy had also written an important earlier decision, *Romer v. Evans*, 517 U.S. 620 (1995), which invalidated a Colorado constitutional amendment that barred all levels of government in the state from enacting legislation to protect gay people from discrimination.

81 See Dale Carpenter, *Flagrant Conduct: The Story of* Lawrence v. Texas (New York: Norton, 2012).

CHAPTER 9: A RELIGIOUS PEOPLE'S COURT

1 343 U.S. 306 (1952).

2 *Engel v. Vitale*, 370 U.S. 421 (1962); *Abington School District v. Schempp*, 374 U.S. 203 (1963).

3 In *Everson v. Board of Education*, 330 U.S. 1 (1947), a landmark decision of the Vinson Court that was the first case to apply the Establishment Clause to the states, the court declared that the Constitution required government "to be neutral in its relations with groups of religious believers and non-believers." Id. at 19.

4 Ten Commandments permissible, *Van Orden v. Perry*, 545 U.S. 677 (2005); Ten Commandments impermissible, *McCreary County v. American Civil Liberties Union*, 545 U.S. 844 (2005); religious claims to exemption, *Employment Division v. Smith*, 494 U.S. 872 (1990), but see *Church of Lukumi Babalu Aye v. City of Hialeah*, 508 U.S. 520 (1993).

5 For example, see two recent 5–4 decisions, *Town of Greece v. Galloway*, 134 S. Ct. 1811 (2014), upholding sectarian legislative prayer, and *Burwell v. Hobby Lobby Stores*, 134 S. Ct. 2751 (2014), permitting a religiously motivated business owner to opt out of a federal requirement to include contraception coverage in the employee health plan.

6 There are many books and articles on the religion clauses. See, e.g., Kent Greenawalt, *Religion and the Constitution: Free Exercise and Fairness* (Princeton: Princeton University Press, 2006) and Kent Greenawalt, *Religion and the*

Constitution: Establishment and Fairness (Princeton: Princeton University Press, 2008).

7 A useful inventory is provided by Bernard Schwartz in the "Church and State" chapter of his *The Ascent of Pragmatism: The Burger Court in Action* (Boston: Addison-Wesley, 1990), 187–214.

8 403 U.S. 602 (1971).

9 *Lamb's Chapel v. Center Moriches Union Free School District*, 508 U.S. 384, 398 (1993) (Scalia, J., concurring). The court held by a vote of 9–0 that the Establishment Clause didn't bar an evangelical Christian church from using public school property after hours to show a series of filmed lectures on Christian family values by James Dobson, founder of the organization Focus on the Family. Scalia agreed, but objected to the fact that the opinion for the court by Justice Byron R. White invoked *Lemon v. Kurtzman* in analyzing the issue.

10 403 U.S. 612–13 (the quotation in the third test is from a 1970 Burger Court decision, *Walz v. Tax Commission of the City of New York*, 397 U.S. 664, which upheld a property tax exemption for churches).

11 403 U.S. at 612.

12 Id. at 623.

13 Id.

14 Data in this paragraph are from John C. Jeffries, Jr., and James E. Ryan, "A Political History of the Establishment Clause," *Michigan Law Review* 100 (2001): 336–37.

15 See Linda Greenhouse and Reva B. Siegel, "Before (and After) *Roe v. Wade*: New Questions About Backlash," *Yale Law Journal* 120 (2011): 2026n141.

16 461 U.S. 574 (1983). See also Olatunde Johnson, "The Story of *Bob Jones University v. United States*: Race, Religion, and Congress' Extraordinary Acquiescence," in *Statutory Interpretation Stories*, eds. William Eskridge, Jr., Philip Frickey, and Elizabeth Garrett (New York: Foundation Press, 2011), 126–63; Kent Greenawalt, *Does God Belong in Public Schools?* (Princeton: Princeton University Press, 2005).

17 461 U.S. at 604.

18 *Committee for Public Education and Religious Liberty v. Nyquist*, 413 U.S. 756 (1973).

19 463 U.S. 388 (1983).

20 Id. at 400–401.

21 Id. at 395.

22 Id. at 405, 409–10 (Marshall, J., dissenting).

23 Id. at 416–17.

24 536 U.S. 639 (2002).

25 Id. at 650.

26 Id. at 689 (Souter, J., dissenting).

27 Id. at 711.

28 Id. at 717.

29 465 U.S. 668 (1984).

30 Id. at 700 (Brennan, J., dissenting).

31 Id. at 679.

32 Id. at 680–81.

33 Id. at 683.

34 Id. at 684–85.

35 Id. at 673, citing *Zorach v. Clauson*, 343 U.S. 306, 314–15 (1952).

36 Id. at 677–78, citing *Zorach*, 343 U.S. 306, 314.

37 Id. at 690 (O'Connor, J., concurring).

38 Id. at 692.

39 Id at 691.

40 E.g. in a 2005 case, *McCreary County v. ACLU*, 545 U.S. 844, O'Connor cast the fifth vote to invalidate Ten Commandments displays on the walls of three Kentucky county courthouses. Each display "conveys an unmistakable message of endorsement to the reasonable observer," she wrote in a concurring opinion. 545 U.S. at 883.

41 465 U.S. at 712 (Brennan, J., dissenting).

42 Brief for the United States as Amicus Curiae Supporting Reversal, *Lynch v. Donnelly*, 465 U.S. 668 (1984) (No. 82-1256), 4.

43 More than thirty years later, controversies over Christmas season displays remain staples of municipal life. A poll conducted in late 2014 by the Pew Religion and Public Life Project found a sharp division in public attitudes. Forty-four percent of respondents said Christian symbols like Nativity scenes should be permitted on public property regardless of whether the display included secular elements or symbols of other faiths; 28 percent said symbols from other faiths should be required; and 20 percent said that "no religious symbols should be allowed." *Pew Forum*, accessed January 20, 2015, http://www.pewforum.org/2014/12/15/most-say-religious-holiday-displays-should-be-allowed-on-public-property/. Courts generally interpret *Lynch v. Donnelly* to permit those displays that follow what has come to be known as the "reindeer rule" of that case.

44 406 U.S. 205 (1972).

45 This political and cultural history of the case is taken from Shawn Francis Peters, *The* Yoder *Case: Religious Freedom, Education, and Parental Rights* (Lawrence: University Press of Kansas, 2003).

46 Reverend William C. Lindholm, "U.S. Supreme Court Case: Is There Religious Freedom in America—for the Amish?," National Committee for Amish Religious Freedom, accessed January 20, 2015, amishreligiousfreedom.org/case.htm.

47 Brief for Respondents, *Wisconsin v. Yoder*, 406 U.S. 205 (1972) (No. 70–110), 15.

48 *Wisconsin v. Yoder*, 406 U.S. 205, 245 (1972) (Douglas, J., dissenting). Douglas went on to suggest that the case should be remanded with instructions to canvas

all school-age Amish children in Wisconsin on whether they preferred to leave school or remain at least until age sixteen.

49 Id. at 213, 222.

50 Id. 222–23n11.

51 Id. at 224–26.

52 Id. at 215.

53 Id. at 218, 228–29. It was important to Burger to make clear that the court was grounding its decision in respect for a particular religious tradition and was not freely sanctioning modern departures from the mainstream. "It cannot be overemphasized that we are not dealing with a way of life and mode of education by a group claiming to have recently discovered some 'progressive' or more enlightened process for rearing children for modern life." Id. at 235.

54 Id. at 231–32 (Douglas, J., dissenting).

55 See Peters, *The* Yoder *Case*, 61–62 (recounting published criticism of the role of the National Committee for Amish Religious Freedom and William Bentley Ball).

56 The vote was 6 to 1; Powell and Rehnquist, who had not yet joined the Court when the case was argued on December 8, 1971, did not vote.

57 455 U.S. 252 (1982).

58 *Lee v. United States Government*, 497 F. Supp. 180 (1980).

59 455 U.S. at 257.

60 Id. at 259.

61 *Braunfeld v. Brown*, 366 U.S. 599 (1961).

62 455 U.S. at 260–61.

63 *Burwell v. Hobby Lobby Stores*, 134 S. Ct. 2751 (2014).

64 Id. at 2784.

65 The *Hobby Lobby* decision was an interpretation of a federal statute, the Religious Freedom Restoration Act, rather than an interpretation of the Free Exercise Clause itself. Those two sources of law are tightly entwined in fascinating ways, outside the scope of this book.

66 455 U.S. at 260.

67 Id. at 263n3 (Stevens, J., concurring).

68 Id. at 262.

69 450 U.S. 707 (1981).

70 *Thomas v. Review Board of the Indiana Employment Security Division*, 391 N.E. 2d 1127 (1979).

71 450 U.S. 718–19.

72 374 U.S. 398 (1963).

73 450 U.S. at 720, 723 (Rehnquist, J., dissenting).

74 Id. at 723.

75 463 U.S. 388 (1983).

INTRODUCTION TO PART IV: BUSINESS

1 Letter from Eugene B. Sydnor, Jr., published in the *Richmond Times-Dispatch* on October 3, 1972, sent by Sydnor to Lewis Powell on October 2, 1972.

2 Douglas Martin, "Jack Anderson, Investigative Journalist Who Angered the Powerful, Dies at 83," *New York Times*, December 18, 2005.

3 Jack Anderson, "FBI Missed Blueprint by Powell," *Washington Post*, September 29, 1972. See also Jack Anderson, "Powell's Lesson to Business Aired," *Washington Post*, September 28, 1972; and Jack Anderson, "Chief Justice Lobbies Against Bill," *Washington Post*, October 5, 1972.

4 Lewis F. Powell, Jr., "Confidential Memorandum: Attack on American Free Enterprise System," to Mr. Eugene B. Sydnor, Jr., Chairman, Education Committee, U.S. Chamber of Commerce, August 23, 1971.

5 Id. (emphasis in original).

6 All the quotes above are from the Powell memorandum.

7 Jack Anderson, "FBI Missed Blueprint by Powell," *Washington Post*, September 29, 1972. See also Jack Anderson, "Powell's Lesson to Business Aired," *Washington Post*, September 28, 1972; and Jack Anderson, "Chief Justice Lobbies Against Bill," *Washington Post*, October 5, 1972.

8 Greg Stohr, "Obama's 10th Justice Kagan Subverts Supreme Court Business Tilt," *Bloomberg.com*, January 11, 2010. Harvard law professor Richard Lazarus describes the Chamber's outsized influence as "an especially remarkable story given that it originated from a recommendation of a private attorney who later himself became a Supreme Court Justice." Richard J. Lazarus, "Advocacy Matters Before and Within the Supreme Court: Transforming the Court by Transforming the Bar," *Georgetown Law Journal* 96 (2008): 1487–1506. Writing in *The New York Times Magazine*, Jeffrey Rosen says that the "origins of the business community's campaign to transform the Supreme Court can be traced back precisely to August 23, 1971"— the date of Lewis Powell's memorandum. Jeffrey Rosen, "Supreme Court Inc.," *New York Times Magazine*, March 16, 2008. Powell's biographer, John Jeffries, on the other hand, regarded the memorandum as trivial. Although Powell himself had provided Jeffries a copy of it while he was serving as Powell's law clerk, Jeffries makes no mention of it in his nearly seven-hundred-page biography of Powell.

9 See, e.g., Michael J. Graetz and Ian Shapiro, *Death by a Thousand Cuts: The Fight over Taxing Inherited Wealth* (Princeton: Princeton University Press, 2005), 85–96.

10 *Diamond v. Chakrabarty*, 447 U.S. 303 (1980).

11 Daniel J. Kevles, "Ananda Chakrabarty Wins a Patent: Biotechnology, Law and Society, 1972–1980," *Historical Studies in the Physical and Biological Sciences* 25 (1994): 111; Rebecca S. Eisenberg, "The Story of *Diamond v. Chakrabarty*: Technological Change and the Subject Matter Boundaries of the Patent System," in *Intellectual Property Stories*, eds. Jane C. Ginsburg and Rochelle Cooper Dreyfuss (New York: Foundation Press, 2006), 327–57.

12 447 U.S. at 309 and 317 (Burger, C.J., majority). Writing for the four dissenting justices, which included Marshall, Powell, and White, Justice Brennan insisted that, given the "relative novelty of patenting a living organism," the issue should be decided by Congress.

13 Kevles, "Ananda Chakrabarty," 133. Unlike the pseudonymous Jane Roe of abortion fame or Oliver Brown, who prevailed over Topeka, Kansas's, Board of Education in the famous school desegregation lawsuit, most legal scholars have never heard of Ananda Chakrabarty. As a postdoctoral biochemist at the University of Illinois and later at General Electric's research center in Schenectady, New York, Chakrabarty pursued his interests in the ability of bacteria to transform organic compounds. Like the alchemists of old, he endeavored to produce an oil-eating bug, a microorganism that could turn petroleum into protein. In 1972, through a process he described to *People* magazine as shuffling genes to create two new strains of bacteria, Chakrabarty succeeded and filed for a patent.

14 See, e.g., *Association for Molecular Pathology v. Myriad Genetics, Inc.*, 133 S.Ct. 2107 (2013).

15 450 U.S. at 175 (1981).

16 Maureen A. O'Rourke, "The Story of *Diamond v. Diehr*: Toward Patenting Software," in *Intellectual Property Stories*, eds. Jane C. Ginsburg and Rochelle Cooper Dreyfuss (New York: Foundation Press, 2006), 194–219.

17 Id. at 219.

18 *Sony Corp. of America v. Universal Studios*, 464 U.S. 417 (1984).

19 See James Lardner, *Fast Forward: Hollywood, the Japanese, and the VCR Wars* (New York: Norton, 1987); and Jessica Litman, "The Story of *Sony v. Universal Studios*: Mary Poppins Meets the Boston Strangler," in *Intellectual Property Stories*, eds. Jane C. Ginsburg and Rochelle Cooper Dreyfuss (New York: Foundation Press, 2006), 358–94.

20 *Flood v. Kuhn*, 407 U.S. 258 (1972). See Robert M. Goldman, *One Man Out: Curt Flood Versus Baseball* (Lawrence: University Press of Kansas, 2008).

21 407 U.S. at 281.

22 Linda Greenhouse, "Justice Blackmun, Author of Abortion Rights, Dies," *New York Times*, March 5, 1999.

23 *Kansas City Royals Baseball Corp. v. Major League Players Association*, 532 F.2d 615 (8th Cir. 1976), affirming 409 F. Supp. 233 (W.D. Mo. 1976).

CHAPTER 10: CORPORATIONS ARE PEOPLE TOO

1 316 U.S. 52 (1942).

2 Id. at 54 (Roberts, J., majority).

3 Id. at 55.

4 376 U.S. 254 (1964).

5 *Virginia Bd. of Pharmacy v. Virginia Citizens Consumer Council*, 425 U.S. 748 (1976).

6 *Bigelow v. Virginia*, 421 U.S. 809 (1975). Much of the discussion of the *Bigelow* case and the quote from Blackmun are based on Linda Greenhouse, *Becoming Justice Blackmun: Harry Blackmun's Supreme Court Journey* (New York: Times Books, 2006), 116–21.

7 421 U.S. at 814, 822 (Blackmun, J., majority).

8 Id.

9 Justice Blackmun's opinion emphasizes how feeble was the state's argument in a footnote pointing out that Virginia had failed even to suggest that advertising low drug prices might lead to their overconsumption. 425 U.S. at 767n.21.

10 Memorandum to Lewis F. Powell, Jr., August 19, 1975 (Lewis F. Powell, Jr.'s, *Virginia State Board of Pharmacy* file, Folder 1, p. 10).

11 425 U.S. at 770. Justice Stevens did not participate.

12 Greenhouse, *Becoming Justice Blackmun*, 119.

13 Id. at 784 (Rehnquist, J., dissenting).

14 Id. at 785. For support he draws on *Nebbia v. New York*, 291 U.S. 502 (1934); and *Olsen v. Nebraska*, 313 U.S. 236 (1941).

15 423 U.S. at 789 (Rehnquist, J., dissenting).

16 Lewis F. Powell, Jr., Handwritten Note on Rehnquist's April 19, 1976 Draft (Lewis F. Powell, Jr.'s *Virginia State Board of Pharmacy* file, Folder 1, p. 56).

17 *Bates v. State Bar of Arizona*, 433 U.S. 350 (1977).

18 Id. at 380.

19 For a history of these developments, see Michael J. Graetz, *The End of Energy* (Cambridge: MIT Press, 2013).

20 447 U.S. 557 (1980).

21 Bruce Ledewitz, "Corporate Advertising's Democracy," *Boston University Public Interest Law Journal* 12 (2003): 400.

22 Few think, for example, that a legislature may constitutionally prohibit misleading or untruthful statements by political officeholders or candidates. Ohio is an exception, but the federal courts have disagreed. See *Susan B. Anthony List v. Driehaus*, 134 S. Ct. 2334 (2014); *Susan B. Anthony List v. Ohio Elections Commission*, Case No. 1:10-cv-720, Southern District of Ohio, September 11, 2014.

23 Memorandum from David O. Stewart to Lewis F. Powell, Jr., June 12, 1980 (titled "Report from the Front") (Lewis F. Powell, Jr.'s, *Central Hudson* file, p. 131).

24 447 U.S. at 563 (Powell, J., majority).

25 Id. at 598–99 (Rehnquist, J., dissenting).

26 *Lochner v. New York*, 198 U.S. 45 (1905).

27 Id. at 62 (Peckham, J., majority).

28 *West Coast Hotel v. Parrish*, 300 U.S. 379 (1973) (minimum wages for women); *National Labor Relations Board v. Jones & Laughlin Steel Co.*, 301 U.S. 1 (1937) (National Labor Relations Act); and *Helvering v. Davis*, 301 U.S. 619 (1937), (Social Security Act).

29 Roosevelt actually made nine appointments but one of those, James F. Byrnes, served only one term. Excellent histories of the Court's transformation during the New Deal include Bruce Ackerman, *We the People, Volume 2: Transformations* (Cambridge: Belknap Press, 1998); William E. Leuchtenburg, *The Supreme Court Reborn: The Constitutional Revolution in the Age of Roosevelt* (Oxford: Oxford University Press, 1995); Howard Gillman, *The Constitution Besieged: The Rise and Demise of* Lochner *Era Police Powers Jurisprudence* (Durham: Duke University Press, 1993); John B. Gates, *The Supreme Court and Partisan Realignment: A Macro and Micro Level Perspective* (Boulder: Westview, 1992).

30 425 U.S. at 775 (Rehnquist, J., dissenting).

31 Id. at 784.

32 Id. at 785, quoting *Ferguson v. Skrupa*, 372 U.S. 726, 730 (1963).

33 447 U.S. at 589 (Rehnquist, J., dissenting).

34 Id. at 591.

35 Id.

36 John C. Jeffries and Thomas H. Jackson, "Commercial Speech: Economic Due Process and the First Amendment," *Virginia Law Review* 65 (1979): 1; Robert Post, "Compelled Commercial Speech" (working paper, Public Law and Legal Theory, Yale Law School, New Haven, 2014).

37 Jeffries and Jackson, "Commercial Speech."

38 The *Virginia Pharmacy* decision was grounded in the adverse economic consequences to consumers of the state's ban on advertising prescription prices. 425 U.S. at 762–65.

39 It may also have added support to the deregulatory efforts of Jimmy Carter's presidency (which, for example, deregulated the trucking and airline industries) and the deregulatory agenda that played a central role in the domestic policies of Ronald Reagan.

40 *Sorrell v. IMS Health Inc.*, 131 S. Ct. 1653, 2661 (Kennedy, J., majority) (2011).

41 Brief of Chamber of Commerce of the United States of America for Respondents as Amici Curiae, *Sorrell v. IMS Health*, 131 S.Ct. 2653 (2011) (No. 10-779), http://www.imsfreespeech.org/resources/Amicus-Brief-Chamber.pdf.

42 131 S.Ct. at 2663 (Kennedy, J., majority).

43 Id. at 2675 (Breyer, J., dissenting).

44 Justice Breyer's dissent described the Court's decision as threatening Food and Drug Administration regulations and calling into question numerous governmental prohibitions on the use of information, including by the Federal Reserve Board, state utility regulators, and other federal and state agencies.

45 131 S. Ct. at 2679 (Breyer, J., dissenting).

46 Yale Law School dean Robert Post, who has written extensively on the creation and expansion of the commercial speech doctrine, describes the Court's recent emphasis on the rights of the "autonomous commercial speaker" as "deeply disturbing." Robert Post, "Compelled Commercial Speech," *West Virginia Law*

Review 117 (2014): 867, 919. He observes that the Burger Court sought to side-step the tension between commercial regulation and autonomous commercial speakers by orienting commercial speech doctrine to the receipt of information by an audience, rather than to the autonomy of a speaker. And he asks, Why do we protect commercial speech in the first place? This, he says, is not about protecting the autonomy of commercial speakers. Instead, it concerns protecting the integrity of public opinion. But the Roberts Court and lower federal courts now have extended the First Amendment protection of commercial speech to benefit businesses by prohibiting state or federal regulations.

47 Archibald Cox, "Foreword: Freedom of Expression in the Burger Court," *Harvard Law Review* 94 (1980): 26.

48 See Id. at 55–56 (The Burger Court, Cox said, had done more "to enhance the political power of money than to promote the goals of the First Amendment").

49 These examples are from Hearings of the House Judiciary Committee cited by Cox, id. at 57.

50 See Julian E. Zelizer, "Seeds of Cynicism: The Struggle over Campaign Finance, 1956–1974," *Journal of Policy History* 14 (2002): 73; and Robert E. Mutch, *Campaigns, Congress, and the Courts: The Making of Federal Campaign Finance Law* (Westport: Praeger, 1988).

51 See, e.g., J. Skelly Wright, "Money and the Pollution of Politics: Is the First Amendment an Obstacle to Political Equality?," *Columbia Law Review* 82 (1982): 609; Harold Leventhal, "Courts and Political Thickets," *Columbia Law Review* 77 (1977): 345; and J. Skelly Wright, "Politics and the Constitution: Is Money Speech?," *Yale Law Journal* 85 (1976): 1001.

52 The act also instituted detailed recordkeeping and reporting requirements by candidates to a new Federal Election Commission, which was given jurisdiction and broad discretion to enforce the law and promulgate additional rules.

53 James L. Buckley, *Gleanings from an Unplanned Life: An Annotated Oral History* (Wilmington: Intercollegiate Studies Institute, 2006), 149, quoted in Richard L. Hasen, "The Nine Lives of *Buckley v. Valeo*," in *First Amendment Stories*, eds. Richard W. Garnett and Andrew Koppleman (New York: Foundation Press, 2012), 356.

54 *Buckley v. Valeo*, 519 F.2d 821 (en banc) (1975).

55 Id. at 897.

56 Id. at 841.

57 Id. at 898.

58 Warren Burger, Memorandum to the Conference, November 18, 1975.

59 Hasen, "Nine Lives," 367.

60 The description of the Justice Department's machinations is from id. at 361–62. See also Richard L. Hasen, "The Untold Drafting History of *Buckley v. Valeo*," *Election Law Journal* 2 (2003): 241.

61 424 U.S. at 48.

62 Id. at 48–49.

63 Id. at 265 (White, J.).

64 Id. at 288 (Marshall, J.).

65 Id. at 241 (Burger, C.J.).

66 The Court of Appeals had previously invalidated—without a government appeal—a disclosure provision that would have required reporting of contributions and spending "by groups whose only connection with the elective process arises from completely nonpartisan public discussion of issues of public importance." 519 F.2d at 821, 832. These are today's notorious 501(c)(4) organizations.

67 For discussion of the cases, see, e.g., Hasen, "The Nine Lives of *Buckley v. Valeo*," at 368–73.

68 Federal Election Campaign Act of 1971, 86 Stat. 3, as amended by the Federal Election Campaign Act Amendments of 1974, 88 Stat. 1263, § 101; see *Buckley v. Valeo*, 424 U.S. at 28n31.

69 The FEC was found to be unconstitutional because of appointment of FEC members by Congress; this was subsequently revised to comply with the *Buckley* opinion.

70 Advisory Opinion 1975–83, November 24, 1975 (Lewis F. Powell, Jr.'s, *Buckley* files, Folder 1, pp. 177–192).

71 Lewis F. Powell, Jr., "Confidential Memorandum: Attack on American Free Enterprise System," to Mr. Eugene B. Sydnor, Jr., Chairman, Education Committee, U.S. Chamber of Commerce, August 23, 1971.

72 435 U.S. 765 (1978).

73 *Trustees of Dartmouth College v. Woodward*, 17 U.S. 518, 636, 4 Wheat. 518 (1819).

74 William J. Brennan, Jr., Memorandum to the Conference (Lewis F. Powell, Jr.'s, *Bellotti* file, Folder 1, p. 60).

75 Powell's clerk assigned to the case, Nancy Bregstein, was, if possible, even more shocked; the next day she wrote a memo to Powell (apologizing for her "highly emotional tone") strongly rejecting Brennan's view and reaffirming Powell's judgment. Lewis Powell, Jr.'s, *Belloti*, file, folder 1, at 64.

76 Id. at 67.

77 435 U.S. at 791 (Powell, J., majority).

78 Id. at 791–92.

79 Id. at 796 (Burger, C.J., concurring).

80 Id. at 803 (White, J., dissenting).

81 Id. at 803–804, 809.

82 Id. at 823 (Rehnquist, J., dissenting).

83 Id. at 828. In 1980, in another decision authored by Powell (handed down on the same day as *Central Hudson*), the Court extended *Bellotti* to strike down an order of the New York Public Service Commission prohibiting Consolidated Ed-

ison, New York's largest electric company, from including in its monthly bills to consumers "inserts discussing controversial issues of public policy." The material prohibited by the utility's regulator had extolled the virtues of nuclear power. New York's highest court upheld the prohibition, but by a 7–2 vote the Supreme Court reversed. *Consolidated Edison Company v. Public Service Commission of New York*, 447 U.S. 530 (1980). Relying on *Bellotti*, the Court determined that the ban was an unconstitutional limitation conditioned on the content or subject matter of the company's speech. Blackmun—surprisingly given his views in *Bellotti* and the commercial speech cases—dissented on the ground that consumers, who paid for the distribution of the company's monthly bills in their electricity rates, were being forced to subsidize the company's distribution of its political views. Rehnquist did not write separately this time, but he, of course, joined Blackmun's dissent.

84 *Citizens United v. Federal Election Commission*, 558 U.S. 310 (2010).

85 435 U.S. at 788n.26.

86 See, e.g., Hasen, "The Nine Lives of *Buckley v. Valeo*," 371.

87 The Court, however, did not invalidate state or federal prohibitions on direct corporate contributions to candidates. The Court also upheld Congress's right to require disclosures of corporate political spending.

88 The case is *McConnell v. Federal Election Commission*, 540 U.S. 93, 115 (2003).

89 Transcript of Oral Argument, *Citizens United v. Federal Election Commission*, 558 U.S. 310 (2010) (No. 08-205), 71.

90 *American Tradition Partnership, Inc. v. Bullock* 132 S.Ct. 2490 (2012).

91 Lucien A. Bebchick and Robert J. Jackson, Jr., "Shining Light on Corporate Political Spending," *Georgetown Law Journal* 101 (2013): 931–32.

92 Claire Hyungyo Chung, "The Rise of the National Chamber Litigation Center" (manuscript, Yale Law School, 2012), 12.

CHAPTER 11: BATTLING WORKPLACE INEQUALITY

1 443 U.S. 193 (1979).

2 Civil Rights Act of 1964, § 703(a) and (c). (The 1964 Civil Rights Act is codified at 42 U.S.C. § 2000e to 2000e-15.)

3 443 U.S. at 197 (Brennan, J., majority). Neither Powell nor Stevens participated in this case.

4 Id. at 208–9.

5 Id. at 220 (Rehnquist, J., dissenting).

6 Id. at 254.

7 Editorial dated June 29, 1979 (Lewis F. Powell, Jr.'s, *Weber* file, Folder 5, p. 14) (from "Racial Quotas" in *The Virginia-Pilot*).

8 Jefferson F. Cowie, *Stayin' Alive: The 1970s and the Last Days of the Working Class* (New York: New Press, 2010), 242.

9 Id. at 243.

10 Judith Stein, *Running Steel, Running America: Race, Economic Policy, and the Decline of Liberalism* (Chapel Hill: University of North Carolina Press, 1988), 191, 243.

11 Lewis F. Powell, Jr., Note on William Brennan's Memorandum to the Conference, June 15, 1979 (Lewis F. Powell, Jr.'s, *Weber* file, Folder 4).

12 Letter from Lewis F. Powell, Jr., to Warren Burger, July 5, 1979 (Lewis F. Powell, Jr.'s, *Weber* file, Folder 5, p. 13) (enclosing *The Virginian-Pilot* editorial of June 29, 1979).

13 *Johnson v. Transportation Agency*, 480 U.S. 616, 642–47 (1987) (Stevens, J., concurring).

14 Id. at 657 (White, J., dissenting). See also Michael J. Yelnosky, "Whither *Weber?*" *Roger Williams University Law Review* 4 (1998): 258–61.

15 443 U.S. at 209 (Blackmun, J., concurring).

16 Katherine Van Wezel Stone, "The Legacy of Industrial Pluralism: The Tension Between Individual Employment Rights and the New Deal Collective Bargaining System," *University of Chicago Law Review* 59 (1992): 579–80 (showcasing the then all-time greatest difference between union and nonunion wages).

17 Burt Neuborne, "Observations on *Weber*," *NYU Law Review* 54 (1979): 546.

18 Jefferson F. Cowie, "How Ronald Reagan Broke the Air Traffic Controllers Union—And Why That Fight Still Matters," *Dissent*, March 25, 2012.

19 Joseph A. McCartin, "A Historian's Perspective on the PATCO Strike, Its Legacy, and Lessons," *Employee Responsibility and Rights Journal* 18 (2006): 215 (first quote); and Joseph A. McCartin, *Collision Course: Ronald Reagan, the Air Traffic Controllers, and the Strike That Changed America* (New York: Oxford University Press, 2011), 245 (second quote).

20 During the Burger era, unions enjoyed little support from the White House even before Reagan become president. Richard Nixon conspicuously tried to induce union leaders and workers to vote Republican. Jimmy Carter in 1977 invoked his powers under the Taft-Hartley Act in an effort to break a strike by the United Mine Workers and offered only tepid support for important 1978 labor law proposals. See Michael J. Graetz, *The End of Energy* (Cambridge: MIT Press, 2013), 87–90, for a discussion.

21 America's workers had lost faith in their political leaders as a result of Watergate and Vietnam. At the same time, employees became distrustful of their union leaders, who were often more interested in lining their own pockets than protecting workers. Congress in 1959 expanded the rights of union members in union elections, required greater financial disclosures, and created both civil and criminal penalties for financial wrongdoing by union leaders (the Labor-Management Reporting and Disclosure Act of 1959, also known as the Landrum-Griffin Act). Jimmy Hoffa, with his famous links to organized crime, his raid on the Teamsters Union pension fund treasury, and his mysterious disappearance in 1975, was the most notorious exemplar of corruption. But Hoffa

was hardly alone. See, e.g., Graetz, *The End of Energy*, 81–82 (the murder of Joseph "Jock" Yablonski, along with his wife and daughter, by assassins hired by the corrupt United Mine Workers president Tony Boyle). Union leadership of the times was often at its best when it was merely sclerotic.

22 The best cultural, political, and economic history is Cowie, *Stayin' Alive.*

23 Lester Thurow, *The Zero-Sum Society* (New York: Basic Books, 2001); see also Jørgen Randers, Dennis Meadows, William W. Behrens III, and Donella Meadows, *The Limits to Growth* (New York: Universe Books, 1972), as the best example.

24 Dwight Yoakum, "I Got You."

25 See, generally, e.g., Clyde W. Summers, "Labor Law as the Century Turns: A Changing of the Guard," *Nebraska Law Review* 67 (1988): 7.

26 "We must have democracy in industry as well as in government," Wagner said. "Democracy in industry," he continued, "means fair participation by those who work in the decisions vitally affecting their lives and livelihood." To ensure this, workers, he said, must be "allowed to organize and bargain collectively through representatives of their own choosing." Quoted in Milton Derber, *The American Idea of Industrial Democracy, 1865–1965* (Champaign: University of Illinois Press, 1970), 321.

27 J. Joseph Huthmacher, *Senator Robert F. Wagner and the Rise of Urban Liberalism* (New York: Holiday House, 1971), 203–4; Clyde W. Summers, "Labor Law as the Century Turns: A Changing of the Guard," *Nebraska Law Review* 67 (1988): 9.

28 NLRA §8(c), 29 U.S.C. §401–53.

29 The bill had passed the House. H.R. 8410 95th Cong. (1977).

30 See Stone, "Industrial Pluralism."

31 See Summers, "Century Turns," 12–14, for examples.

32 Bureau of Labor Statistics, *Union Members 2014*, January 23, 2015. Public sector workers are unionized at more than five times the rate (35.7 percent) of private workers (6.6 percent). Today, African American workers are more likely to be unionized than white workers, but that wasn't always so. When employees unionized, their unions were able to secure collective bargaining contracts from previously nonunion employers only about half the time in the 1980s, compared to nearly 90 percent in the 1950s.

33 The decline of unions is also offered as a reason why ongoing increases in labor productivity are showing up as increases in business profits, rather than wages. See, e.g., Alan B. Krueger, Chairman of the Council of Economic Advisers, Speech, "Land of Hopes and Dreams: Rock and Roll, Economics and Rebuilding the Middle Class," Cleveland, Ohio (June 12, 2013).

34 In the early 1930s, before the Wagner Act, only 15 percent of private sector workers were represented by unions. By the mid-1950s, union representation had grown to its peak of 40 percent. By the end of the 1980s, it had declined

to less than 15 percent. Paul C. Weiler, "Hard Times for Unions; Challenging Times for Scholars," *University of Chicago Law Review* 58 (1991): 1017, 1019. In the mid-1950s, unions won elections covering nearly 75 percent of eligible workers; by the 1980s the percentage of workers covered by victorious elections had fallen to less than 40 percent. Id. at 1018.

35 Seth Stern and Stephen Wermiel, *Justice Brennan: Liberal Champion* (New York: Houghton Mifflin Harcourt, 2012), 6–9.

36 Id. at 30–41.

37 Id. at 33.

38 Id. at 43.

39 Id.

40 Brenda Haugen, *Thurgood Marshall: Civil Rights Leader and Supreme Court Justice* (Minneapolis: Compass Point, 2007), 45.

41 Mark V. Tushnet, *Making Civil Rights Law* (New York: Oxford University Press, 1996), 76–79.

42 Tinsley E. Yarbrough, "Justice Potter Stewart: Decisional Patterns in Search of Doctrinal Moorings" in *The Burger Court: Political and Judicial Profiles*, eds. Charles M. Lamb and Steven C. Halpern (Champaign: University of Illinois Press, 1991), 404n4.

43 *NLRB v. Bell Aerospace Co.*, 416 U.S. 267, 281–82n11 (1974) (Powell, J., majority) (quoting the House Report on the Taft-Hartley Act, H.R. Rep. No. 245, 80th Cong., 1st Sess., 16–17 [1947]).

44 Harry T. Edwards, "The Coming of Age of the Burger Court: Labor Law Decisions of the Supreme Court During the 1976 Term," *Boston College Law Review* 19 (1977): 2.

45 William B. Gould IV, "Some Reflections on Fifty Years of the National Labor Relations Act: The Need for Labor Board and Labor Law Reform," *Stanford Law Review* 38 (1986): 941.

46 James J. Brudney, "The Changing Complexion of Workplace Law: Labor and Employment Decisions of the Supreme Court's 1999–2000 Term," *The Labor Lawyer* 16:151 (2000), 159–61. Public employees fared somewhat worse than those in the private sector. Workplace controversies during the Burger years accounted for about 10 percent of the Court's business until about 1974 and about 17 percent after that, a total of 379 decisions. Id. at 152n3 and 4; 153, Figure 7. Labor-management relations cases comprised more than half of these. Id. at 153. Race or sex discrimination cases accounted for about a third, and the rest involved interpretation of specific employee protection statutes such as OSHA and ERISA. Id. at 153–54, 157. As unions declined, so did the Court's labor business. The Rehnquist Court, by comparison, decided only seven labor-management cases in the four terms 1990–1993, and only eight race or sex discrimination cases in its 1996–1999 terms. Id. at 155–56.

47 See, e.g., Max Zimny, "Reagan Stacks the Deck at the NLRB," *Business and Society Review* 45 (Spring 1983): 153.

48 *NLRB v. Gissel Packing Co.*, 395 U.S. 575 (1969). The employers had fired union advocates, threatened economic reprisals, and offered employees benefits for opposing the unions—all violations of the Wagner Act. See, e.g., Laura J. Cooper and Dennis R. Nolan, "The Story of *NLRB v. Gissel Packing*: The Practical Limits of Paternalism," in *Labor Law Stories*, eds. Laura Cooper and Catherine Fisk (New York: Foundation Press, 2005); and Daniel M. Carson, "The *Gissel* Doctrine: When a Bargaining Order Will Issue," *Fordham Law Review* 41 (1972): 85.

49 *Linden Lumber Division, Summer & Co. v. NLRB*, 419 U.S. 301 (1974). In addition to Douglas, the majority included Burger, Brennan, Blackmun, and Rehnquist. Justice Stewart dissented, joined by Marshall, Powell, and White, but even the dissenters would have permitted employers to refuse to recognize a union based on a majority of authorization cards and to require an election. The Court's decision provides employers considerable time after a majority of employees has signaled its desire to join a union, but before an election, to oppose unionization. Robert L. Douglas, *"Linden Lumber Division, Summer & Co. v. NLRB,"* *Hofstra Law Review* 3 (1975): 854n10. See, generally, e.g., Paul C. Weiler, "Promises to Keep: Securing Workers' Rights to Self-Organization Under the NLRA," *Harvard Law Review* 96 (1983): 1804–22.

50 Employee Free Choice Act of 2009, H.R. 1409 111th Cong. (2009); S. 560, 111th Cong. (2009). The Burger Court also constricted unions' ability to organize by adopting a broad view of the class of "managerial employees" whom the Taft-Hartley Act excludes from protections against upper management's retaliation for supporting union activity. In a case involving parts buyers for an aerospace manufacturer, the 5–4 majority endorsed a sharp distinction between rank-and-file workers and managers, asserting that protecting union activity by those with "true" managerial responsibilities would create a conflict of interest and "would eviscerate the traditional distinction between labor and management." *NLRB v. Bell Aerospace Co.*, 416 U.S. 267, 284 (1974). Powell's opinion for the Court worried that joining a union would lead managerial employees to become disloyal to their employer and that unionization would hinder the productivity and ambition of managers. That characterization speaks volumes about the majority's view of labor unions. In a related 5–4 opinion, also by Justice Powell (for a slightly different majority), the Court treated university faculty as managerial employees and barred them from forming a union. *NLRB v. Yeshiva University*, 444 U.S. 672 (1980). See, e.g., David M. Rabban, "Distinguishing Excluded Managers from Covered Professionals Under the NLRA," *Columbia Law Review* 89 (1989): 1775.

51 *Hudgens v. NLRB*, 424 U.S. 507 (1976), overruling *Amalgamated Food Employees, Local 590 v. Logan Valley Plaza, Inc.*, 391 U.S. 308 (1968). The Court sent

the case back to the NLRB to determine whether the picketers enjoyed any legal protections under the Wagner Act. See Frederick F. Schauer, "*Hudgens v. NLRB* and the Problem of State Action in First Amendment Adjudication," *Minnesota Law Review* 61 (1977): 433, 460 (describing *Hudgens* as a "regrettable decision"). Subsequently, after years of case-by-case adjudication of such disputes, which had balanced the rights of the unions against those of property owners, the Rehnquist Court, in *Lechmere, Inc. v. NLRB*, 502 U.S. 527 (1992), made clear that the rights of the owners of private property trump union organizing efforts by nonemployees in the absence of "unique obstacles" to "nontrespassory means of communication." Id. at 535.

52 In 1964, the Warren Court upheld picketing by striking Washington state fruit packers of grocery stores selling Washington apples. *NLRB v. Fruit and Vegetable Packers and Warehousemen, Local 760*, 377 U.S. 58 (1964) (known as the *Tree Fruits* case). Such picketing was banned by the Burger Court in *NLRB v. Retail Store Employees Union, Local 1001*, 447 U.S. 607 (1980) (known as the *Safeco* case).

53 447 U.S. at 616.

54 *Howard Johnson Co. v. Detroit Local Joint Executive Board*, 417 U.S. 249 (1974). See James Severson and Michael Willcoxon, "Successorship Under *Howard Johnson*: Short Order Justice for Employees," *California Law Review* 64 (1976): 795; and Christopher Michael Russo, "Navigating the Labor Law Successorship Doctrine: Why 'Substantial Continuity' Is Insufficient to Find a Duty to Arbitrate Under a Preexisting Collective Bargaining Agreement" (Paper 271, Seton Hall Repository, 2013). This rule does not apply when the transaction is just a paper transaction without any meaningful impact on the ownership or operation of the business. Douglas Leslie, *Labor Law in a Nutshell*, 5th ed. (St. Paul: West Group, 2008), 297. When the successor corporation reemploys a majority of its predecessor's employees, however, it must bargain with the predecessor's union even though it is not bound by the previous collective bargaining agreement. *NLRB v. Barns International Securities Services, Inc.*, 406 U.S. 272 (1972). See also *Fall River Dyeing and Finishing Corp. v. NLRB*, 482 U.S. 27 (1987).

55 See Leslie, *Labor Law in a Nutshell*, 297–98.

56 Weiler, "Hard Times for Unions," 1019. The Warren Court in 1962 had determined that there is no statutory basis for an employer to successfully enjoin a strike even when the strike violates a no-strike clause in the collective bargaining agreement. *Sinclair Refining Co. v. Atkinson*, 370 U.S. 195 (1962). Then, the only remedy for employers was damages. In 1970, the Burger Court overruled that decision, concluding that an employer may enjoin a strike over any grievance that the union and the employer have agreed to arbitrate. *Boys Markets, Inc. v. Retail Clerks Local 770*, 398 U.S. 235 (1970). Douglas Leslie, a University of Virginia labor law professor, in his *Labor Law*, 286, says that by allowing

employers to enjoin strikes, the Court ignored legislative history and "brushed aside with little difficulty" any regard for precedent.

57 The Court suggested that the bankruptcy court should do so "if the debtor [employer] can show that the collective agreement burdens [it], and that after careful scrutiny, the equities balance in favor of rejecting the labor contract." *NLRB v. Bildisco & Bildisco*, 465 U.S. 513, 526 (1984). By a 5–4 vote (with Brennan, White, Marshall, and Blackmun dissenting), the Court also concluded that an employer in bankruptcy may unilaterally alter the terms of its collective bargaining agreement even before the bankruptcy court authorizes rejection of the agreement. Id. at 528. This essentially would make collective bargaining agreements unenforceable anytime an employer files a bankruptcy petition. Congress reversed this aspect of the Burger Court's decision, and the law now requires the bankruptcy court's approval for a debtor to reject a collective bargaining agreement. Bankruptcy Amendments and Federal Judgeship Act of 1984, Public Law No. 98-353, § 541, codified at 11 U.S.C. § 1113. This law allows the bankruptcy court to permit the employer to reject the agreement based on the "balance of equities" only if the union has refused the employer's proposed modifications "without good cause."

58 See, e.g., "American Airlines Seeks to Cancel Labor Contracts," Associated Press, March 27, 2012.

59 452 U.S. 666 (1981).

60 Alan Hyde, "The Story of *First National Maintenance Corp. v. NLRB*: Eliminating Bargaining for Low-Wage Service Workers," in *Labor Law Stories*, eds. Laura Cooper and Catherine Fisk, 281; 452 U.S. at 669–70.

61 Hyde, "The Story of *First National Maintenance Corp. v. NLRB*," 295–96. The Chamber offered FNM's lawyer $50,000 to let Frankel argue the case, but the lawyer refused. Id. at 297.

62 Id. at 285. The AFL-CIO filed a "totally ineffectual" *amicus* brief in the case. Id. at 296.

63 452 U.S. at 682–83 (Blackmun, J., majority), quoting *Fireboard Paper Products Corporation v. NLRB*, 379 U.S. 203, 223 (1964) (Stewart, J., concurring). See also Hyde, "The Story of *First National Maintenance Corp. v. NLRB*," 283, 299.

64 Lower court cases and NLRB decisions subsequent to *First National Maintenance* are difficult even for labor law specialists to reconcile, but they generally provide great flexibility to management.

65 Hyde, "The Story of *First National Maintenance Corp. v. NLRB*," 310; and Armen A. Alchian, "Decision Sharing and Expropriable Specific Quasi-Rents: A Theory of *First National Maintenance Corp. v. NLRB*," *Supreme Court Economic Review* 1 (1982): 235. Under *FNM*, the union has no right to bargain over decisions to close or move business operations, but it can bargain over the "effects" of such decisions, including, for example, severance pay or the employer's ability to transfer to another location.

66 The AFL-CIO's support of the Vietnam War and neglect of, if not outright hostility to, women's rights also split the Democrats' New Deal coalition.

67 For discussion of this history, see William P. Jones, *The March on Washington: Jobs, Freedom, and the Forgotten History of Civil Rights* (New York: Norton, 2014), 121–200.

68 Id. at 130–31; 140–41, 145–47.

69 Id. at 148, quoting reports from *The New York Times.*

70 These quotations are from United States Commission on Civil Rights, *1961 Civil Rights Report, Book 3, Employment* (October 13, 1961), 128, 131, 136, 142, 151, 161.

71 William P. Jones, *The March on Washington*, 158.

72 Randolph had been president of the Brotherhood of Sleeping Car Porters. For years he had lobbied for such a march. For more information on race relations in unions, see Jones, *The March on Washington.*

73 The act's coverage was originally limited to employers with at least one hundred employees, but this was subsequently reduced to fifteen; the act also applies to unions and employment agencies.

74 Martin Luther King, Jr., "Address to the Fourth Constitutional Convention of the American Federation of Labor-Congress of Industrial Organizations (AFL-CIO)," December 11, 1961, Bal Harbour, Florida.

75 Civil Rights Act of 1964, section 703(h).

76 Daniel T. Rodgers, *Age of Fracture* (Cambridge: Harvard University Press, 2011): 93.

77 Tessa Bialek, "The Burger Court's Treatment of Seniority Systems Under Title VII" (unpublished manuscript, Yale Law School, February 1, 2012): 14–15.

78 William B. Gould, *Black Workers in White Unions: Job Discrimination in the United States* (Ithaca: Cornell University Press, 1977), 19–20.

79 Herbert Hill and James E. Jones, *Race in America: The Struggle for Equality* (Madison: University of Wisconsin Press, 1993), 306–7.

80 See, e.g., *Quarles v. Philip Morris, Inc.*, 279 F. Supp 505, 510 (E.D. Va. 1968); Berta E. Hernandez, "Title VII v. Seniority: The Supreme Court Giveth and the Supreme Court Taketh Away," *American University Law Review* 35 (1986): 348–51; and David Benjamin Oppenheimer, "Employment Discrimination: Rightful Place Seniority Under Title VII and Section 1981: The Teamsters Roadblock May Be Only a Detour," *Hamline Law Review* 2 (1979): 15.

81 *Franks v. Bowman Trans. Co., Inc.*, 424 U.S. 747 (1976). On retroactive seniority awards, see also *Zipes v. Trans World Airlines, Inc.*, 455 U.S. 385 (1982); and *Ford Motor Co. v. EEOC*, 458 U.S. 219 (1982).

82 Lewis F. Powell, Jr., Memorandum to the Conference, February 12, 1976 (Lewis F. Powell, Jr.'s, *Franks* file, Folder 4, p. 13).

83 *Franks*, 424 U.S. at 781 (Burger), 789 (Powell).

84 Id. at 790. Burger suggested that the majority was "robbing Peter to pay Paul." Id. at 781.

85 431 U.S. 324 (1977).

86 Id. at 328.

87 Theodore J. St. Antoine, "Individual Rights in the Workplace: The Burger Court and Labor Law," in *The Burger Court: The Counter-Revolution That Wasn't*, ed. Vincent Blasi (New Haven: Yale University Press, 1983), 157, 159 ("bombshell"); Hernandez, "Title VII v. Seniority" 352 ("overruled a decade of legal precedent").

88 431 U.S. at 355–56. In *Teamsters*, the lack of discriminatory purpose was conceded and that the seniority system "did not have its genesis in racial discrimination." Id. In the decision involving female flight attendants, the same majority upheld a seniority system even when the discrimination occurred after the enactment of Title VII. *United Air Lines, Inc. v. Evans*, 431 U.S. 553 (1977). See, generally, Bialek, "Seniority Systems," 27–29.

89 E.g., *Trans World Airlines, Inc. v. Hardison*, 432 U.S. 63 (1977); and *California Brewers Association v. Bryant*, 444 U.S. 598 (1980).

90 *American Tobacco Co. v. Patterson*, 456 U.S. 63 (1982).

91 *Pullman-Standard Co. v. Swint*, 456 U.S. 273 (1982).

92 456 U.S. at 281.

93 456 U.S. at 275, quoting *Swint v. Pullman-Standard*, 624 F.2d 525, 533–34 (1980).

94 456 U.S. at 289–90 (White, J., majority). See also, e.g., Mark S. Brodin, "The Role of Fault and Motive in Defining Discrimination: The Seniority Question Under Title VII," *North Carolina Law Review* 62 (1984): 943.

95 *Firefighters Local Union No. 1784 v. Stotts*, 467 U.S. 561 (1984). For more detail, see Lawrence K. Hoyt, "*Firefighters Local Union No. 1784 v. Stotts*: Are Seniority Systems Approaching Inviolability in Title VII Actions," *Denver University Law Review* 62 (1985): 503; and Hernandez, "Title VII v. Seniority," 360–74.

96 Robert Belton, *The Crusade for Equality in the Workplace: The* Griggs v. Duke Power *Story* (Lawrence: University Press of Kansas, 2014), 280.

97 *Wygant v. Jackson Board of Education*, 476 U.S. 267 (1986).

98 476 U.S. at 274 (Powell, J., majority). Powell's opinion was joined in full by Burger and Rehnquist. O'Connor joined most of Powell's opinion, but wrote a lengthy concurrence diverging from some of Powell's analysis. White wrote a brief opinion concurring in the result. Marshall dissented, joined by Brennan and Blackmun, and Stevens dissented in a separate opinion.

99 Id. at 282. See Chapter 4 (school desegregation) and Chapter 5 (higher education).

100 Id. at 282–83.

101 Id. at 283–84.

102 Id. at 307 (Marshall, J., dissenting).

103 *AT&T Corp. v. Hulteen*, 556 U.S. 701 (2009).

104 Id. at 719 (Ginsburg, J., dissenting).

105 Marcia Coyle, "Seeking to Undo Bias in Pension: Pregnancy Leave Policy at Issue," *National Law Journal* 31 (2008): 14.

106 John David Skrentny, *The Ironies of Affirmative Action* (Chicago: University of Chicago Press, 1996), 6.

107 Executive Order 10925, March 6, 1961, §§ 201 (federal government) and 301(1) (government contractors).

108 Civil Rights Act of 1964, § 706(g).

109 Executive Order 11246, September 24, 1965, § 202(1). See also Lyndon B. Johnson, Commencement Address at Howard University, "To Fulfill These Rights," in *Public Papers of the President of the United States, 1965* (Washington, D.C.: Government Printing Office, 1966), 635.

110 Nixon's Philadelphia Plan is described in Skrentny, *The Ironies of Affirmative Action*, 193–98. See also Richard Nixon, "Statement About Congressional Action on the Philadelphia Plan," in *Public Papers of the President of the United States, 1969* (Washington, D.C.: Government Printing Office, 1970), 1040.

111 Skrentny, *The Ironies of Affirmative Action*, 197–98.

112 E.g., Kevin L. Yull, *Richard Nixon and the Rise of Affirmative Action: The Pursuit of Racial Equality in an Era of Limits* (Lanham: Rowman & Littlefield, 2006).

113 Rick Perlstein, *Nixonland: The Rise of a President and the Fracturing of America* (New York: Simon & Schuster, 2009), 515–16.

114 Ackerman, *We the People, Volume 3*, 88.

115 Skrentny, *The Ironies of Affirmative Action*, Chapter 5; and John David Skrentny, *The Minority Rights Revolution* (Cambridge: Harvard University Press, 2004), 88–89. See also Ackerman, *We the People, Volume 3*, 180.

116 Michael I. Sovern, *Legal Restraints on Racial Discrimination in Employment* (New York: Periodicals Service, 1966), 124, quoted in Skrentny, *The Minority Rights Revolution*, 105. See also Ackerman, *We the People, Volume 3*, Chapter 9.

117 *Griggs v. Duke Power Company*, 401 U.S. 424 (1971). For a detailed account of this litigation, see Belton, *The Crusade for Equality in the Workplace*.

118 Belton, *The Crusade for Equality in the Workplace*, 109.

119 401 U.S. 426–27. See also Belton, *The Crusade for Equality in the Workplace*, 109–15, detailing Duke Power's segregation policies.

120 Belton, *The Crusade for Equality in the Workplace*, 110–15.

121 401 U.S. at 428.

122 Harry Blackmun Papers (Box 125, Folder 1), quoted in Belton, *The Crusade for Equality in the Workplace*, 181.

123 Belton, *The Crusade for Equality in the Workplace*, 181–82.

124 401 U.S. at 432 (Burger, C.J., majority).

125 Id. at 431. See Belton, *The Crusade for Equality in the Workplace*, 162–87, for a detailed discussion of each justice's views.

126 Brief of the United States as Amicus Curiae, *Griggs v. Duke Power Company*, 401 U.S. 424 (1971) (No. 124), 12.

127 See, e.g., Reva B. Siegel, "Foreword: Equality Divided," *Harvard Law Review* 127 (2013): 13–15.

128 *Washington v. Davis*, 426 U.S. 229 (1976). On school desegregation, see Chapter 4.

129 *McCleskey v. Kemp*, 481 U.S. 279 (1987). See Chapter 1.

130 *Wesley v. Collins*, 791 F. 2d 1255 (CA6, 1986).

131 Harry A. Blackmun Papers, Preliminary Memo from Kenneth W. Starr (Box 224, Folder 5).

132 Harry A. Blackmun Notes, Harry A. Blackmun Papers (Box 224, Folder 5).

133 Byron R. White Papers, Letter from Harry A. Blackmun to Warren Burger, February 19, 1976 (Box 348, Folder 10).

134 Lewis F. Powell, Jr. Papers, Bench Memorandum, February 23, 1976 (Lewis F. Powell, Jr., *Washington* file, Folder 1, p. 35).

135 The discussion at conference is taken from Lewis F. Powell, Jr.'s, *Washington* file, Folder 1, and from Harry A. Blackmun Papers (Box 224, Folder 5).

136 426 U.S. at 238 (White, J., majority).

137 Id. at 238–39.

138 Id. at 242.

139 Id. at 245.

140 Id. at 248.

141 Id. at 241.

142 Id. at 242.

143 Id. at 254 (Stevens, J., concurring).

144 Id. at 253.

145 Id. at 253. See also *Arlington Heights v. Metropolitan Housing Development Corp.*, 429 U.S. 252 (1977) (using evidence of disparate impact to prove a discriminatory purpose).

146 *Personnel Administrator of Massachusetts v. Feeney*, 442 U.S. 256 (1979).

147 Skrentny, *The Ironies of Affirmative Action*, 32–57.

148 442 U.S. at 265.

149 See, e.g., Siegel, "Foreword: Equality Divided"; and Serena Mayeri, *Reasoning from Race: Feminism, Law, and the Civil Rights Revolution* (Cambridge: Harvard University Press, 2011), 133–41.

150 Mayeri, *Reasoning from Race*, 141 (quoting Smeal); 442 U.S. at 269 (Stewart, J., majority).

151 Id. at 270.

152 Id. at 271–72.

153 Id. at 279.

154 Siegel, "Foreword: Equality Divided," 19–20.

155 Robert Pear, "Changes Weighed in Federal Rules on Discrimination," *New York Times*, December 3, 1984.

156 E.g., Clarence Thomas, *My Grandfather's Son: A Memoir* (New York: Harper Collins, 2007), 80.

157 See, e.g., *Texas Department of Housing v. Inclusive Communities Project*, Slip. Op. No 13-1371, June 25, 2015 (dissenting opinion of Thomas, J. at 5–12) ("disparate impact jurisprudence was erroneous from its inception," Id. at 12).

158 Office of Legal Policy, U.S. Department of Justice, *The Constitution in the Year 2000: Choices Ahead in Constitutional Interpretation* (1988), discussed in Siegel, "Foreword: Equality Divided," 26–28.

159 See *Ward's Cove Packing Co. v. Atonio*, 490 U.S. 642 (1989). See also, e.g., Belton, *The Crusade for Equality in the Workplace*, 282–95.

160 Civil Rights Act of 1991, §105.

161 In 2015, disparate impact analysis survived in a statutory interpretation of the Fair Housing Act by a 5–4 vote. See *Texas Department of Housing*.

162 *Ricci v. DeStefano*, 557 U.S. 557 (2009).

163 Id. at 562–64 (Kennedy, J., majority).

164 Id. at 582–83.

165 Id. at 609 (Ginsburg, J., dissenting).

166 Id. at 613, 580.

167 Id. at 592–93 (Kennedy, J., majority).

168 Brief of General Motors as Amicus Curiae in Favor of Respondents, *Grutter v. Bollinger*, 539 U.S. 306 (2003) (Nos. 02-241 and 02-516). See, generally, Jennifer Delton, *Racial Integration in Corporate America, 1940–1990* (New York: Cambridge University Press, 2009).

169 E.g., Mike Isaac, "Behind Silicon Valley's Self-Critical Tone on Diversity, a Lack of Progress," *New York Times* (June 28, 2015); Vindu Goel, "Facebook Mirrors Tech Industry's Lack of Diversity," *New York Times* (June 25, 2014); Nick Wingfield, "Intel Allocates $300 Million for Workplace Diversity," *New York Times* (January 6, 2015); Elizabeth Olson, "Black Lawyers Lose Ground at Top Firms," *New York Times* (May 29, 2014); Tanzina Vega, "With Diversity Still Lacking, [Advertising] Industry Focuses on Retention," *New York Times* (September 3, 2012); Richard Pérez-Peña, "To Enroll More Minority Students, Colleges Work Around the Court," *New York Times* (April 1, 2012).

INTRODUCTION TO PART V: THE PRESIDENCY

1 Woodrow Wilson, *Constitutional Government in the United States* (New York: Columbia University Press, 1911), 56–57.

2 The phrase "Imperial Presidency" is the title of White House historian Arthur M. Schlesinger, Jr.'s, *The Imperial Presidency* (New York: Houghton Mif-

flin, 1973). The description is from Megan McArdle, "Richard Nixon's Palace Guard," *Bloomberg*, August 16, 2013, citing Richard Reeve.

3 See Louis Fisher, *Presidential Spending Power* (Princeton: Princeton University Press, 1975), 150–51, 168–70; Note, "Impoundment of Funds," *Harvard Law Review* 86 (1973): 1505.

4 *Train v. New York*, 420 U.S. 35 (1975) (rejecting the executive's power to control spending under the Federal Water Pollution Control Act). After Nixon left office, Congress enacted the Congressional Budget and Impoundment Control Act of 1974 to limit the president's ability to impound appropriated funds and to assert greater congressional control over the federal budget. 2 U.S.C. §§ 601–88, July 12, 1974. That legislation established House and Senate Budget Committees, created the Congressional Budget Office (CBO), and provided procedures for enactments of budget legislation.

5 Richard Nixon, interview by David Frost, May 20, 1977, available at: http://www.streetlaw.org/en/Page/722/Nixons_views_on_presidential_power_excerpts_from_a_1977_interview_with_David_Frost; and "Excerpts from Interview with Nixon About Domestic Effects of Indochina War," *New York Times*, May 20, 1977, A16. For a partial defense of Nixon's position, see Henry Monaghan, "The Protective Power of the Presidency," *Columbia Law Review* 93 (1993): 47–56.

6 See "Excerpts from Interview with Nixon About Domestic Effects of Indochina War," A16.

7 The War Powers Resolution of 1973 limits the time for deployment of U.S. troops without congressional approval. It was enacted in November 1973 when Congress overrode Nixon's veto. Public Law 93-148 (H.J. Res. 542), 50 U.S.C. § 1541–48, November 7, 1973. Nixon maintained that the law was unconstitutional, an issue that has been vigorously debated in the academic literature, but that law has survived, despite injury inflicted on it by the Burger Court. See *INS v. Chadha*, 462 U.S. 919 (1983) (White's dissent lists the War Powers Act as among the laws affected). See also Stephen L. Carter, "The Constitutionality of the War Powers Resolution," *Virginia Law Review* 70 (1984): 101.

8 *Marbury v. Madison*, 5 U.S. (Cranch) 137, 177 (1803) ("It is emphatically the province and duty of the judicial department to say what the law is"). The existence of this power was one of many issues disputed between Alexander Hamilton and Thomas Jefferson. Compare Alexander Hamilton, "Federalist No. 78," in *The Federalist Papers* (New York: Bantam, 1982) (explaining the courts' expansive powers), with Thomas Jefferson, Letter to William Jarvis, September 28, 1820 (describing judges as "the ultimate arbiters of all constitutional questions" as "a very dangerous doctrine indeed" leading to "the despotism of an oligarchy").

9 Alexander Bickel, *The Least Dangerous Branch: The Supreme Court at the Bar of Politics* (Indianapolis: Bobbs-Merrill, 1962) (attributing the "achievement" to Chief Justice John Marshall), 1.

CHAPTER 12: POWER AND ITS ABUSE

1 William Safire, *Before the Fall: An Inside View of the Pre-Watergate White House* (New York: Doubleday, 1975), 342.

2 Sanford J. Ungar, *The Papers and the Papers* (New York: E.P. Dutton & Co., 1989); John Prados and Margaret Pratt Porter, eds., *Inside the Pentagon Papers* (Lawrence: University Press of Kansas, 2004). See also Peter E. Quint, "The Separation of Powers Under Nixon: Reflections on Constitutional Liberties and the Rule of Law," *Duke Law Journal* 1981 (1981): 5–9.

3 David Rudenstine, *The Day the Presses Stopped: A History of the Pentagon Papers Case* (Berkeley: University of California Press, 1998), 64.

4 Rick Perlstein, *Nixonland: The Rise of a President and the Fracturing of America* (New York: Simon & Schuster, 2000), 574.

5 Conversation between Nixon and Rogers, 1-15-71, 6:44 p.m., quoted in Prados and Porter, *Inside the Pentagon Papers*, 114.

6 Id.

7 The text of Mitchell's telegram is set forth in Rudenstine, *The Day the Presses Stopped*, 92.

8 Id. at 81.

9 Id. at 128, 136; Ungar, *The Papers and the Papers*, 151.

10 Ungar, *The Papers and the Papers*, 151–52.

11 Id. at 158.

12 Rudenstine, *The Day the Presses Stopped*, 385n14; Ungar, *The Papers and the Papers*, 164–69.

13 Del Dickson, *The Supreme Court in Conference, 1940–1985: The Private Discussions Behind Nearly 300 Supreme Court Decisions* (New York: Oxford University Press, 2001), 369n1. Dickson describes this initial conference as occurring on June 26 but it actually took place on June 24.

14 *New York Times Co. v. United States*, 403 U.S. 713, 753 (1971).

15 For further discussion of the opinion, see Rudenstine, *The Day the Presses Stopped* (New York: Fordham University Press, 2001), 301; and Kate Stith, "Alexander Bickel and the *Pentagon Papers*" (unpublished manuscript, Yale Law School).

16 Dickson, *The Supreme Court in Conference*, 370.

17 403 U.S. at 753 (Harlan, J., dissenting).

18 403 U.S. at 715 (Black, J., concurring).

19 Dickson, *The Supreme Court in Conference*, 370n5, quoting Howard Ball, *Hugo L. Black: Cold Steel Warrior* (New York: Oxford University Press, 1996), 197.

20 403 U.S. at 723–24 (Douglas, J., concurring).

21 Dickson, *The Supreme Court in Conference*, 371.

22 403 U.S. at 726–27 (Brennan, J., concurring).

23 Dickson, *The Supreme Court in Conference*, 370.

24 403 U.S. at 725–26 (Brennan, J., concurring).

25 Id. at 727 (Stewart, J., concurring).

26 Id. 727–28 (Stewart, J., concurring).

27 Dickson, *The Supreme Court in Conference*, 371.

28 403 U.S. 729 (Stewart, J., concurring).

29 Dickson, *The Supreme Court in Conference*, 371.

30 403 U.S. 732–33 (White, J., concurring).

31 Dickson, *The Supreme Court in Conference*, 371n8.

32 403 U.S. 742 (Marshall, J., concurring).

33 Rudenstine, *The Day the Presses Stopped*, 298.

34 For an especially nuanced analysis, see John C. Jeffries, Jr., "Rethinking Prior Restraint," *Yale Law Journal* 92 (1983): 409.

35 Id. at 437; 403 U.S. at 761 (Blackmun, J., dissenting).

36 Rudenstine, *The Day the Presses Stopped*, 297.

37 See, e.g., *Snepp v. United States*, 444 U.S. 507 (1980) (upholding restraining book publication under contract permitting review and approval); and *Haig v. Agee*, 453 U.S. 280 (1981).

38 Rudenstine, *The Day the Presses Stopped*, 288–89.

39 David E. Pozen, "The Leaky Leviathan: Why the Government Condemns and Condones Unlawful Disclosures of Information," *Harvard Law Review* 127 (2013): 516.

40 The Holder description and "twice as many" are from Sharon LaFraniere, "Math Behind Leak Crackdown: 153 Cases, 4 Years, 0 Indictments," *New York Times*, July 20, 2013, A1. The number eight is from Pozen, "The Leaky Leviathan," 534, 536.

41 Pozen, "The Leaky Leviathan," 535.

42 Don Van Natta, Jr., et al., "The *Miller* Case: A Notebook, A Cause, a Jail Cell and a Deal," *New York Times*, October 16, 2005, at A1.

43 Margaret Sullivan, "A Blow for the Press and for Democracy," *New York Times*, July 27, 2013, at 12.

44 For a discussion of these guidelines, see Pozen, "The Leaky Leviathan," 535.

45 *United States v. Sterling*, 724 F.3d 482 (4th Cir. 2013), 492.

46 Matt Apuzzo, "Times Reporter Will Not Be Called to Testify in Leak Case," *New York Times*, January 12, 2015, A1.

47 Rudenstine, *The Day the Presses Stopped*, 342.

48 Erwin N. Griswold, "Secrets Not Worth Keeping," *Washington Post*, February 15, 1989, A25.

49 Id. See also Rudenstine, *The Day the Presses Stopped*, 327.

50 For detailed discussion see id. at 343. See also Prados and Porter, *Inside the Pentagon Papers*.

51 A point emphasized by Perlstein, *Nixonland*, 575.

52 Pun Plamondon recounts his life story in his autobiography, *Lost from the Ottawa: The Story of the Journey Back* (Victoria: Trafford, 2004). See also Trevor W.

Morrison, "The Story of *United States v. United States District Court (Keith)*: The Surveillance Power," in *Presidential Power Stories*, eds. Christopher Shroeder and Curtis Bradley (New York: Foundation Press, 2000), 291–3; and Robert Downes, "The Last Outlaw: Pun Plamondon's Radical Odyssey," *Northern Express*, January 27, 2005, www.northernexpress.com/michigan/article-1351-the-last-outlaw-pun-plamondons-radical-odyssey.html.

53 Marsha Low, "'60s Radical Takes Long Trips Back to His Roots: White Panthers' Plamondon Surfaces with Memoir," *Detroit Free Press*, October 27, 2004, B1, quoted in Morrison, "The Surveillance Power," 293.

54 *United States v. United States District Court for Eastern District of Michigan, Southern Division*, 407 U.S. 297, 300 (1972) contains the affidavit.

55 Id.

56 Id. at 301.

57 *Katz v. United States*, 277 U.S. 347 (1967).

58 407 U.S. at 299 (Powell, J., majority).

59 Id. at 303.

60 Id. at 320–22.

61 Dickson, *The Supreme Court in Conference*, 473.

62 For a detailed discussion of Powell's previous statements, see Morrison, "The Surveillance Power," 299–305.

63 *United States v. United States District Court*, 444 F.2d 651, 653n1 (6th Cir. 1971).

64 Morrison, "The Surveillance Power," 296.

65 Lewis F. Powell, Jr., Confidential Memorandum to the File, March 13, 1972 (Lewis F. Powell, Jr.'s, *Keith* file, Folder 4, p. 14).

66 *United States v. United States District Court*, 444 F.2d 651, 670 (6th Cir. 1971).

67 The information on COINTELPRO here is based on Richard Powers, "A Bomb with a Long Fuse: 9/11 and the FBI 'Reforms' of the 1970s," *American History* (December 2004): 43–47.

68 Betty Medsger, *The Burglary: The Discovery of J. Edgar Hoover's Secret FBI* (New York: Knopf, 2014). See also Margaret Talbot, "Opened Files," *The New Yorker*, January 20, 2014, 19–20.

69 Final Report of the Senate Select Committee to Study Government Operations with Respect to Intelligence Activities and Rights of Americans, S. Rep. No. 94-94-755, pt. 2, 186–87.

70 Powers, "A Bomb with a Long Fuse," 45.

71 S. Rep. 95-604 (I), 8, quoted in Morrison, "The Surveillance Power," 34.

72 50 U.S.C. §1801 (e) and (f).

73 50 U.S.C. §1805.

74 Chief Justice Roberts was criticized when it became known that almost all of the judges he had selected for the FISA Court had been appointed by Republican presidents. Charles Savage, "Roberts' Picks Reshaping Secret Surveillance

Court," *New York Times*, A1, July 25, 2013. Roberts subsequently began to fill vacancies in a more evenhanded manner. Tal Kopan, "Roberts Names 2 New FISA Court Judges," February 7, 2014, http://www.politico.com/blogs/under-the-radar/2014/roberts-names-new-fisa-court-judges-182921.html.

75 Morrison, "The Surveillance Power," 325.

76 *Smith v. Maryland*, 442 U.S. 735 (1979).

77 Id. See also Linda Greenhouse, "We've Got Your Number," *New York Times*, January 22, 2014.

78 442 U.S. at 743 (Blackmun, J., majority).

79 Greenhouse, "We've Got Your Number."

80 *United States v. Jones*, 132 S. Ct. 945 (2012).

81 132 S. Ct. at 957 (Sotomayor, J., concurring).

82 *Riley v. California*, 134 S.Ct. 2473 (2014).

83 134 S. Ct. at 2489, 2493 (Roberts, C.J., majority).

84 *Nixon v. Fitzgerald*, 457 U.S. 731 (1982); *Harlow v. Fitzgerald*, 457 U.S. 800 (1982).

85 *Kissinger v. Halperin*, 452 U.S. 713 (1981).

86 Rudenstine, *The Day the Presses Stopped*, 73.

87 *Halperin v. Kissinger*, 606 F.2d 1192 (D.C. Cir. 1979). Litigation over the Pentagon Papers leak was how Halperin learned that his family's phone had been wiretapped.

88 *Kissinger v. Halperin*, 452 U.S. 713 (1981).

89 Memorandum from Byron White to Lewis F. Powell, Jr., March 18, 1981 (Potter Stewart's *Halperin* files, Box 367, Folder 4471).

90 Thurgood Marshall, Memorandum to the Conference, March 11, 1981 (Potter Stewart's *Halperin* files, Box 272, Folder 6).

91 Brennan and Blackmun, for example, regarded the settlement agreement and its concealment as "deceptive and manipulative." Dickson, *The Supreme Court in Conference*, 192.

92 Lewis F. Powell, Jr., Conference Notes (Lewis F. Powell, Jr.'s *Fitzgerald* files, Folder 3, p. 11); and Dickson, *The Supreme Court in Conference*, 191–95.

93 457 U.S. 731. (Powell, J., majority) "In view of the special nature of the President's constitutional office and functions," Powell wrote, "we think it appropriate to recognize absolute Presidential immunity from damages liability for acts within the 'outer perimeter' of his official responsibility." Id. at 749. Burger wrote a gratuitous concurrence emphasizing that the president's absolute immunity is firmly grounded in the constitutional separation of powers.

94 Id. at 765 (White, J., dissenting).

95 Id. at 765n1–2. Blackmun also wrote separately, in a dissent joined by Brennan and Marshall, to complain that the case was not dismissed because of the settlement agreement. "Surely," he said, "had the details of this agreement been known at the time the petition for certiorari came before the Court, certiorari

would have been denied." "For me," Blackmun added, "the Court leaves unanswered the unanswerable argument that no man, not even the President of the United States, is absolutely and fully above the law." Id. at 797 (Blackmun, J., dissenting).

96 "Supreme Court Rules on *Nixon v. Fitzgerald*," *NBC Nightly News*, June 24, 1982, http://archives.nbclearn.com/portal/site/k-12/flatview?cuecard=40951. The Supreme Court has only once after *Nixon v. Fitzgerald* addressed presidential immunity. This occurred in 1997 when the Rehnquist Court unanimously decided that Bill Clinton had no immunity in a civil lawsuit filed by Paula Jones for sexual misconduct by Clinton before he became president. *Clinton v. Jones*, 520 U.S. 681 (1997). The Court concluded that the Constitution does not prevent lawsuits against a sitting president for unlawful conduct before he took office nor require that such civil lawsuits be delayed until the president leaves office. This decision required Clinton to testify before a grand jury in connection with the Jones affair, and that testimony ultimately led to the House of Representatives voting Articles of Impeachment for perjury and obstruction of justice. Clinton was acquitted by the Senate, but his presidency suffered serious damage, and the episode ultimately rang the death knell for the special prosecutor law that had been enacted in 1978, five years after Archibald Cox had been fired in Nixon's "Saturday Night Massacre." 28 U.S.C. §591–99 (now expired). (In 1988 the Rehnquist Court upheld the 1978 law over a strong dissent by Justice Scalia. *Morrison v. Olson*, 487 U.S. 654 [1988].) Following the bitter political battle over Clinton's impeachment, Congress allowed the law to expire on June 30, 1999. For a history of the independent counsel law, see Ken Gormley, "Monica Lewinsky, Impeachment, and the Death of the Independent Counsel Law: What Congress Can Salvage from the Wreckage—a Minimalist View," *Maryland Law Review* 60 (2001): 97.

97 *Harlow v. Fitzgerald*, 457 U.S. 800 (1982).

98 Burger alone claimed that Harlow and Butterfield, as presidential aides, also enjoyed absolute immunity from civil damages—immunity he regarded as derived from that of the president. Burger insisted that such immunity was essential for the president to discharge his duties effectively. 457 U.S. 822 (Burger, C.J., dissenting).

99 403 U.S. 388 (1971).

100 *Scheuer v. Rhodes*, 416 U.S. 232, 246–49 (1974) (Burger, C.J., majority). The court of appeals had dismissed the lawsuit, finding that all of the defendants enjoyed absolute immunity from a claim for damages while acting within the scope of their official duties. Three years later, in a more mundane suit by Arthur Economou, a commodities futures dealer, against Earl Butz, the secretary of agriculture, and other federal officials, Justice White, writing for a five-vote majority (including Brennan, Marshall, Blackmun, and Powell), provided more comprehensive guidance about how determinations of qualified immu-

nity should be resolved. *Butz v. Economou*, 438 U.S. 478 (1978). Justice Rehnquist dissented, in an opinion joined by Burger, Stewart, and Stevens, urging a broader scope of absolute immunity for federal officials.

101 Martha Weil, "Joseph Kelner, Attorney Who Sued Sitting Ohio Governor over Kent State Slayings, Is Dead at 98," *ABA Journal*, March 8, 2013.

102 *Harlow v. Fitzgerald*, 457 U.S. at 818.

103 *Mitchell v. Forsyth*, 472 U.S. 511 (1985).

104 Subsequent decisions by the more conservative Courts made the defense of qualified immunity even more difficult to overcome. See, e.g., *Anderson v. Creighton*, 483 U.S. 635 (1987).

105 *Halperin v. Kissinger*, 723 F. Supp. 1535 (D.D.C. 1989).

106 *Halperin v. Kissinger*, 807 F.2d. 180 (D.C. Cir. 1986).

107 This occurred in two unreported decisions. See "Halperin Settles Suit with Kissinger," *First Principles* 17, nos. 3 and 4 (December 1992), http://www.cnss.org/data/files/resources/FirstPrinciples/FirstPrinciplesVol17No3-4.pdf.

108 Walter Pincus, "20-Year-Old Wiretap Suit Against Kissinger Settled," *Washington Post*, November 13, 1992.

CHAPTER 13: RICHARD NIXON IN WARREN BURGER'S COURT

1 For a detailed account of the Watergate Committee's work, see Rick Perlstein, *The Invisible Bridge: The Fall of Nixon and the Rise of Reagan* (New York: Simon & Schuster, 2014).

2 Id. at 267.

3 Kutler, *The Wars of Watergate: The Last Crisis of Richard Nixon* (New York: Knopf, 1992), 340.

4 J. Anthony Lukas, *Nightmare: The Underside of the Nixon Years* (New York: Viking, 1976), 289.

5 See Carol Kilpatrick, "President Refuses to Turn Over Tapes; Ervin Committee, Cox Issue Subpoenas," *Washington Post*, July 24, 1973. There are many good books on the Watergate incident. The most famous, of course, is Bob Woodward and Carl Bernstein, *All the President's Men* (New York: Simon & Schuster, 1974). See also Christopher Schroeder, "The Story of *United States v. Nixon*: The President and the Tapes," in Christopher Schroeder and Curtis R. Bradley, eds., *Presidential Power Stories* (St. Paul: Foundation Press, 2009).

6 Perlstein, *The Invisible Bridge*, 188.

7 For the Judiciary Committee's discussion of impeachment, see id. at 259–65.

8 506 U.S. 224 (1974). The account that follows is largely based on Lukas, *Nightmare*, 517–20.

9 *New York Times*, July 20, 1974, quoted in Bob Woodward and Scott Armstrong, *The Brethren: Inside the Supreme Court* (New York: Simon & Schuster, 1979), 334.

10 Lukas, *Nightmare*, 520.

11 Perlstein, *The Invisible Bridge*, 268.

12 Lukas, *Nightmare*, 520.

13 Id. at 522.

14 Richard Nixon, "Address to the Nation Announcing Decision to Resign the Office of President of the United States," in *Public Papers of the President of the United States: Richard Nixon, 1974* (Washington, D.C.: Government Printing Office, 1975), 633.

15 Burger and his colleagues were also blissfully unaware that the *Nixon* case would inspire Bob Woodward, and his colleague Scott Armstrong to write a bestselling, behind-the-scenes chronicle of the early years of the Burger Court. Their book, *The Brethren: Inside the Supreme Court* (New York: Simon & Schuster, 1979), contains over sixty pages describing every step along the way to the Court's opinion in *United States v. Nixon*, far more detail than they devote to any other decision. Woodward and Armstrong, *The Brethren*, 283–347. *The Brethren*'s account of the case has proved to be quite accurate. John Jeffries, who served as a clerk to Powell when *United States v. Nixon* was before the Court, makes a few small clarifications to *The Brethren*'s account in his biography of Lewis Powell. (John C. Jeffries, Jr., *Justice Lewis F. Powell, Jr.* [New York: Fordham University Press, 2001], 389–98.)

16 See, e.g., Louis Henkin, "Is There a Political Question Doctrine?," *Yale Law Journal* 85 (1975): 597; Michael E. Tigar, "Judicial Power, the 'Political Question' Doctrine and Foreign Relations," *UCLA Law Review* 17 (1970): 1135; and Rachel E. Barkow, "More Supreme than Court? The Fall of the Political Question Doctrine and the Rise of Judicial Supremacy," *Columbia Law Review* 102 (2002): 737.

17 *O'Brien v. Brown*, 409 U.S. 1 (1972).

18 506 U.S. 224 (1993).

19 Dickson, *The Supreme Court in Conference*, 184.

20 Lewis F. Powell, Jr., Notes, September 13, 1973 (Lewis F. Powell, Jr.'s, *Nixon* file, Folder 1, p.1); see also John C. Jeffries, Jr., *Justice Lewis F. Powell, Jr.*, 382–83.

21 Lewis F. Powell, Jr., Memorandum, September 13, 1973 (Lewis F. Powell, Jr.'s, *Nixon* file, Folder 1).

22 Woodward and Armstrong, *The Brethren*, 307.

23 Id. at 303–4.

24 Lewis F. Powell, Jr., Notes for Conference, July 9, 1974 (Lewis F. Powell, Jr.'s, *Nixon* file, Folder 8).

25 Woodward and Armstrong, *The Brethren*, 286, 295–97.

26 For details, see Woodward and Armstrong, *The Brethren*.

27 The phrase is from Louis Henkin, "Executive Privilege: Mr. Nixon Loses but the Presidency Largely Prevails," *UCLA Law Review* 22 (1974): 40.

28 *United States v. Nixon*, 418 U.S. 683, 708 (1974) (Burger, C.J., majority).

29 Id. at 711.

30 Id. at 714.

31 Id. at 712.

32 Id. at 714–15.

33 See Woodward and Armstrong, *The Brethren*, 311–46.

34 *United States v. Burr*, 25 F. Cas. 187 (No. 14, 694) (C.C. Va. 1807).

35 An excellent account of the Burr conspiracy and trial is R. Kent Newmyer, *The Treason Trial of Aaron Burr: Law, Politics, and the Character Wars of a New Nation* (Cambridge: Cambridge University Press, 2012).

36 See Michael S. Paulson, "The Most Dangerous Branch: Executive Power to Say What the Law Is," *Georgetown Law Journal* 83 (1994): 217; and John C. Yoo, "The First Claim: The Burr Trial, *United States v. Nixon* and Presidential Power," *Minnesota Law Review* 83 (1998): 1435.

37 E.g., Paul A. Freund, "The Supreme Court 1973 Term—Forward: On Presidential Privilege," *Harvard Law Review* 88 (1974): 31.

38 Del Dickson, *The Supreme Court in Conference, 1940–1985: The Private Discussions Behind Nearly 300 Supreme Court Decisions* (New York: Oxford University Press, 2001), 183.

39 Lewis F. Powell, Jr., Memorandum to the File, June 30, 1974 (Lewis F. Powell, Jr.'s, *Nixon* file, Folder 4, p. 18) (marked tentative and confidential).

40 Ken Gormley, *Archibald Cox: Conscience of a Nation* (New York: Da Capo, 1999), 386.

41 "Familiar objects" in his office is from a note Burger taped to the back of this painting. For a view of the painting in color, see Warren Burger Online Exhibit—Earl Gress Swem Library, accessed January 7, 2015, at http://cf.swem.wm.edu/exhibits/burger/artist.cfm.

42 Gormley, *Archibald Cox*, 385–87.

43 See, e.g., Phillip B. Kurland, "*United States v. Nixon*: Who Killed Cock Robin?," *UCLA Law Review* 22 (1974): 68; Akhil Reed Amar, "Nixon's Shadow," *Minnesota Law Review* 83 (1998): 1405; and Bernard Schwartz, "Bad Presidents Make Hard Law: Richard M. Nixon in the Supreme Court," *Rutgers Law Review* 31 (1978): 22. For a bibliography, see Mark J. Rozell, "Executive Privilege: A Bibliographic Essay," *Journal of Law and Politics* 4 (1987): 639.

44 Gerald Ford, "Remarks on Taking the Oath of Office," in *Public Papers of the President of the United States: Gerald Ford, 1974* (Washington, D.C.: Government Printing Office, 1975), 1, quoted in Jeffries, *Justice Lewis F. Powell, Jr.*, 382.

45 In a case described by Justice Brennan as raising important constitutional issues in "a context unique in the history of the Presidency and [presenting] issues that the Court has heretofore had no occasion to address," the Court, by a 7–2 vote, upheld the Presidential Recording and Materials Act, signed by President Ford on December 19, 1974. *Nixon v. Administrator of General*

Services, 433 U.S. 421, 439 (1977) (Brennan, J., majority). That statute ordered FSA to take custody of Nixon's papers and tapes, to arrange for government archivists to examine them and return to Nixon those that were private, and to issue regulations setting forth conditions for public access to those materials not returned to Nixon. This controversy produced seven separate opinions, spanning 140 pages, with Brennan writing for the majority. Burger and Rehnquist dissented. Burger describes the majority as repudiating "nearly 200 years of judicial precedent and historical practice" and tearing "into the fabric of our constitutional framework." Id. at 505 (Burger, C.J., dissenting). Rehnquist described the case as "a real threat to the ability of future presidents to receive candid advice and to give candid instructions," and described it as "a veritable Sword of Damocles over every succeeding President and his advisors." Id. at 546 (Rehnquist, J., dissenting). The Court's decision revealed Richard Nixon's secrets and provided researchers unparalleled access to his presidency's achievements and its downfall. For an excellent discussion of the case and the events leading up to it, see Pamela R. McKay, "Presidential Papers: A Property Issue," *Library Quarterly* 52 (1982): 21. (In 1978, Congress enacted the Presidential Records Act of 1978, providing that presidential papers and other records are now owned by the government and generally available to the public twelve years after a president leaves office.)

A year later, the Court gave Nixon a victory, barring commercial exploitation of the tapes that had been played in the criminal conspiracy trial of Nixon's closest aides. In a 5–4 vote, with Potter Stewart and Nixon's four appointees in the majority, the Court rejected Warner Communications' request for copies of the twenty-two hours of tapes of White House conversations, which—pursuant to the Court's decision in *United States v. Nixon*—had been played in Judge Sirica's courtroom to the jury and the public and had been admitted into evidence in the criminal conspiracy trial. *Nixon v. Warner Communications, Inc.*, 435 U.S. 589 (1978). Transcripts of the tapes had also been made available to reporters and the public. The trial resulted in the conviction of four of Nixon's co-conspirators: three of his closest associates—John Mitchell, Bob Haldeman, and John Ehrlichman—and Robert Mardian, who had served as an assistant attorney general under Mitchell. Warner Communications wanted the tapes to copy and distribute commercially based on the longstanding right of public access to judicial records. What was unique here was Warner's insistence that it was legally entitled to audio copies of the tapes, not just the transcripts. The Supreme Court denied the tapes to Warner Communications. Given the risks of distortion through cutting, erasing, and modification of the tapes, the Court determined that neither the free press guarantee of the First Amendment nor the public trial requirement of the Sixth Amendment demanded a different result. Writing for the Court, Justice Powell gave short shrift to the company's First Amendment claims, saying that they were being advanced simply to satisfy private spite and promote public scandal. 435 U.S. at 598 (Powell, J., majority). Powell was, of course, right about the company's intentions. Judge Sirica had said much the same thing in response to Warner Communications' demand for immediate access to the tapes.

Justice Stevens dissented, emphasizing the "great historical interest" in the tapes and remarking on the irony that a statute designed to produce and promote public access to Nixon's tapes was now being used as a basis for denying that access. Justice Stevens said that the "risk that some people will reproduce the recordings and exploit them for commercial purposes" is "the risk of a free society." 435 U.S. 617, n. 5 (Stevens, J., dissenting).

46 A notable instance when the Burger Court was called on to validate presidential power in a crisis involved its affirmation of Jimmy Carter's settlement of the Iranian hostage crisis in the Algiers Accords agreed to on January 19, 1981, by the Iranian government and the outgoing president. *Dames & Moore v. Regan*, 453 U.S. 654 (1981). The Supreme Court took the *Dames & Moore* case on June 11, 1981. The case was argued on June 24, and demonstrating his exceptional ability, Rehnquist's opinion for the Court, upholding the validity of the Algiers agreement and the executive orders and regulations implementing it, was issued just eight days later on July 2. Brennan and Powell both described the opinion as "splendid;" Stevens later described it as one of his two favorite Rehnquist opinions. Letters praising Rehnquist in *Dames & Moore* can be found in Lewis F. Powell, Jr.'s file on the case, and Stevens is quoted in Lyle Dennison, "WHR Enters Court's Pantheon," December 10, 2009, www.Scotusblog.com/2009/12/whr-enters-courts-pantheon/. Insisting that the extraordinary press of time made it a "necessity to rest this decision on the narrowest possible grounds," Rehnquist looked for statutes demonstrating Congress's approval of the president's actions. At conference, he told his colleagues that by deciding the case on statutory rather than constitutional grounds, the Court would allow Congress to respond if it wanted to. Lewis F. Powell, Jr., Conference Notes, June 24, 1981 (Lewis F. Powell, Jr.'s, *Dames and Moore* file, Folder 7). For more detail, see Harold H. Bruff, "The Story of *Dames & Moore*: Resolution of an International Crisis by Executive Order," in *Presidential Power Stories*, ed. Christopher Shroeder and Curtis Bradley (New York: Foundation Press, 2008), 392.

Worth noting here are two additional significant decisions that strengthened the presidency. In the area of administrative law, *Chevron U.S., Inc. v. Natural Resources Defense Council*, 467 U.S. 837 (1984), one of the most frequently cited of all Supreme Court decisions, requires courts to defer to Executive Branch agencies in the interpretation of ambiguous statutes. On the subject of the constitutional separation of powers, *Immigration and Naturalization Service v. Chadha*, 462 U.S. 919 (1983) invalidated a cherished congressional device known as the legislative veto, by which Congress could disapprove an Executive Branch action without actually passing a law. In both cases, the Court handed high-profile victories to the Reagan administration.

CONCLUSION

1 Remarks of Lewis F. Powell, Jr., Before the American Bar Association Litigation Section Meeting (Lewis F. Powell, Jr.'s, *Bowers* file, Folder 1, p. 135).

2 Had Powell read Vincent Blasi's *The Burger Court: The Counter-Revolution That Wasn't* (New Haven: Yale University Press, 1986), published three years earlier? (See Introduction). We don't know. But talk of a Burger Court "counterrevolution" had been in the air since Burger's nomination in 1969.

3 Powell, Remarks Before the American Bar Association, 5.

4 A long footnote to the criminal justice section of Powell's speech, perhaps added by a law clerk in the interests of accuracy, does provide an inventory of the decisions by which the Burger Court constricted access to habeas corpus, concluding: "Fairly read, the Burger Court's decisions represent an effort to accommodate the States' interest in finality of criminal convictions, on which many important aspects of a rational criminal justice system are founded." Powell, Remarks Before the American Bar Association, 5–6n3. Referring to the Court's criminal procedure docket as a whole, Powell's text itself acknowledges: "I think it is fair to say that the record of the Burger Court in this area reflects a higher sensitivity to the public interest in law enforcement than that reflected in some of the decisions of the Warren Court." Powell, Remarks Before the American Bar Association, 5.

5 418 U.S. 717 (1974).

6 411 U.S. 1 (1973).

7 Powell, Remarks Before the American Bar Association, 13.

8 "Sally—put in *Bowers v. Hardwick* File."

9 Id. at 11.

10 Id. at 14.

11 Ronald Reagan, "State of the Union Address to Congress, February 6, 1985," in *Public Papers of the President of the United States: Ronald Reagan, 1985* (Washington, D.C.: Government Printing Office, 1986), 146.

12 Ronald Reagan, "State of the Union Address to Congress, February 18, 1981," in *The American Presidency Project*, www.presidency.ucsb.edu/ws/index .php?pid=43425. Shifting power to the states elevates state policy preferences over nationwide equality, as the experience with Medicaid and the Affordable Care Act amply demonstrates.

13 For discussion of this memorandum, see the introduction to Part IV.

14 For an excellent description of this movement, see Steven M. Teles, *The Rise of the Conservative Legal Movement: The Battle for Control of the Law* (Princeton: Princeton University Press, 2008).

15 Memorandum from Patrick J. Buchanan to Richard Nixon, November 10, 1972, quoted in Teles, *The Rise of the Conservative Legal Movement*, 1. Even Teles, however, repeats the no-counter-revolution dogma. Id.

16 Across district lines: *Milliken v. Bradley*, 418 U.S. 717 (1974). Share of the state's wealth: *San Antonio Independent School District v. Rodriguez*, 411 U.S. 1 (1973).

APPENDIX: THE MEMBERS OF THE BURGER COURT

1 Sources for this Appendix: Lee Epstein, Thomas Walker, Jeffrey Segal, and Harold Spaeth, *The Supreme Court Compendium: Data, Decisions, and Developments*, 6th ed. (Washington, D.C.: CQ Press, 2015); Joan Biskupic and Elder Witt, *Guide to the U.S. Supreme Court*, 3rd ed. (Washington, D.C.: Congressional Quarterly, 1997); Leon Friedman and Fred L. Israel, *Justices of the United States Supreme Court: Their Lives and Major Opinions*, 4th ed. (New York: Infobase Publishing, 2013).

Photo Credits

Photo Credits

Page 329: AP Photo/File

Page 336: In private hands. Copy provided by Special Collections Research Center, Swem Library, College of William & Mary

Page 344: White House Photo, Collection of the Supreme Court of the United States

Page 345: Collection of the Supreme Court of the United States

Index

Page numbers in *italics* refer to illustrations.